ATLAS
OF
BRITISH SOCIAL
AND ECONOMIC HISTORY
SINCE C. 1700

ATLAS
OF
BRITISH SOCIAL
AND ECONOMIC HISTORY
SINCE C. 1700

EDITED BY REX POPE

MACMILLAN PUBLISHING COMPANY
NEW YORK

Copyright © 1989 by Rex Pope

First American edition published in 1989 by Macmillan Publishing Company, A Division of Macmillan, Inc.

Macmillan Publishing Company
866 Third Avenue, New York, N.Y. 10022

First published in Great Britain by
Routledge
London

Library of Congress Catalog Card Number: 88-37915

Printed and bound in Great Britain by
Butler & Tanner Ltd, Frome and London
printing number
1 2 3 4 5 6 7 8 9 10

Library of Congress Cataloging-in-Publication Data

Atlas of British social and economic history since
   c. 1700 / edited by Rex Pope.—1st American ed.
     p.   cm.
   Bibliography: p.
   Includes index.
   ISBN 0-02-897341-0
   1. Great Britain—Economic conditions. 2. Great
Britain—Industries—History. 3. Great Britain—Social conditions. 4. Great
Britain—Economic conditions—Maps. 5. Great
Britain—Industries—History—Maps. 6. Great Britain—Social
conditions—Maps.   I. Pope. Rex.
   HC253.A86   1989
   330.941—dc19   88-37915
                        CIP

CONTENTS

Maps and diagrams   vi

Introduction   xi

Acknowledgements   xiii

1   *Agriculture*   1
Peter Dewey, Royal Holloway and
Bedford New College, University of
London

2   *The textile and chemicals industries*   23
Geoff Timmins and Rex Pope,
Lancashire Polytechnic

3   *Metal, vehicle, and engineering industries*   45
Rex Pope, Lancashire Polytechnic

4   *Coal, gas, and electricity*   68
Carol Jones, University of Southampton

5   *Transport and trade*   96
John Armstrong, Ealing College of
Higher Education

6   *Demographic changes 1701–1981*   134
Stephen Jackson, Liverpool Polytechnic,
and Geoff Timmins, Lancashire
Polytechnic

7   *Employment and unemployment*   150
Rex Pope, Lancashire Polytechnic

8   *Urbanization and living conditions*   170
Callum Brown, University of Strathclyde

9   *Labour movements*   183
Keith Laybourn, Huddersfield
Polytechnic

10   *Education: late nineteenth-century disparities in provision*   198
Bill Marsden, University of Liverpool

11   *Religion*   211
Callum Brown, University of Strathclyde

12   *Leisure*   224
Stephen G. Jones, Manchester
Polytechnic

Further reading   236

Index   246

v

MAPS AND DIAGRAMS

1.1 England: land without common or common field at the end of the seventeenth century

1.2 English parliamentary enclosure to 1845: open-field arable

1.3 English parliamentary enclosure to 1845: commons and wastes

1.4 Changes in income tax Schedule B assessments, 1874/5–1892/3

1.5 Percentage decline in corn crop area, 1870–1914

1.6 Percentage rise in milking herds (cows and heifers in milk or calf), 1870–1914

1.7 Regional agricultural wages, 1902

1.8 Tillage increases, 1914–18

1.9 Tillage increases, 1939–45

1.10 Increase in barley production, 1945–81

1.11 Increase in dairy herd (cows and heifers in milk), 1945–81

1.12 Changes in average size of farm holding, 1945–81

1.13 Percentage increases in the number of fowls, 1945–81

1.14 Percentage changes in wheat yields per hectare, 1945–81

2.1 Woollen and worsted industries, 1835 and 1867

2.2 Yorkshire wool textile area, c.1800

2.3 Lancashire and the West Riding: local textile specialization, c.1900

2.4 Arkwright-type mills in Nottinghamshire and Derbyshire, 1788

2.5 Blackburn: cotton mills in operation, 1894

2.6 Wool textile industry, Location map, October, 1946

2.7 Lancashire textile districts, 1818–22: proportions of bridegroom weavers

2.8 Leyland and Croston districts of Lancashire: weaver groups as proportions of total labour force, 1851

2.9 Leyland and Croston districts of Lancashire: weaver groups as proportions of total labour force, 1861

2.10 Textile trades, 1838: power derived from steam and water

2.11 Textile trades, 1870: power derived from steam and water

2.12 Locations of alkali manufacturers, 1864

2.13 Chemical plants in the St Helens, Widnes, and Runcorn districts, 1882

2.14 Tyneside chemical plants, 1882

2.15 Plant producing alkali, hydrochloric acid, bleaching powder or chlorine, 1882

2.16 Nitric and sulphuric acid production, 1882

2.17 Chemical manure plant, 1882

2.18 Plant producing sulphate of ammonia, 1882

2.19 Heavy organic chemicals, 1982, plant and productive capacity

2.20 Heavy inorganic chemicals, 1982, plant and productive capacity

2.21 Chemical works, 1982, showing the importance of coastal locations

2.22 Chemicals: gross output and number of units of production, 1983

2.23 Chemical plant in the area of the Mersey, 1982

2.24 Teesside chemical plant, 1982

3.1 English and Welsh iron production, 1720

3.2 Pig iron production: major centres, 1839

3.3	Pig iron production: major centres, 1875	4.1	Regional coal output, 1700–1830
3.4	Pig iron production: major centres, 1913	4.2	Tyne collieries, 1780s–1800
3.5	Pig iron production by region, 1937	4.3	Regional coal output, 1830–1913
3.6	Steel production by region, 1880	4.4	North-east collieries, mid-nineteenth century
3.7	Steel production by region, 1913		
3.8	Steel production by region, 1951	4.5	Yorkshire coalfield, 1947
3.9	Steel production by region, 1973 and 1983	4.6	North-east collieries, 1940s
		4.7	Regional coal output, 1920–65
3.10	Principal centres of merchant shipbuilding, 1825	4.8	North-east deep mines, 1987
		4.9	Yorkshire coalfield: deep mines South and North Yorkshire, 1987
3.11	Principal centres of merchant shipbuilding, 1870		
		4.10	Gas undertakings: England and Wales, 1882
3.12	Principal centres of merchant shipbuilding, 1913, 1938, 1953, and 1963		
		4.11	London: gas companies, 1882
3.13	Merchant shipbuilding: average tonnage launched, 1985–6	4.12	Gas undertakings, 1945
		4.13	Gas undertakings supplying London area, 1945
3.14	River Wear: shipbuilding, marine engineering, and ship repair in the early 1920s with dates of yard or works closures		
		4.14	National gas transmission system, 1987
		4.15	Public electricity supply undertakings, 1896
3.15	River Tyne: shipbuilding, marine engineering, and ship repair in the early 1920s with dates of yard works closures		
		4.16	Electricity supply undertakings in London, 1907
3.16	Motor car manufacturers, 1913		
3.17	Major car manufacturing plant, 1960s–1980s	4.17	National Grid, 1934
		4.18	Typical power flow pattern during maximum Midlands–South transfer, winter 1982–3
3.18	Major British airframe and aero-engine makers, 1937		
3.19	British Aerospace establishments in Britain, 1985	4.19	National Grid, 1980s
		4.20	Location of power stations by regions, 1985
3.20	Railway companies: major locomotive and carriage workshops, early twentieth century		
		5.1	River navigation, c.1750
		5.2	The principal waterways of the North-west and Midlands, c.1830
3.21	Private locomotive, carriage, and wagon works, 1910		
		5.3	Coach journey times from London, c.1750
3.22	Major textile engineering firms, 1914	5.4	Coach journey times from London in the 1830s
3.23	Boilermakers, 1910		
3.24	Agricultural Engineers, 1910	5.5	The turnpike road network in 1750
3.25	Eastern England: location of agricultural and mechanical engineering works (including engine-makers), 1910	5.6	The turnpike road network in 1770
		5.7	Top six ports in the coastal trade, 1841
		5.8	Top six ports in the coastal trade, 1912
		5.9	Top six ports in the coastal trade, 1938
3.26	Electrical engineering: manufacturers of cables, 1910	5.10	Coal received coastwise, top ten ports, 1780–5
3.27	Electrical engineering: manufacturers of transformers, 1910	5.11	Coal received coastwise, top ten ports, 1885
		5.12	Coal shipped by coaster, top ten ports, 1885
3.28	Electrical engineering: manufacturers of dynamos and/or electric motors, 1910	5.13	London's docks, opened 1802–28
		5.14	Liverpool dock building, 1715–1836
3.29	Gross output (£'000): mechanical engineering and electrical engineering, 1935	5.15	The railway system, c.1850
		5.16	The completed railway network, c.1890
3.30	Engineering: capital expenditure, by region, 1983	5.17	Railway grouping in 1921
		5.18	British Rail passenger network, 1986–7

5.19 Trunk roads, 1936
5.20 Motorways in England and Wales, 1986
5.21 The Park Royal estate, London
5.22 Principal domestic air routes, 1930s
5.23 Principal domestic air routes, 1970s
5.24 UK airports, 1984 (millions of passengers p.a.)
5.25 UK imports by region (percentage of total value), 1770–4
5.26 UK exports by region (percentage of total value), 1770–4
5.27 UK imports by region (percentage of total value), 1866–70
5.28 UK exports by region (percentage of total value), 1866–70
5.29 UK imports by region (percentage of total value), 1908–12
5.30 UK exports by region (percentage of total value), 1908–12
5.31 UK imports by region (percentage of total value), 1933–7
5.32 UK exports by region (percentage of total value), 1933–7
5.33 UK imports by region (percentage of total value), 1955–9
5.34 UK exports by region (percentage of total value), 1955–9
5.35 UK imports by region (percentage of total value), 1980–4
5.36 UK exports by region (percentage of total value), 1980–4
5.37 Imports by type of commodity
5.38 Exports by type of commodity
5.39 Top ten ports in foreign trade, 1872 (by value of imports)
5.40 Top ten ports in foreign trade, 1872 (by value of exports)
5.41 Top ten ports in foreign trade, 1902–6 (by value of imports)
5.42 Top ten ports in foreign trade, 1902–6 (by value of exports)
5.43 Top ten ports in foreign trade, 1933–7 (by value of imports)
5.44 Top ten ports in foreign trade, 1933–7 (by value of exports)
5.45 Top ten ports in foreign trade, 1985 (by value of imports)
5.46 Top ten ports in foreign trade, 1985 (by value of exports)

5.47 Top ten ports despatching coal abroad, 1870
5.48 Top ten ports despatching coal abroad, 1910

6.1 Population growth: England and Wales, 1701–1981
6.2 Age–sex structure: England and Wales, 1821–1981
6.3 Population distribution: Britain, 1801
6.4 Population distribution: Britain, 1861
6.5 Population distribution: Britain, 1921
6.6 Population distribution: Britain, 1981
6.7 Passengers to/from UK ports from/to extra-European countries, 1815–1935
6.8 International migration, 1981
6.9 Concentration of Irish-born in Britain, by county, 1851
6.10 Concentration of Welsh-born in England and Scotland, by county, 1851
6.11 Concentration of Scots-born in England and Wales, by county, 1851
6.12 Population growth in the North-west, 1841–1981
6.13 Population distribution in the North-west, 1801
6.14 Population distribution in the North-west, 1851
6.15 Population distribution in the North-west, 1901
6.16 Population distribution in the North-west, 1951
6.17 Population change in North-west districts, 1961–81
6.18 Country of birth of immigrants in North-west districts, 1981

7.1 Male employment in agriculture in nine northern counties, 1851
7.2 Male employment in the manufacture of cotton, silk, woollens and worsteds in nine northern counties, 1851
7.3 Male employment in coal-mining in nine northern counties, 1851
7.4 Male employment in shipping and in ship-building in nine northern counties, 1851
7.5 Highest and lowest percentages of males employed in agriculture, 1911

7.6 Highest percentages of males employed in textile manufacture, 1911

7.7 Highest percentages of males employed in mining and quarrying, 1911

7.8 Highest percentages of males employed in metal manufacture and engineering (including electrical workers), 1911

7.9 Highest and lowest percentages of males employed in administrative and professional occupations, 1911

7.10 Highest percentages of males employed in agriculture, 1971

7.11 Highest percentages of males employed in mining and quarrying, 1971

7.12 Highest percentages of males employed in metal manufacture and engineering (including electrical and electronics industries), 1971

7.13 Highest and lowest percentages of males in administrative, professional, and other service occupations, 1971

7.14 'Occupied' women in nine northern counties, 1851

7.15 Female employment in domestic service in nine northern counties, 1851

7.16 Female employment in the manufacture of cotton, silk, woollens, and worsteds in nine northern counties, 1851

7.17 Female employment in agriculture in nine northern counties, 1851

7.18 Girls aged 10–15 in England and Wales designated 'occupied', 1891

7.19 Highest and lowest percentages of females in employment, 1911

7.20 Highest percentages of females employed in textile and clothing manufacture, 1911

7.21 Highest and lowest percentages of females employed in domestic service, 1911

7.22 Highest percentages of females employed in agriculture, 1911

7.23 Highest and lowest percentages of females economically active, 1971

7.24 Highest percentages of females employed in textile and clothing manufacture, 1971

7.25 Highest and lowest percentages of females in administrative, professional, and other service occupations, 1971

7.26 Unemployment by county, June 1932

7.27 Unemployment by county, June 1937

7.28 Lancashire unemployment levels, June 1930, 1932, 1937

7.29 Warwickshire unemployment levels, June 1932, 1937

7.30 Unemployment by region, 1964

7.31 Unemployment by county, October 1984

7.32 Special Areas, 1934

7.33 Development Areas between 1945 and 1960

7.34 Special Development, Development, and Intermediate Areas, 1978

7.35 Development and Intermediate Areas, 1984

8.1 Growth of cities, 1801

8.2 Growth of cities, 1851

8.3 Growth of cities, 1901

8.4 Growth of cities, 1951

8.5 Growth of cities, 1981

8.6 New towns

8.7 The growth of Glasgow, 1700–1980

8.8 House overcrowding, Scotland, 1861

8.9 House overcrowding, Scotland, 1901

8.10 House overcrowding, Britain, 1951

8.11 Houses without piped water supply, 1951

8.12 Houses without cooking stoves, 1951

8.13 Houses without water closets, 1951

8.14 Houses without fixed baths, 1951

8.15 Infant mortality rate, 1841

8.16 Infant mortality rate, 1872

8.17 Infant mortality rate, 1901

8.18 Infant mortality rate, 1951

8.19 Infant mortality rate, 1980

9.1 Luddite areas in the North of England, c.1811–17

9.2 Main Luddite attacks in West Yorkshire, 1812

9.3 Main Chartist areas in Britain, c.1838–48

9.4 Bradford Chartist activity, 1848

9.5 Trade union strength, 1867

9.6 Number of trade unionists per hundred people, 1891

9.7 The Labour movement in the West Riding of Yorkshire, 1890–1914

9.8 Syndicalism and militant industrial acts in the United Kingdom, 1910–14.

9.9 The effectiveness of trade union organization in the General Strike, 3–12 May 1926

9.10 Yorkshire and the General Strike, 1926

10.1 Elementary day schools, 1858: percentage Church of England schools

10.2 Elementary day schools, 1858: percentage British schools

10.3 Elementary day schools, 1858: percentage Roman Catholic schools

10.4 Lancashire registration districts: children at school census day 1851 as percentage of school-age population

10.5 Cumberland and Westmorland registration districts: children at school, census day 1851, as percentage of school-age population

10.6 Herefordshire and Monmouthshire registration districts: children at school census day 1851, as percentage of school-age population

10.7 Towns with more day-school pupils than 1 in 6 of the population, 1851

10.8 Urban School Boards, November 1870

10.9 Bootle, 1871: spatial variations in socio-economic grouping of children, 3–15

10.10 Bootle, S.W. corner: spatial variations in socio-economic grouping of children, 3–15

10.11 Bootle: aspects of school attendance after 1870

11.1 Levels of church-going, 1851

11.2 Levels of church-going, 1979–84

11.3 Denominational alignments in England and Wales, 1851: Church of England

11.4 Denominational alignments in England and Wales, 1851: Methodist Churches

11.5 Denominational alignments in England and Wales, 1851: Nonconformists

11.6 Denominational alignments in England and Wales, 1851: Roman Catholic Church

11.7 Denominational alignments in England, 1979, and Wales, 1982: Church of England and the Church in Wales

11.8 Denominational alignments in England, 1979, and Wales, 1982: Methodist Church

11.9 Denominational alignments in England, 1979, and Wales, 1982: Nonconformists

11.10 Denominational alignments in England, 1979, and Wales, 1982: Roman Catholic Church

11.11 Denominational alignments in Scotland, 1851: Church of Scotland

11.12 Denominational alignments in Scotland, 1851: Free Church of Scotland

11.13 Denominational alignments in Scotland, 1851: United Presbyterian Church and other Churches

11.14 Denominational alignments in Scotland, 1851: Roman Catholic Church

11.15 Denominational alignments in Scotland, 1984: Church of Scotland

11.16 Denominational alignments in Scotland, 1984: Free Church, Free Presbyterian Church, and Reformed Presbyterian Church

11.17 Denominational alignments in Scotland, 1984: other Protestant Churches

11.18 Denominational alignments in Scotland, 1984: Roman Catholic Church

12.1 Total stock and number of books per head of population in selected public libraries, 1913

12.2 Drinking places in York city centre, c.1900

12.3 The English Football League, 1888–9

12.4 The main seaside resorts of England and Wales as listed by the 1901 Census

12.5 The English and Scottish Football Leagues, 1935–6

12.6 Public places of recreation/culture and urban transport systems in Manchester city centre, c. early 1930s

12.7 Cinemas in the textile districts of the North-west, 1919 and 1939

12.8 National Parks and other Areas of Natural Beauty, c.1985

INTRODUCTION

All students of history use maps. Sometimes, these maps are simply used to illustrate a point, for example the layout of a medieval town or the placing of armies before a battle. Frequently though, and particularly in the case of economic and social history, maps play a more positive role. They can show the importance of raw materials, sources of power, transport facilities, or economic linkages, including proximity to consumer markets, in determining the location of an industry. Taken in sequence, maps can be used to indicate the expansion of eighteenth-century roads, nineteenth-century railways, or twentieth-century electricity supply, the decline of the coal-mining industry, the shift, over time, in the location of the iron and steel or chemicals industries, the concentration of production in wool textiles or motor vehicles, and regional contrasts of product within a sector such as agriculture or engineering. Maps, too, can be used to demonstrate changing patterns of trade, by direction or commodity, and the significance of particular ports.

On social issues, maps can indicate contrasts, between areas and over time, in densities of population, in occupational distribution, of unemployment, in religious observance or in the provision of denominational schools, in overcrowding or in infant mortality levels, in labour unrest or in leisure activity. These, and other issues, are dealt with in this Atlas. The end-product offers some support for those historians who question the usefulness of thinking in terms of *national* economic histories.

The different sections of the Atlas contain roughly equal proportions of maps and supporting text. In most instances, they contain, too, maps indicating developments at the local level, e.g. the closing shipyards of the Tyne, the growth of Glasgow, the socio-economic groupings of children in a district of Bootle. These case studies are selected to draw attention to variations in experience within quite small areas and to the impact of change on particular localities.

The Atlas is designed primarily for the use of students of social and economic history at undergraduate and GCE advanced level. For this reason, the contributors are all subject specialists who have taught in higher education institutions, and a large proportion of the maps and text are based on their own original research using primary sources. However, we also hope to reach a wider readership. Thus contributors have sought to avoid undue complexity in chapter structure, text, or maps and, by naming, for instance, pits, shipyards or textile mills in local case studies (not strictly necessary in economic history terms), have tried to impress on readers the fact that these are real places, well remembered in many cases by those who live in, or come from, the areas concerned.

Inevitably, there are omissions. Some subjects are left out intentionally, if contentiously, on the grounds that they do not constitute sufficiently important areas of economic or social activity (e.g. the footwear industry) or that they do not lend themselves to useful spatial analysis (e.g. a universal economic activity like building). Others are victims of constraints of space (e.g. banking or various forms of savings activity in the eighteenth and nineteenth centuries, or regional studies of retailing). On balance, we have opted to cover a limited range of areas at reasonable length rather than to include a wider range of topics and run the risk of fragmentation.

One final point of explanation is required regarding coverage. The Atlas covers Britain, not the United Kingdom. Thus Ireland (or, from 1922, Northern Ireland) is omitted. Such action could be seen as indicating a political position. In this instance, it does not. The changing definition of the United Kingdom and the very different economic and social history of Ireland are the reasons for restricting the Atlas to Britain. It has to be said that this was not a decision to which all contributors agreed.

ACKNOWLEDGEMENTS

Acknowledgement of individuals and organizations contributing to particular parts of this Atlas is made in the notes to the section concerned. It remains to thank those who have contributed to the work as a whole.

Three members of what was originally Croom Helm Ltd have been involved: Richard Stoneman, Alan Jarvis, and Anita Roy. All have been unfailingly helpful. The successful publication of the Atlas is substantially their achievement.

Cartography has been undertaken by Jayne Lewin. To Jayne goes the credit for a clear and consistent presentation in spite of constraints of medium and space. If any maps or diagrams are considered to have failed in their objective, this must be in spite, not because, of Jayne's efforts.

Contributors of the different sections have also played their part. One or two even delivered their material on time. Most kept close to their schedules and all proved tolerant of an occasionally indecisive editor. Sadly, one of their number, Stephen Jones, died before publication was achieved. I'm sure I speak for many in praising the work of Stephen who was one of the most promising young social historians of leisure.

As ever, I have been well served by the staff and students of Lancashire Polytechnic. Particular thanks are due to the staff of the Library, especially Hilary Higgins who organizes Inter-Library Loans, and to the clerical staff of the Schools of Language and Literature, and Historical and Critical Studies: Ann Hitchen, Maureen Aspinwall, and Teresa Smith. Ann, Maureen, and Teresa never, well rarely, flinched in the face of what must have seemed, at times, a never-ending task.

All concerned have done their best to produce a successful work. It remains to be said, of course, that any failure to achieve that object is wholly my responsibility as editor.

Rex Pope
School of Historical and Critical Studies
Lancashire Polytechnic

1 AGRICULTURE
Peter Dewey

English open-field farming *c.* 1700

At the beginning of the eighteenth century, large areas of England were still cultivated under the system of 'open' fields. This system, which predated the Norman Conquest, involved organizing the arable land around a village into two or three large fields. In order to ensure an equitable distribution of land of differing qualities, each farmer worked a number of strips of land which were widely scattered about the large fields. Usually, one of the fields would be devoted to fallow, and the other(s) to corn crops. There resulted a two- or three-course rotation, which served to maintain crop yields. Animals would be kept on the common land of the village, on the stubbles left after harvest, and on any available waste land.

This system had never been universal. Its heart was the lowland region of central and southern England (see Map 1.1), and this remained true on the eve of the parliamentary enclosure movement of the eighteenth century. But there were large tracts of England where it had never been in force, or only on a modest scale. The reasons for this are conjectural. In areas where much of the new land for medieval farming was obtained by clearing woodland (Devon, Kent, Essex, Suffolk), the creation of new farms was bound to be a piecemeal process, leading to the formation of individual farmsteads and hamlets rather than the large fields and nucleated villages of the Midlands. In other areas, the small-farm nature of pastoral agriculture or regional inheritance systems may have played a part. Whatever the reason, there existed in the late Middle Ages a peripheral belt, concentrated in the South-east, South-west and North-west, where the open-field system was of little importance.

In the ensuing centuries this belt grew, as existing open fields were enclosed into individual holdings by a process of agreement amongst farmers. By 1600, Essex, Kent, Suffolk, Hertfordshire, Surrey, and Sussex were largely enclosed, as were the coastal lowlands of Durham, Cumberland, Lancashire, and Cheshire. In addition, much of the Welsh border land was enclosed, as was Somerset, apart from its unreclaimed wastes. While the motives for enclosure varied, the main one before 1700 was probably the demand for pasture; this would certainly seem to be the spur to the much-discussed enclosures of the fifteenth and sixteenth centuries. More generally, the spread of enclosure may be seen as the response to population and market growth, entailing a shift away from a system whose rationale was to provide adequate land for subsistence farming, to one more oriented to providing opportunities for success in an expanding market. The result was that, by 1700, only about half of the agricultural land of England was still farmed on the open-field system.

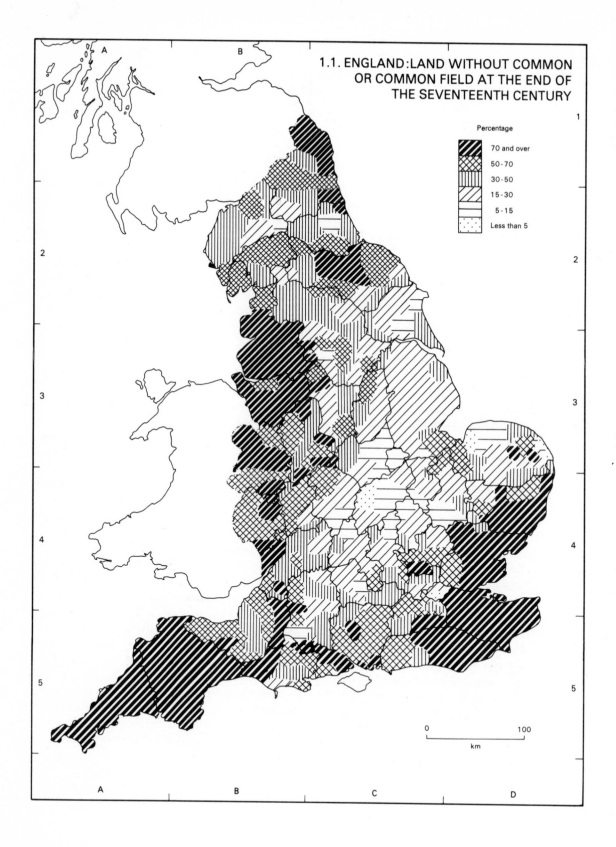

1.1. ENGLAND: LAND WITHOUT COMMON
OR COMMON FIELD AT THE END OF
THE SEVENTEENTH CENTURY

Percentage

70 and over

50 - 70

30 - 50

15 - 30

5 - 15

Less than 5

0   100
km

Parliamentary enclosure

Between the early eighteenth and the mid-nineteenth century there occurred the greatest agrarian reorganization since the Norman Conquest: the enclosure of the remaining open fields of England. After 1850, only a handful of unenclosed villages remained. There is now only one (Laxton, Nottinghamshire), preserved only with the aid of the Ministry of Agriculture. While in the early part of the eighteenth century, enclosure still proceeded by agreement, this soon gave way to the use of Acts of Parliament, and the bulk of enclosure after *c.* 1750 was by Act. The scale of the movement was enormous; some 5,300 Acts were passed (from the first in 1614), the bulk falling in the period 1750–1850. About 3,100 dealt with cases involving some proportion of arable land, and the remainder dealt with commons and wastes. The total area involved was about 6.8 million acres (4.5 million being arable, the rest commons and wastes), or about one-fifth of the land area of England. The result was not just an agrarian reorganization, but also a topographical one, in which the enclosed areas (chiefly the Midland plain) acquired their large fields, straight hedgerows, and farmsteads separated from the village, lying in the newly-created enclosed fields.

The general reasons for the spread of enclosure were the same as they had always been; the desire to free the individual farmer from the constraints of scattered strips and communal practices. On the livestock side, enclosure made possible the evolution of herds and flocks of more uniform quality than was possible under the old intercommoning which accompanied the open fields. Likewise, the spread of disease was limited. Perhaps of most immediate importance for farmers was that enclosure made possible a rapid expansion in the grazing area, which previously had been confined to the commons, wastes, and the post-harvest stubbles of the open fields. On the arable side, consolidation of lands under enclosure avoided the loss of time and energy involved in working scattered strips of plough-land, and reduced the possibility of damage from straying animals and weeds from neighbouring farmers' strips. Most importantly in the long run, it permitted farmers to experiment with the new fodder crops of the 'Agricultural Revolution' such as 'artificial' grasses (clover, lucerne, sainfoin) and turnips, which permitted a higher stock/land ratio. This in turn led to a larger supply of natural manure, and thus to higher corn yields per acre.

While the years 1750–1850 saw the greatest recourse to parliamentary enclosure, it was not spread uniformly over the century. In particular, two peaks stand out; the 1760s and 1770s, and the war years 1793–1815. These were roughly two comparable periods of about twenty years, in each of which about 40 per cent of all parliamentary enclosure took place, so that about 80 per cent of all parliamentary enclosure took place in those forty years. While in both periods it was mainly open-field arable land which was being enclosed, a certain proportion was of commons and waste, and this became somewhat more important during the war years; before 1793, 1.85 million acres of open-field and 0.71 million acres of commons and wastes were enclosed, whereas from 1793 to 1815 the figures were 1.99 and 0.91 million acres respectively.

Maps 1.2 and 1.3 reveal substantial differences between the counties affected by open-field arable and commons/waste enclosure. The former were, as might be expected, concentrated in the pre-existing Midland open-field belt, the chief counties affected being Oxfordshire, Northamptonshire, Bedfordshire, Huntingdonshire and Cambridgeshire. Surrounding these counties lay a further belt of intensive enclosure, stretching in the South to include Wiltshire, and in the North-east to include the East Riding of Yorkshire. By contrast, it was the peripheral counties which were most affected by the enclosure of commons and wastes. In some, especially during wartime, the

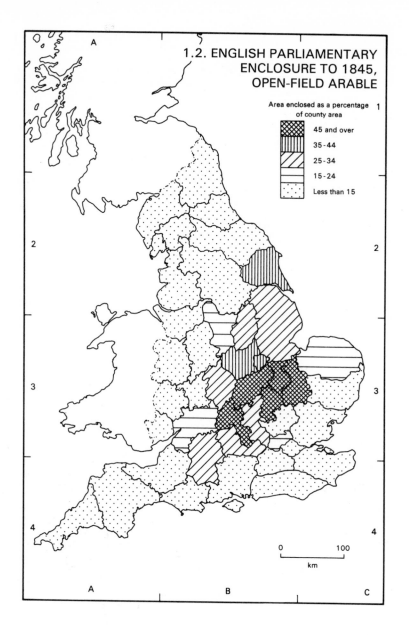

1.2. ENGLISH PARLIAMENTARY ENCLOSURE TO 1845, OPEN-FIELD ARABLE

Area enclosed as a percentage of county area

- 45 and over
- 35 - 44
- 25 - 34
- 15 - 24
- Less than 15

enclosure movement was almost entirely concerned with commons and wastes; this was so in Cheshire, Cornwall, Devon, Durham, Kent, Lancashire, Monmouthshire, and Westmorland. It was largely the case also in Cumberland, Northumberland, Salop, Staffordshire, and the North Riding of Yorkshire. Yet it was even a factor in southern, largely arable counties such as Hampshire and

Surrey, which still had notable examples of common or waste land.

The specific reasons for the spectacular peaking of the enclosure movement between 1750 and 1850 are still controversial. Generally, this was a period when the population was growing at an unprecedented rate. In addition, the beginning of the industrial revolution may have contributed to the

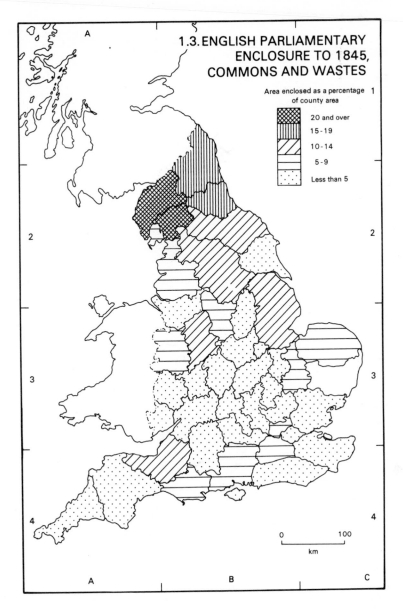

1.3. ENGLISH PARLIAMENTARY ENCLOSURE TO 1845, COMMONS AND WASTES

Area enclosed as a percentage of county area

	20 and over
	15 - 19
	10 - 14
	5 - 9
	Less than 5

0   100
km

pressure by stimulating a rise in money incomes (and perhaps also real incomes in its early stages). More specifically, the wars of 1793–1815 led to a startling rise in food prices (the price of wheat more than doubled between 1790 and the peaks of 1800/1 and 1812/13). The financial incentive to increase output by means of enclosure was thus considerable, and private Acts of Parliament provided the method of expediting the process.

The agricultural depression of the late nineteenth century

The period from the early 1870s until the late 1890s was widely regarded by contemporaries as one of national economic depression. Strictly, this was not the case; national output rose substantially, and, although the average level of unemployment was slightly higher, it was scarcely at a level to constitute a depression. What was occurring was rather a general period of price deflation, as a result of increased industrial development and international competition.

In this situation, the greatest sufferers were entrepreneurs and investors, rather than workers and consumers. There seems little doubt that farmers were the hardest hit of all entrepreneurs. Unlike industrial producers, their market was not expanding, due to the inroads of foreign competition on the domestic market. In addition, they had to cope with price falls which, in some important cases, were much greater than the national average. This was particularly the case for crops, and especially wheat, the largest of the corn crops. Thus, while the general national price level fell by 31 per cent between 1874/5 and 1892/3, the price of wheat fell by almost 60 per cent, barley by 46 per cent, and oats by 43 per cent. The price of livestock fell less, by an average of about 15 per cent, as probably did the price of milk (although the information on these products is imperfect).

The effect on farms was to reduce incomes and profits substantially. While regional variations in these are not precisely known, some indication of the regional impact of the depression can be gained from mapping the reductions in rent which landowners were obliged to offer to their tenants. These are reflected in the assessments for income tax (Schedule B), which are shown in Map 1.4. Overall, they show that rents had fallen by 17 per cent in Britain between 1874/5 and 1892/3. However, this was largely an English experience; English rents fell by 18 per cent, while Scottish rents only fell by 8 per cent, and Welsh rents actually rose, by 5 per cent. The more favourable experiences of Scotland and Wales may be attributed to a lesser reliance on cereals and a keen competition for farms (especially in Wales), which the depression seems hardly to have affected. The latter factor may also have operated in Cornwall, the only English county to show a rise in rent, and one noted for its large number of small farmers. The most severely affected were certain Midland and eastern counties, especially Cambridgeshire, Huntingdonshire, Essex and Wiltshire, where rents fell by 40 per cent or more. The least affected were the north-western counties of Lancashire, Cheshire, Westmorland and Cumberland, all noted for stock-raising and dairying rather than cereals, and not far from the expanding urban markets for meat and milk to be found in Lancashire and the West Riding of Yorkshire. In addition, livestock producers benefited in one important respect from the general deflation, since it lowered the cost of purchased animal feed and so cheapened production. For the cereal producer, however, the largest cost was labour, and money wages did not fall in the same proportion as product prices.

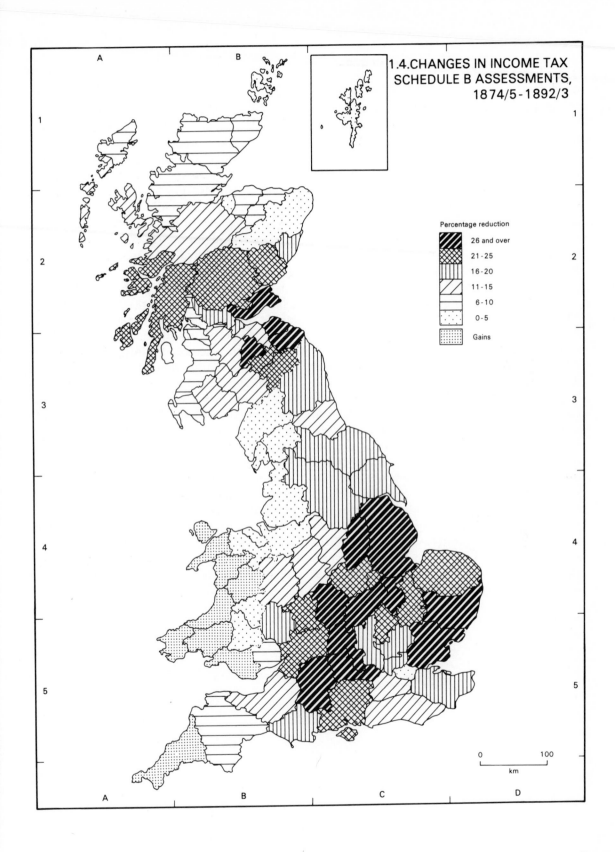

1.4. CHANGES IN INCOME TAX SCHEDULE B ASSESSMENTS, 1874/5-1892/3

Percentage reduction

- 26 and over
- 21 - 25
- 16 - 20
- 11 - 15
- 6 - 10
- 0 - 5

Gains

0   100
km

The changing product structure, 1870–1914

From the 1870s until the First World War, British farming underwent a substantial transformation. The main reason for this was a large increase in foreign competition, chiefly in the form of cereals from the USA; by 1914, only about one-fifth of the British bread supply came from domestic sources. Competition was also felt in the meat and dairy trades, although to a lesser extent. Milk, however, was almost immune to foreign competition and faced a rising demand from the rapidly growing urban population.

These factors lay behind the large changes which farmers were forced to make in this period. The greatest, and most apparent to contemporaries, was the fall in the cereal area. Between 1870 and 1914, the area of corn crops fell by 2.4 million acres (27 per cent). This was largely due to the fall in the wheat area, but barley also declined. This process was offset to some extent by a slight rise in oats, a response to the growing number of urban horses and an increasing reliance by farmers on horse-drawn implements. The decline in corn (see Map 1.5) was greatest in South Wales, certain Midland counties, and Northumberland, but most southern and Midland counties were seriously affected. The least affected were the large-farm areas of eastern England, where wheat was climatically suitable, and economies of scale could be achieved. In Lancashire and Che-

shire, the decline in wheat was largely offset by the expansion of oats. In the Scottish Highland counties, the small reduction in corn is explained by the overwhelming predominance (for climatic reasons) of oats, against which even large reductions in wheat and barley could not have much effect.

Dairying, which was largely unaffected by foreign competition, was the most dynamic element in British farming in this period, when the milking herd grew by one-third. However, this was unevenly distributed (see Map 1.6). The main influences were the proximity of large towns and the existence or absence of rail links. While the traditional western dairying districts remained important, and expanded to meet the rising demand of towns like Manchester, Birmingham, and Leeds, the largest and most rapidly expanding market was London. This led to the fastest growth in dairying being in the southern and south-eastern counties, although Lincolnshire and Northamptonshire also showed rapid growth. In Scotland, the border counties proved most adept at responding to the rising demand of Edinburgh and Glasgow. Conversely, West Wales and certain northern and Scottish counties, disadvantaged by poor rail links and a limited capacity to grow their own fodder, failed to hold their own.

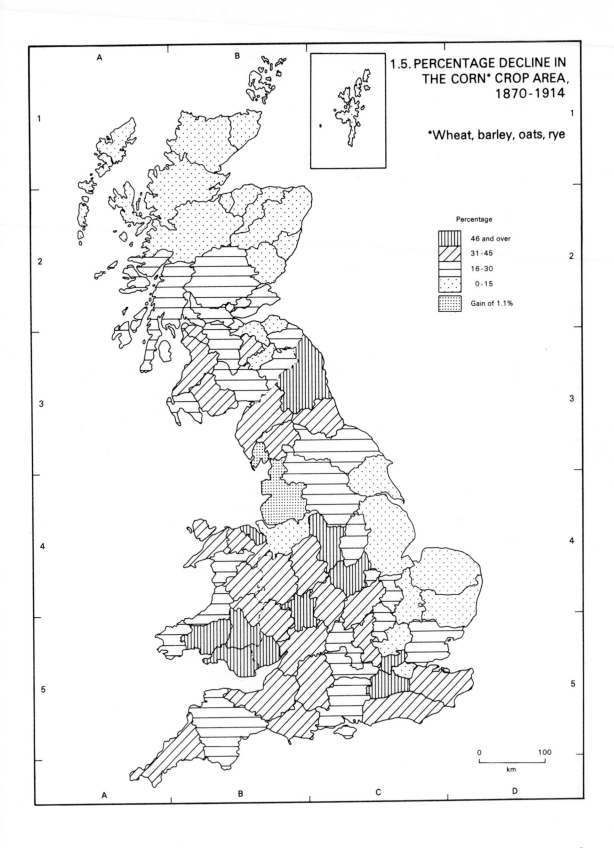

1.5. PERCENTAGE DECLINE IN
THE CORN* CROP AREA,
1870-1914

*Wheat, barley, oats, rye

Percentage

46 and over
31 - 45
16 - 30
0 - 15

Gain of 1.1%

0   100
km

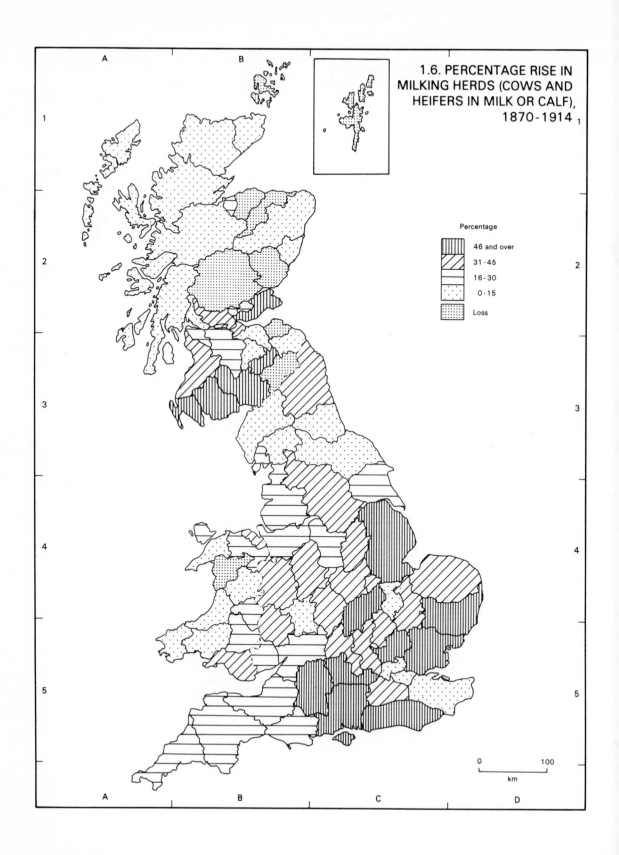

1.6. PERCENTAGE RISE IN
MILKING HERDS (COWS AND
HEIFERS IN MILK OR CALF),
1870-1914

Percentage

46 and over
31 - 45
16 - 30
0 - 15

Loss

0   100
km

Regional agricultural wages, 1902

Nineteenth-century industrialization, which had brought changes in the way of life and economic position of farmers and landowners, also affected the agricultural labourer. There were two aspects to this change: agricultural earnings fell below those of other groups, and there were considerable regional differences in farm wages.

Prior to industrialization, farm labourers' earnings had been roughly comparable with those in other occupations. However, by the end of the nineteenth century, they were amongst the lowest-paid groups in society. In 1902 (see Map 1.7) the average cash wages of ordinary agricultural labourers (those without special responsibility for livestock) was about 17 shillings (85p) a week. While this was supplemented in certain cases by extra payments at hay and corn harvest, and perhaps a subsidized or rent-free cottage, it is unlikely that over the whole year these were equivalent to more than an extra shilling or two per week in England and Wales (although they were higher in Scotland). Overall, the earnings of the farm labourer compared badly with those in the towns, being below even those of the unskilled urban labourer, earning about £1.00 a week.

While contemporaries were inclined to attribute this state of affairs to such factors as the reduction in the demand for agricultural labour as a result of increasing farm mechanization (especially in harvesting), this is now seen as part of the longer-term process of industrialization, whereby demand for non-agricultural products rises more rapidly than for farm products. In the long run, this implies that real incomes in the agricultural sector will not rise as rapidly as those elsewhere.

The considerable regional differences in agricultural earnings (Map 1.7) stem from the effects of industrialization and urban growth on the labour market. The general pattern is a gradient from north to south; the industrial areas of Lancashire, the West Riding of Yorkshire, and Durham generated competition for labour, which led to agricultural wages being higher there than in the southern and Midland counties. The same effect is seen in South Wales, and near London (in the case of Kent and Surrey). It is notable that the two lowest-wage counties in England are Oxfordshire and Rutland, which were neither industrialized to any extent nor near large industrial or urban areas. In Scotland, the high-wage areas are the Lowland counties (except Aberdeen), which were not far from the heavily industrialized area of Glasgow and Edinburgh.

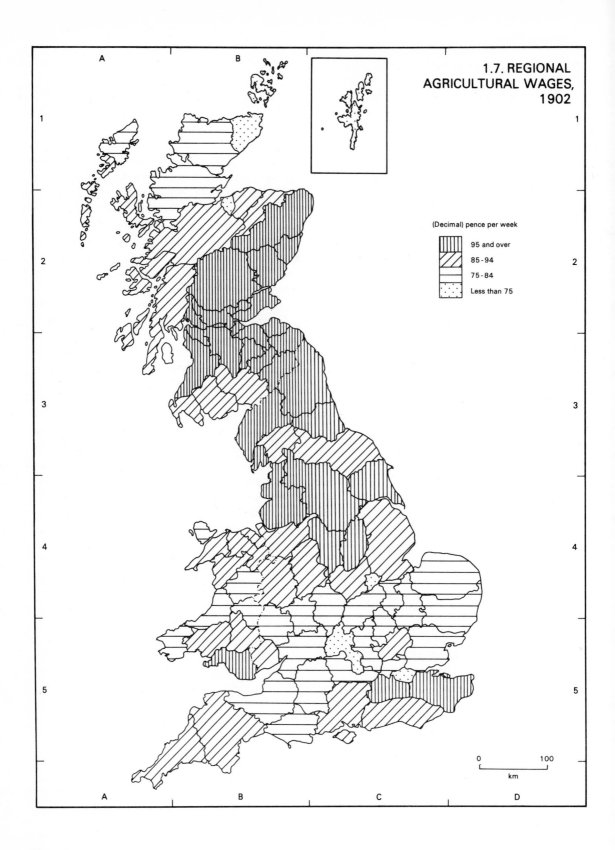

1.7. REGIONAL
AGRICULTURAL WAGES,
1902

(Decimal) pence per week

95 and over
85 - 94
75 - 84
Less than 75

0   100
    km

Wartime changes: tillage, 1914–18 and 1939–45

By 1914, British farming had settled down into a pattern dictated by the reality of foreign competition, in which the greater part of the population's grain supply and a substantial part of its meat supply were obtained from abroad. In overall terms, measured in calories (the energy in the food supply), about 60 per cent of UK food came from abroad. This situation, acceptable on commercial grounds in peacetime, became a source of concern during both the world wars and led to radical changes in policy.

During the First World War, this change occurred in 1917, following the decision of the German government to intensify submarine warfare. To counter this potential threat, the British government decided to pursue a policy of producing at home as much food as possible. This was to be achieved by ploughing extra land in order to grow more cereals and potatoes. The scientific reason for this was that it is possible to maintain many more people per acre if the land is devoted to producing crops for direct human consumption rather than indirect consumption (i.e. via meat and milk).

In drawing up its targets, the government had as its slogan 'Back to the Seventies', a conscious reference to the high-water mark of tillage in the early 1870s. It was envisaged that the bulk of the 3 million or so acres laid down to grass after 1870 would be reconverted into arable land. This target was not achieved, since the new policy was in effect confined to the agricultural year 1917/18; the British tillage area in 1918 was only 1.9 million acres more than in 1909–13. However, this may be reckoned a fairly substantial achievement in the time available, being an increase of some 18 per cent.

Second World War policy was based on the same principle. The differences were that the policy was imposed as soon as the war commenced, and that much greater effort was put into supplying farmers with essential machinery and labour. Given these advantages, it is not surprising that performance in the second war was superior; overall, tillage in Britain in 1945 was 55 per cent greater than on average in the years 1935–9.

If policy was similar in both wars, the geographical results were less so. In the first war, significant changes in the tillage area were confined to the North and West of England, Wales and the South-west of Scotland (see Map 1.8). This reflects the previously low proportion of tillage in these predominantly grassland regions, and the difficulties which farmers in the arable counties of the South and East of England experienced in finding labour, machinery, and fertilizers. In the second war these areas also extended their tillage substantially, but were joined by a large belt of Midland counties and some southern counties (Map 1.9). Clearly, the impact of the second war was much more universal, as well as more substantial.

These differences are reflected in the degree of national self-sufficiency achieved. The effort during the first war served only to restore it to its pre-war level (it had fallen below this in 1914–16). Between the wars, the policy was abandoned, and the degree of self-sufficiency fell to about one-third. However, the effort made during the Second World War restored it again to 40 per cent.

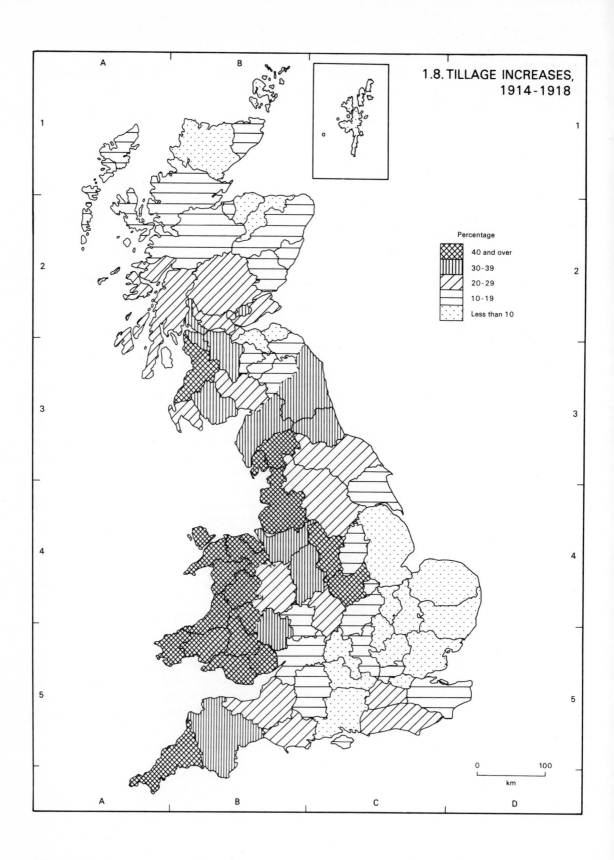

1.8. TILLAGE INCREASES, 1914-1918

Percentage

40 and over
30 - 39
20 - 29
10 - 19
Less than 10

0   100
km

14

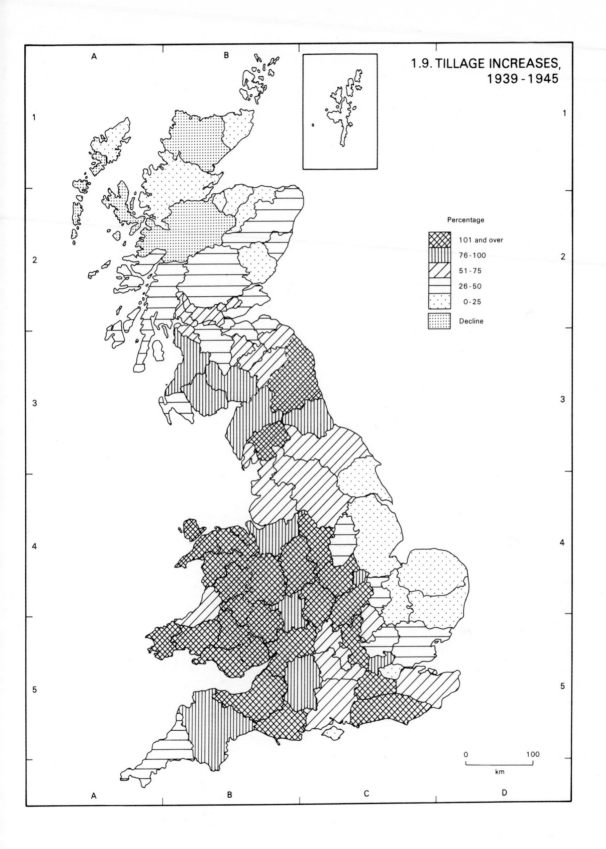

1.9. TILLAGE INCREASES,
1939-1945

Percentage

101 and over
76 - 100
51 - 75
26 - 50
0 - 25

Decline

0   100
km

A   B   C   D

15

Product changes, 1945–81

Crops (barley)

Whereas the arable gains of the First World War were quickly lost, those of the Second World War have been largely maintained; by 1945, the arable area was 17.9 million acres (not far off its recorded peak in 1873), and only fell slowly, to 16.3 million acres in 1980/1; a far cry from the depths of depression in the late 1930s, when it fell below 12 million acres.

Within this greater emphasis on arable farming, substantial changes took place in the types of crops grown. The greatest change has been in barley, which has extended considerably as a result of the demand for animal feeds, and now dominates the corn crop to a

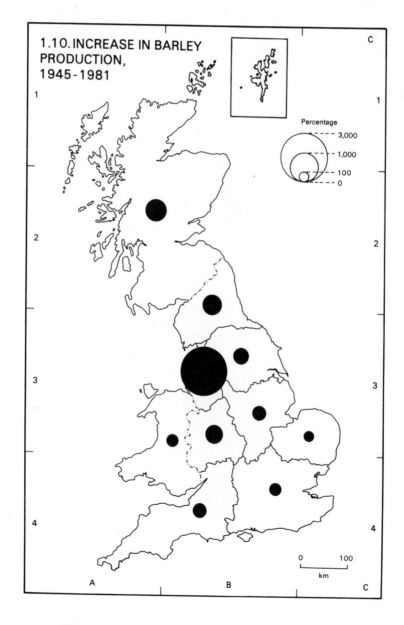

1.10. INCREASE IN BARLEY PRODUCTION, 1945-1981

Percentage
3,000
1,000
100
0

0   100
km

greater extent even than wheat in the nineteenth century, occupying 5.6 million acres in 1980/1 (wheat = 3.6 million acres).

The expansion of barley (see Map 1.10) has not been uniform. Growth has been least in traditional malting barley areas of South and East England (especially Kent and East Anglia), although even here the acreage has at least doubled. The greatest rise has been in the production of barley for animal feed, chiefly in North and West England, and in Scotland, where it has largely replaced oats.

Livestock (dairying)

Dairying is the most important livestock enterprise, and one of the most important branches of the industry as a whole, currently accounting for about one-quarter of the value of all agricultural output. Much of this

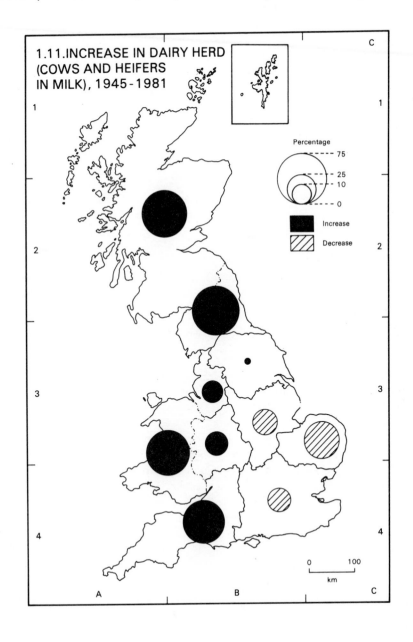

1.11. INCREASE IN DAIRY HERD (COWS AND HEIFERS IN MILK), 1945-1981

dominant position has been achieved in the post-1945 period, as rising real incomes generated demand for milk and other dairy products. This demand has been met partially by expansion of the dairy herd (+ 16 per cent, 1945–81), but chiefly by a rise in the yield of milk per cow, due to improved feeding and selective breeding, so that total milk production rose by 93 per cent between 1945 and 1981.

Traditionally, the industry was centred around four main regions; the North-west and South-west of England, South-west Wales and South-west Scotland. In the late nineteenth and early twentieth centuries, emphasis shifted to the South and East of England, which had developed as large suppliers of liquid milk. However, much of the history of dairying after 1945 is that of the relative decline of the South and East, so that the traditional dairying regions have reasserted their dominance (see Map 1.11). This really is a reflection of the general policy of post-war support for agriculture, which has permitted the farmers of South and East England to concentrate more on arable products, for which their regions are more suited by reason of climate and soil, and from which they had reluctantly departed in the late nineteenth century.

Post-1945 intensification

Changes in average farm size, 1945–81

The post-1945 period has been one of considerable change, both technically and organizationally. This is strikingly apparent when considering the size of the British farm; from 1945 to 1981, the average farm increased in size by 94 per cent, from 26.6 hectares to 51.6 hectares. Such rapid change in such a comparatively short historical period is unprecedented in modern British history.

This change has not been due to an expansion of the cultivated area, which has continued to shrink under the continuing pressure of industrial, urban, and transport developments. In 1945 the cultivated area (crops and grass, excluding rough grazing) was 11.6 million hectares and in 1981 it had fallen to 11.1 million hectares. The main change has been in the number of farmers, which has more than halved – from some 438,000 to 216,000. There are many reasons for this. The supply of potential farmers has been curtailed by the years of full employment (roughly until the early 1970s), which permitted non-farm employment (and higher earnings) to be found more easily than in the depressed years of the 1920s and 1930s. Culturally, the attractions of the town continued to exert a powerful influence on rural dwellers, and the spread of car ownership gave easier access to employment outside the village community.

At the same time, the demand for farmland from existing farmers has been very high, by historical standards, throughout the period. This is largely the result of the change in agriculture's position, from an industry unprotected from foreign competition to one which was heavily subsidized after 1945. The accession of the UK to the EEC in 1973 led to the level of subsidy being raised further. Thus cushioned, farmers and landowners have invested heavily in new machinery, fertilizers, drainage, and buildings. In order to make the most efficient use of this investment, farmers have been obliged to seek greater economies of scale through the amalgamation of farms. Thus, while the number of new entrants to the industry has declined, retiring farmers have not been replaced, but their holdings absorbed by neighbouring farmers.

This process of enlargement has been most marked in the eastern regions of England, and in Scotland. Here farm amalgamation has pro-

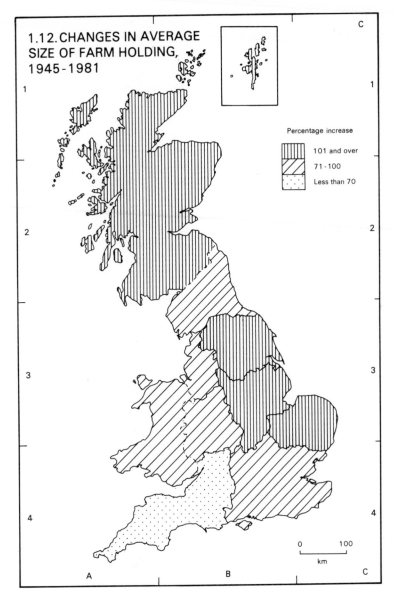

1.12. CHANGES IN AVERAGE
SIZE OF FARM HOLDING,
1945-1981

Percentage increase

101 and over

71 - 100

Less than 70

ceeded apace, most rapidly in East Anglia (see Map 1.12), where the average farm size has increased by 116 per cent in this period. At the other extreme lies South-west England, where farm size has only increased by 64 per cent. The reasons for the different regional experiences are largely the suitability of a region for cereal growing, and the ease with which adjacent holdings can be physically amalgamated. In East Anglia, this may involve nothing more than grubbing up hedges on the farms to be joined up; such a process is much more difficult and expensive in the West Country, with its substantial stone walls. Even there, however, the abandoned farmstead is a not uncommon sight.

Intensive livestock enterprise since 1945: poultry

The rise of the modern poultry industry must be accounted one of the outstanding success stories of post-war farming, leading to the creation of what is virtually a new industry. Here the interest centres on fowls, which account today for about 93 per cent of all poultry. In 1945 there were 40.6 million fowls on farms. By 1981 their numbers had almost trebled, to 111.3 million. At the same time, considerable changes had occurred in the industry. To start with, it was comparatively small, unspecialized flocks which were almost universally found on farms.

The first sector to rationalize was egg production. By the late 1950s, the market for eggs was almost saturated, so that attention among producers turned to cost reduction. This was achieved by adopting the battery system of management. Almost simultaneously, the breeding sector turned to mass production in order to keep pace with the demand for low-priced laying stock. Finally, the meat sector turned to mass production of a new commodity – the broiler chicken, fed on

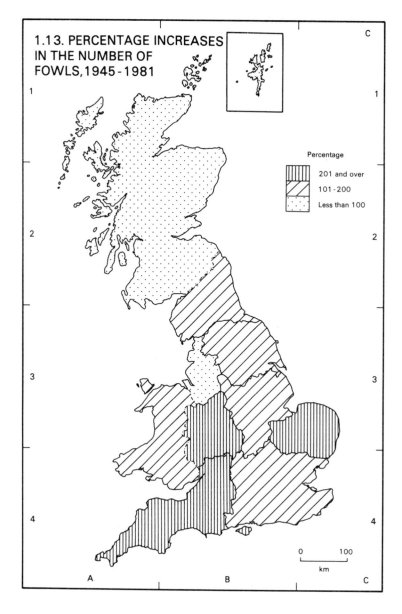

1.13. PERCENTAGE INCREASES IN THE NUMBER OF FOWLS, 1945-1981

Percentage

201 and over

101-200

Less than 100

0   100
km

compound feeds so as to fatten early, and thus reduce costs. The success of the broiler industry can be gauged from the facts that almost half of all fowls are broilers, and that consumption of poultry meat has risen from about 0.6 ounces per head weekly in the mid-1950s to 6.4 ounces (1980).

Geographically, the emphasis has altered from the industry's concentration on areas such as Lancashire and Sussex, which had developed strongly in the inter-war period.

The most dynamic areas (see Map 1.13) have been the West Midlands, the South-west and East Anglia, largely as a result of the expansion of southern industry and population, and the improvement of road transport.

Changes in wheat yields per hectare, 1945–81

As noted earlier, the virtual disappearance of oats in Britain has left arable farmers with the choice of barley or wheat only as major cereal

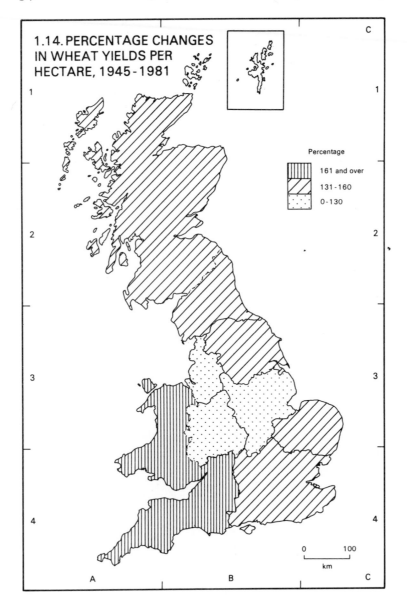

1.14. PERCENTAGE CHANGES IN WHEAT YIELDS PER HECTARE, 1945-1981

Percentage

161 and over

131 - 160

0 - 130

crops. While in terms of area barley predominates, the expansion of wheat has been almost as striking, and yields per hectare have increased more than in the case of barley. In 1945, wheat occupied some 2.2 million acres. After some mild fluctuations in the 1950s, it began to rise slowly, and expanded rapidly after the accession of Britain to the EEC, so that in 1980/1 it covered 3.6 million acres, or about as much as at its nineteenth-century peak around 1870. Yields per hectare rose continuously, and had roughly doubled by the mid-1970s; a further surge took them by 1981 to 152 per cent above their 1945 level.

The principal reason for higher yields has been the development of improved varieties of seed. These have been evolved so as to maximize yields, at the same time offering greater resistance to disease. The outstanding feature of the new varieties has been their responsiveness to greater use of artificial fertilizers, especially nitrogenous ones. In addition, the chemical industry has provided a further benefit in the form of sprays to combat diseases and harmful insects. Both fertilizers and chemicals have become much more important to farmers in recent years; in 1939, they accounted for only about 4 per cent of farmers' costs of production, but by 1985 this had risen to about 13 per cent.

In addition to biological improvements, yields have been boosted by the spread of mechanization. Here the most significant innovation is the combine harvester, which has almost universally replaced the system of reaper/binder and portable threshing box which was dominant in the 1940s. Combining is particularly successful in gathering crops laid low by adverse weather. In addition, it provides immediate threshing; thus grain which is too high in moisture can be put through a drying machine at once, without the risk of spoilage.

In regional terms, the most impressive yield increases have occurred in Wales and South-west England, rather than in the traditional grain-growing counties of the South and East (see Map 1.14). The explanation for this is that the new strains of seed have had more impact on these formerly low-yield areas than on the regions where yields have usually been high. However, it is the general rise in yields in the post-war period which is striking, rather than regional variations.

Notes

Map 1.1 is taken from E. C. K. Gonner, *Common Land and Inclosure* (London, 1912); Maps 1.2 and 1.3 are based on data in M. E. Turner, *English Parliamentary Enclosure: Its Historical Geography and Economic History* (Folkestone, 1980); Map 1.4 is based on data from the Royal Commission on Agricultural Depression, 1894–6, *Final Report*, Appendix D. Maps 1.5, 1.6, and 1.8–1.14 are based on the annual Agricultural Statistics collected successively by the Statistical Department of the Board of Trade (from 1866), the Board of Agriculture (from 1889), and the Ministry of Agriculture (from 1919). They are currently published by the Ministry of Agriculture and Fisheries. Map 1.7 is based on material originally compiled for the Board of Trade by Arthur Wilson-Fox and published as the *Report on Wages, Earnings and Conditions of Employment of Agricultural Labourers in the United Kingdom*, Cd. 2376 (1905), p. 68.

2 THE TEXTILE AND CHEMICALS INDUSTRIES
Geoff Timmins and Rex Pope

Textiles

In the early and middle eighteenth century, domestically organized textile manufacture was to be found throughout the country. None the less, certain areas (for a variety of reasons which could include good local wool supplies, fast-flowing streams to power fulling mills, soft water for finishing processes, or freedom from controls) were, or had been, pre-eminent. These included East Anglia (especially Suffolk), the West Country (Gloucestershire, Oxfordshire, Wiltshire, Somerset and Devon), and the West Riding of Yorkshire (with adjacent areas of Lancashire). The East Midlands counties of Nottinghamshire (cotton), Leicestershire (wool), and Derbyshire (silk) were centres for hosiery while London was a centre of the specialized finishing trades.

The middle years of the eighteenth century saw rapid growth in the wool textile industries, particularly those of the West Riding. Of a product valued at *c*. £10 million in 1770, about a third (worsted £1.4 million, woollens £1.9 million) came from this area. Due largely to Yorkshire competition, much of the East Anglian industry (though not, as yet, the fine worsted manufacture of Norwich) was, by this time, in absolute decline. In the West Country, the coarser trade suffered from the effects of the War of American Independence and fluctuations in purchases by the East India Company, but demand for superfine Gloucester broadcloths held up until the early nineteenth century. Thereafter, however,

failure to respond to changing fashions (in colour or weave) led to the region being replaced by Scotland as the main centre for the manufacture of high-grade and more costly woollen cloths, the latter benefiting particularly from the demand for outdoor leisure wear and tartans.

The West Riding remained the major area of growth during the late eighteenth and the nineteenth centuries. The area gained from a commitment to the right products (worsted at the more expensive end of the market, 'low woollens' for bulk sales in cheaper fabrics) and from substantial involvement in the more dynamic export trade. There were also advantages, albeit marginal, in the availability of water power and in coal prices for steam power. Latterly the growth of local merchanting facilities and machinery manufacture reinforced the tendency to geographical concentration. By 1867, of 1,717 British woollen mills, 899 employing 54 per cent of millworkers in the industry were to be found in Yorkshire; Somerset, Wiltshire and Gloucestershire contained 116 mills, Scotland 193, and Lancashire 125. In 1867–8, Yorkshire contained 626 of the United Kingdom's 703 worsted mills (employing 92 per cent of worsted millworkers); Lancashire contained 10 and Norfolk 4 (see Map 2.1). Yorkshire domination of worsted manufacture continued, while, in the woollen sector, the industry in Lancashire and Scotland thrived until the 1870s whereas that of East Anglia and

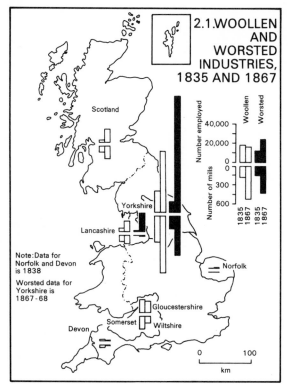

2.1. WOOLLEN AND WORSTED INDUSTRIES, 1835 AND 1867

Note: Data for Norfolk and Devon is 1838

Worsted data for Yorkshire is 1867-68

2.2. YORKSHIRE WOOL TEXTILE AREA, c. 1800

the West Country continued a decline which had been already under way. Within Yorkshire, by the late eighteenth century, the worsted industry had become centred on Halifax and, latterly, Bradford. Woollen cloth manufacture predominated in an area lying north of Huddersfield and Wakefield and between Leeds (its major centre) and Bradford. In this area, the western district (mainly the Calder Valley and the region to the north) concentrated on white cloths whilst to the east (mainly the Aire Valley) emphasis was on coloured cloth (see Map 2.2). The degree of specialization can, though, be overstated. Halifax, for example, produced as much woollen as worsted cloth while Leeds, for a time, had quite an extensive worsted industry. Nor was any emphasis constant. By the late nineteenth century, while Bradford had come to dominate in worsted weaving and merchanting and in tops (combed wool), Halifax was probably more noted for its carpets. Indeed the latter town, which also had a cotton

as well as worsted and woollen industries, could hardly be said to demonstrate any local specialization. The use of waste (shoddy and mungo) characterized the area around Dewsbury, Batley, and Ossett, while Leeds, no longer pre-eminent in the woollen sector, had developed a substantial clothing industry (Map 2.3).

The cotton industry, until the coming of machine-spun yarn (using jenny, water frame or mule), between 1760 and 1790, was unimportant. Following mechanization, many of the early mills were established in Nottinghamshire or Derbyshire (see Map 2.4), meeting the demand for yarn from the knitting industries. South-west Scotland, too, saw the establishment of early cotton mills. Like Lancashire, this region had port facilities, water supplies, an established textile industry and, along with that, marketing arrangements.

Lancashire also developed as the centre of technological innovation while Liverpool, by

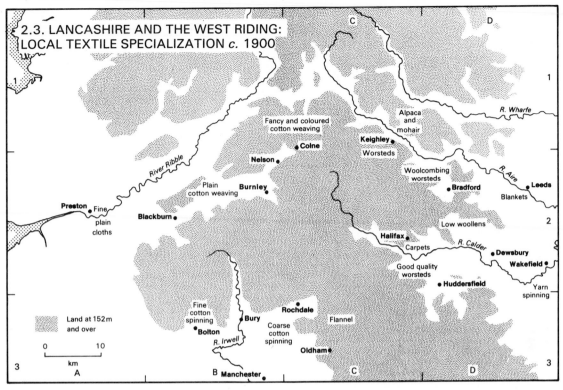

2.3. LANCASHIRE AND THE WEST RIDING: LOCAL TEXTILE SPECIALIZATION *c.* 1900

Alpaca and mohair

Fancy and coloured cotton weaving

Keighley
Worsteds

Colne

Nelson

Woolcombing worsteds

Bradford

Leeds

Blankets

Plain cotton weaving

Burnley

River Ribble

R. Wharfe

R. Aire

Preston • Fine plain cloths

Blackburn •

Low woollens

Halifax

Carpets

R. Calder

Dewsbury

Wakefield

Good quality worsteds

Huddersfield

Yarn spinning

Land at 152 m and over

Fine cotton spinning

Bury

Rochdale

Flannel

R. Irwell

Coarse cotton spinning

Bolton

0   10
km

Oldham

Manchester

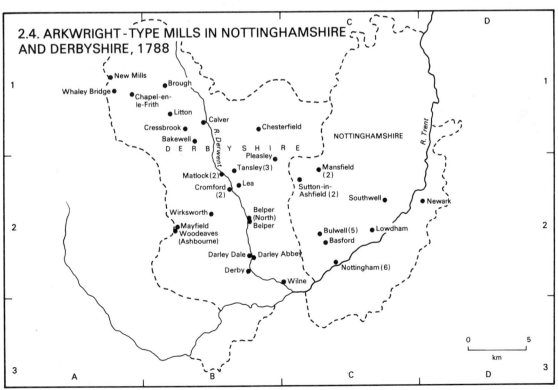

2.4. ARKWRIGHT-TYPE MILLS IN NOTTINGHAMSHIRE AND DERBYSHIRE, 1788

New Mills

Brough

Whaley Bridge

Chapel-en-le-Frith

Litton

Calver

Chesterfield

NOTTINGHAMSHIRE

Cressbrook

Bakewell

D E R B Y S H I R E

R. Derwent

R. Trent

Pleasley

Tansley (3)

Mansfield (2)

Matlock (2)

Lea

Cromford (2)

Sutton-in-Ashfield (2)

Southwell

Newark

Wirksworth

Belper (North)
Belper

Bulwell (5)

Lowdham

Mayfield Woodeaves (Ashbourne)

Basford

Darley Dale

Darley Abbey

Derby

Wilne

Nottingham (6)

0   5
km

25

1835, was taking 90 per cent of raw cotton imports. Lancashire's humid climate was another benefit, especially after the mule made the machine-production of finer yarn counts practicable, although artificial humidification was easily achieved in steam-powered mills. Additionally water, or later coal, for power, and soft water suitable for boilers, helped dictate the concentration of the industry in the east of Lancashire.

Once concentration was established, transport economies and the development of technical and commercial facilities led to its reinforcement. Thus Lancashire had less than one-third of all cotton mills in 1790 but over half (nearly all modern and steam-driven) by 1835; the county had 59 per cent of all cotton operatives in 1835, 76 per cent by the end of the nineteenth century. A substantial proportion of the remaining operatives were to be found, moreover, in adjoining areas of the West Riding and Cheshire.

Within the cotton districts, further specialization developed (see Map 2.3). Initially, the introduction of the powerloom had encouraged the unification of weaving and spinning. In the early 1840s, some 58 per cent of Lancashire cotton mill operatives worked in establishments engaged in both spinning and weaving, 37 per cent were employed in mills solely devoted to spinning (mostly south of Rochdale) and the remainder were in weaving-only mills (mostly north of Rochdale). The advantages of specialization, however, led to segregation by process. By the 1880s, 78 per cent of all spindles lay to the south of Rochdale, 62 per cent of all looms to the north. The great new mills of the early twentieth century, plus the effects of the inter-war slump, accentuated specialization. By 1937, 90 per cent of spindles were south of Rochdale, 75 per cent of looms lay to the north. This was in marked contrast to the practice of the Yorkshire wool textile industries. In worsted, although there was movement towards greater specialization, the late 1880s saw 44 per cent of operatives still employed in integrated spinning and weaving mills. In the woollen industry, the powerloom led to integration, 77 per cent of operatives being employed in spinning *and* weaving mills by 1889.

As in wool textiles, there was local specialization in cotton products. Within the spinning district, the division was between areas producing coarser 'American' yarns (the main product of Oldham, Royton, Rochdale, Ashton, or Wigan) and those, notably Bolton and Leigh, specializing in finer 'Egyptian' yarns. In the weaving district, Preston, Blackburn, and Burnley concentrated on plain cloths mainly for export, while Nelson and Colne produced coloured cloths and apparel fabrics, largely for home consumption.

Both the cotton and the wool textile industries underwent contraction in the interwar years but the decline in Lancashire's cotton industry was much the more marked. Cotton piece goods, of which in 1913 three-quarters of all production had been sold abroad, constituted the major export. Grey cloths, for India and the Far East, were most important of all. By the late 1930s, total piece good exports were running at a quarter of their 1913 volume and at about half their value. The greatest loss had been in the Indian market where tariffs, exchange rate difficulties, falling agricultural incomes, and political activity combined with increased competition from native and Japanese producers to reduce grey cloth exports, by 1937, to under 15 per cent of their 1909–13 level. The 1930s saw planned (and forced) rationalization; 22 million spindles and 251,000 looms were scrapped and the cotton workforce reduced from 564,000 to 398,000. Contraction was most marked in weaving areas catering for Asian markets. Half of Blackburn's mills closed between 1919 and 1939 (Map 2.5); the town, along with neighbouring Great Harwood, Accrington, and Darwen, lost a similar proportion of its looms. The resulting unemployment is indicated in Map 7.28.

Industrial concentration in war led to the permanent closure of a further 250 Lancashire cotton mills but 1945–51 saw a brief boom for the industry. Thereafter, the record was one of decline which even the development of large-scale, vertically integrated firms like Courtaulds or Viyella, or the 1959 Cotton Industry Reorganisation Act failed to check. The Act encouraged re-equipment and reduced capacity – in spinning by almost 50 per cent, in weaving and finishing by almost 40 per cent. Import penetration grew rapidly with Britain becoming a net importer from 1958. In a bid to survive, Lancashire firms moved increasingly into synthetic yarns, knitted fabrics, and specialist production, leaving cotton manufacture to other countries. By the mid-1980s, 76 per cent of the cotton cloth consumed in this country came from abroad and imports were running at six times exports.

Another characteristic of the post-1951 period was the undermining of the division between spinning and weaving districts. Areas with weaving *and* spinning, notably Rossendale or the relatively late-developing Wigan area, did rather better than traditional centres with a heavy emphasis on one process. Once again, the northern weaving towns fared worst, notably Blackburn (see Map 2.5) where, in 1985, there were just five cotton mills left working. The finishing trades did not fare as badly as the manufacturing processes since much untreated cotton cloth still needed to be bleached, dyed, or printed.

The wool textile industries had not been as export-orientated as cotton. Though experiences varied, and worsteds in particular had suffered from tariffs and fashion changes in the late nineteenth century, overseas sales of woollen and worsted tissues (easily the most important wool exports) accounted for just under half total output during the 1920s. By 1937, these exports (at 124.5 million square yards compared with 221.6 million in 1924) had fallen to a little more than a quarter of the industry's production. The major loss was in the export-led woollen sector but this was more than made up in home markets. Part of the home market gain was at the expense of worsteds as male tastes in clothing changed; more came from replacement of imports

following the introduction of tariffs in 1932. None the less, there was a shake-out of equipment and labour. Between 1919 and 1939 the industries lost 10 per cent of their spindles and 31 per cent of their looms, while between 1912 and 1937 their labour force fell by 11 per cent. In the same period, by contrast, the cotton labour force fell by 42 per cent.

During and after the Second World War, the wool textile industries continued to fare rather better than cotton. Imports, while making up 56 per cent of home consumption of woollen and worsted cloth by 1985, never equalled exports. Exports in fact have accounted for an increasing proportion of overall output – 59.7 per cent by 1984. The problem for the industries has been falling home demand. Car ownership and declining use of overcoats, warmer homes leading to lighter clothing and increased informality reducing the demand for men's suits have all affected output of woollen and worsted cloth. This fell from over 300 million linear yards in the 1930s to 113 million in 1977 and 67 million in 1984. The industry lost approximately 20 per cent of its workforce as a result of wartime concentration and more attractive alternative job opportunities in the post-war period. This provided the stimulus to long-overdue technological innovation which, along with industrial concentration and the reduction of the labour force, gathered pace in the 1960s and 70s.

Although firms engaged in wool textile manufacture were still to be found in different parts of the country in the post-war period, the overwhelming concentration of workers and equipment was in Yorkshire (Map 2.6). In 1945, 101,340 out of a total workforce of 126,700 was located in the West Riding while, in November 1943, 6.1 million out of 7 million woollen and worsted spindles and 67,200 out of 78,000 mules were in Yorkshire and Lancashire. In consequence, the impact of decline has been felt in a limited geographical area. Bradford was aptly named 'the wool capital of the world'. In 1939, 70,987 people in Bradford and Keighley (now part of Bradford

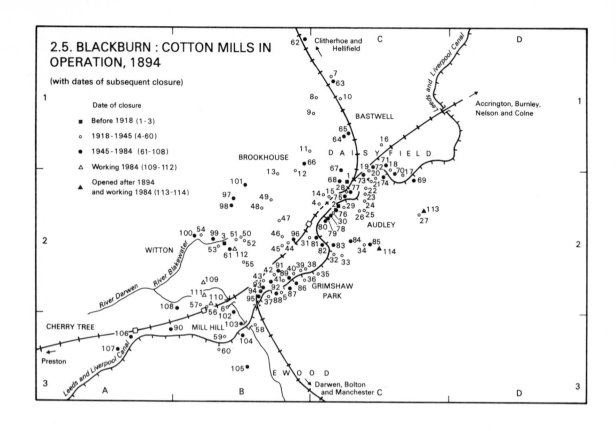

2.5. BLACKBURN : COTTON MILLS IN OPERATION, 1894

(with dates of subsequent closure)

Date of closure

- ■ Before 1918 (1–3)
- ○ 1918–1945 (4–60)
- ● 1945–1984 (61–108)
- △ Working 1984 (109–112)
- ▲ Opened after 1894 and working 1984 (113–114)

Manufacturing ceases pre-1918

1	Melbourne	(1899)
2	Eanam Bridge	(1914)
3	Phoenix	(1900)

Manufacturing ceases 1918–45

4	Foundry Hill	(1925)
5	Albert, Hall St	(1930)
6	Waterloo	(1930)
7	Carr Cottage	(mid-1930s)
8	Royshaw	(1928)
9	Oozebooth	(1928–9)
10	Boundary	(1927)
11	Brookhouse	(1934)
12	Brookhouse Fields	(1930)
13	Limbrick	(1923)
14	Quarry Street	(1930)
15	Canal New	(1927)
16	Moss St	(1924)
17	Gorse Bridge	(1936–7)
18	Burmah, Gladstone St	(1922–3)
19	Springfield	(1929)
20	Green Bank, Harwood St	(1933)
21	India	(by 1945)
22	Ordnance	(1934)
23	Bank Field	(1936)
24	Paradise	(1933)
25	Jubilee, Gate St	(1931)
26	Albert, Copy Nook	(1928–9)
27	Furthergate	(1929)
28	Navigation New	(1928)
29	Rose Hill	(1927–8)
30	Canton	(1939–40)
31	Carlisle St	(1936)
32	Audley Bridge	(1929)
33	Audley Hall No. 1	(1930–1)
34	Alexandra	(1933–4)
35	Crossfield	(1929)
36	Park Bridge	(1931–2)
37	Infirmary	(1933)
38	Cumpstey St	(1938)
39	Mossley	(1938)
40	Nova Scotia	(1930)
41	Rockfield	(1933)
42	Wellington Old	(1929)
43	Chadwick St	(1932)
44	Bath	(1930)
45	Brunswick	(1933)
46	Unity	(1939)
47	Gladstone	(1927)
48	St Paul's	(1928)
49	Duke St	(1928)
50	George St West	(1931)
51	Duckworth Field	(1929–30)
52	Royal Albert	(1931)
53	Garden Street	(1933–41)
54	Wensley Fold Old	(1930)
55	Shakespeare	(1936)

Key to map 2.5, cont.

56	Mill Hill Works	(1933)
57	Woodfield	(1929–30)
58	Hollin Bank	(1938)
59	Bridge	(1925)
60	Moorgate Fold	(late 1920s)

Manufacturing ceases 1945–84

61	Whalley Bank	(1960)
62	Roe Lee	(1981)
63	Florence	(1971)
64	Wellfield	(1955–6)
65	Bastfield	(1959)
66	Swallow St	(1959)
67	Fisher St	(1955)
68	Daisyfield	(1959)
69	Hole House	(1959)
70	Green Bank, Gladstone St	(1980)
71	Cobden St	(1975)
72	Stanley St	(1959)
73	Plantation	(1959)
74	Greenlow	(1959–60)
75	Navigation Old	(1962)
76	Wharf St	(1972)
77	Appleby St	(1967)
78	Bridgewater	(1959)
79	Alma	(1975)
80	Cicely Bridge	(1983)
81	Walpole St	(1956)
82	Audley	(1955)
83	Higher Audley	(1959)
84	Dewhurst St	(1969)
85	Audley Range	(1970s)
86	Rockcliffe	(1955)
87	Highfield	(1959)
88	Atlantic	(1971)
89	Commercial	(1968)
90	Victoria	(1957–8)
91	Britannia	(1955–6)
92	Wellington New	(1956)
93	Lower Hollin Bank	(1973–4)
94	America	(1973–4)
95	Columbia	(1963)
96	Canterbury St	(1955)
97	Peel	(1959)
98	Belle Vue	(1960)
99	Bank Top	(1970)
100	Wensley Fold New	(1965)
101	Havelock	(1960)
102	Cardwell	(1983)
103	Albert, Livesey	(1958)
104	Albion	(1975)
105	Ewood	(1962)
106	Cherry Tree	(1959)
107	Bank	(1959)
108	Primrose	(1962)

Mills working, 1984

109	Witton
110	Waterfall
111	Griffin
112	Fir Mill

Mills opened after 1894 and still working in 1984

113	Didsbury St Mill
114	Prospect Mill

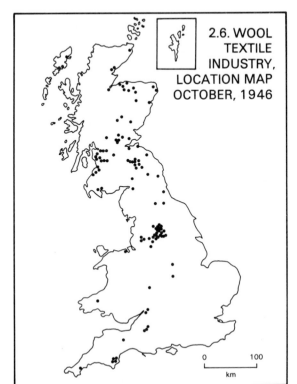

2.6. WOOL TEXTILE INDUSTRY, LOCATION MAP OCTOBER, 1946

0   100
km

District) were employed in the woollen and worsted industries. The highest post-war figure for all textile employment in the district was 55,734 in 1951 and numbers remained at over 50,000 into the early 1960s. After that they fell rapidly. Between 1971 and 1981 alone, 24,207 jobs were lost in textiles and clothing. By 1984, the number of textile workers was down to 14,506. This figure how-ever, along with the thirty-one weaving establishments still operating in the district, demonstrates that the plight of the West Riding's wool textile industries is not as bad as that of Lancashire's cotton.

Handloom weaving

Conventional wisdom maintains that handloom weaving declined quite slowly in the woollen cloth industry, more rapidly in worsted cloth manufacture and quickest of all in cotton. In this section we examine the contrasting pace of change and, in particular, the role of the handloom in the cotton industry.

The powerloom certainly came late to woollen cloth manufacture, though not as late in Lancashire as in Yorkshire. The fragility of woollen yarn and the great width of the broadcloth web (108 inches before milling) meant that, in this branch at least, powerlooms were no quicker than handlooms before the mid-nineteenth century. Also important was the delayed development of a mechanized drawloom acceptable to manufacturers of fancy woollen cloths. From the 1850s, however, changes in the relative costs of steam power and labour, along with improved technology, brought a rapid transition to powerloom weaving. Even so, pockets of handloom weaving remained. In Yorkshire, these were concentrated around the fancy woollens centre of Huddersfield where, during the late 1880s, handloom weaving was still the main occupation in the villages of Skelmanthorpe, Shelley, and Scissett. In the West Country, handlooms continued in use on some narrow fancy cloths. In parts of Scotland they remained in use into the twentieth century in the Harris tweed trade. In West Wales, too, handlooms survived.

In worsteds, where powerlooms could work at a much higher speed than in woollens, the changeover was much more rapid. By 1857, it was reported that 'comparatively few pieces are woven by hand in Bradford parish'. By the 1870s, the few worsted handloom weavers remaining appear to have been of little importance.

Neither contemporaries nor more recent commentators have suggested that long-term decline in the number of handloom weavers in Britain took place before the mid-1820s. Until then, mechanized cotton weaving made limited progress, in part because of the technical difficulties encountered. During the following decade, however, the powerloom spread comparatively rapidly, especially in the production of plainer and coarser grades of cotton cloth. Factory inspectors' returns show

that by 1835 over 100,000 cotton powerlooms were in use throughout the country. By 1850, this figure had reached almost 250,000.

Some indication of the importance achieved by the Lancashire handloom weaving trade before large-scale mechanization occurred may be obtained by calculating the proportions of bridegroom weavers recorded annually in Anglican marriage registers. The result for the quinquennium 1818–22 are shown in Map 2.7.

It is clear from Map 2.7 that handloom weaving was most heavily concentrated in central Lancashire, especially along the Ribble valley, and in the southern and eastern parts of the county. Here, marriage registers commonly described between one-third and a half of all bridegrooms as weavers, whilst, in several cases, bridegroom weavers outnumbered those of all other occupational groups taken together. Since hand weaving was neither age- nor gender-specific, it seems

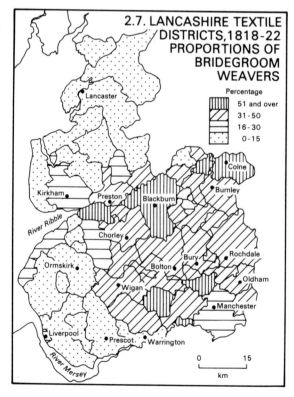

2.7. LANCASHIRE TEXTILE DISTRICTS, 1818-22 PROPORTIONS OF BRIDEGROOM WEAVERS

Percentage
51 and over
31-50
16-30
0-15

probable that most towns and villages throughout these districts would have depended on the trade to a remarkably high degree.

Elsewhere in Lancashire, comparatively little weaving took place, though few registers failed to make at least some reference to the trade. In places, too, appreciable weaver concentrations were found, as at Kirkham parish, in the Fylde, where 28 per cent of bridegrooms were estimated to have been weavers, and at North Meols, the present-day Southport area, where the estimate was 23 per cent.

One approach to explaining the locational pattern shown in Map 2.7 is to consider physical variations within Lancashire, especially in terms of soil and climate. With few exceptions, the strongest concentrations of weavers occurred in the upland districts of the county, where soils were too cold, damp, and acidic for arable cultivation. Here pastoral farming developed, giving limited employment opportunities. Accordingly, as the textile industry prospered during the sixteenth and seventeenth centuries, surplus labour was readily available to work in spinning and weaving. This took place on a domestic basis using hand machines and was largely concerned with producing fustians. By the time the manufacture of cotton cloth became commercially viable during the later decades of the eighteenth century, this proto-industry had assumed considerable importance, especially, but not exclusively, in the eastern half of the county.

As far as climatic aspects are concerned, stress has been laid on the high levels of rainfall and humidity required to spin and weave cotton efficiently. In both these respects, the uplands of east Lancashire were more favourably placed than the western lowlands, though whether or not the difference was marked enough to be a significant influence is uncertain. It is also plain from field evidence that cotton handloom weavers generally preferred cellar or ground-floor loomshops to those in the upper storey, where humid conditions were difficult to establish and maintain.

How long the handloom weaver concentrations shown in Map 2.7 were maintained is uncertain. Debate on the rate of decline in the cotton handloom weaving trade has been conducted largely at a theoretical level, without the benefit of detailed empirical analysis. Yet revealing insights can be obtained from examination of mid-nineteenth century census schedules, despite the all too frequent failure of enumerators to distinguish clearly between hand and power workers.

In all probability, Lancashire's handloom weavers were superseded in some districts much more gradually than is usually acknowledged. Well into the third quarter of the nineteenth century, significant concentrations could be found, especially in rural areas and small towns. This can be seen in the case of several enumeration districts in the Leyland and Croston areas, to the south of Preston (Maps 2.8 and 2.9). In only one of these districts had the powerloom made any significant inroads in 1851. Moreover, in some instances the handloom weavers remained of greater numerical importance than any other occupational group. A decade later, powerloom weavers were much more evident, sometimes outnumbering the handloom weavers. Yet this was by no means the case in every district. Indeed, in some of the more rural areas the hand weavers continued to predominate and to remain the largest element in the labour force. Nor, as might be expected in a declining trade, were they all middle-aged or elderly. By 1871, it seems likely that comparatively few handloom weavers would have been found in these districts, though inadequate census details make the position hard to judge. The enumerators for Croston provided the fullest information, recording between 72 and 114 handloom weavers, some 10 to 15 per cent of the total labour force. Even by this date, therefore, handloom weaving could still provide significant employment opportunities in Lancashire.

Influences on the gradual rate at which handloom weaving declined include the difficulties involved in adapting the powerloom for

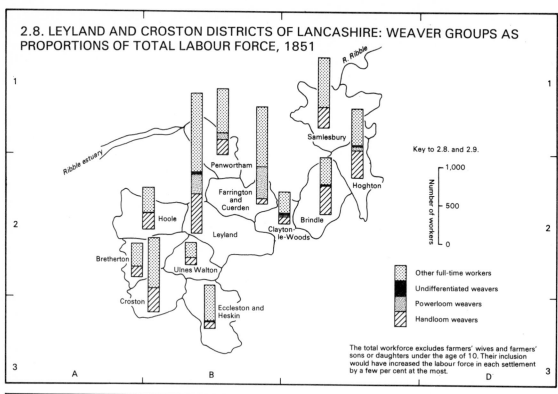

2.8. LEYLAND AND CROSTON DISTRICTS OF LANCASHIRE: WEAVER GROUPS AS PROPORTIONS OF TOTAL LABOUR FORCE, 1851

R. Ribble

Ribble estuary

Samlesbury

Penwortham

Farrington and Cuerden

Hoghton

Hoole

Brindle

Leyland

Clayton-le-Woods

Bretherton

Ulnes Walton

Croston

Eccleston and Heskin

Key to 2.8. and 2.9.

Number of workers

1,000

500

0

Other full-time workers

Undifferentiated weavers

Powerloom weavers

Handloom weavers

The total workforce excludes farmers' wives and farmers' sons or daughters under the age of 10. Their inclusion would have increased the labour force in each settlement by a few per cent at the most.

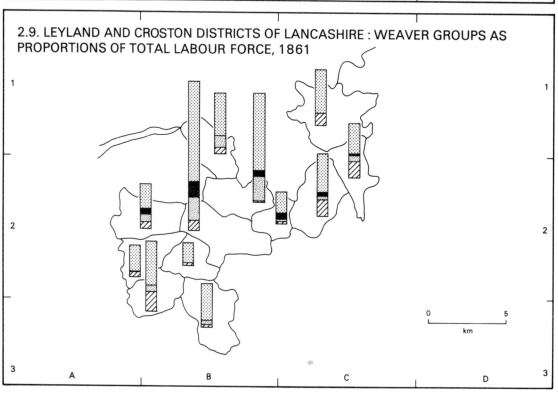

2.9. LEYLAND AND CROSTON DISTRICTS OF LANCASHIRE : WEAVER GROUPS AS PROPORTIONS OF TOTAL LABOUR FORCE, 1861

0   5
km

32

use in the production of finer and more fancy cotton goods. These included counterpanes and bed-quilts of the Bolton area; silk cloth, woven to the north and west of Manchester, and mixture cloths, principally mousseline-de-laine (a dress fabric made from cotton and worsted) which was extensively produced in the Colne district. Even when powerlooms became capable of weaving a particular type of cloth, it did not necessarily mean that they quickly replaced the hand weavers. In part, this may have reflected a desire on the part of the handloom weaver to avoid factory labour, even if it meant working for a meagre wage. Equally, manufacturers may have been willing to retain at least some handloom weavers, because they believed the costs of installing powerlooms was high, especially when compared with those arising from the continued use of handlooms. Such a comparison would have been brought into sharp focus during trade recessions, when the fixed capital costs of powerlooms would still have to be met, even though they were not being used to full capacity. Finally, it should not be overlooked that some handloom weavers would have been unable to find alternative work, either because local employment opportunities were limited, or because they were deemed too old to transfer jobs easily, especially into factory work.

Steam and water power in the textile industries

In considering Britain's industrial growth during the late eighteenth and early nineteenth centuries, emphasis has often been placed on improvements in steam-engine technology. Particular attention has been given to the savings in fuel costs arising from the introduction of Watt's separate condenser, and to the benefits of his rotative engine which allowed direct application of steam power to mill machinery. Both these developments, it has been suggested, were of fundamental importance in textiles and iron-making, then Britain's leading manufacturing industries.

Recent research by von Tunzelmann,[1] how-ever, has challenged these views. He argues that the social savings which would have been achieved by using Watt engines instead of atmospheric engines would only have amounted to about 0.11 per cent of national income in 1800. In von Tunzelmann's view, substantial economies in power costs were not achieved until high-pressure stationary engines became widely used during the mid-nineteenth century.

Coupled with the limited savings achieved by the improved steam-engine was its relatively slow adoption by industrialists, at least in certain parts of the country. This may be demonstrated using evidence obtained from factory inspectors' returns. Those of 1838 provide the earliest reliable details, though they relate only to textiles. The data they yield are presented in Map 2.10.

It is clear from the map that, taking the country as a whole, steam had become the predominant form of power in the textile trades. In Yorkshire and Lancashire, by far the most important of Britain's textile regions, it was extensively used, supplying, in the former county, around 75 per cent of textile mill requirements and in the latter almost 90 per cent.

As far as other leading textile areas were concerned, a varied picture emerged. In Cheshire, in South-west Scotland (chiefly Lanarkshire and Renfrewshire), and in North-east Scotland (mainly Angus and Aberdeenshire) steam had also made considerable progress, providing, in each case, about 75 per cent of requirements. Elsewhere, however, progress was much slower. In Derbyshire, in the South-west counties of England and in the central counties of Scotland (with Fifeshire and Stirlingshire predominating) water still supplied around two-thirds of the total power used in textile mills, whilst in the West Midlands (where Gloucestershire was the chief centre) the figure was well over half. A varied picture was also apparent in those districts with relatively small textile industries. Thus in Wales, dependence on water power remained high – in South

33

Wales hardly any steam power was employed in textile mills – whereas in the textile trades of East Anglia and the East Midlands steam-engines were generating some three to four times as much power as waterwheels.

In explaining the differing rates at which improved steam-engines were adopted in the textile trades, both between and within regions, emphasis has been placed on the relative costs of steam and water power. It has been suggested that in districts where low-grade boiler fuel was plentiful, the incentive to install steam power at an early date was strong. In some instances, it has been noted, pit-head prices were quadrupled by the time deliveries were made to the final customer. Conversely, in districts remote from coalfields, the high cost of importing coal, coupled with the uncertainties of supply, would have encouraged entrepreneurs to continue with water power. It seems, too, that the relatively high costs of steam-engine installation, the advances that continued to be made in waterwheel technology, and the cheapness of land and labour in rural areas, would have been additional constraints on any decision to switch from water to steam.

On the whole, the data shown in Map 2.10 are consistent with the view that coal availability was a significant factor in the decision to install steam-engines. In most of the leading textile districts, major coalfields were to be found, though North-east Scotland and the South-west of England provided notable exceptions. Industrialists in the former area, however, may have obtained coal relatively cheaply by sea, an advantage which would have encouraged their early conversion to steam power. Meanwhile, textile entrepreneurs in the South-west and in the West Midlands (largely Gloucestershire) continued to rely heavily on waterwheels. This was true also of their counterparts in Derbyshire, despite the apparent nearness to local coal supplies. Here, though, difficult terrain over which to transport bulky goods, coupled with high and reliable rainfall, would have reduced incentives to install steam-engines.

As far as other areas were concerned, similar considerations operated. In East Anglia and South-east England (mainly the London area) textile entrepreneurs would probably have obtained cheap supplies of sea-coal. Besides, they operated in a region where rainfall was limited, and where land was generally too flat to install the more efficient overshot or back-shot waterwheels. Consequently, they mostly favoured steam power. In Wales, though, rainfall and relief were far more conducive to the use of waterwheels, so that steam power made little headway.

In explaining the continued use of water power, a further point should be made. Even where coal could be obtained regularly and cheaply, waterwheels might still be used in conjunction with steam-engines. This occurred when textile mills occupying coalfield sites were equipped with steam-driven pumping engines, the function of which was to replenish water supplied in reservoirs during periods of dry weather.

How long beyond 1838 water power remained significant in the textile industry is hard to assess. Other surveys showing amounts of power derived from water and steam were made in subsequent decades, culminating in the 1870 returns. Yet differing methods of calculating horse-power ratings for steam engines, as well as uncertainty over whether the returns gave figures of power in use as opposed to power available, make comparisons over time rather hazardous. Nevertheless, for the textile trades they can be used to show the likely geographical variation in water power usage, even though it seems likely that the importance of steam power would have been somewhat understated. This is attempted in Map 2.11 which is based on the 1870 returns.

Comparison of Maps 2.10 and 2.11 shows clearly that the use of steam power in textile manufacturing was greatly extended during the middle decades of the nineteenth century, even if the precise rate of growth cannot be measured. By 1870, mills in each of the leading production areas depended on steam-engines

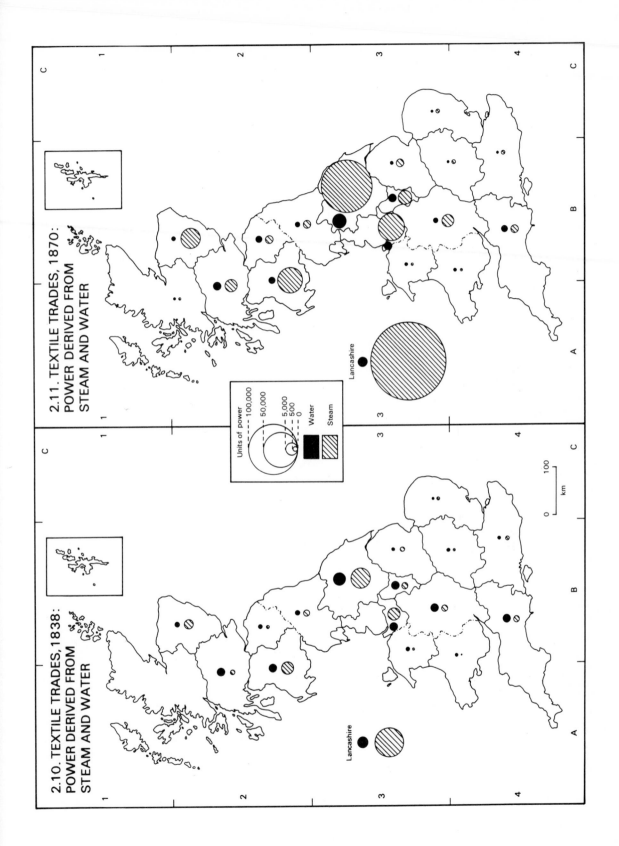

2.11. TEXTILE TRADES, 1870: POWER DERIVED FROM STEAM AND WATER

2.10. TEXTILE TRADES, 1838: POWER DERIVED FROM STEAM AND WATER

Units of power

100,000
50,000
5,000
500
0

Water
Steam

Lancashire

0   100
km

to generate well over 90 per cent of power needs. In other areas, too, steam power made significant advances, a reflection of price reductions in coal and in its transportation. Even so, water power had yet to be superseded. Generally, it seems, the amount of power supplied by waterwheels showed relatively little change during the middle decades of the nineteenth century and in some districts it even increased. It is plain that, throughout this period, numerous water-powered textile mills were still able to compete effectively, despite, in many instances, being of limited capacity and having inconvenient locations.

Chemicals

The advance of the chemical industries in the late eighteenth and early nineteenth centuries was largely to meet the needs of textile manufacture. In more recent times, many important developments have been in the field of dyestuffs or of new materials to replace traditional textiles. Of course, the chemical industries have important links with metal manufacture (indeed much of the manufacture of metals is based on chemical processes) as well as with the coal and oil industries. Chemical inputs and processes are important, too, in the manufacture of soap, glass, and fertilizers. Nevertheless, the placing of the chemical industries in a section alongside textiles would seem to be appropriate.

For much of the nineteenth century, the production of sodium carbonate (soda alkali) by the Le Blanc process formed the nucleus of the British heavy chemical industry. The bulk of sulphuric acid production was reacted with salt in furnaces to produce sodium sulphate (saltcake). Most of this was reacted with limestone and coal in Le Blanc furnaces to produce 'black ash' from which soda was extracted. Increasingly, legislative regulation of pollution (in the form of the Alkali Acts), along with economic motives, led to the recovery and use of waste products, in particular hydrochloric or muriatic acid for the manufacture of bleaching powder, much of which was exported to America.

The second half of the nineteenth century saw a great expansion in the British chemical industries but, towards the end of the century, powerful rivals emerged and market conditions deteriorated. A major area of growth was in the synthetic fertilizer (chemical manure) industry. From the 1840s superphosphates, involving the treatment of bones and imported phosphate rock with sulphuric acid, were produced. Ammonium sulphate, a by-product of gasworks, had been available since early in the century but its widespread use was more a feature of the 1870s and 1880s. By this time, too, potassium sulphate was also being produced on a large scale. These products replaced natural manures and, after 1870, the diminishing supply of Peruvian guano. Imports of the latter fell from 280,000 tons to under 20,000 tons in the twenty years after 1870. From the 1860s, Britain was an exporter of artificial fertilizers, holding virtually a world monopoly until the 1890s.

Large-scale conversion of salt to soda using ammonia (generally known as the Solvay process) was introduced into this country by the Brunner, Mond partnership in 1872. By 1889, British ammonia-soda output had reached 219,000 tons compared to the 584,000 tons produced by the established Le Blanc soda process. The Solvay method was cheaper in fuel and labour but did waste chlorine, a valued product of the Le Blanc method. Brunner, Mond's British patent rights to the Solvay process (which only expired in 1886) and the extent of existing Le Blanc investment were further obstacles to change. As a means of defence, Lancashire Le Blanc manufacturers formed the Bleaching Powder Association (1883), the nucleus of the United Alkali Company of 1890. To the competition for the Solvay process was added the impact of overseas protectionist policies, notably the

American McKinley Tariff which reduced British alkali exports to the United States by four-fifths between 1890 and 1898. The United Alkali Company (which came to contain all but one of the British Le Blanc firms), though never very successful, did, contrary to its original intent, permit the gradual conversion of the British heavy chemical industry to new production processes.

In the mid-nineteenth century, Britain had been the world leader in chemicals production. By 1913, with an estimated 11 per cent of world output, she had fallen behind the United States (34 per cent) and Germany (24 per cent). There were areas, including the manufacture of soaps, paints, coal tar intermediates, and explosives, where the British industry performed well. Sulphuric acid production (widely considered a measure of a country's industrialization) had reached a million tons by 1900 – still a quarter of the world total. The initiative, however, in new techniques had

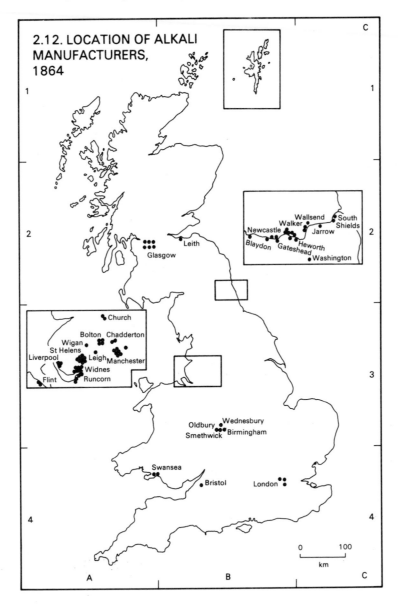

2.12. LOCATION OF ALKALI MANUFACTURERS, 1864

passed to the United States and Germany. The former country led in electro-chemical processes, Germany in the application of organic chemistry to the production of synthetic materials. The manufacture of synthetic dye-stuffs, in spite of early British successes with amiline and alizarin dyes, had become German-dominated. Germany led, too, in the production of synthetic drugs (an offshoot of the dyestuffs industry) and in artificial fibres and plastics. Much of this achievement resulted from the flow of trained scientists produced by the German education system.

Central Scotland, the West Midlands and London were early centres of the chemical industries. Though chemical manufacture remained in these districts, they were superseded in importance during the first half of the nineteenth century, first by Tyneside and later by the area around the lower and middle Mersey. Of the 81 registered alkali manufacturers in England, Wales, and Scotland in 1846, 20 were on Tyneside, 21 were in Liverpool, Widnes, or Runcorn, and another 17 were located elsewhere in Lancashire (see Map 2.12). Maps 2.13 and 2.14 reveal the concentration of plant around the middle Mersey and the Tyne in 1882. The shifting

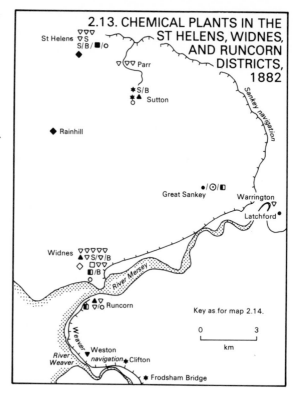

2.13. CHEMICAL PLANTS IN THE ST HELENS, WIDNES, AND RUNCORN DISTRICTS, 1882

Key as for map 2.14.

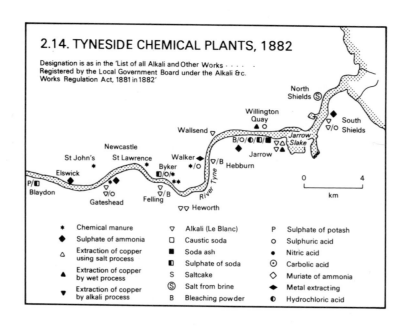

2.14. TYNESIDE CHEMICAL PLANTS, 1882

Designation is as in the 'List of all Alkali and Other Works · · · · · Registered by the Local Government Board under the Alkali &c. Works Regulation Act, 1881 in 1882'

✳	Chemical manure	▽ Alkali (Le Blanc)	P	Sulphate of potash
◆	Sulphate of ammonia	▢ Caustic soda	o	Sulphuric acid
△	Extraction of copper using salt process	■ Soda ash	●	Nitric acid
▲	Extraction of copper by wet process	◨ Sulphate of soda	⊙	Carbolic acid
▼	Extraction of copper by alkali process	S Saltcake	◇	Muriate of ammonia
		Ⓢ Salt from brine	◆	Metal extracting
		B Bleaching powder	◖	Hydrochloric acid

location of the chemical industries was dictated by its raw materials and its markets. The replacement of natural alkali by synthetic soda favoured the Mersey area, close to coal, Cheshire salt, limestone from Derbyshire and North Wales, or to imported raw materials through Liverpool. The area was also close to centres of the textile industry, the main domestic consumer of chemicals; the proximity of Liverpool was also important for exports, e.g. of bleaching powder. Glass and soap manufacture, as on Tyneside, constituted further markets. Map 2.15 shows the concentration of alkali, hydrochloric acid, bleaching powder and chlorine close to industries (principally textiles) that make use of these products. Production of nitric and sulphuric acids (Map 2.16) is slightly less geographically concentrated due to the use of the latter product in the making of chemical manures. Chemical manure plant (Map 2.17) and plant producing sulphate of ammonia (Map 2.18) (generally a by-product of gas-works) are widely dispersed. This reflects the scattered agricultural market and the widespread production of gas. Concentration around ports, however, notably London, is a consequence of dependence on imported raw materials.

The First World War, in particular the demands for explosives, dyestuffs, and drugs, had a substantial and lasting impact on the British chemical industry. The contact method of producing sulphuric acid was introduced in government factories at Queensferry (North Wales), Gretna, and Avonmouth as well as in the works of the Stavely Coal and Iron Company and a United Alkali Company plant at Widnes. The need for toluene for TNT gave rise to a British petro-chemical industry. The Asiatic Petroleum Company's refining plant was moved from neutral Holland to Portishead (near Bristol); nitration of the crude toluene produced was then undertaken at plant in Oldbury and Queensferry. Toluene resources could also be conserved by the use of mixtures of TNT and ammonium nitrate (amatols). Thus Brunner, Mond & Co. were encouraged to develop new methods of producing ammonium nitrate including double-decomposition of sodium nitrate with ammonium sulphate. By 1918, in the quest for ammonia, the government had embarked on the establishment of a nitrogen fixation plant at Billingham (Co. Durham). The government initiative was abandoned when the war ended and the site and 'all relevant . . . information' on nitrogen fixation bought by Brunner, Mond. This firm had also dominated government commissions to the German BASF nitrogen fixation plants, though the value of these trips (given German sabotage) is open to question. Brunner, Mond's newly established subsidiary 'Synthetic Ammonia and Nitrates' began ammonia production at Billingham in 1924.

The war also led to expansion in cellulose acetate production (dope for aircraft wings, use in the manufacture of window substitutes for battle zones) and the establishment of the British Cellulose and Chemical Manufacturing Company (later British Celanese) at Spondon, Derby. War, by cutting off German supplies, also reinvigorated the British dyestuffs industry. Government funding aided the creation of the British Dyestuffs Corporation and James Morton's Scottish Dyers Ltd in 1919. In 1925, these two firms amalgamated. New products, including the first really fast green dye and dyes suitable for man-made fibres, had already appeared in the early 1920s. The dyestuffs industry was protected from foreign competition by the Dyestuffs (Import Regulations) Act of 1920, other sections of the chemical industry by the Safeguarding of Industries Act (1921).

New techniques and government protection were both clearly linked to the experience of war; so was amalgamation. Chemical industries, internationally, were large-scale and capital-intensive. British firms to compete needed to be similar in size and resources. Brunner, Mond, by stages (1916–19) took over the Castner-Kellner Alkali Company, operators at Weston Point (Runcorn) of electrolytic plant. Most of the rest of the alkali-

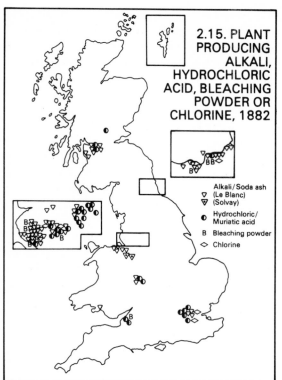

2.15. PLANT PRODUCING ALKALI, HYDROCHLORIC ACID, BLEACHING POWDER OR CHLORINE, 1882

Alkali/Soda ash
△ (Le Blanc)
▽ (Solvay)
◑ Hydrochloric/Muriatic acid
B Bleaching powder
◇ Chlorine

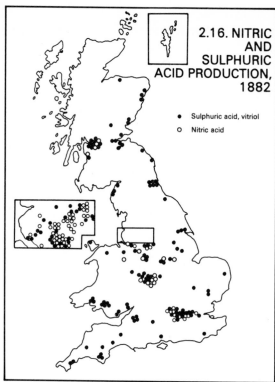

2.16. NITRIC AND SULPHURIC ACID PRODUCTION, 1882

● Sulphuric acid, vitriol
○ Nitric acid

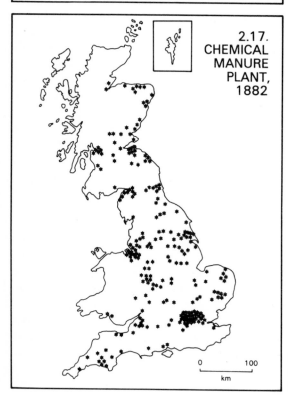

2.17. CHEMICAL MANURE PLANT, 1882

0   100
km

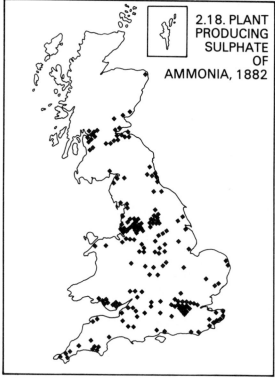

2.18. PLANT PRODUCING SULPHATE OF AMMONIA, 1882

manufacturing industry was in the hands of the United Alkali Company. Different British explosives firms merged, in 1918, into Nobel Industries. Brunner, Mond, the United Alkali Company, Nobel Industries and the British Dyestuffs Corporation came together as Imperial Chemical Industries (ICI) in 1926 with an issued capital of £57 million.

ICI had virtually a monopoly in alkali and explosives production. In other sectors of the industry, including dyestuffs, fertilizers, fine chemicals, pharmaceuticals, paints and lacquers, other firms were present and, in some cases, dominant. Albright and Wilson, Beechams, Courtaulds, Distillers, Fisons and, from 1929, Unilever were among a number of major producers of chemical or chemical-related products which were themselves to become centres of amalgamation.

ICI's record, before 1939, was patchy. The 1930s did see the discovery of carbolan dyes (able to be used in the dyeing of wool and colour-fast in light and water), of poly-methylmethacrylate (marketed as Diakon, Kallodent, or Perspex) and, at the very end of the decade, of polyethylene. Otherwise, the company diverted much of its resources first into a huge development of the capacity to produce ammonium sulphate by nitrogen fixation, then into the production of petrol by hydrogenation of coal, both at Billingham. World over-production of fertilizer and the collapse of agriculture prices in the slump of 1929–32 led to a 50 per cent cut in ammonium sulphate production and the writing-off of £10 million of investment. Petrol production, aided by a duty on imported petrols (at first 4d, later 8d), began in 1936. ICI also participated in international cartels, notably those relating to nitrogen (1930), hydrogenation (1931), and dyestuffs (1932), as well as in other agreements aimed at reducing competition.

By the eve of the Second World War, the British chemical industries, largely due to protection, were in a healthier state than they had been twenty-five years earlier. Production of rayon yarn had risen from under 4 million lbs in 1918 to 170 million in 1939. The viscose process, developed by Courtaulds, pre-dominated but about one-third of the market was met by cellulose acetate yarn, mostly produced by British Celanese. In 1939, too, ICI and Courtaulds combined to set up British Nylon Spinners Ltd, producing nylon under licence from the American firm, Du Pont. Output of synthetic dyestuffs had risen from 5,000 tons in 1913 to 29,000 in 1937. Imports, at 5 per cent of domestic demand, were only half the volume of exports. Production of synthetic pharmaceuticals had also grown strongly. There had been rapid growth in the output of celluloid and bakelite, of chloro-hydrocarbons (mainly as solvents) and of soap powders. On the other hand gross output, at £206 million in 1935, was still less than half that of textiles. Traditional heavy inorganic production still predominated. Since most petrol was imported into the country already refined, the great development of petro-chemicals still lay in the future.

Increased use of petrol as the basis of production stemmed partly from the quest for an abundant and stable-priced raw material; oil appeared to meet these requirements while coal or molasses (originally used by The Distillers Company at Hull for producing ethyl alcohol) did not. More significant was the growing domestic demand for petrol and the transition, for economic and strategic reasons, to UK refining. By-product hydrocarbons were available for use in increasingly large quantities. In the late 1940s, petrol provided just 6 per cent of the raw materials for organic chemical manufacture; by the mid-1960s it provided 60–70 per cent.

Abundant, cheap supplies of raw materials were the prerequisites of a heavy organic chemicals industry. By 1982, British chemical companies produced over 1,115,000 tonnes of ethylene, 770,000 tonnes of propylene, 229,000 tons of butadiene, and 570,000 tonnes of benzene (see Map 2.19 for plant and capacity). From these were produced a huge range of products including rayon, terylene, pvc, polythene, polystyrene, synthetic rubbers, solvents, epoxy resins for bonding or coating

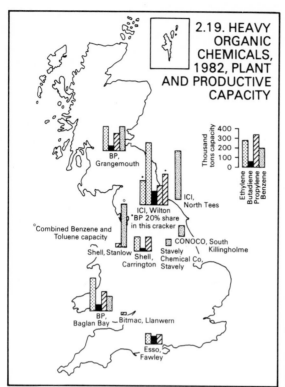

2.19. HEAVY ORGANIC CHEMICALS, 1982, PLANT AND PRODUCTIVE CAPACITY

Thousand tons capacity

400 300 200 100 0

Ethylene
Butadiene
Propylene
Benzene

BP, Grangemouth

ICI, Wilton
*BP 20% share in this cracker

ICI, North Tees

°Combined Benzene and Toluene capacity

Shell, Stanlow

Shell, Carrington

Stavely Chemical Co, Stavely

CONOCO, South Killingholme

BP, Baglan Bay

Bitmac, Llanwern

Esso, Fawley

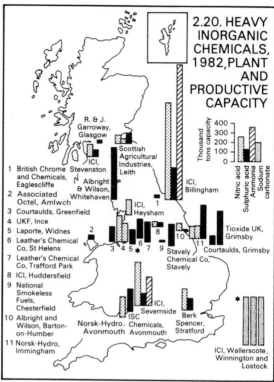

2.20. HEAVY INORGANIC CHEMICALS, 1982, PLANT AND PRODUCTIVE CAPACITY

R. & J. Garroway, Glasgow

Scottish Agricultural Industries, Leith

ICI, Stevenston

Albright & Wilson, Whitehaven

ICI, Heysham

ICI, Billingham

Thousand tons capacity

400 300 200 100 0

Nitric acid
Sulphuric acid
Ammonia
Sodium carbonate

1 British Chrome and Chemicals, Eaglescliffe
2 Associated Octel, Amlwch
3 Courtaulds, Greenfield
4 UKF, Ince
5 Laporte, Widnes
6 Leather's Chemical Co, St Helens
7 Leather's Chemical Co, Trafford Park
8 ICI, Huddersfield
9 National Smokeless Fuels, Chesterfield
10 Albright and Wilson, Barton-on-Humber
11 Norsk-Hydro, Immingham

Tioxide UK, Grimsby

Courtaulds, Grimsby

Stavely Chemical Co, Stavely

Norsk-Hydro, Avonmouth

ISC Chemicals, Avonmouth

ICI, Severnside

Berk Spencer, Stratford

ICI, Wallerscote, Winnington and Lostock

2.21. CHEMICAL WORKS, 1982, SHOWING THE IMPORTANCE OF COASTAL LOCATIONS

o Place
• Chemical works

Grangemouth

Teesside (See map 2.24.)

Barton-on-Humber

Hull

Stallingborough
Immingham
Grimsby

Mersey-Manchester (See map 2.23.)

Machen
Caerphilly Newport
Baglan Bay
Barry Llanwern
Avonmouth Hythe Totton
Fawley

0   100
km

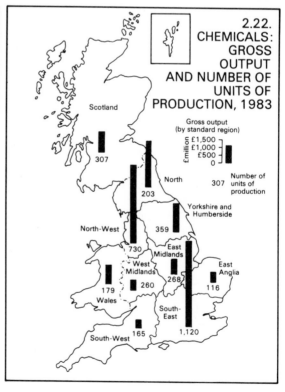

2.22. CHEMICALS: GROSS OUTPUT AND NUMBER OF UNITS OF PRODUCTION, 1983

Scotland

Gross output (by standard region)

£million
£1,500
£1,000
£500

307 Number of units of production

North
307
203

Yorkshire and Humberside
359

North-West
730

East Midlands
268

East Anglia
116

West Midlands
260

Wales
179

South-East
1,120

South-West
165

42

materials, drugs, dyes, and detergents. Detergents also incorporate, in large quantities, inorganic chemicals e.g. sodium silicate, phosphate, sulphate, and perborate. This serves to remind us of the continuing importance of heavy inorganic chemical manufacture. Thus in 1982, 3.1 million tonnes of nitric acid was produced, along with 2.6 million tonnes of sulphuric acid, some 2 million tonnes of ammonia and 1.5 million tonnes of sodium carbonate. Map 2.20 shows plant and their capacity for these products.

The use of petrol as a chemical raw material had major implications for the structure and location of the chemical industries. By 1982, BP Chemicals was, in terms of turnover, the third largest firm in the British chemical industries (after ICI and Courtaulds). Shell

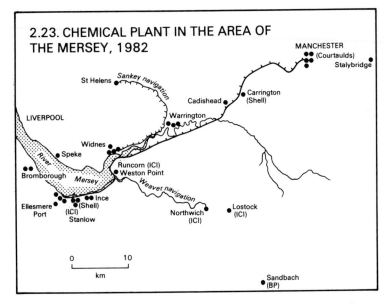

2.23. CHEMICAL PLANT IN THE AREA OF THE MERSEY, 1982

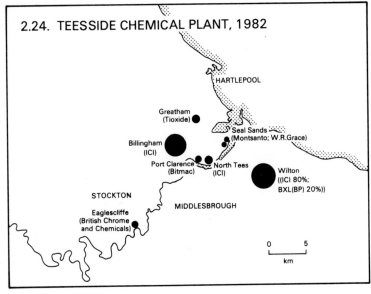

2.24. TEESSIDE CHEMICAL PLANT, 1982

Chemicals and Esso Chemicals were also among the giants of organic chemical production. The association of chemical processes with petrol refining led to the development of new industrial complexes at points where the oil was landed, e.g. at Grangemouth, Baglan Bay (Port Talbot), Fawley, the Humber, Severnside, or on the south bank of the Mersey (see Map 2.21). In the case of the Mersey, developments led to the traditional south–north axis of the local chemical industry, linking Cheshire salt and Lancashire coal via the Weaver and Sankey Navigations, being replaced by an east–west link from Elles-mere Port and Stanlow, via Runcorn and Widnes, to the giant Shell chemicals plant at Carrington near Manchester (see Map 2.23). In other instances, including the ICI development to the south side of the Tees at Wilton (see Map 2.24), availability of a labour force and proximity to other elements of the company's production processes (at Billingham) were probably more significant. The importance of proximity to markets, especially in the case of pharmaceuticals and other fine chemicals, is brought out by the restored importance of the South-east as an area of production (see Map 2.22).

Notes

1 G. N. von Tunzelmann, *Steam Power and British Industrialisation* (Oxford, 1978), p. 149.

Map 2.1 is based on Figures from D. Jenkins and K. G. Ponting, *The British Wool Textile Industry, 1770–1914* (London, 1982). Maps 2.2 and 2.3 are from various sources including H. Heaton, *The Yorkshire Woollen and Worsted Industries* (Oxford, 1965) and Jenkins and Ponting, op. cit. Map 2.4 is based on that by S. D. Chapman in 'The Arkwright mills – Colquhoun's census of 1788 and archaeological evidence', *Industrial Archaeology Review*, VI (1981), pp. 5–26. This map is reproduced with kind permission of Professor Chapman who points out that over 200 Arkwright-type mills (not the usual figure of 143) have now been identified as in existence by 1788. Map 2.5 is based largely on material from Barrett's *General and Commercial Directory of Blackburn* (Preston, 1894) and M. Rothwell, *Industrial Heritage: Part 1 The Textile Industry* (Hyndburn, 1985). Thanks are also due, in respect of this map, for the help given by the staff of Blackburn Reference Library. Map 2.6 is reproduced, with permission of the Controller of Her Majesty's Stationery Office, from the *Report of the Board of Trade Working Party on Wool* (London, 1946). Map 2.7 is based on Parish Register entries and Maps 2.8 and 2.9 on Census Enumerators' Returns for 1851 and 1861. Maps 2.10 and 2.11 use information from *Factory Inspectors' Returns*, 1838 (BPP 1839, XLII) and 1870 (BPP 1870, LXII). Map 2.12 is based on evidence from the *Alkali Act, 1863: First Annual Report* (1865), BPP 1865, XX, p. 1, and Maps 2.15–2.18 on the *List of all Alkali and Other Works in England, Scotland and Ireland Registered by the Local Government Board under the Alkali & C. Works Regulation Act, 1881 in 1882*, BPP 1882, LVII, p. 1. Maps 2.19–2.21 and 2.23–2.24 depend largely on material from *Chemfacts 1983* (London, 1983), Map 2.22 is based on statistics in *Regional Trends* (London, 1986).

3 METAL, VEHICLE, AND ENGINEERING INDUSTRIES

Rex Pope

The iron and steel industry

The iron industry of the early eighteenth century was scattered and small-scale. The need for large quantities of charcoal in the smelting process and the impracticality of transporting this any distance, along with dependence on water power, dictated geographical dispersion. The limited output of individual furnaces meant that local ore supplies normally sufficed though there is evidence of ore from the Furness region being shipped to the Scottish Highlands, the Forest of Dean, and elsewhere. In so far as there was geographical concentration, this was generally in the area served by the River Severn (especially the Forest of Dean and Shropshire) (see Map 3.1). Overall, this area provided some two-thirds of the 20–25,000 tons of pig iron produced. The refining section of the industry was rather more concentrated. The particularly high cost of transporting bar iron encouraged proximity to markets (e.g. Birmingham) situated on the coalfields.

The geographical location of the industry, and its scale, were transformed by a series of innovations involving the substitution of coke for charcoal and the use of steam-powered blowing engines. Darby's method of producing pig iron using coke as fuel (1709) only seems to have spread beyond Shropshire after the mid-century and yet by 1806 there were only eleven charcoal-powered furnaces left in operation. Even more important was the introduction of coke into the process of converting pig iron into bar (or puddled) iron. Experi-

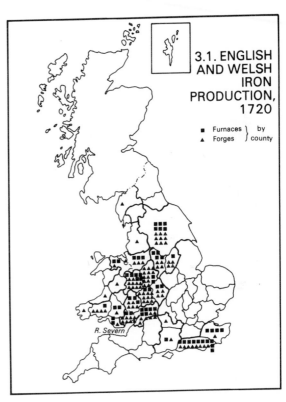

3.1. ENGLISH AND WELSH IRON PRODUCTION, 1720

■ Furnaces } by
▲ Forges } county

R. Severn

ments in the period after 1760 led to Cort's patenting the puddling process (1783) and using grooved rollers from 1784.

Use of coke meant that by 1820 some 90 per cent of pig iron production (and with it puddled iron) was concentrated on the coalfields. The increasing scale of operation, a result of the interaction of new techniques with new markets including, by the mid-nineteenth century, railways, meant that good local supplies of iron ore were also important. The fuel economies resulting from Neilson's 'hot blast' (1829) further enhanced the importance of ore. Thus, in spite of ample and good-quality coking coal, there was no great success in establishing the iron industry in the North-east of England before the discovery of the Cleveland iron ore deposits. Those areas where coal and ore were available were South Wales, Staffordshire, and Scotland (once the hot blast allowed use of local black-band, i.e. coal measures ore). Together, in 1839, these areas produced 83.5 per cent of the national pig iron output of 1.24 million tons (see Map 3.2).

In the second half of the nineteenth century, further developments in fuel economy, including the regenerative hot blast (1860) and increased furnace size, made ore not fuel the greater influence on location. Added to this, coalfield ore deposits were approaching exhaustion. New areas grew in importance, notably the North-east coast of England (where supplies of low-grade jurassic ores lay in close proximity to the Durham coalfield) and the North-west (Cumberland and Lancashire) with supplies of high-grade haematite ore. By 1875, the North-east coast was producing over 2 million tons of pig iron a year (one-third of national output) while the North-west's output of approximately a million tons equalled that of Scotland (see Map 3.3). Increasingly, too, there was dependence on high-grade imported ores, particularly from Spain. South Wales, especially, became dependent on imports and this contributed to a coastward shift of the iron industry in that region.

Steel manufacture, hitherto small-scale, became the dynamic sector of the iron and steel industry after 1860. By 1880, output stood at 1.3 million tons; by 1913 it was 7.7 million. Bessemer's first successful operation of his converter was in Sheffield in the 1860s. Siemens' open hearth furnace was first used in Birmingham in 1866 and in South Wales in 1869. With these processes, it was practicable to mass-produce 'acid' steel using pig iron made from domestic or imported haematite ores. Thomas and Gilchrist's 'basic process' (1879) made possible the use of cheaper low-grade phosphoric ores. For economic, technological, and marketing reasons, however, British firms were slow to switch to the new process; by 1913 under 37 per cent of British steel was manufactured by the basic method. Maps 3.6 and 3.7 indicate regional growth patterns during this period. The North-west and South Wales became major centres of Bessemer production; the North-east and Scotland centres of the more widely adopted open hearth process.

The twentieth century, as a result of war needs and the development of interventionist economic policies, has added government influence to the traditional factors, raw material supplies and markets, which affect the size and distribution of the iron and steel industry. Subsidized additional blast furnace and steel-making facilities contributed to a general overcapacity in the period 1920–33. Government influence and subsidies were also to be responsible, in the 1930s, for the development of Richard, Thomas, and Baldwin's integrated plant at Ebbw Vale (an inland site in South Wales) rather than in Lincolnshire. Use of scrap and shortages of haematite ores led to a continued increase in the proportion of steel made by the basic process (79 per cent by 1939), while the East Midlands, with cheap, if low-grade, ore supplies, continued an expansion in pig iron output begun before 1914, and by 1937 was responsible (with Essex) for 35 per cent of UK output (see Maps 3.4 and 3.5). Developments in this area such as Stewart's and Lloyd's integrated steel-making plant at Corby and United Steel's Appleby-Froding-ham complex (Lincolnshire) made rather more *economic* sense than either the Ebbw Vale plant or 1920s reconstructions such as those at Consett or Irlam. Finally, the middle years of the 1930s saw recovery for the industry aided by protection and by price-fixing, quota, and export agreements between the newly formed

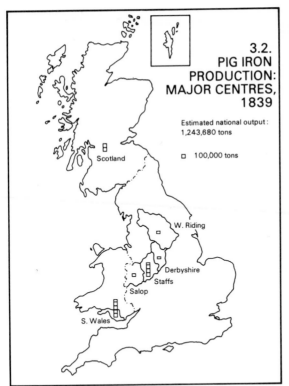

3.2.
PIG IRON
PRODUCTION:
MAJOR CENTRES,
1839

Estimated national output:
1,243,680 tons

□ 100,000 tons

Scotland

W. Riding

Derbyshire
Staffs

Salop

S. Wales

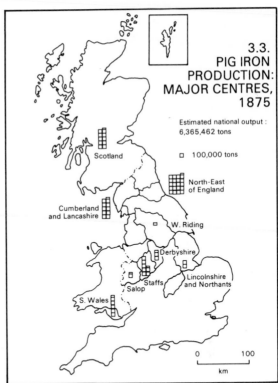

3.3.
PIG IRON
PRODUCTION:
MAJOR CENTRES,
1875

Estimated national output:
6,365,462 tons

□ 100,000 tons

Scotland

North-East
of England

Cumberland
and Lancashire

W. Riding

Derbyshire

Lincolnshire
and Northants

Salop Staffs

S. Wales

0   100
        km

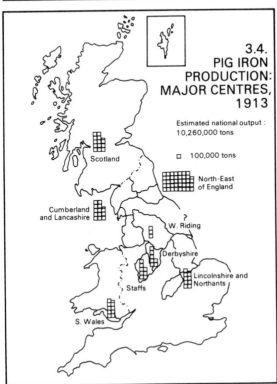

3.4.
PIG IRON
PRODUCTION:
MAJOR CENTRES,
1913

Estimated national output:
10,260,000 tons

□ 100,000 tons

Scotland

North-East
of England

Cumberland
and Lancashire

W. Riding

Derbyshire

Lincolnshire and
Northants

Staffs

S. Wales

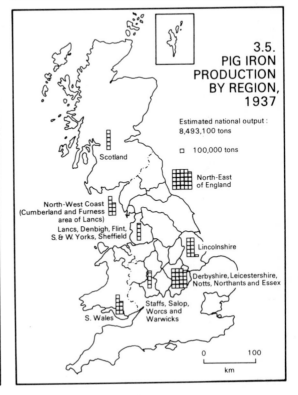

3.5.
PIG IRON
PRODUCTION
BY REGION,
1937

Estimated national output:
8,493,100 tons

□ 100,000 tons

Scotland

North-East
of England

North-West Coast
(Cumberland and Furness
area of Lancs)

Lancs, Denbigh, Flint,
S. & W. Yorks, Sheffield

Lincolnshire

Derbyshire, Leicestershire,
Notts, Northants and Essex

Staffs, Salop,
Worcs and
Warwicks

S. Wales

0   100
        km

47

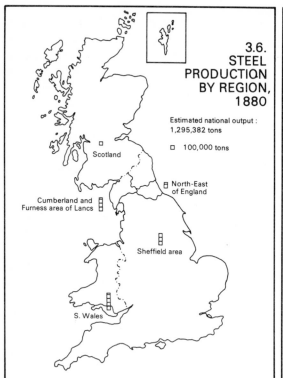

3.6.
STEEL
PRODUCTION
BY REGION,
1880

Estimated national output :
1,295,382 tons

☐   100,000 tons

Scotland

North-East
of England

Cumberland and
Furness area of Lancs

Sheffield area

S. Wales

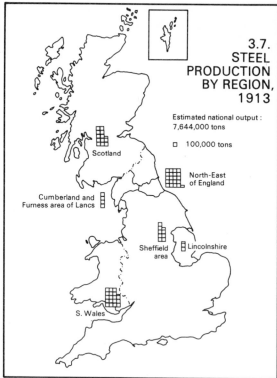

3.7.
STEEL
PRODUCTION
BY REGION,
1913

Estimated national output :
7,644,000 tons

☐   100,000 tons

Scotland

North-East
of England

Cumberland and
Furness area of Lancs

Sheffield
area

Lincolnshire

S. Wales

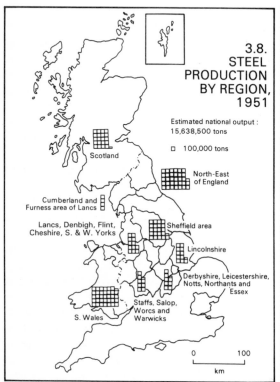

3.8.
STEEL
PRODUCTION
BY REGION,
1951

Estimated national output :
15,638,500 tons

☐   100,000 tons

Scotland

North-East
of England

Cumberland and
Furness area of Lancs

Lancs, Denbigh, Flint,
Cheshire, S. & W. Yorks

Sheffield area

Lincolnshire

Derbyshire, Leicestershire,
Notts, Northants and
Essex

Staffs, Salop,
Worcs and
Warwicks

S. Wales

0   100
km

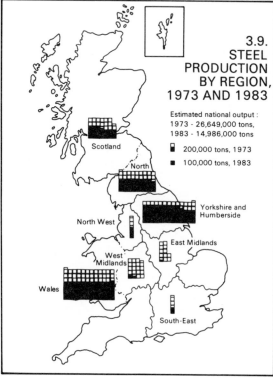

3.9.
STEEL
PRODUCTION
BY REGION,
1973 AND 1983

Estimated national output :
1973 - 26,649,000 tons,
1983 - 14,986,000 tons

▮   200,000 tons, 1973

■   100,000 tons, 1983

Scotland

North

North West

Yorkshire and
Humberside

East Midlands

West
Midlands

Wales

South-East

48

British Iron and Steel Federation and the European Steel Cartel. Output peaked at nearly 13 million tons in 1937 and, after a fall in the depression of 1937–8, recovered (aided by rearmament) to 13.2 million tons in 1939.

First World War experience had taught that expansion of production took time and diverted resources. Therefore, there was no attempt to do this during the Second World War. The post-war period, however, saw rapid expansion of output from 11.8 million tons in 1945 to 15.6 million in 1951 (see Map 3.8) and 27 million by 1965. By the latter date, acid steel was a mere 2.4 per cent of the total while electric arc and induction processes, used for high-grade steels, contributed 13 per cent. By the 1960s, too, the more efficient basic oxygen process was being generally adopted in hot metal establishments. The later part of the period saw, in addition, the establishment (as part of a revived regional economic policy) of the Ravenscraig (Scotland) and Llanwern (South Wales) strip mills.

The establishment of the British Steel Corporation (covering $c.90$ per cent of steel-making) in 1967 was followed by ambitious plans for rationalization but further expansion of capacity. In fact, BSC has presided over falling demand and successive moves to concentrate and reduce production. Appleby-Frodingham and Ebbw Vale were the largest closures in the Heritage programme of the early 1970s. Later casualties included major works at Shotton, Hartlepool, Consett, Corby, and Workington. By 1983, steel production, concentrated largely at Ravenscraig, South Teesside, Port Talbot, Llanwern, Scunthorpe, and Sheffield (special steels) was down to 15 million tons (see Map 3.9). Prospects, however, given an estimated 200 million tons excess capacity in the non-Communist world, were still not encouraging. Even remaining establishments were therefore at risk.

Shipbuilding

In the eighteenth century, British shipbuilding was a craft industry of small-scale units, mainly located in the south, building wooden sailing ships. At the beginning of the nineteenth century, the industry had the capacity to construct about 150,000 tons of shipping a year and the Thames, traditionally the major shipbuilding river was being challenged by the Tyne and Wear where the growth of the seaborne coal trade stimulated the local industry. By 1825 (see Map 3.10), the Wear (and therefore Sunderland) had emerged as the leading shipbuilding centre, concentrating on cheap eight-year vessels.

The first half of the nineteenth century saw erratic and limited growth in the industry. Yards remained small; in 1851 only 11 out of 317 English and Welsh firms claimed to employ more than 100 men. None the less, changes in hull and bow design and in construction materials (iron or composite ships), particularly in evidence by the 1850s, regained British pre-eminence in sailing ship construction and maintained, for the time being, the superiority of sail for long-distance bulk carriage. By contrast, though some yards on the Thames, Mersey, and Clyde had begun to specialize in steamship construction, such ships were small (averaging only 140 tons in 1850), uneconomical in fuel, and could only compete with sail on short-distance mail and passenger carriage.

The development of the screw propeller in the 1830s, the compound engine (by Elder and Randolph in 1853), Howden's cylindrical 'Scotch' boiler (1862), coupled with the availability of cheap malleable iron plates, allowing for lighter yet stronger construction, changed the position. Iron construction was greater than that in wood from 1862 and though building of sailing vessels continued (peak UK construction at 258,700 net tons occurring as late as 1892), it was overtaken by steam construction at the beginning of the 1870s.

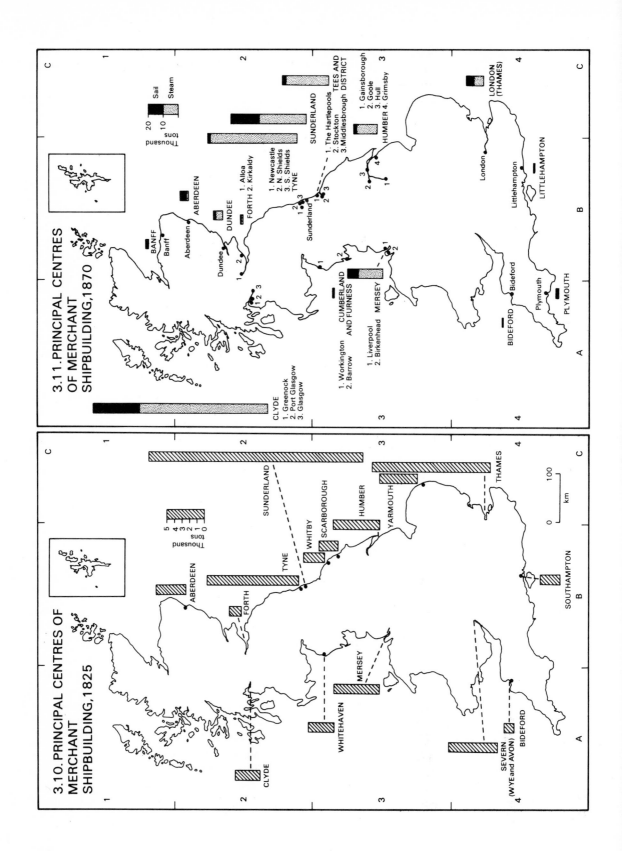

3.10. PRINCIPAL CENTRES OF MERCHANT SHIPBUILDING, 1825

ABERDEEN
FORTH
TYNE
SUNDERLAND
WHITBY
SCARBOROUGH
HUMBER
YARMOUTH
THAMES
SOUTHAMPTON
MERSEY
WHITEHAVEN
CLYDE
SEVERN (WYE and AVON)
BIDEFORD

Thousand tons
5
4
3
2
1
0

km
0   100

3.11. PRINCIPAL CENTRES OF MERCHANT SHIPBUILDING, 1870

CLYDE
1. Greenock
2. Port Glasgow
3. Glasgow

BANFF
Banff

ABERDEEN
Aberdeen

DUNDEE
Dundee

FORTH
1. Alloa   2. Kirkaldy

TYNE
1. Newcastle
2. N. Shields
3. S. Shields

Sunderland

SUNDERLAND

TEES AND TEES DISTRICT
1. The Hartlepools
2. Stockton
3. Middlesbrough

HUMBER
1. Gainsborough
2. Goole
3. Hull
4. Grimsby

LONDON (THAMES)

London

Littlehampton
LITTLEHAMPTON

Bideford
BIDEFORD

Plymouth
PLYMOUTH

CUMBERLAND AND FURNESS
1. Workington
2. Barrow

MERSEY
1. Liverpool
2. Birkenhead

Sail
Steam

Thousand tons
20
10

50

The Wear, with its established labour force and traditions, was slower than the major rivers to abandon either wood or sail. None the less Map 3.11 shows the extent to which the centre of shipbuilding had shifted to the North-east of England and the Clyde.

The conversion to iron and steam led to bigger yards; in 1871 the ninety British iron yards listed by the Factory Inspectors employed on average some 550 men. A complex of marine engineering industries developed around the major northern rivers. Cheap steel, from companies geared to the needs of the industry, triple- and quadruple-expansion engines, twin screws, plus new steam-powered, hydraulic, pneumatic, and electrical equipment in the yards contributed to a growth in the size and capacity of vessels (with ships of 10–15,000 tons on Atlantic routes by 1900), to their speed, to economies in construction, and to the domination, by British shipbuilders, of the world market. The position of Britain at the centre of a rapidly expanding world trade and the sheer scale of the UK merchant shipping fleet (c. 12.1 million tons in 1913, of which just 847,000 tons was sail) added to the demand for British-built ships. By 1913, output stood at 1.2 million tons, four times the 1870 figure (see Map 3.12).

Though British shipbuilders have been seen as slow to adapt to new techniques or types of ship (e.g. motor vessels), experienced management, a large, skilled, and productive labour force and a readiness to specialize or develop standardized vessels made British yards highly competitive. Not only did they meet virtually all home demand but, by 1913, some 30 per cent of output was sold abroad.

The First World War and the years immediately after saw a great expansion of shipbuilding capacity and output not only in Britain but also overseas, notably in the United States, Japan, and Sweden. Thus 5.9 million tons of shipping were produced, world-wide, in 1920 and 4.4 million tons in 1921. Trade, however, was stagnant, only reaching 1913 levels in 1925. In consequence, the capacity of the world mercantile fleet was greater than the demands imposed on it. Ships were laid up and freight rates cut; investment in new vessels was limited and it was 1938 before mercantile construction climbed back to the 3 million tons mark. Only in 1929 and 1937 did carrying capacity and trade approach balance; on each occasion economic slump restored the shipping surplus. Greater efficiency in ships (reducing the numbers needed), subsidies and protection for foreign shipbuilders, loss of leadership in design, poor organization of British yards, the absence of any productivity gains, and a 10 per cent fall, in the 1930s, in the size of the British merchant fleet (while that of other countries was growing), all added to British shipbuilders' difficulties. So, possibly, did an over-commitment to steam as opposed to motor vessels, though approximately half British output in the 1930s was motor-driven, and superheating and the use of oil-fired boilers had added to the efficiency of ships. National Shipbuilding Securities Ltd (1930), funded by a levy on firms in the industry, was one response to over-capacity. By 1934 NSS had bought up and dismantled 137 berths with a capacity of a million tons per annum. These included several on the Tyne and Wear (see Maps 3.14 and 3.15). Many of the yards acquired were, however, already effectively out of production. The government-backed 'Scrap and Build' scheme of 1935 was similarly limited in overall effect.

Though Britain was restored as the major shipbuilder of the world (a position briefly usurped by the USA in 1919–20), the percentage of world tonnage constructed in the UK fell from the 60 per cent of 1913 to just over 50 per cent in the late 1920s and 34 per cent in 1937–8. The fall in tonnage produced, particularly in the period 1931–4 when annual output was half a million tons or less, was more drastic. Even in the relatively healthy years of 1937–8 (see Map 3.12), output of the ship-building centres of North-east England and on the Clyde was generally one- to two-thirds below that of 1913.

The inter-war years had seen the beginning

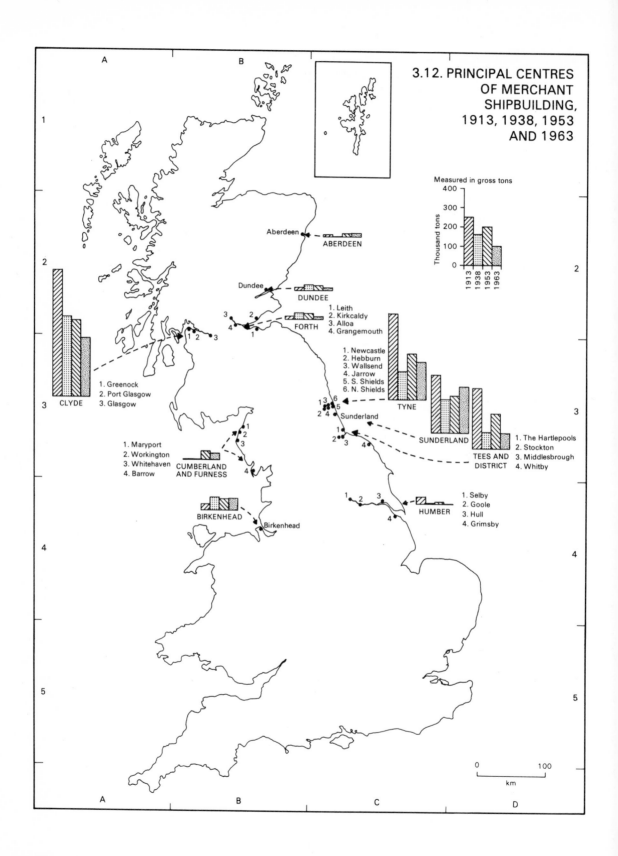

3.12. PRINCIPAL CENTRES OF MERCHANT SHIPBUILDING, 1913, 1938, 1953 AND 1963

Measured in gross tons

ABERDEEN

DUNDEE

FORTH
1. Leith
2. Kirkcaldy
3. Alloa
4. Grangemouth

CLYDE
1. Greenock
2. Port Glasgow
3. Glasgow

TYNE
1. Newcastle
2. Hebburn
3. Wallsend
4. Jarrow
5. S. Shields
6. N. Shields

SUNDERLAND

TEES AND DISTRICT
1. The Hartlepools
2. Stockton
3. Middlesbrough
4. Whitby

CUMBERLAND AND FURNESS
1. Maryport
2. Workington
3. Whitehaven
4. Barrow

BIRKENHEAD

HUMBER
1. Selby
2. Goole
3. Hull
4. Grimsby

0   100
km

of the long-term collapse of the British ship-building industry. The years after the Second World War were to see the completion of that process. Shortages of labour, of steel, and of berths (due to inter-war policy) meant that shipbuilding responded slowly to wartime demands. Mercantile output never exceeded the 1.3 million gross tons of 1942; construction of naval and landing craft peaked at 0.6 million deadweight tons in 1943. After the war there was a sellers' market for ships, and though British shipbuilders for a time retained leadership in output (50.9 per cent of the world total in 1948) and in export (41 per cent in 1948 but compared to 86.2 per cent in 1913 and 96.4 per cent in 1896), they failed to take opportunities to modernize yards or marine engineering workshops. Gross tonnage built was above 1.2 million tons throughout the period 1948–61, exceeding 1.4 million tons in 1954 and 1956–8. Britain's figure of just over one million (see Map 3.12 for distribution) represented about 12 per cent of the total; Japan's share was 22 per cent. Export share, meantime, had fallen to 4 per cent, traditional markets like Norway had been lost and foreign builders were invading British markets.

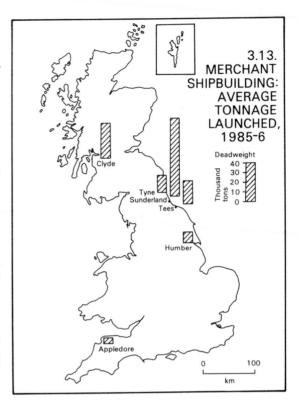

3.13.
MERCHANT SHIPBUILDING: AVERAGE TONNAGE LAUNCHED, 1985-6

Government subsidies were used to prop up large sections of the industry but weak management, bad industrial relations (often, in the 1950s and 1960s, centring on demarcation issues), outdated yards (especially when compared to those of Japan or Sweden), a poor record in meeting delivery dates plus, by the 1970s, a huge world over-capacity in ship-building berths led to a spectacular and absolute decline of the industry in the 1970s and 1980s. There were notable exceptions, for example the modernized Wearside yards of Austin and Pickersgill (probably the most successful shipyard in Europe in the 1970s) and Sunderland Shipbuilders. The general picture, though, in the industry, by now largely nationalized, has been one of dramatic contraction. The closure of other Wearside yards and of most of those on the south bank of the Tyne is shown in Maps 3.14 and 3.15. The closure of Smith's Dockyard on the Tees, in 1986, meant the end of shipbuilding on that river. On the Clyde, only Govan still builds ships, though Scott Lithgow builds drilling rigs. The shipbuilding and ship-repairing labour force, some 220,000 in November 1946 and over 20,000 on the Wear alone in the early 1960s, had fallen to 14,900 (5,100 in the Wear) by 1984 and the decline has continued. In 1985 and 1986, annual British production averaged just over 170,000 deadweight tons (see Map 3.13 for distribution of construction). The 172,000 tons of 1985 meant that Britain was now the seventeenth largest shipbuilder in the world: Japan, with 9.5 million tons (52 per cent of world output), built most.

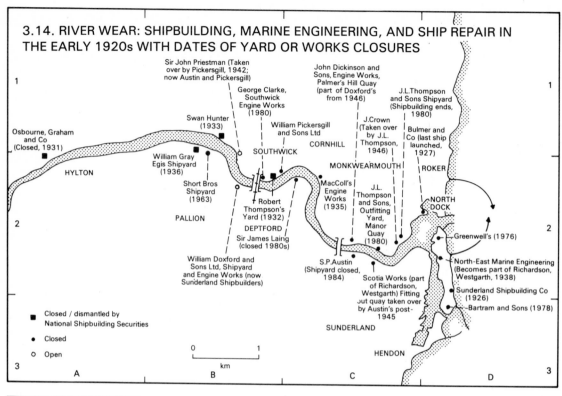

3.14. RIVER WEAR: SHIPBUILDING, MARINE ENGINEERING, AND SHIP REPAIR IN THE EARLY 1920s WITH DATES OF YARD OR WORKS CLOSURES

Sir John Priestman (Taken over by Pickersgill, 1942; now Austin and Pickersgill)

John Dickinson and Sons, Engine Works, Palmer's Hill Quay (part of Doxford's from 1946)

J.L. Thompson and Sons Shipyard (Shipbuilding ends, 1980)

George Clarke, Southwick Engine Works (1980)

Swan Hunter (1933)

William Pickersgill and Sons Ltd

J. Crown (Taken over by J.L. Thompson, 1946)

Bulmer and Co (last ship launched, 1927)

Osbourne, Graham and Co (Closed, 1931)

CORNHILL

SOUTHWICK

MONKWEARMOUTH

ROKER

William Gray Egis Shipyard (1936)

HYLTON

MacColl's Engine Works (1935)

J.L. Thompson and Sons, Outfitting Yard, Manor Quay (1980)

NORTH DOCK

Short Bros Shipyard (1963)

Robert Thompson's Yard (1932)

PALLION

DEPTFORD

Sir James Laing (closed 1980s)

Greenwell's (1976)

North-East Marine Engineering (Becomes part of Richardson, Westgarth, 1938)

William Doxford and Sons Ltd, Shipyard and Engine Works (now Sunderland Shipbuilders)

S.P.Austin (Shipyard closed, 1984)

Scotia Works (part of Richardson, Westgarth) Fitting Out quay taken over by Austin's post-1945

Sunderland Shipbuilding Co (1926)

Bartram and Sons (1978)

■ Closed / dismantled by National Shipbuilding Securities

• Closed

○ Open

SUNDERLAND

HENDON

0   1
km

A   B   C   D

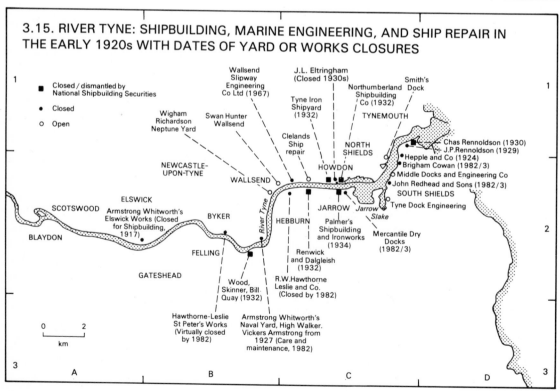

3.15. RIVER TYNE: SHIPBUILDING, MARINE ENGINEERING, AND SHIP REPAIR IN THE EARLY 1920s WITH DATES OF YARD OR WORKS CLOSURES

■ Closed / dismantled by National Shipbuilding Securities

• Closed

○ Open

Wallsend Slipway Engineering Co Ltd (1967)

J.L. Eltringham (Closed 1930s)

Smith's Dock

Northumberland Shipbuilding Co (1932)

Tyne Iron Shipyard (1932)

TYNEMOUTH

Wigham Richardson Neptune Yard

Swan Hunter Wallsend

Clelands Ship repair

NORTH SHIELDS

Chas Rennoldson (1930)
J.P.Rennoldson (1929)

NEWCASTLE-UPON-TYNE

HOWDON

Hepple and Co (1924)
Brigham Cowan (1982/3)
Middle Docks and Engineering Co
John Redhead and Sons (1982/3)

WALLSEND

SOUTH SHIELDS

ELSWICK

SCOTSWOOD

Armstrong Whitworth's Elswick Works (Closed for Shipbuilding, 1917)

BYKER

River Tyne

HEBBURN

JARROW

Jarrow Slake

Tyne Dock Engineering

BLAYDON

Palmer's Shipbuilding and Ironworks (1934)

Mercantile Dry Docks (1982/3)

FELLING

Renwick and Dalgleish (1932)

GATESHEAD

Wood, Skinner, Bill Quay (1932)

R.W.Hawthorne Leslie and Co. (Closed by 1982)

0   2
km

Hawthorne-Leslie St Peter's Works (Virtually closed by 1982)

Armstrong Whitworth's Naval Yard, High Walker. Vickers Armstrong from 1927 (Care and maintenance, 1982)

A   B   C   D

Motor vehicles

The British motor vehicle industry was initially slow to develop. The first manufacturing group, Harry Lawson's British Motor Syndicate, was only registered in November 1895 and its first manufacturing subsidiary, the Daimler Motor Company, was established two months later. In part, this slow start might be ascribed to the efficiency of steam technology in this country and to cheap and plentiful supplies of coal; a consequence of this was the slow development of gas or oil-powered internal combustion engines. The lack of a market on the scale of that in the United States could also have been a factor, though that does not explain the much more impressive performance of the French motor vehicle industry. The 'Red Flag' Act (repealed 1896) was not important nor, probably, was any shortage of capital, though the general failure of large engineering firms to engage in early motor manufacture could have been. Most important was the stress on traditional engineering practices, on individualism and technical quality rather than on production techniques and the market.

None the less, there was substantial expansion in the industry and in its output after 1900. In 1900 there were 59 motor manufacturers in Britain. A further 339 were established between then and 1914 though the casualty rate among such companies was high. Only 113 firms remained in 1914 including 21 of the original 59, and Richardson lists 48 firms in Coventry alone which failed to survive beyond 1914. Twelve thousand motor vehicles (cars and commercials) were produced in 1907 (many, though, assembled from French components) and 34,000 in the particularly successful year, 1913. By the latter date Ford, producing over 6,000 Model T cars at Trafford Park from American components, was by far the biggest producer; Wolseley (Birmingham), controlled since 1901 by Vickers, Son, and Maxim, produced 3,000 vehicles and Humber (originally Beeston, now Coventry) 2,500. Eight other firms produced between 1,000 and 2,000 cars. Though output was, by this time, 75 per cent of that of France, it compared ill with the 485,000 cars produced in the USA in 1914.

Motor manufacture became centred on the West Midlands, in particular Coventry (see Map 3.16), largely because of its links with the earlier mass-produced cycle industry. This had depended heavily on components produced by metalworking firms in the area. A substantial components industry also developed in connection with motor vehicle production, particularly in radiators, carburettors, wheels, tyres, and electrical equipment. Major firms like Rover, Austin, or Wolseley, however, made most parts for themselves. The growth of the West Midland industry owed less, in fact, to economic necessity than to historical accident, including the success of two of the earliest firms in the area, Daimler at Coventry and Wolseley in Birmingham. Saul[1] has estimated that in 1913 there were 13 car-makers in London (all on a small scale), 12 in Coventry (producing 9,000 cars), 8 in Birmingham (producing up to 5,000), 4 in Wolverhampton (3,000) and 3 in Scotland (2,400). Manchester, at that time, had 3 firms producing 4,700 cars, plus Ford (6,139). Others, though, were scattered throughout the country.

Following the dislocation of the war and immediate post-war years, the 1920s and 1930s saw a marked growth in motor vehicle production. Tariff protection in the home market, combined with the growing efficiency of the product and the introduction, in imitation of Ford, of production-line techniques (thereby cutting costs and prices), served to increase sales. So did the growing emphasis, especially during the 1930s, on light, low-horsepower cars, a development encouraged by the horsepower and petrol taxes. In the latter period, especially, first-time purchasers of small-engined cars constituted a large part of the home market. By 1937 exports, too, were important, taking more than one-fifth of

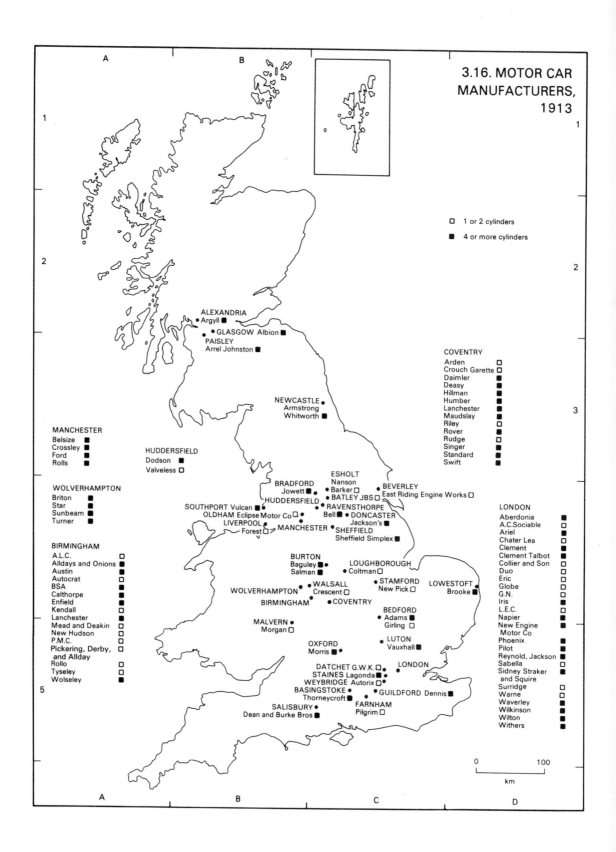

3.16. MOTOR CAR MANUFACTURERS, 1913

□ 1 or 2 cylinders

■ 4 or more cylinders

COVENTRY
Arden □
Crouch Garette □
Daimler ■
Deasy ■
Hillman ■
Humber ■
Lanchester ■
Maudslay ■
Riley □
Rover ■
Rudge □
Singer ■
Standard ■
Swift ■

MANCHESTER
Belsize ■
Crossley ■
Ford ■
Rolls ■

WOLVERHAMPTON
Briton ■
Star ■
Sunbeam ■
Turner ■

HUDDERSFIELD
Dodson ■
Valveless □

BIRMINGHAM
A.L.C. □
Alldays and Onions ■
Austin ■
Autocrat □
BSA ■
Calthorpe ■
Enfield ■
Kendall ■
Lanchester ■
Mead and Deakin □
New Hudson □
P.M.C. □
Pickering, Derby, □
 and Allday
Rollo □
Tyseley □
Wolseley ■

LONDON
Aberdonia ■
A.C.Sociable □
Ariel □
Chater Lea □
Clement ■
Clement Talbot ■
Collier and Son □
Duo □
Eric □
Globe □
G.N. ■
Iris ■
L.E.C. ■
Napier ■
New Engine ■
 Motor Co
Phoenix ■
Pilot ■
Reynold, Jackson ■
Sabella ■
Sidney Straker ■
 and Squire
Surridge □
Warne □
Waverley ■
Wilkinson ■
Wilton ■
Withers ■

ALEXANDRIA
• Argyll ■
GLASGOW Albion ■
PAISLEY
Arrel Johnston ■

NEWCASTLE
Armstrong
Whitworth ■

BRADFORD
Jowett ■
ESHOLT
Nanson
Barker □
BATLEY JBS ■
HUDDERSFIELD
RAVENSTHORPE
Bell ■ DONCASTER
SOUTHPORT Vulcan ■
OLDHAM Eclipse Motor Co □
LIVERPOOL Jackson's ■
Forest □ MANCHESTER
SHEFFIELD
Sheffield Simplex ■
BEVERLEY
East Riding Engine Works □

BURTON
Baguley ■ ■
Salman ■
LOUGHBOROUGH
Coltman □
STAMFORD
New Pick □
LOWESTOFT
Brooke ■

WALSALL
Crescent □
WOLVERHAMPTON
BIRMINGHAM
COVENTRY

BEDFORD
Adams ■
Girling □

MALVERN
Morgan □

OXFORD
Morris ■
LUTON
Vauxhall ■

DATCHET G.W.K. ■
STAINES Lagonda ■
WEYBRIDGE Autorix □
BASINGSTOKE
Thorneycroft ■
SALISBURY
Dean and Burke Bros ■
FARNHAM
Pilgrim □
LONDON
GUILDFORD Dennis ■

0   100
km

56

cars produced. In 1924, Britain produced 146,000 motor vehicles (116,600 cars and taxis; 30,000 commercial vehicles). Output grew each year until 1929 (238,805 vehicles including 182,347 cars and 56,458 commercial vehicles), and even in the trough of the slump in 1931 only declined by 5 per cent on the 1929 figure (partly because commercial vehicle output continued to rise). The 1930s saw renewed and more vigorous expansion to a peak of 507,749 vehicles (389,633 cars and 118,116 commercial vehicles) in 1937, 60 per cent of the cars being, by now, 10 h.p. or less.

Increased output was accompanied by amalgamation of companies. The 96 car-manufacturing companies of 1922 shrank to 41 by 1929, when Morris (35 per cent), Austin (25 per cent), and Singer (15 per cent) dominated output. By 1939 there were perhaps 20 independent companies and 33 manufacturers. Six firms now shared 90 per cent of output: Nuffield (incorporating Morris, M. G., Riley and Wolseley) had 26.6 per cent, Ford (17.8 per cent), Austin (17 per cent), Vauxhall (10.1 per cent), Rootes (Hillman, Sunbeam Talbot and Humber) had 9.6 per cent, and Standard 9 per cent. This trend had been accompanied by enhanced concentration of car manufacturing in the West Midlands and the South-east, close to the London market and to components manufacturers ('bought-out' components accounting, by now, for some 60 per cent of the costs of car production). Commercial vehicle manufacture, with its greater dependence on traditional heavy engineering, was mainly based in Lancashire and north Cheshire.

At the peak of Second World War mobilization, in 1943, car manufacture (at 1,649) had almost ceased but that of commercial vehicles (147,669) had continued to rise. The post-war period saw rapid expansion in both sections, principally for export. In the absence of European competition and in a world lacking the dollars to purchase American vehicles, Britain became the world's leading exporter, selling abroad some 70 per cent of the 783,672 vehicles (522,515 cars and 261,157

commercial vehicles) produced in 1950. Continued growth saw output reach 1,722,045 cars and 455,216 commercial vehicles by 1965. Thereafter, increasing competition, including in home markets, along with the poor productivity and product reliability record of the British motor-manufacturing industry, took its toll. Imports took 5 per cent of the domestic market in 1965, 35 per cent in 1974, 50 per cent in the 1980s. By 1984, car production was down to 908,906 and that of commercial vehicles, which until the mid-1970s had fared quite well, down to 224,825.

The process of amalgamation continued. The model range was reduced by some 60 per cent in the immediate post-war years. Austin and the Nuffield organization merged into the British Motor Corporation in 1952 and, with government support, BMH (as it had become) was linked to the successful Leyland company, forming British Leyland in 1968. The intention was to create a rationalized British volume car vehicle producer at a time when the three

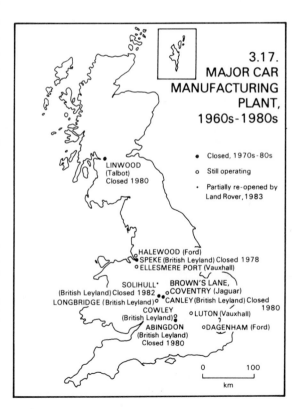

3.17.
MAJOR CAR
MANUFACTURING
PLANT,
1960s–1980s

• Closed, 1970s–80s

○ Still operating

∙ Partially re-opened by Land Rover, 1983

LINWOOD (Talbot) Closed 1980

HALEWOOD (Ford)
SPEKE (British Leyland) Closed 1978
○ ELLESMERE PORT (Vauxhall)

SOLIHULL∙
(British Leyland) Closed 1982
LONGBRIDGE (British Leyland)○

BROWN'S LANE,
○COVENTRY (Jaguar)
∙CANLEY (British Leyland) Closed 1980

COWLEY (British Leyland)
○LUTON (Vauxhall)

ABINGDON (British Leyland) Closed 1980
○DAGENHAM (Ford)

0   100
km

remaining major manufacturers in this country (Ford, Vauxhall, and Rootes) were all in American hands. The new company was not successful; in 1975, when it became 95 per cent state-owned in return for a huge infusion of state resources, there were still over sixty separate plants in different parts of the country. The report, in the same year, by the Central Policy Review Staff on *The Future of the British Car Industry* blamed the problems of the British industry as a whole on over-capacity, too great a range of models, engines, and body types, poor labour productivity (the result of over-manning, slow line speeds, frequent stoppages) and poor plant maintenance. None the less, the motor industry remained Britain's biggest exporter and, for economic as well as social reasons, government support, albeit with strings attached, continued.

During the expansionist period of the early 1960s, government pressure led to car-manufacturing firms establishing plant on Merseyside and in Scotland rather than in preferred West Midlands locations (see Map 3.17). In the severe cutbacks of the late 1970s and early 1980s (BL alone shedding 36,400 jobs between 1976 and 1981), outlying plants were worst affected. Talbot (who had taken over the Rootes group from Chrysler) closed Linwood in Scotland; BL closed plant at Speke. More traditional centres, however, were also hit with BL also ceasing operations at Abingdon, Canley (Coventry), and Solihull.

Aerospace

In aircraft manufacture, as in motor vehicles, Britain lagged behind France in the years before the First World War. There were, perhaps, a dozen small-scale airframe manufacturers; aero engines, if not imported, were left to firms mainly engaged in motor manufacture. War brought great expansion but post-war cancellation of military contracts and the availability, through the Aircraft Disposals Company, of surplus machines, co-inciding as this did with burdensome demands for Excess Profits Duty, put many firms in difficulty. Some disappeared, e.g. Airco and Sopwith whose design teams reformed later as De Havilland and Hawker. Others diversified into motor manufacture, general engineering, or air transport. From 1920 to 1934, the air-frame industry survived on small and irregular supplies of work and with a labour force of under 24,000. The government was, for military reasons, the major purchaser of British planes and, through the ring of approved suppliers, kept close controls over the industry. Only De Havilland, concentrating in peacetime exclusively on civil aircraft, escaped this tutelage. In aero engines, too, the Ministry adopted particular manufacturers: Armstrong Siddeley and Bristol for air-cooled engines, Napier and Rolls Royce for water-cooled. One reaction to scarcity of orders was amalgamation, notably Vickers' takeover of Supermarine in 1928 or the chain of mergers (including A. V. Roe, Saunders, Armstrong Siddeley, Gloster and Hawker) leading to the emergence of Hawker Siddeley in the mid-1930s. Even where amalgamations occurred, however, separate organizations, including design staff, were maintained, thus meeting the Air Ministry's requirement that the industry should be geared to rapid expansion.

This expansive capacity was demonstrated in rearmament. Between 1934 and 1943 employment in the industry increased forty-fold to over one million and output of aircraft rose from 1,108 machines in 1934 to 7,940 in 1939 and 26,263 in 1943. Some of this production was in 'shadow' factories established by car firms like Rootes or Austin with mass-production experience; much of it though, was through established airframe or aero-engine makers. New models, mainly metal mono-planes, required engineering skills which were scarce in some of the traditional centres of the

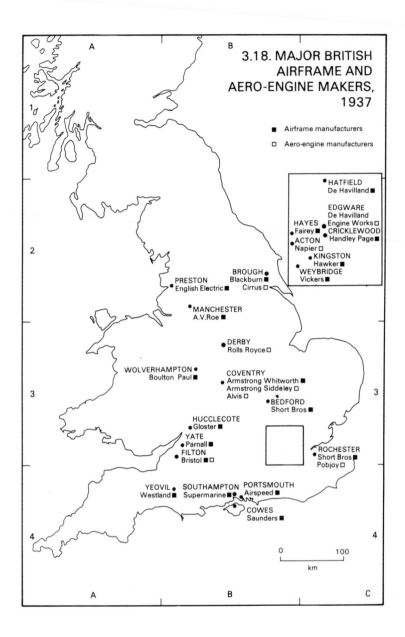

3.18. MAJOR BRITISH AIRFRAME AND AERO-ENGINE MAKERS, 1937

■ Airframe manufacturers

□ Aero-engine manufacturers

HATFIELD
De Havilland ■

EDGWARE
De Havilland
HAYES Engine Works □
Fairey ■ CRICKLEWOOD
ACTON Handley Page ■
Napier □
KINGSTON
Hawker ■
WEYBRIDGE
Vickers ■

BROUGH
Blackburn ■
PRESTON Cirrus □
English Electric ■

MANCHESTER
A.V.Roe ■

DERBY
Rolls Royce □

WOLVERHAMPTON
Boulton Paul ■ COVENTRY
Armstrong Whitworth ■
Armstrong Siddeley □
Alvis □
BEDFORD
Short Bros ■

HUCCLECOTE
Gloster ■
YATE
Parnall ■
FILTON ROCHESTER
Bristol ■□ Short Bros ■
Pobjoy □

YEOVIL SOUTHAMPTON PORTSMOUTH
Westland ■ Supermarine ■□ Airspeed ■
COWES
Saunders ■

0   100
km

industry. Thus Boulton Paul moved from Norwich to Wolverhampton. Location of plant however, remained more southern-based than that of motor vehicles (see Map 3.18).

Though the period 1943–8 saw a rapid run-down of the aircraft industry, the labour force never fell below 167,000 (six times the 1934 figure). At its post-war peak, in 1957, it stood at 303,000 and was still over a quarter of a million in 1965. The 1970s and 1980s saw the workforce fall to 139,380 in 1985 of which 72,900 worked in British Aerospace operating on twenty sites, virtually all of them in north-west or southern England (see Map 3.19). As pre-war, government money supported an industry that was important on strategic and balance-of-payments grounds and was at the forefront of technological advance.

Both before and during the war, the USA

**3.19.
BRITISH
AEROSPACE
ESTABLISHMENTS
IN BRITAIN,
1985**

Divisions

* Air weapons
▽ Army weapons
○ Civil aircraft
□ Electronic systems and equipment
■ Military aircraft
△ Naval weapons
● Space and communications

Prestwick

Preston
Warton   Brough
Lostock (Bolton)   Salmesbury
Manchester
Woodford
Chester   (Cheshire)

Stevenage
Bracknell   Hatfield
Weybridge   Kingston
Filton (Bristol)   Dunsfold
Hamble   (Godalming)
Weymouth
Plymouth

0   100
km

had taken a big lead in developing civilian airliners. Anachronistic thinking (flying boats, Brabazon), engineering failure (Comet), the effect of government policy on airline purchases (e.g. BOAC and the VC 10) and the large-scale American home market – all ensured that the US industry stayed ahead, with only the occasional British plane (e.g. the De Havilland Dove or the Vickers Viscount) meeting with any real international success. Achievements were much greater in the aero-engine field (in spite of early problems with the RB 211) and, until recently, in helicopters. Military aircraft (from the post-war Vampire and Meteor, via the Hunter and the Canberra, to the Harrier) have also sold successfully in world markets.

During the 1970s and 1980s, missile systems and, to a lesser extent, satellite equipment have provided major growth areas, illustrating the increasing overlap between the aircraft and advanced electronics industries.

Most recently, huge Research and Development costs, plus the international nature of the market (British Aerospace sells over 60 per cent of its products, by value, abroad) have led British companies into participation in international consortia: Rolls Royce with the US aero-engine giants or British Aerospace in Airbus Industrie, in the development of the Tornado with Italian and German companies or in production of the Hawk or Harrier II with the American firm, McDonnell Douglas.

Other engineering industries

Other branches of the engineering industries give further evidence of the twentieth-century southward shift in location apparent in iron and steel, motor vehicle and aircraft manufacture. In the case of the industries considered in this section, this tendency is largely a consequence of the changing structure of the industry; older, often northern-based textile, railway, and marine engineering branches declined, the electrical and electronic engineering industries grew.

During the late nineteenth and early twentieth centuries, the British engineering industry was dominated by those sectors which had grown up with industrialization. The 1907 Census of Production showed manufacture of railway carriages and wagons (£15.8 million), of textile machinery (£13 million) and of railway locomotives (£12.4 million) as the biggest sectors. The manufacture of steam-engines, boilers, and of agricultural machinery was also important. Total output of all branches of the electrical engineering industry only amounted to £14.1 million.

The location of the railway companies' locomotive and carriage workshops related to their areas of operation (Map 3.20) but private locomotive manufacturers were to be found primarily in the North of England or Scotland, where three Glasgow firms (Sharp Stewart, Neilson, and Dubs) combined to form the North British Locomotive Company in 1902 (Map 3.21). Private railway carriage and equipment building was centred on Birmingham, the base by 1914 of the Metropolitan Amalgamated Carriage and Wagon Company (Map 3.21). Textile machinery manufacture was based on Lancashire (where six major firms dominated) and, in the case of worsted, on Keighley (see Map 3.22). Steam-engine manufacture was more widespread. Much, of course, was to be found in Scotland or the North of England (e.g. the world-renowned boiler manufacturers, Babcock and Wilcox of Glasgow or Adamsons and Galloway of Manchester) (see Map 3.23). Manufacture of

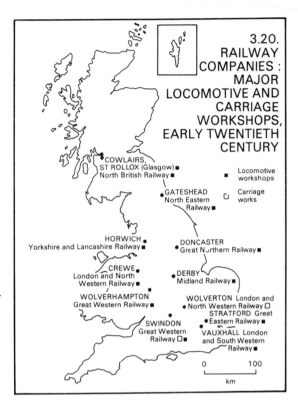

3.20.
RAILWAY COMPANIES : MAJOR LOCOMOTIVE AND CARRIAGE WORKSHOPS, EARLY TWENTIETH CENTURY

COWLAIRS, ST ROLLOX (Glasgow) North British Railway ■

■ Locomotive workshops

□ Carriage works

GATESHEAD North Eastern Railway ■

HORWICH Yorkshire and Lancashire Railway ●

DONCASTER ● Great Northern Railway ■

CREWE London and North Western Railway ●

DERBY ● Midland Railway ■

WOLVERHAMPTON Great Western Railway ●

WOLVERTON London and ● North Western Railway □ STRATFORD Great ● Eastern Railway ■

SWINDON Great Western Railway □ ■

VAUXHALL London and South Western Railway ■

0   100
km

portable steam-engines, however, tended to be based on agricultural engineering firms which were more evenly distributed across the country (see Map 3.24). Marshalls (Gainsborough), Rushtons (Lincoln) and Hornsby's (Grantham), all in Lincolnshire, and Garrett and Sons (Leiston) and Ransome, Sims, and Jefferies (Ipswich) were among the most important of such firms located in the agricultural East of England (Map 3.25). The largest electrical firms by 1910 were to be found not only in traditional heavy engineering areas like the North-west (thus the American-owned Westinghouse Company in Manchester and the successful British firm, Dick, Kerr, and Co. in Preston) but also in new centres on the fringe of the West Midlands, e.g. the British Thompson-Houston Co. (American GEC) at Rugby or Siemens' dynamo plant at Stafford (see Maps 3.26–3.28).

Changes in the relative importance of

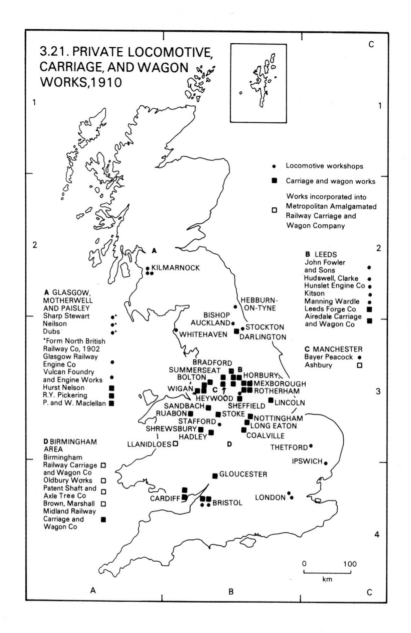

3.21. PRIVATE LOCOMOTIVE, CARRIAGE, AND WAGON WORKS, 1910

· Locomotive workshops

■ Carriage and wagon works

□ Works incorporated into Metropolitan Amalgamated Railway Carriage and Wagon Company

KILMARNOCK

HEBBURN-ON-TYNE

BISHOP AUCKLAND
STOCKTON
WHITEHAVEN
DARLINGTON

B LEEDS
John Fowler and Sons
Hudswell, Clarke
Hunslet Engine Co
Kitson
Manning Wardle
Leeds Forge Co
Airedale Carriage and Wagon Co

A GLASGOW, MOTHERWELL AND PAISLEY
Sharp Stewart
Neilson
Dubs
*Form North British Railway Co, 1902
Glasgow Railway Engine Co
Vulcan Foundry and Engine Works
Hurst Nelson
R.Y. Pickering
P. and W. Maclellan

C MANCHESTER
Bayer Peacock
Ashbury

BRADFORD
SUMMERSEAT
BOLTON
HORBURY
WIGAN
MEXBOROUGH
ROTHERHAM
HEYWOOD
LINCOLN
SANDBACH
SHEFFIELD
RUABON
STOKE
NOTTINGHAM
STAFFORD
LONG EATON
SHREWSBURY
COALVILLE
HADLEY
LLANIDLOES
THETFORD
IPSWICH

D BIRMINGHAM AREA
Birmingham Railway Carriage and Wagon Co
Oldbury Works
Patent Shaft and Axle Tree Co
Brown, Marshall
Midland Railway Carriage and Wagon Co

GLOUCESTER
CARDIFF
BRISTOL
LONDON

0   100
km

different engineering sectors led to a shifting geographical distribution of the industry. The inter-war period brought sharply contrasting fortunes. We have already seen the varying experiences of the hard-hit shipbuilding industry, the rapidly expanding motor vehicle industry (6.6 per cent p.a. growth in gross output 1920–38) and the erratic yet still considerable advance of aircraft manufacture (160 per cent increase in output in the ten years before rearmament began in 1934). Makers of textile machines and locomotives, faced with increased overseas competition and a sharp fall in the home market, declined in relative importance. So did marine engineering (though here an overall decline of 8 per cent in the value of output, 1924–35, masked a 30 per cent increase in the value of marine internal-combustion engines). The output of reciprocating steam-engines collapsed; by

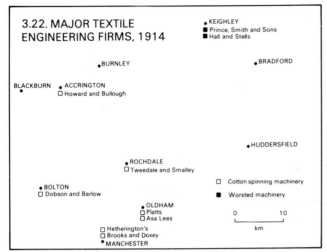

3.22. MAJOR TEXTILE ENGINEERING FIRMS, 1914

- KEIGHLEY
  - ■ Prince, Smith and Sons
  - ■ Hall and Stells
- BURNLEY
- BRADFORD
- BLACKBURN
- ACCRINGTON
  - □ Howard and Bullough
- HUDDERSFIELD
- ROCHDALE
  - □ Tweedale and Smalley
- BOLTON
  - □ Dobson and Barlow
- OLDHAM
  - □ Platts
  - □ Asa Lees
- □ Hetherington's
- □ Brooks and Doxey
- MANCHESTER

□ Cotton spinning machinery
■ Worsted machinery

0   10
km

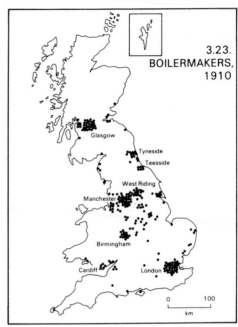

3.23. BOILERMAKERS, 1910

Glasgow
Tyneside
Teesside
West Riding
Manchester
Birmingham
Cardiff
London

0   100
km

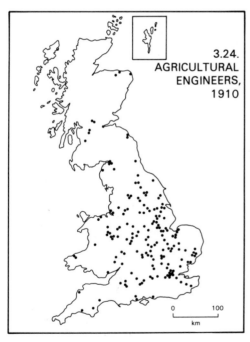

3.24. AGRICULTURAL ENGINEERS, 1910

0   100
km

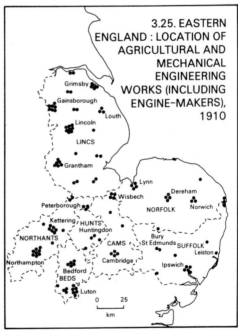

3.25. EASTERN ENGLAND : LOCATION OF AGRICULTURAL AND MECHANICAL ENGINEERING WORKS (INCLUDING ENGINE-MAKERS), 1910

Grimsby
Gainsborough
Louth
Lincoln
LINCS
Grantham
Lynn
Dereham
Wisbech
NORFOLK
Norwich
Peterborough
Kettering
HUNTS
Huntingdon
NORTHANTS
CAMS
Bury
St Edmunds
SUFFOLK
Leiston
Northampton
Cambridge
Ipswich
Bedford
BEDS
Luton

0   25
km

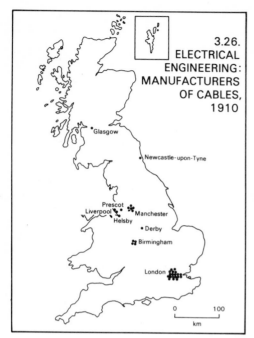

3.26.
ELECTRICAL
ENGINEERING:
MANUFACTURERS
OF CABLES,
1910

Glasgow

Newcastle-upon-Tyne

Prescot
Liverpool
Helsby
Manchester
Derby
Birmingham

London

0   100
km

3.27. ELECTRICAL
ENGINEERING:
MANUFACTURERS OF
TRANSFORMERS, 1910

C
1

2   2

ALLOA
British
Electrical Plant Ltd

BARROW
Vickers, Son and Maxim

3   OLDHAM   LEEDS   3
     J.P.Hall   Birch Bros
     MANCHESTER   SHEFFIELD
British Westinghouse   Vickers, Son and Maxim
Ferranti Ltd   W.E.Burnand
Cowans Ltd
     STAFFORD   LOUGHBOROUGH
Siemens Dynamo Works   Brush Engineering
     WOLVERHAMPTON   RUGBY
The Electrical Construction Co   British Thompson-Houston Co

British Electrical Transformer Co
Fuller Elec. and Manufac. Co
Home and Rowland   LONDON
Johnson and Phillips
Neville, Williams and Co
Union Electric Co
Vickers, Son and Maxim

4   4

A   B   C

0   100
km

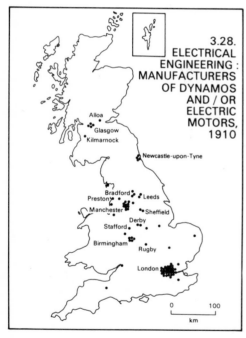

3.28.
ELECTRICAL
ENGINEERING :
MANUFACTURERS
OF DYNAMOS
AND / OR
ELECTRIC
MOTORS,
1910

Alloa
Glasgow
Kilmarnock

Newcastle-upon-Tyne

Bradford
Preston   Leeds
Manchester
Sheffield
Derby
Stafford
Birmingham
Rugby

London

0   100
km

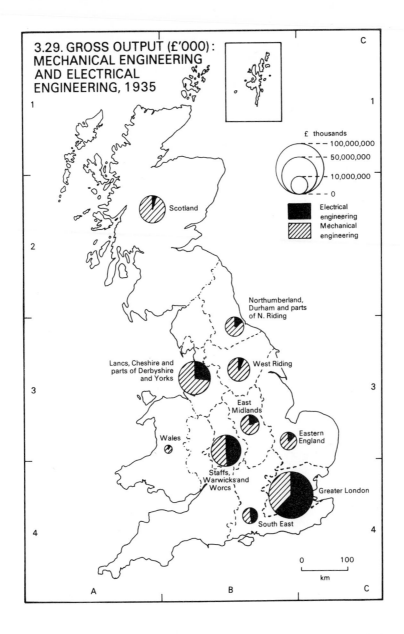

3.29. GROSS OUTPUT (£'000): MECHANICAL ENGINEERING AND ELECTRICAL ENGINEERING, 1935

£ thousands
— 100,000,000
— 50,000,000
— 10,000,000
— 0

Electrical engineering
Mechanical engineering

Scotland

Northumberland, Durham and parts of N. Riding

Lancs, Cheshire and parts of Derbyshire and Yorks

West Riding

East Midlands

Wales

Eastern England

Staffs, Warwicks and Worcs

Greater London

South East

0   100
km

1935 it was only 30 per cent that of 1924. Conversely, makers of boilers and of steam turbines (boosted by the demand from electricity generating stations) grew in importance as, more impressively, did electrical engineering; its 4.7 per cent growth in gross output, 1920–38, was second only to that of vehicle makers. Electrical engineering was heavily South- and Midlands-orientated. In 1935, whereas nationally electrical engineering (by value of gross output) was 62.2 per cent the size of mechanical engineering, in Greater London it was 164.7 per cent, in the South-east 93.1 per cent, and in Warwickshire, Worcestershire, and Staffordshire 98.3 per cent. By contrast, in North-west England electrical engineering output was 36.3 per cent that of mechanical and in Scotland just 4.9 per cent (see Map 3.29).

The period after the Second World War saw

the continued relative advance of electrical and electronic engineering. In the post-demobilization period, 1948–55, electrical engineering output rose 96 per cent, that of mechanical engineering 47 per cent. In spite of increased overseas competition from the mid-1950s and the small-scale units and technical conservatism of the strategically crucial machine-tool industry, both mechanical and electrical engineering performed well until at least 1980, with the electrical sector achieving a 4 per cent p.a. growth rate even during the difficult period 1974–80. By 1983, the £15,153 million sales of electrical and electronic engineering products (which excludes £4.9 million sales of electronic data-processing equipment and instrument engineering products, or the electronics input into aerospace) amounted to 86.1 per cent of the sales by the mechanical engineering sectors. With this went a further concentration of the industry in South-east England; the £435 million capital invested in the engineering industries of that region in 1983 was more than three times the next largest regional investment, Scotland (see Map 3.30). Much of the investment in Scotland was by overseas firms in the rapidly developing electronics field; electronics firms were important, too, in the South-east, though perhaps the most spectacular expansion was in

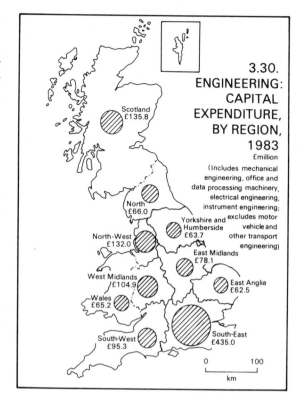

3.30.
ENGINEERING:
CAPITAL
EXPENDITURE,
BY REGION,
1983
£million

(Includes mechanical
engineering, office and
data processing machinery,
electrical engineering,
instrument engineering;
excludes motor
vehicle and
other transport
engineering)

Scotland £135.8
North £66.0
Yorkshire and Humberside £63.7
North-West £132.0
East Midlands £78.1
West Midlands £104.9
East Anglia £62.5
Wales £65.2
South-East £435.0
South-West £95.3

0   100
km

Cambridgeshire (in East Anglia) where 135 firms producing computer-ware had been established by 1984.

Notes

1 S. B. Saul, 'The motor industry in Britain to 1914', *Business History*, V (1962–3), pp. 22–44. Saul's estimates are generally lower than the numbers indicated on Map 3.16, which is based on W. C. Bersey and W. V. Foucard, *List of Motor Cars and Cycle Cars Manufactured or Sold in the United Kingdom, 1907–1913* (London, 1913).

Maps on the iron and steel industry are based largely on figures reproduced in P. Riden, 'The output of the British iron industry before 1870', *Economic History Review*, 2nd ser., XXX

(1977), 3, pp. 442–59 (Map 3.1); H. G. Roepke, *Movements of the British Iron and Steel Industry – 1720–1951* (Urbana, 1956) and *Regional Trends 1986* (London, 1986) (Maps 3.2–3.9). The sources of maps on shipbuilding are as follows: BPP 1826–7, XVIII (Map 3.10); BPP 1871 (329), LX, p. 29 (Map 3.11); *Annual Statement of the Navigation and Shipping of the United Kingdom*, Cmd. 7616 (London, 1914), Lloyd's *Annual Summary of the Merchant Shipbuilding of the World* (London, 1938, 1953) and *Fairplay Shipping Journal* (January 1964) (Map 3.12); *Fairplay Shipping Journal* (1985–7)

(Map 3.13). Maps 3.14 and 3.15 are based on a variety of materials held in the Local Studies Collections of the Sunderland, South Shields, and Newcastle-upon-Tyne Central Libraries. Thanks are due to the staff of those libraries, in particular F. W. Manders (Local Studies Librarian, Newcastle) and J. P. Hall (Sunderland Central Library) and to Joe Clarke, Principal Lecturer in the School of Geography and Environmental Studies, Newcastle Polytechnic. Maps on the motor industry are based on Bersey and Foucard, op. cit. (Map 3.16), and on material in S. Fothergill and J. VIncent, *The State of the Nation* (London, 1985) and K. Williams, J. Williams, and C. Haslam, *The Breakdown of Austin-Rover* (Leamington Spa, 1987) (Map 3.17). Aerospace maps are based on information from *'The Aeroplane' Directory of the Aviation and Allied Industries* (London, 1937) (Map 3.18) and on material supplied by British Aerospace (Map 3.19). Map 3.20 rests heavily on material in S. B. Saul, 'The engineering industry', in D. H. Aldcroft (ed.), *The Development of British Industry and Foreign Competition, 1875–1914* (London, 1968); Maps 3.21–3.26 are based largely on information from *The British and Foreign Guide to the Engineering, Steel and Hardware Trades* (London, 1910). Maps 3.26–3.28, on the electrical engineering industry, use material from *'The Electrician' Electrical Trades Directory and Handbook* (London, 1910). The *Final Report of the 5th Census of Production and the Import Duties Inquiry, 1935*, Pt II (London, 1939) is the source for Map 3.29 and *Regional Trends, 1986* (London, 1986) for Map 3.30.

4 COAL, GAS, AND ELECTRICITY
Carol Jones

Coal

The development of the coal industry was a crucial factor in promoting the economic expansion and industrial diversification which characterized Britain during the industrial revolution. Indeed, coal remained the primary source of fuel in Britain until after the Second World War. The initial stimulus to growth came in the seventeenth century when a shortage of wood forced domestic consumers to burn the hitherto despised sea-coal on their hearths. Annual output rose from 210,000 tons in 1560 to 2,985,000 tons by 1700, of which 43 per cent came from the advanced Tyne and Wear collieries which continued to dominate the trade into the twentieth century (see Map 4.1). The main market was London, and by 1720 63 per cent of the North-east's output was shipped into the city. Although in the North-east, by the late eighteenth century, pits were being sunk at depths of over 750 feet, many early pits were small-scale and shallow and some older collieries had already been depleted of their coal stocks to the limits of existing technology. Dependence on water transport also restricted colliery development, as reflected in the concentration of the oldest North-east pits (see Map 4.2) close to the River Tyne in areas where thick seams of coal lay near to the surface.

Much of the early growth of the industry, therefore, occurred without any great technological advances being made. In the late eighteenth century, however, two developments contributed to the expansion of the industry: the adoption of the Newcomen engine for pumping, thus overcoming the serious drainage problems associated with deeper mining and enabling new seams to be exploited, and the construction of canals and railways (the so-called 'Newcastle roads') which enabled inland collieries to expand their markets. Steam-driven winding machinery and the Davy safety lamp also facilitated the development of deeper mines.

North-east producers bitterly opposed the extension of the railways, perceiving that it would threaten their monopoly of the domestic trade. However the first rail-borne coal from inland collieries reached London by 1840. Twenty years later this coal had replaced sea-borne coal from the North-east and by the 1870s the region's share of national output declined to less than 22 per cent (see Map 4.3) as the Lancashire and South Wales coalfields, stimulated by the demand from industrial consumers, began to challenge its supremacy.

The period 1830 to 1870 was one of rapid growth in the coal-mining industry, particularly in response to the demands of industries like cotton, iron and steel, milling, brewing, and pottery. South Wales, for example, had increased its production from less than 5 million tons per year in the 1830s to over 30 million by the 1890s, representing 17 per cent of national production, only 4 per cent behind the North-east and surpassing the Scottish coalfields (see Map 4.3). Within the regions colliery development was dispersed as

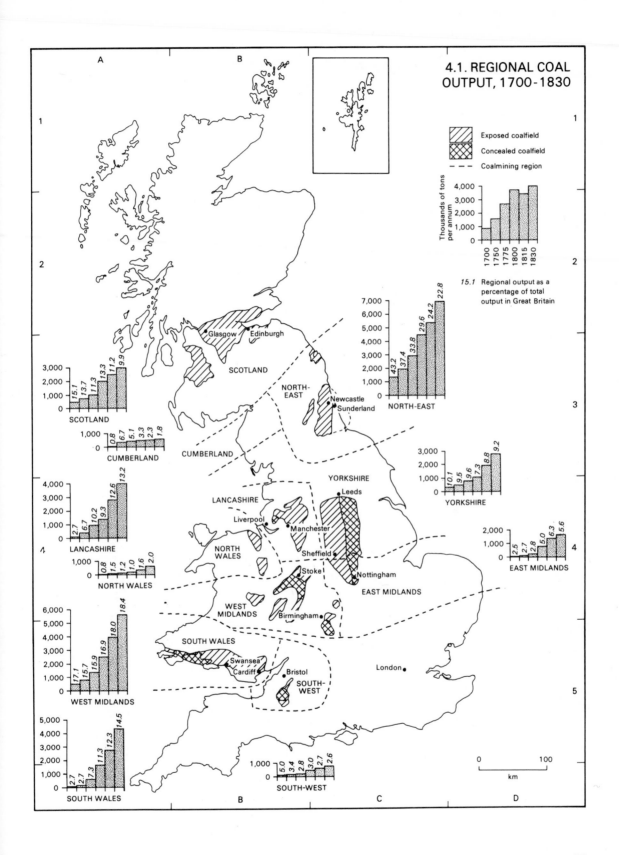

4.1. REGIONAL COAL OUTPUT, 1700-1830

Exposed coalfield
Concealed coalfield
Coalmining region

Thousands of tons per annum

1700 1750 1775 1800 1815 1830

15.1 Regional output as a percentage of total output in Great Britain

SCOTLAND
15.1 13.7 11.3 13.3 11.2 9.9

CUMBERLAND
0.8 6.7 5.1 3.3 2.3 1.8

LANCASHIRE
2.7 6.7 10.2 9.3 12.6 13.2

NORTH WALES
0.8 1.5 1.2 1.0 1.6 2.0

WEST MIDLANDS
17.1 15.7 15.9 16.9 18.0 18.4

SOUTH WALES
2.7 2.7 7.3 11.3 12.3 14.5

SOUTH-WEST
5.0 3.4 2.8 3.0 2.7 2.6

NORTH-EAST
43.2 37.4 33.8 29.6 24.2 22.8

YORKSHIRE
10.1 9.5 9.6 7.3 8.8 9.2

EAST MIDLANDS
2.5 2.7 2.8 5.0 6.3 5.6

Glasgow Edinburgh
SCOTLAND
NORTH-EAST
Newcastle
Sunderland
CUMBERLAND
YORKSHIRE
Leeds
LANCASHIRE
Liverpool Manchester
Sheffield
NORTH WALES
Stoke
Nottingham
WEST MIDLANDS
EAST MIDLANDS
Birmingham
SOUTH WALES
Swansea
Cardiff Bristol
SOUTH-WEST
London

0   100
km

69

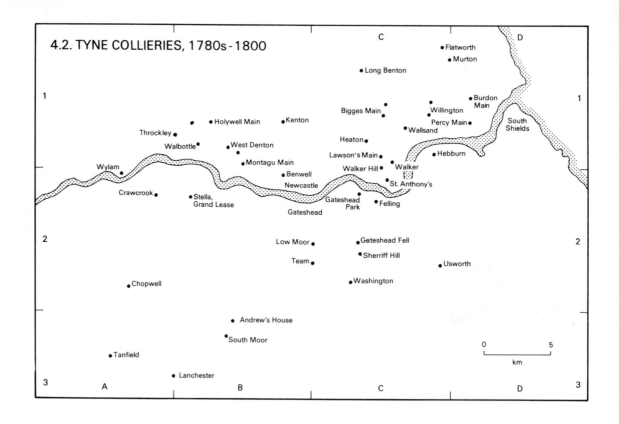

4.2. TYNE COLLIERIES, 1780s-1800

the railways removed the need to be close to rivers or the coast (see Map 4.4). The expansion of the Durham coalfield had also been fuelled by the success of Hetton colliery in 1822; the first sinking under the limestone at a depth of 1,080 feet. The North-east coalfield was not only shifting southwards, with the opening of the Tees coalfield in the 1820s, but also northwards away from Newcastle in response to the demands of the gas and iron industries. A similar drift away from the older, more accessible seams can also be seen in the Yorkshire coalfield in the period after 1870 (see Map 4.5), where output had increased from only 3 million tons in 1830 to over 21 million tons by the 1890s.

Mining costs had also risen steadily. Monkwearmouth colliery near Sunderland, for example, cost its owners an estimated £250,000 between 1826 and 1843, when they sold out before coal had even been mined. Within a few years, however, the colliery had become one of the most successful on the coalfield. Despite the highly speculative nature of coal-mining, investors continued to be attracted to the industry by the lure of high profits, noting, no doubt, that Hetton had made its owners £80,000 in the first year of production. By 1850 there were an estimated 3,000 mines in the country (see Maps 4.4 and 4.5) and although the industry faced repeated crises of over-production, output continued to rise, doubling between 1850 and 1880, and again between 1880 and 1913 (see Map 4.3). The proliferation of small pits in the nineteenth century made the structure of the industry inefficient and cumbersome.

The problems facing the industry were becoming apparent by the 1870s, when industries like iron and steel, which had been heavy consumers of coal, began to adopt new fuel-saving production methods. Part of this loss was offset by the increased foreign trade and by 1913 over 30 per cent of coal output was

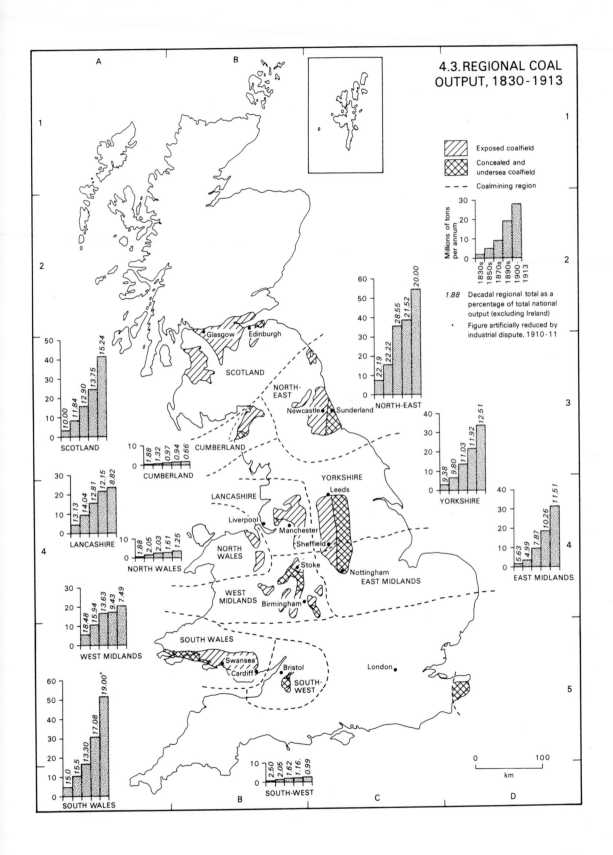

4.3. REGIONAL COAL OUTPUT, 1830-1913

Exposed coalfield

Concealed and undersea coalfield

Coalmining region

Millions of tons per annum

1830s 1850s 1870s 1890s 1900-1913

1.88 Decadal regional total as a percentage of total national output (excluding Ireland)

• Figure artificially reduced by industrial dispute, 1910-11

SCOTLAND
10.00 11.84 12.90 13.75 15.24

NORTH-EAST
22.19 22.22 28.55 21.52 20.00

CUMBERLAND
1.88 1.32 0.97 0.94 0.66

YORKSHIRE
9.38 9.80 11.03 11.92 12.51

LANCASHIRE
13.13 14.04 12.81 12.15 8.82

NORTH WALES
1.88 2.05 2.03 1.61 1.25

EAST MIDLANDS
5.63 4.99 7.87 10.26 11.51

WEST MIDLANDS
18.48 15.94 13.63 9.43 7.49

SOUTH WALES
15.0 15.5 13.30 17.08 19.00*

SOUTH-WEST
2.50 2.05 1.62 1.16 0.99

Glasgow   Edinburgh

SCOTLAND

NORTH-EAST

Newcastle   Sunderland

CUMBERLAND

YORKSHIRE   Leeds

LANCASHIRE

Liverpool   Manchester

Sheffield

NORTH WALES

Stoke

Nottingham

WEST MIDLANDS   Birmingham

SOUTH WALES

Swansea   Bristol

Cardiff   SOUTH-WEST

London

0   100
km

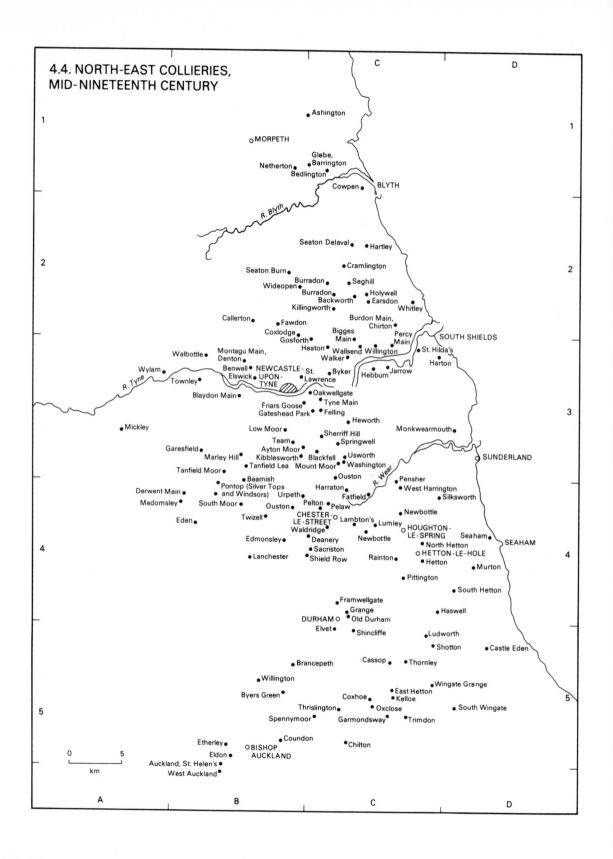

4.4. NORTH-EAST COLLIERIES, MID-NINETEENTH CENTURY

Ashington

○ MORPETH

Glebe,
Barrington
Netherton
Bedlington
Cowpen
BLYTH

R. Blyth

Seaton Delaval
Hartley

Seaton Burn
Cramlington
Burradon
Seghill
Wideopen
Burradon
Holywell
Backworth
Earsdon
Whitley
Killingworth
Burdon Main,
Chirton
Callerton
Fawdon
Percy
Coxlodge
Bigges
Main
SOUTH SHIELDS
Gosforth
Heaton
Wallsend Willington
St. Hilda's
Walbottle
Montagu Main,
Denton
Walker
Harton
Wylam
Benwell
NEWCASTLE - St.
Byker
Townley
Elswick
UPON-
Lawrence
Hebburn
Jarrow
TYNE
Blaydon Main
Oakwellgate
Friars Goose
Tyne Main
Gateshead Park
Felling
Mickley
Heworth
Low Moor
Monkwearmouth
Sherriff Hill
Garesfield
Team
Springwell
SUNDERLAND
Ayton Moor
Marley Hill
Blackfell
Usworth
Tanfield Moor
Tanfield Lea
Mount Moor
Washington
Beamish
Ouston
Pontop (Silver Tops
Harraton
Pensher
Derwent Main
and Windsors)
Urpeth
Fatfield
West Harrington
Medomsley
South Moor
Ouston
Pelton
Silksworth
Eden
Twizell
Pelaw
Newbottle
CHESTER-
Lambton's
LE-STREET
Lumley
HOUGHTON-
Waldridge
LE-SPRING
Seaham
Deanery
Newbottle
SEAHAM
Edmonsley
North Hetton
Sacriston
Rainton
HETTON-LE-HOLE
Lanchester
Shield Row
Hetton
Murton
Pittington
South Hetton
Framwellgate
Grange
Haswell
DURHAM ○
Old Durham
Elvet
Shincliffe
Ludworth
Shotton
Castle Eden
Brancepeth
Cassop
Thornley
Willington
East Hetton
Wingate Grange
Byers Green
Coxhoe
Kelloe
Thrislington
Oxclose
South Wingate
Spennymoor
Garmondsway
Trimdon
Etherley
Coundon
Chilton
Eldon
○ BISHOP
Auckland, St. Helen's
AUCKLAND
West Auckland

0   5
km

exported. But, as other countries began to develop their own coal industries, it was apparent that the British coal industry's increased dependence on foreign trade made it particularly vulnerable to competition. Between 1880 and 1913 its share of world output declined from 41 per cent to only 25 per cent. Unlike their competitors, the British coal-owners were slow to adopt new production techniques. With labour relatively cheap, increased demand was met by taking on more men – shedding them or cutting wages when recession set in, with all the implications this had for soured industrial relations. As a result little attention was paid to output per man-shift and, unlike in America where the relatively high cost of labour encouraged the use of mechanized cutting equipment and conveyor systems, technical innovation was not a priority. As late as the 1930s, less than 40 per cent of Britain's coal was cut mechanically, compared to 97 per cent in Germany and 99 per cent in Belgium.

The First World War marked a turning-point for the industry and in spite of the government's taking effective control between 1917 and 1921 in an effort to curtail spiralling prices, many foreign markets were lost and output declined as the export price of coal fell by 50 per cent. Despite a brief revival due to the American and Ruhr coal strikes of 1922–3, and government subsidies of £3 million in 1921 and £10 million in 1926, the inter-war years were marked by contraction, increased foreign competition and bad industrial relations in the pits, culminating in the General Strike in 1926. Nationalization, which had been suggested by the Sankey Commission in 1919, now became a public issue.

A further problem was that the declining demand for coal from the hard-pressed staple industries was not offset by the increased demands of the gas and electricity industries. Governments were aware of the need for rationalization and the benefits of focusing production on large collieries,[1] but the already high levels of unemployment in mining areas made them reluctant to adopt more extreme

measures. The 1926 Mining Industry Act, based on the recommendations of the Samuel Commission, attempted to promote voluntary reorganization, but although some amalgamations were achieved, the output quotas established under the 1930 Coal Mines Act actually protected smaller pits and deterred the coal-owners from making any radical changes. As early as 1936 the government was aware that they would have to be prepared to take control of the coal industry in the event of war. The depression years had not left the industry well placed to respond to the demands of a wartime economy and by 1941 there was a national coal shortage. Manpower shortages, lack of investment, and declining production continued to be a problem throughout the war years. In 1942, in response to the recommendations of the Anderson Committee, power over distribution and production had already centralized in the National Coal Board, and after considerable debate about the future of the industry in the post-war world, the coal industry passed into state control on 1 January 1947, with 1,500 pits (see Maps 4.5 and 4.6) at a cost of over £200 million, along with a holiday camp, cinema, mortuary, swimming baths, shops and hotels, and ancillary industries.

The booming post-war economy found the coal industry in a sellers' market, but facing repeated crises like that of 1946–7. Working on projected demands for coal of 250 million tons by the 1960s, the 1950s were years of expansion and prosperity, and improvements in coal production were achieved by the widespread introduction of coal-cutting equipment, power loading, and hydraulic pit props. However, production costs were ignored and the continuing high price of coal, coupled with recurring shortages, convinced industries which had been heavily dependent on it, including the other energy industries, to begin the process of switching to cheaper fuels. Thus, while power station consumption increased between 1950 and 1975 from 43.5 million tons to 73.4 million tons per year, the electricity industry was also developing oil and nuclear

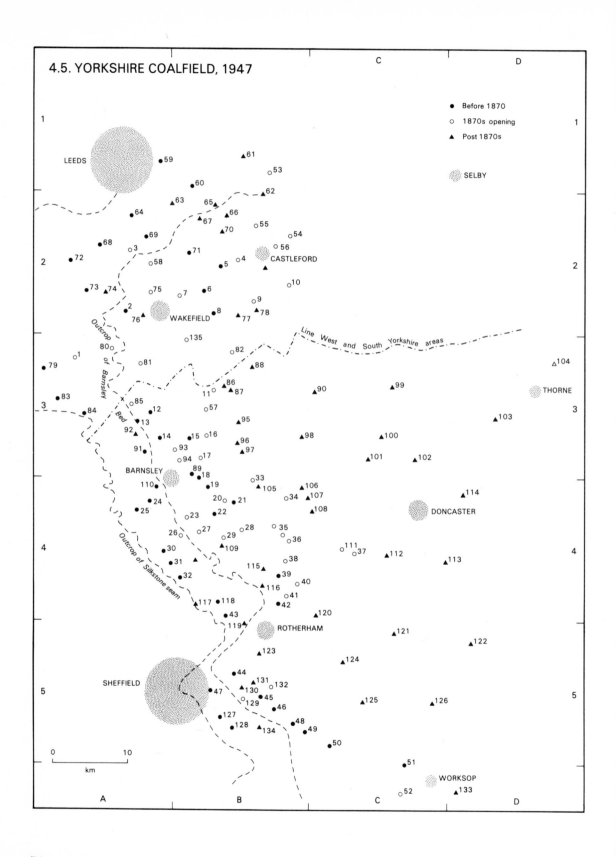

4.5. YORKSHIRE COALFIELD, 1947

● Before 1870
○ 1870s opening
▲ Post 1870s

SELBY

LEEDS
●59
▲61
○53
●60
▲62
▲63
65▲
●64
66▲
▲67
●69
○55
▲70
●68
○54
○3
○56
●72
○58
CASTLEFORD
●71
5● ●4
○10
●73 ▲74
○75 ●7 ●6
○9
2● ●8 ○78
76▲ WAKEFIELD ●77
80○ ○135
○82
○1 Line West and South Yorkshire areas
●79 ○81 ▲88 △104
○86 THORNE
11○ ▲87 ▲99
●83 ○85 ●90
84▲ 12● ○57 ▲103
13▲ ●95
92▲ 14● ○15 ○16 ●98 ▲100
91● ○93 ▲96 ▲101 ▲102
○94 ○17 ●97
BARNSLEY 89● ○33 ●114
110● ○18 ▲105 ▲106
19● ○34 ▲107
●24 20○ ●21 ▲108 DONCASTER
●25 ○23 ●22 ○35
26● ○27 ○28 ○36
●30 29○ ○111
▲109 ○37 ▲112
●31 ○38 ▲113
▲32 115▲ ●39 ▲116 ○40
117▲ ●118 ○41
●43 ●42
119▲ ▲120
ROTHERHAM ▲121
▲123 ▲122
SHEFFIELD ▲124
44● ▲125 ▲126
●47 ▲131 ○132
130▲ ○45
129○ ●46
127● ●48
128● 134▲ ●49
●50
●51
WORKSOP
○52 ▲133

0   10
km

A   B   C   D

1 Denby Main Cophouse
2 Old Roundwood
3 East Ardsley
4 Whitwood
5 West Riding
6 St John's
7 Park Hill
8 Sharlston
9 Featherstone Main
10 Prince of Wales
11 Ryhill
12 Wheatley Wood
13 Woolley
14 North Gawber
15 Wharncliffe Woodmoor
16 Carlton Main
17 Monkbretton
18 Old Oaks
19 New Oaks
20 Mitchell Main
21 Darfield Main
22 Wombwell Main
23 Barrow
24 Strafford
25 Wentworth Silkstone
26 Rockingham
27 Hoyland Silkstone
28 Cortonwood
29 Hemmingfield Pumping Pit
30 Wharncliffe Silkstone
31 Tankersley
32 Thorncliffe
33 Houghton Main
34 Highgate
35 Wath Main
36 Manvers Main
37 Denaby Main
38 Swinton Common
39 Warren Vale
40 Thyberg
41 Roundwood
42 Aldwarke
43 Grange
44 Tinsley Park
45 Gargreave

46 Fence
47 Nunnery
48 Aston
49 Waleswood
50 Riveton Park
51 Shireoaks
52 Steetley
53 Peckfield
54 Fryston
55 Allerton Bywater
56 Wheldale
57 New Monkton
58 Lofthouse
59 Osmanthorpe
60 Waterloo Main Temple
61 Garforth Sisters
62 Ledstone Luck
63 Rothwell Haigh Fanny
64 Middleton Broom
65 Primrose Hill
66 Allerton Main
67 Water Haigh
68 West Ardsley
69 Robin Hood Jane
70 Whitwood Saville
71 Newmarket Nelson
72 Howley Park
73 Shaw Cross
74 Low Laithes
75 Wrenthorpe
76 Manor
77 Smydale
78 Acton Hall
79 Shuttle Eye
80 Hartley Bank
81 Crigglestone
82 Rostell
83 Emley
84 Park Mill
85 Haigh
86 New Monkton
87 Hodroyd
88 Hemsworth
89 Barnsley Main
90 Upton

91 Barugh
92 Darton
93 Staincross
94 Mottram Wood
95 Brierley
96 Ferry Moor
97 Grimethorpe
98 Frickley
99 Askern Moor
100 Bridgecraft Main
101 Brodsworth Main
102 Bentley
103 Hatfield Main
104 Thorne
105 Dearnvalley
106 Mickleton Main
107 Goldthorpe
108 Barnborough
109 Elsecar
110 Round Hill
111 Sareby Main
112 Yorkshire Main
113 Rossington Main
114 Markham Main
115 Warrenhouse
116 New Stubbin
117 Smithy Wood
118 Scholes
119 Bradgate
120 Silverwood
121 Maltby Main
122 Haworth Main
123 Rotherham Main
124 Thurcroft Main
125 Dinnington Main
126 Firbrick Main
127 Woodthorpe
128 Birley West
129 Handsworth
130 Hazels
131 Waverley
132 Treeton
133 Manton Main
134 Birley East
135 Sharlston West

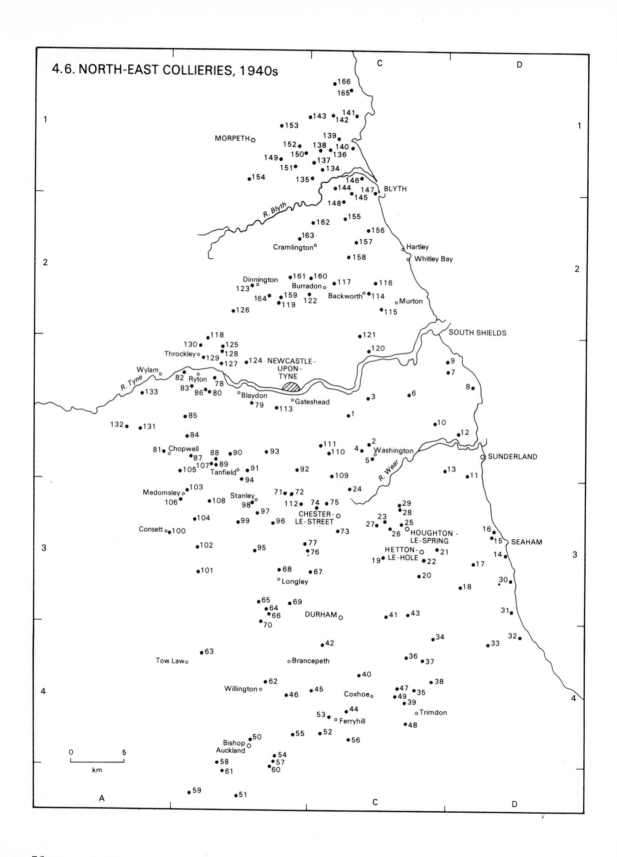

4.6. NORTH-EAST COLLIERIES, 1940s

MORPETH

BLYTH

Hartley
Whitley Bay

SOUTH SHIELDS

R. Blyth

Cramlington

Dinnington
Burradon
Backworth
Murton

Throckley
NEWCASTLE-
UPON-
TYNE

Wylam
R. Tyne
Ryton
Blaydon
Gateshead

SUNDERLAND

Chopwell
Tanfield
R. Wear

Washington

Medomsley
Stanley
CHESTER-
LE-STREET

Consett
HOUGHTON-
LE-SPRING
SEAHAM

HETTON-
LE-HOLE

Longley

DURHAM

Tow Law
Brancepeth

Willington
Coxhoe
Trimdon

Ferryhill

Bishop
Auckland

0   5
km

1 Heworth
2 Usworth
3 Wardley
4 Washington 'F'
5 Washington Glebe
6 Boldon
7 Harton
8 Whitburn
9 Westoe
10 Hylton
11 Ryhope
12 Wearmouth
13 Silksworth
14 Dawdon
15 Seaham
16 Vane Tempest
17 Murton
18 South Hetton
19 Adventure
20 Elemore
21 Eppleton
22 Hetton Lyons
23 Burnmoor
24 Harraton
25 Houghton
26 Lambton
27 Lumley 'Sixth'
28 Dorothea Philadelphia
29 Herrington
30 Easington
31 Horden
32 Blackhall
33 Castle Eden
34 Shotton
35 Deaf Hill, Wingate
36 Thornley
37 Wheatley Hill
38 Wingate Grange
39 Trimdon Grange
40 Bowburn
41 Lady Durham, Sherburn
42 Littleburn
43 Sherburn Hill
44 Thrislington
45 Tudhoe Park
46 Whitworth Park
47 East Hetton
48 Fishburn
49 Kelloe Winning
50 Auckland Park
51 Brusselton
52 Chilton
53 Dean and Chapter
54 Eldon, Shildon
55 Leasingthorne
56 Mainsforth
57 Princes Street 1 & 2, Shildon

58 Ramshaw 1 & 2, West Auckland
59 Randolph & Gordon House, Evenwood
60 South Shildon
61 West Auckland
62 Brancepeth A & C, Willington
63 East Hedley Hope
64 Esh
65 Hamsteels
66 Hill Top Harvey, Esh
67 Kimblesworth
68 Langley Park
69 Ushaw Moor
70 Waterhouses
71 Beamish Mary
72 Beamish Second & Park
73 Chester South Moor
74 Pelton
75 South Pelaw
76 Witton & Shield Row
77 Sacriston
78 Addison
79 Axwell Park, Blaydon
80 Blaydon Burn 'Bessie' & 'Mary'
81 Chopwell 1, 2, & 3
82 Clara Vale, Ryton
83 Emma, Ryton
84 Garesfield 'Bute' & 'Ruler'
85 Greenside
86 Stargate
87 Victoria, Garesfield
88 Bryan's Leap, Burnopfield
89 Burnopfield
90 Byermoor
91 East Tanfield
92 Kibblesworth New (Glamis) & Old (Robert)
93 Marley Hill
94 Tanfield Lea
95 Burnhope
96 Craghead 'Busty' & 'Oswold'
97 Hedley
98 Louisa, Stanley
99 Morrison Busty
100 Crookhall 'Victory'
101 Crookhall 'Humber Hill'
102 Crookhall 'Woodside'
103 Derwent
104 Eden
105 Hamerstley
106 Medomsley
107 South Garesfield
108 South Medomsley
109 Ouston 'E'
110 Ravensworth 'Ann' & 'F'
111 Ravensworth 'G'
112 Urpeth 'C'

113 Watergate, Wickham
114 Backworth, 'Eccles' & 'Maud'
115 Backworth, 'Algernon' & 'Prosperous'
116 Backworth 'Fenwick'
117 Burradon
118 Callerton
119 Hazelrigg
120 Wallsend 'G'
121 Wallsend 'Rising Sun'
122 Weetslade
123 East Walbottle
124 Montagu Main
125 North Walbottle
126 Prestwick
127 Throckley, 'Blucher'
128 Throckley, 'Coronation'
129 Throckley, 'Isabella'
130 Throckley, 'Maria'
131 Hedley Park
132 Mickley
133 West Wylam
134 Bedlington 'A'
135 Bedlington 'D'
136 West Sleekburn
137 Barrington
138 Bomarsund
139 North Seaton
140 Cambois
141 Newbiggin
142 Woodhorn
143 Ashington
144 Horton Grange
145 Isabella
146 Bates
147 Mill
148 New Deleval
149 Barmoor
150 Choppington 'A'
151 Netherton Howard
152 Choppington 'B'
153 Pegswood
154 West Clifton
155 'Gloria'
156 New Hartley
157 Seaton Deleval
158 Seghill
159 Dinnington
160 Dudley
161 Seaton Burn
162 Hartford
163 Nelson
164 Williams
165 Lynemouth
166 Ellington

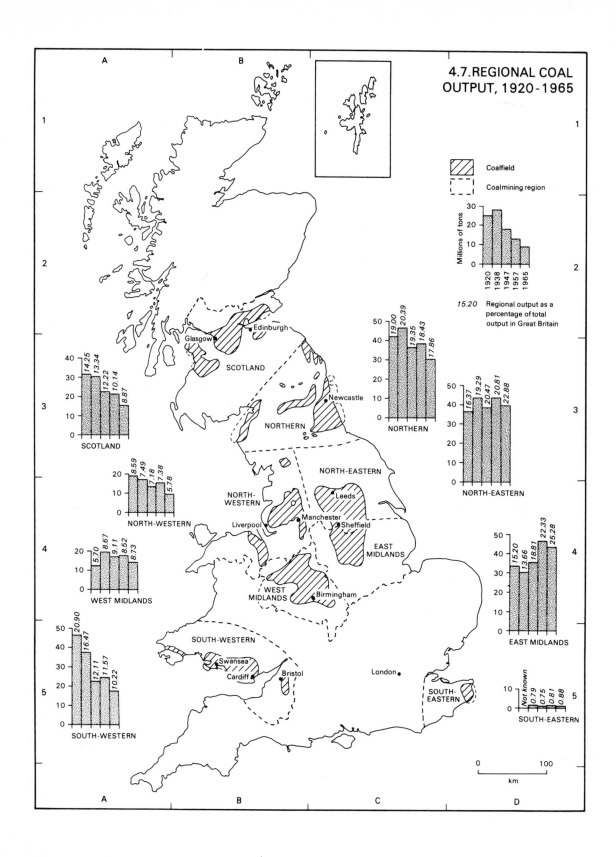

4.7. REGIONAL COAL OUTPUT, 1920-1965

Coalfield

Coalmining region

15.20 Regional output as a percentage of total output in Great Britain

SCOTLAND
14.25 13.34 12.22 10.14 8.87

NORTHERN
19.00 20.39 19.35 18.43 17.86

NORTH-EASTERN
16.37 19.29 20.47 20.81 22.88

NORTH-WESTERN
8.59 7.49 7.18 7.38 5.78

WEST MIDLANDS
5.70 8.67 9.11 8.52 8.73

EAST MIDLANDS
15.20 13.66 18.81 22.33 25.28

SOUTH-WESTERN
20.90 16.47 12.11 11.57 10.22

SOUTH-EASTERN
Not known 0.79 0.75 0.81 0.88

0   100 km

78

stations to reduce its dependence on coal. The 28.2 million tons used in gas production was lost to natural gas, while sales to industry, the railways, and domestic consumers declined by approximately 80, 86, and 70 per cent respectively. As the projected demand failed to materialize, stockpiles of coal mounted. In 1967 the Coal Industry Act attempted to encourage the gas and electricity industries to use coal, but many believed that the age of cheap energy had dawned and the closure of pits proceeded at the rate of one per week. In County Durham alone, 75 pits closed in the 1960s, and by 1974 only 246 pits remained nationally, employing 246,000 men. New areas of production in Nottinghamshire and Kent signalled a further shift in colliery development. By 1965, the Yorkshire and East Midlands coalfields accounted for nearly half total production (see Map 4.7); by the 1970s

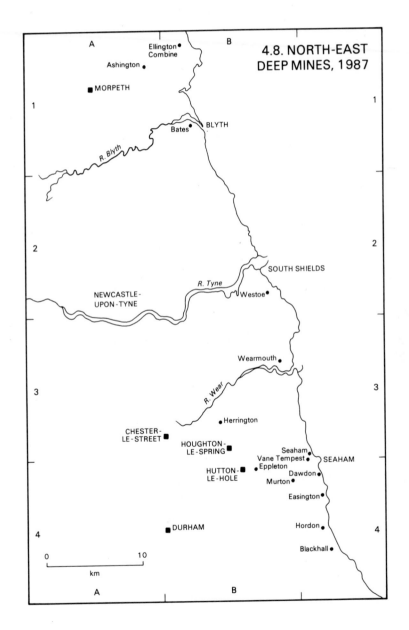

4.8. NORTH-EAST DEEP MINES, 1987

they were responsible for over 60 per cent.

While the falling price of oil had contributed to the recession in the coal industry in the 1960s, in the 1970s the sharp increase in oil prices together with delays in the completion of the nuclear power programme led to a brief recovery in the industry's fortunes. The 1974 Plan For Coal projected an increase of 42 million tons per year by the mid-1980s and new supermines were planned for Leicester-shire and Yorkshire. However, the run-down of the industry in the 1960s led to many former users of coal switching to other forms of energy and the long-term investment necessary for sustained recovery was not forthcoming. The economic recession of the 1980s again proved the planners' targets to have been optimistic and by 1983 the National Coal Board was losing £143 million per year, with only the Yorkshire and East Midlands coalfields

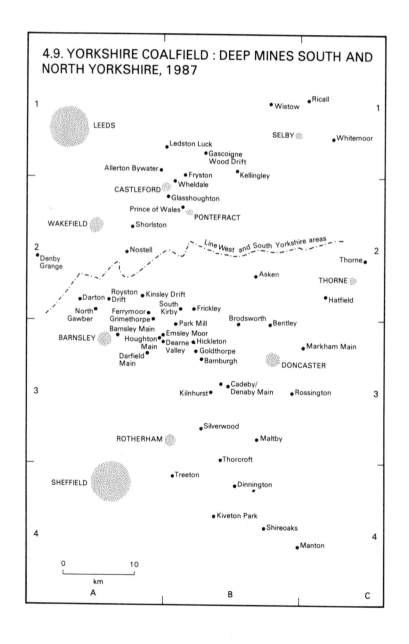

4.9. YORKSHIRE COALFIELD : DEEP MINES SOUTH AND NORTH YORKSHIRE, 1987

producing at a profit. A further phase of rationalization was embarked upon under the chairmanship of Ian MacGregor, provoking a bitter dispute with the miners in 1984–5. By 1986 only 154 deep pits remained, employing 181,000 men. The Scottish, South Wales, and North-east (see Map 4.8) coalfields were particularly badly affected, with only 17 mines remaining in Wales, 13 in the North-east and 10 in Scotland. Only the Yorkshire (see Map 4.9) and East Midlands coalfields emerged relatively unscathed and with their supremacy as coal producers firmly established. In 1986 the National Coal Board was renamed British Coal. By the 1980s coal provided only 35 per cent of the country's energy needs, as compared to 90 per cent as late as the 1940s. Most of the industry's output is now consumed by the electricity industry. As part of a four-fuel economy (gas, electricity (including nuclear power), oil, and coal), coal has thus moved from being the main source of energy to become a supplier of fuel to the other major energy producers.

Gas

Although William Murdock had lit his office at Redruth with coal gas as early as 1792 and Boulton and Watt's Soho works at Birmingham in 1798, it was the German, Frederick Winsor's theatrical lectures on the properties of gas which did much to break down public hostility. London's Corporations, fearful both of the cost of installation and of the possible consequences of what was seen as a highly volatile form of fuel, continued to resist the logic of accepting gas as a means of lighting public buildings and streets until after 1812, when streets were being dug up anyway to lay sewage pipes. This reluctance was not shared by industrialists, who were keen to have their factories lit by gas, and as early as 1806 Whitbread's had a coal-gas plant attached to their brewery in London. It was also in 1812 that the Gas Light and Coke Company, established by Murdock and Winsor two years earlier, received a Royal Charter to supply gas to the London and Westminster area. Other towns were also beginning to recognize the advantages of gas for street lighting and by 1815 major towns as far apart as Preston, Leeds, Bath, Bristol, Liverpool, Glasgow, Cheltenham, Manchester, Exeter, Chester, Macclesfield, and Kidderminster had this provision. By 1829 London could boast six gas companies: the Gas Light and Coke Company, the City, the Imperial, the Ratcliffe, the Phoenix, and the Independent. In 1850, there were twelve.

It has been estimated that by 1830 there were 200 gas undertakings in Britain, all of them private concerns. The industry was hampered before the 1860s by the belief that the number of undertakings operating in any area should be unrestricted. Unfettered competition, it was believed, was healthy for the industry and the consumer. As a result undertakings proliferated to such an extent that even small towns found themselves with companies competing for custom, digging up streets to enlarge or replace mains, with all the attendant inconvenience this caused. Nor did this competition have the effect of maintaining a fair price for gas. No sooner had rivals been undercut to the point of bankruptcy than the victor increased the price to the consumer. Eventually public outcry over the discrepancy between prices charged by the various companies led to clauses being inserted into the companies' charters limiting prices and dividends. In London, public disquiet finally led to a series of amalgamations in the 1870s. This reduced the number of companies competing for business in the City from nine to three in the space of a year, but left the survivors (namely the Gas Light and Coke Company, the Commercial Company, and the South Metropolitan) with a monopoly in the now

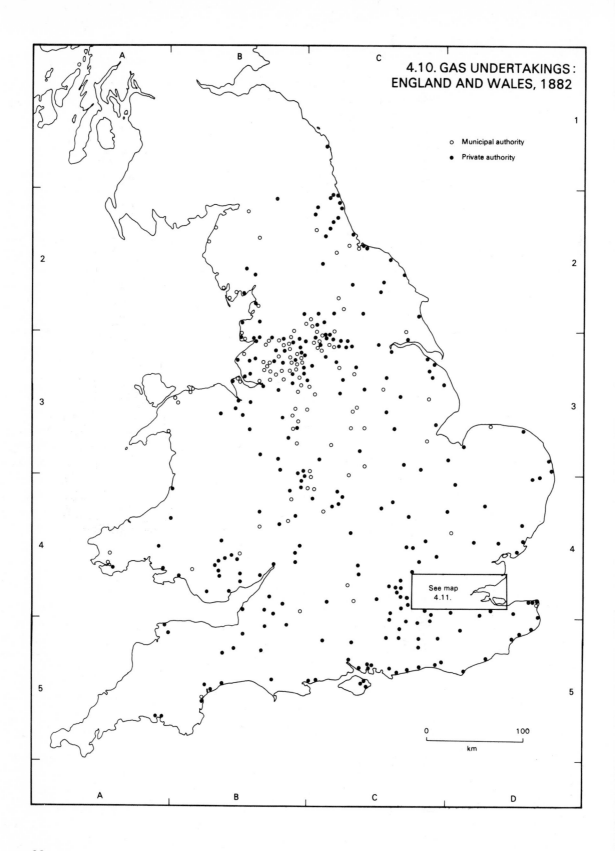

4.10. GAS UNDERTAKINGS :
ENGLAND AND WALES, 1882

○ Municipal authority
● Private authority

See map
4.11.

0   100
km

extensive areas which they controlled.

By 1882 (Map 4.10), the year for which the first reliable statistical evidence for the distribution of gasworks is available, the number had risen to 500,[2] reflecting a capital investment of £50 million. A third of these were municipal undertakings, heavily concentrated in the northern and Midlands industrial towns. This contrasts strongly with the situation in the London area (Map 4.11) and the South, which continued to be dominated by private companies. In both areas the largest gas undertakings were to be found located near major centres of population, while smaller, non-statutory companies proliferated in Wales, Scotland, and more rural areas of England; a situation that remained largely unchanged in the 1940s (see Map 4.12). Although domestic gas appliances had begun to appear by 1870, the bulk of the gas sold was still used for street lighting and in public buildings. The much-needed boost to domestic sales only came in the 1880s with widespread

introduction of the brighter and more effective incandescent gas mantle, and the pre-payment gas meter. As a result of these developments, and of a fall in the price of gas, the industry continued to expand. By 1912 the number of undertakings had reached 826, while the amount of gas sold increased threefold and the number of customers rose from 1,972,000 to 6,876,000. But while few major towns were without a supply of gas, the lack of standardization and co-operation between undertakings remained unresolved.

A major beneficiary of the expanding gas sales was the coal industry. By 1869 approximately 6 per cent of annual coal production was used by the gas industry; by 1903 this had increased to 9 per cent. Industries were developed to utilize gas by-products like ammonia and coal-tar in a wide range of products, including rubberized fabric for mackintoshes, creosote for railway sleepers, and, eventually, synthetic dyes, drugs, and chemicals. By the 1880s, annual sales of coke amounted to

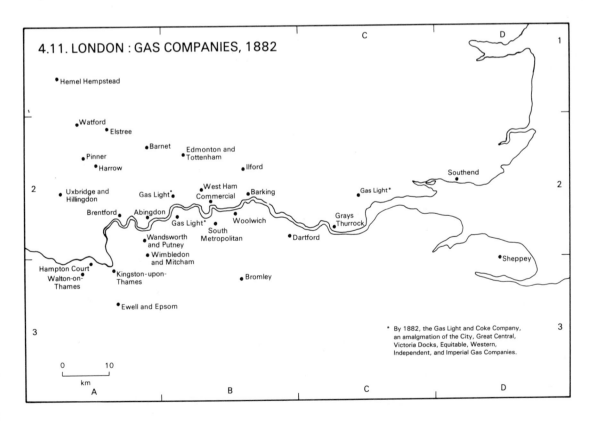

4.11. LONDON : GAS COMPANIES, 1882

* By 1882, the Gas Light and Coke Company, an amalgmation of the City, Great Central, Victoria Docks, Equitable, Western, Independent, and Imperial Gas Companies.

10 million tons. Although the First World War gave a boost to the demand for explosives, dyes, and chemicals it also presented the gas industry with several problems, not least the increased cost of coal and the shortage of labour.

During the inter-war years the gas industry came under increased competition from electricity. Although the number of gas consumers increased by 50 per cent between 1920 and 1938 to over 11 million, electricity was successfully replacing gas as the commonest source of public and domestic lighting, accounting for 44 per cent of street lighting by 1939. In response to this challenge the gas industry mounted a sales drive to persuade people to use gas refrigerators, fires, and water heaters. Amalgamations continued and many small companies disappeared. The Gas Light and Coke Company alone had absorbed a further six smaller concerns and by 1945 it accounted for 12 per cent of national gas production. Gas production was geographically concentrated in major urban conurbations and, by 1944, 65 of the 969 undertakings manufacturing and supplying gas produced 70 per cent of the total sales.[3] However, unlike the electricity industry, which was moving towards integration via the National Grid, the gas industry was far from being in a position to consider linking gas mains between areas or even within areas. One notable exception was the Sheffield Gas Company whose high-pressure grid system connected gas, coking, and industrial plant, resulting in a 30 per cent fall in prices. By the 1930s many companies were using coke and carburetted water-gas to supplement their supplies during peak demand.

During the Second World War the gas industry was particularly vulnerable to air attacks and also to a disruption of its sea-borne coal stocks. By 1945 it was clear that if the industry was to respond to the needs of the post-war world, a massive programme of reorganization would be necessary. Acting on the recommendations of the Heyworth Committee of 1944, and conscious of the extensive regional grids which had already

been established in the Ruhr Valley and in Belgium, the government took the decision to nationalize the industry. The situation pertaining in the British gas industry in the 1940s is reflected in Map 4.12, with the large number of very small non-statutory companies clearly dominating rural areas, the private statutory undertakings most visible in the South-east, in London (Map 4.13) and southern provincial towns, and the municipal concerns centred around the northern and Midlands industrial areas: a picture little changed since 1882.

Under the Gas Industry Act of 1948, on 1 May 1949, 1,050 undertakings were placed under the control of the Gas Council, supported by twelve autonomous regional Area Boards, responsible for manufacturing and supplying gas and for ensuring that the demand was met. In the next decade £500 million was invested in the industry as pipelines were extended, plant updated and the number of undertakings reduced by nearly 60 per cent. But despite the extension of the mains system from 74,000 to 90,000 miles by 1956, gas was being overtaken as a source of power by the now more flexible electricity industry. The gas industry's dependence on coal, the price of which had increased steadily since the war, was reflected in high prices and lost custom, both domestic and industrial. Although drilling for natural gas had been under way since the 1930s, the immediate solution was felt to lie in liquefied natural gas (LNG), frozen to take less storage space. Beginning in 1959, this was imported from America and Algeria in specially converted tankers, using a storage terminal established on Canvey Island. In order to convey this gas to other areas of the country a high-power transmission system (Map 4.14) was constructed; initially only to Leeds but soon with access points for eight of the Area Boards. A massive selling campaign was launched to demonstrate the advantages of gas domestic heating and soon the words 'high speed gas' were familiar to the public.

It was also in 1959 that the important Schlochteren gasfield was discovered in

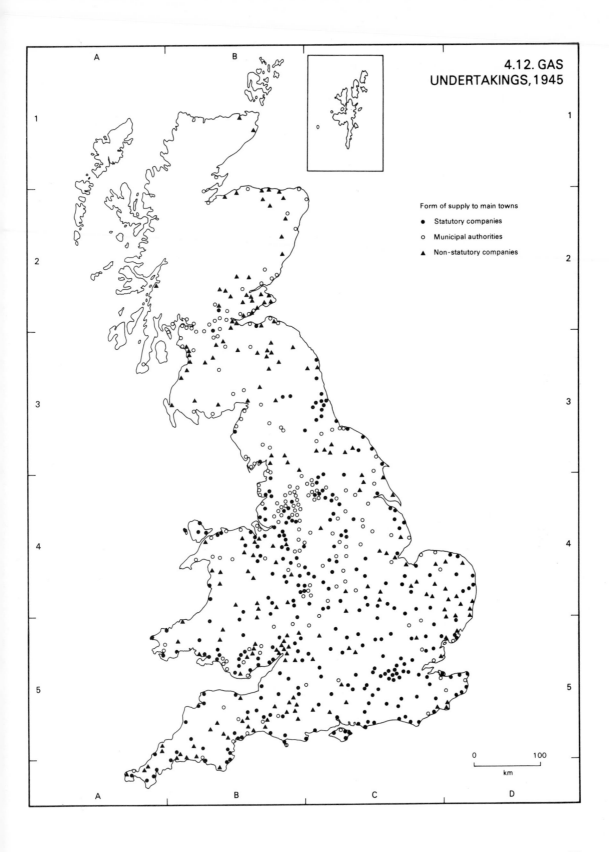

4.12. GAS UNDERTAKINGS, 1945

Form of supply to main towns
● Statutory companies
○ Municipal authorities
▲ Non-statutory companies

0   100
km

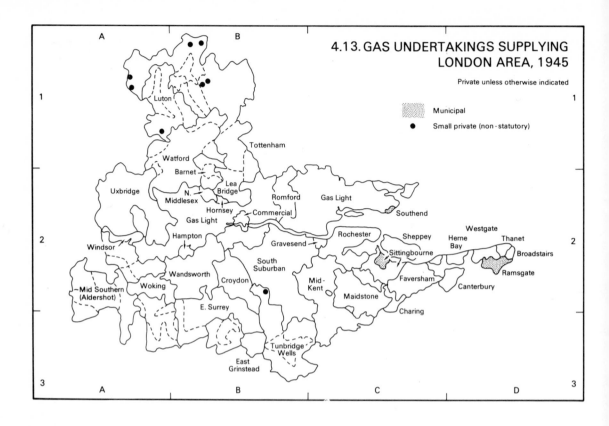

4.13. GAS UNDERTAKINGS SUPPLYING LONDON AREA, 1945

Private unless otherwise indicated

Municipal

● Small private (non-statutory)

Holland, leading to speculation about other untapped reserves under the North Sea. Indeed, these reserves of gas were to result in a complete reversal of the industry's fortunes. The first major British discovery occurred in the West Sole field off the Humber only a year after licences to drill were first issued in 1964. In 1967 natural gas was being piped ashore at Easington, now connected to the high-pressure system, and the Gas Council announced plans to convert all gas users to natural gas, beginning in the East Midlands. Only two years later the pipeline supplied 10 per cent of gas sales and 1.5 million households were receiving natural gas.

When the conversion programme was completed in 1977, at an estimated total cost of £1,000 million, 2,915 miles of high-pressure pipeline had been installed and ten compressor stations built to ensure that the pressure was maintained throughout the system (Map 4.14). Thus by the early 1970s the gas industry supply system was centralized, and to reflect this the British Gas Corporation replaced the Gas Council and the Area Boards. By 1973 the number of gasworks had fallen to only eighty-one and the conversion to natural gas continued to reduce this number still further. Alternative storage facilities were utilized, for example the cavities left by salt workings, and the once-familiar gas holders were demolished. By 1984/5, 16 million homes were connected to the gas mains and the industry met 20 per cent of the country's energy needs. In November 1986 the industry was privatized by the Conservative government and five million people exercised the option to buy shares.

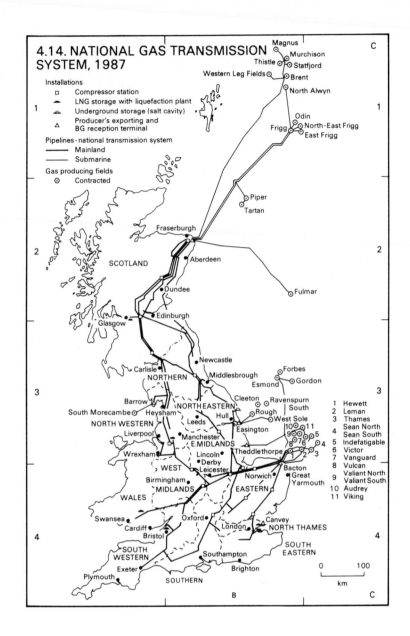

4.14. NATIONAL GAS TRANSMISSION SYSTEM, 1987

Installations
- □ Compressor station
- ▬ LNG storage with liquefaction plant
- ▲ Underground storage (salt cavity)
- △ Producer's exporting and BG reception terminal

Pipelines - national transmission system
— Mainland
— Submarine

Gas producing fields
- ⊙ Contracted

Magnus
Murchison
Thistle
Statfjord
Western Leg Fields
Brent
North Alwyn
Odin
Frigg
North-East Frigg
East Frigg

Piper
Tartan

Fraserburgh
Aberdeen
SCOTLAND
Dundee
Edinburgh
Glasgow

Fulmar

Newcastle
Carlisle
Middlesbrough
NORTHERN
Forbes
Esmond
Gordon

Barrow
South Morecambe
Heysham
NORTH EASTERN
Cleeton
Ravenspurn South
Rough
West Sole
NORTH WESTERN
Leeds
Hull
Liverpool
Manchester
Easington
E. MIDLANDS
Wrexham
Theddlethorpe
Lincoln
Derby
Leicester
WEST
Birmingham
MIDLANDS
Bacton
Norwich
Great Yarmouth
EASTERN
WALES

Swansea
Oxford
Canvey
Cardiff
London
NORTH THAMES
Bristol
SOUTH EASTERN
SOUTH WESTERN
Southampton
Exeter
Brighton
Plymouth
SOUTHERN

1 Hewett
2 Leman
3 Thames
4 Sean North
  Sean South
5 Indefatigable
6 Victor
7 Vanguard
8 Vulcan
9 Valiant North
  Valiant South
10 Audrey
11 Viking

0   100
km

Electricity

The initial impetus to the development of the British electricity supply industry came in the late 1870s when Joseph Swan and Thomas Edison's patented the electric light bulb. Unlike the arc lighting used in lighthouses, London theatres, Blackpool's illuminations, and Sheffield's floodlit football matches, this new glass globe made it possible to harness electricity as a viable form of domestic lighting. Businessmen were quick to realize electricity's potential and despite the relatively speculative nature of the early undertakings many new companies were formed. By 1888, sixty-four private companies and seventeen

87

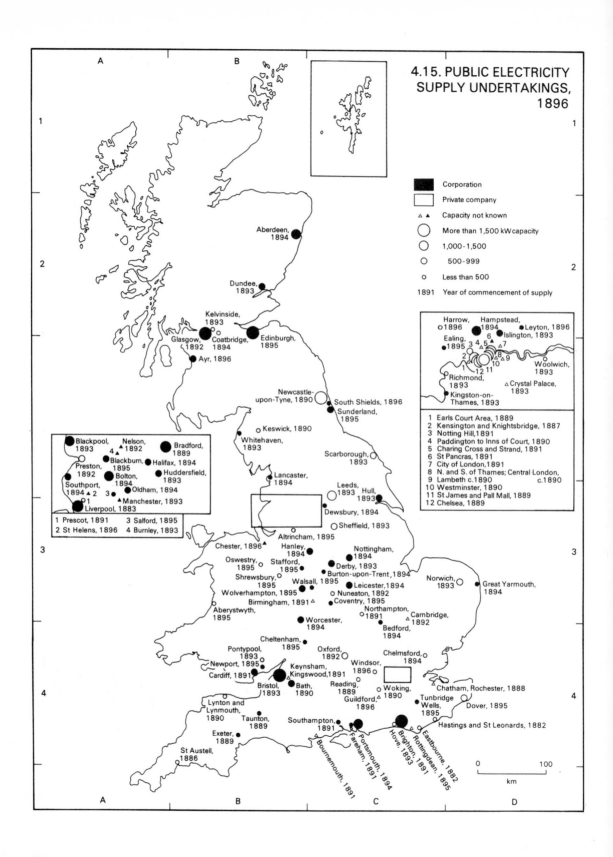

4.15. PUBLIC ELECTRICITY SUPPLY UNDERTAKINGS, 1896

Corporation
Private company
△ ▲ Capacity not known
◯ More than 1,500 kW capacity
◯ 1,000 - 1,500
○ 500 - 999
○ Less than 500
1891 Year of commencement of supply

Aberdeen, 1894

Dundee, 1893

Kelvinside, 1893
Glasgow, 1892 Coatbridge, 1894 Edinburgh, 1895
Ayr, 1896

Newcastle-upon-Tyne, 1890 South Shields, 1896
Sunderland, 1895

Keswick, 1890
Whitehaven, 1893

Scarborough, 1893

Lancaster, 1894

Leeds, 1893 Hull, 1893

Dewsbury, 1894

Sheffield, 1893

Blackpool, 1893 Nelson, 1892 Bradford, 1889
4 ▲
Blackburn, 1895 Halifax, 1894
Preston, 1892
Bolton, 1894 Huddersfield, 1893
Southport, 1894 ▲ 2
Oldham, 1894
○ 1 3 ▲ Manchester, 1893
Liverpool, 1883

1 Prescot, 1891 3 Salford, 1895
2 St Helens, 1896 4 Burnley, 1893

Chester, 1896 Hanley, 1894 Nottingham, 1894
Oswestry, 1895 Stafford, 1895 Derby, 1893
Shrewsbury, 1895 Burton-upon-Trent, 1894
Walsall, 1895 Leicester, 1894 Norwich, 1893 Great Yarmouth, 1894
Wolverhampton, 1895 Nuneaton, 1892
Birmingham, 1891 △ Coventry, 1895
Aberystwyth, 1895 Northampton, 1891 Cambridge, 1892
Worcester, 1894 Bedford, 1894

Cheltenham, 1895
Pontypool, 1893 Oxford, 1892 Chelmsford, 1894
Newport, 1895 Windsor, 1896
Cardiff, 1891 Keynsham, Kingswood, 1891 Reading, 1889 Woking, 1890 △ Chatham, Rochester, 1888
Bristol, 1893 Bath, 1890 Guildford, 1896 Tunbridge Wells, 1895 Dover, 1895
Lynton and Lynmouth, 1890
Taunton, 1889 Southampton, 1891 Hastings and St Leonards, 1882
Exeter, 1889 Portsmouth 1894 Eastbourne, 1882
St Austell, 1886 Bournemouth, 1891 Fareham, 1891 Brighton, 1891 Rottingdean, 1895
Hove, 1893

Harrow, 1896 Hampstead, 1894 Leyton, 1896
Ealing, 1895 6 Islington, 1893
3 4 5 △7
2 8
△ 9
1 10 Woolwich, 1893
12 11
Richmond, 1893 △ Crystal Palace, 1893
Kingston-on-Thames, 1893

1 Earls Court Area, 1889
2 Kensington and Knightsbridge, 1887
3 Notting Hill, 1891
4 Paddington to Inns of Court, 1890
5 Charing Cross and Strand, 1891
6 St Pancras, 1891
7 City of London, 1891
8 N. and S. of Thames; Central London, c.1890
9 Lambeth c.1890
10 Westminster, 1890
11 St James and Pall Mall, 1889
12 Chelsea, 1889

local authorities had been granted franchises by the government to supply electricity. Eight years later (see Map 4.15) most towns had access to electricity supplies. In the northern industrial areas many towns continued to be supplied by large private companies. But in London, while the wealthy residential districts of Kensington, Knightsbridge, Chelsea, and Westminster were supplied by private concerns, the newly developing suburbs of Islington, Hampstead, and Ealing were dominated by local authority undertakings (see Map 4.15). By the early twentieth century (see Map 4.16), electrification was continuing to spread into the suburbs (with municipal concerns often dominating the development), while the existing undertakings had considerably extended their generating capacity: the City of London Company, for example, had increased its station size from 1.5 MW in 1896 to 23 MW by 1907. However, although wealthy men like Lord Armstrong and Lord

Salisbury had had electricity installed in their homes in the 1880s, the general public were more usually served by the cheaper and more reliable gas suppliers. As late as 1919 less than 6 per cent of the homes in Britain were wired for electricity, and it was in the electrification of tramways and railways and in the use of electricity as a means of lighting public streets and buildings that the impact was most noticeable.

Despite the progress which had been made, the electricity industry was hampered by several factors. There was no co-ordination of development, and in London alone there were fifty supply companies, using twenty-four voltages and ten different frequencies. Although there had been some attempts by both municipal and private concerns to produce regionally based, integrated, and standardized supply systems (for example, the Joint Tramways and Electricity Board in Lancashire, and the North-east Electricity

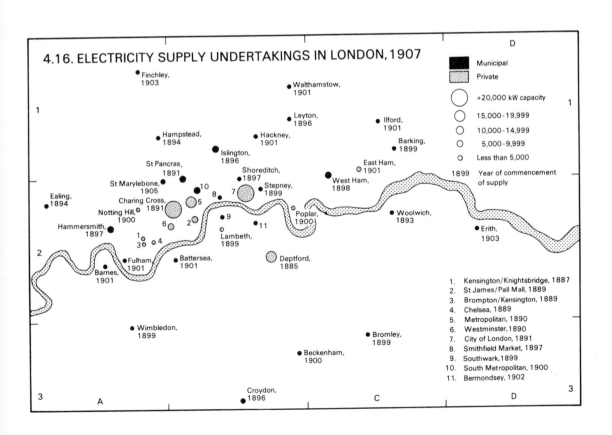

4.16. ELECTRICITY SUPPLY UNDERTAKINGS IN LONDON, 1907

Municipal
Private

+20,000 kW capacity
15,000-19,999
10,000-14,999
5,000-9,999
Less than 5,000

1899 Year of commencement of supply

Finchley, 1903
Walthamstow, 1901
Leyton, 1896
Ilford, 1901
Hampstead, 1894
Hackney, 1901
Barking, 1899
Islington, 1896
St Pancras, 1891
Shoreditch, 1897
East Ham, 1901
St Marylebone, 1905
10
Stepney, 1899
West Ham, 1898
Ealing, 1894
Charing Cross, 1891
8 7
Notting Hill, 1900
5
Poplar, 1900
Woolwich, 1893
Hammersmith, 1897
6 2
9
Erith, 1903
1 3 4
11
Lambeth, 1899
Fulham, 1901
Battersea, 1901
Deptford, 1885
Barnes, 1901

Wimbledon, 1899
Bromley, 1899
Beckenham, 1900

Croydon, 1896

1. Kensington/Knightsbridge, 1887
2. St James/Pall Mall, 1889
3. Brompton/Kensington, 1889
4. Chelsea, 1889
5. Metropolitan, 1890
6. Westminster, 1890
7. City of London, 1891
8. Smithfield Market, 1897
9. Southwark, 1899
10. South Metropolitan, 1900
11. Bermondsey, 1902

Supply Company, private companies continued to be effective in their attempts to preserve their position intact, thus delaying positive state intervention and integration. As late as 1924, seventeen different frequencies were used throughout Britain and while Britain could boast the largest gas industry in Europe, the British electricity industry remained less advanced than those of both America and Germany.

Unlike gas, electricity could not be stored and the power companies had to keep a reserve generating capacity to cover peak periods and breakdowns. Inevitably, despite the introduction in 1900 of off-peak charges to try to encourage users to spread the load themselves, this increased the unit price of electricity to the consumer. The first step towards comprehensive reorganization, directed by the state but with private companies retaining their autonomy, came in 1926, when the Weir Committee's proposals finally passed into statute. Under the chairmanship of Andrew Duncan, the Central Electricity Board was set up to act as a co-ordinating body, promoting the idea of a National Grid of 132 kV (see Map 4.17). 140 selected stations were interlinked at regional level, with control centres at Newcastle-upon-Tyne, Birmingham, Leeds, Manchester, Bristol, London, and Glasgow. This new structure enabled stations connected to the Grid to develop a regional response to shifts in the level of demand for power. In Lancashire, for example, surges in the demand for power were known to occur on Mondays with the family wash, and, less predictably, when Gracie Fields was due to sing on the radio. Because all the stations linked to the Grid worked to exactly the same frequency, stations could also be taken out of the system for maintenance work without disrupting supply. The National Grid was completed in September 1933 and by 1938 the annual saving amounted to £3.25 million, with further savings as larger stations were built. By the 1930s the average size of station was 60 MW, as compared to 0.1 MW in the 1890s and 25–55 MW in the 1920s. Battersea power

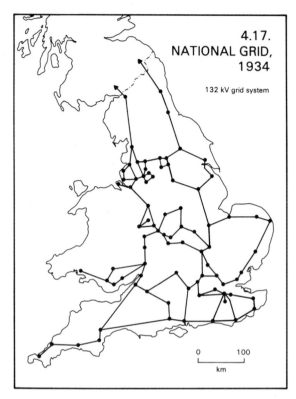

4.17.
NATIONAL GRID,
1934

132 kV grid system

0   100
km

station in London was the biggest in Europe at this time, at 105 MW.

The increased efficiency and the reductions in costs were reflected in the numbers of homes connected to the supply and in the use of mass-produced electrical appliances bought on hire-purchase terms from local electricity board offices. By 1938 two-thirds of the houses in Britain were wired for electricity, although often this merely meant that they had electric lighting. Ironically, demand was increasing most rapidly in areas which lacked sufficient generating capacity (for example, the South-east of England), while the North of England and Scotland had excess generating capacity. The implications of this were graphically demonstrated in 1934 when a series of London stations were disconnected from the Grid and 12,000 square miles of the South-east were left without power for a day. Eventually the regions were linked together into a truly national grid system in October 1937. Power

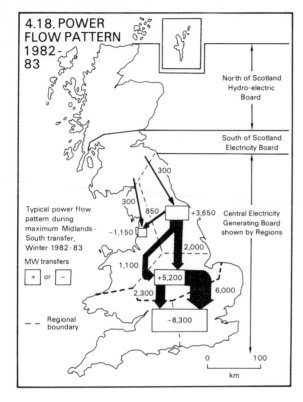

4.18. POWER FLOW PATTERN 1982-83

North of Scotland Hydro-electric Board

South of Scotland Electricity Board

Typical power flow pattern during maximum Midlands - South transfer, Winter 1982-83

MW transfers

$\boxed{+}$ or $\boxed{-}$

Central Electricity Generating Board shown by Regions

300

300   850   +3,650

−1,150

2,000

1,100

+5,200

2,300   6,000

−8,300

− − Regional boundary

0   100
km

get coal themselves, switched over to electric fires for heating. Despite prioritizing industry, introducing power cuts and reducing voltage, the electricity industry could not meet the demand and factories were closed, exports lost and unemployment increased briefly to 15 per cent.

After the electricity industry was nationalized in 1948, the British Electricity Authority[4] became directly responsible both for power stations and for upgrading the system, with a planned investment pro-gramme of £650 million. Although the deficit in capacity had been identified and a pro-gramme of power station building embarked upon, construction bottlenecks, particularly the diversion of essential materials like steel to the housing sector, plus the necessary time-lag between the commissioning, building, and completion of new stations, meant that power cuts continued until 1956. The BEA priori-tized electrification, particularly in rural areas, and the number of domestic consumers rose between 1948 and 1958 from 9.7 million to 14.3 million. Sales of washing machines, refrigerators, and televisions rose accordingly. Industries like chemicals, steel, and pottery were also being won over to public supply, leading by 1958 to a decline of 23 per cent in the number of industries generating their own electricity.

Although major advances had been made in the distribution of electricity with the National Grid – upgraded in the 1950s to the six-times more powerful 275 kV supergrid and again in the 1970s to a 400 kV system (see Map 4.19) – the Central Electricity Authority still faced difficulties associated with attempting to plan on the basis of projected fuel supplies, costs, and levels of demand. By the mid-1950s, as coal prices increased and the National Coal Board suggested that it would be unable to meet the projected demand for coal, planners began to consider other sources of power. Oil-fired power stations were commissioned to take advantage of the fall in the price of oil, but the long-term solution was perceived to lie in the development of nuclear power. The

could then be transferred from areas with more electricity output than they required to areas where the demand outstripped the supply (see Map 4.18).

Despite the changing pattern of demand during the Second World War, as industries moved to more rural locations and the black-out cut public consumption, the electricity industry responded well to the strictures of a wartime economy. After the war the lack of investment in new plant had to be remedied and problems were exacerbated by recurring coal shortages. At the very time that many power stations were left with insufficient supplies of fuel and with inefficient and run-down plant, the public demand for electricity was further boosted by artificially reduced prices and by coal rationing. By 1948 sales to the public had increased by 300 per cent on the pre-war figure. The result of these convergent trends had been obvious in the harsh winter of 1946/7, when many householders, unable to

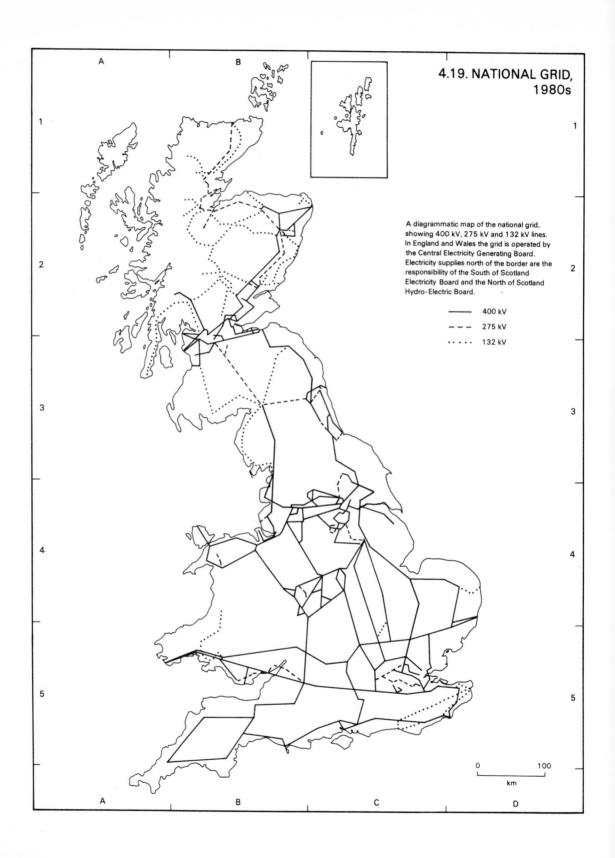

4.19. NATIONAL GRID, 1980s

A diagrammatic map of the national grid, showing 400 kV, 275 kV and 132 kV lines. In England and Wales the grid is operated by the Central Electricity Generating Board. Electricity supplies north of the border are the responsibility of the South of Scotland Electricity Board and the North of Scotland Hydro-Electric Board.

———— 400 kV

– – – 275 kV

· · · · · 132 kV

0   100
km

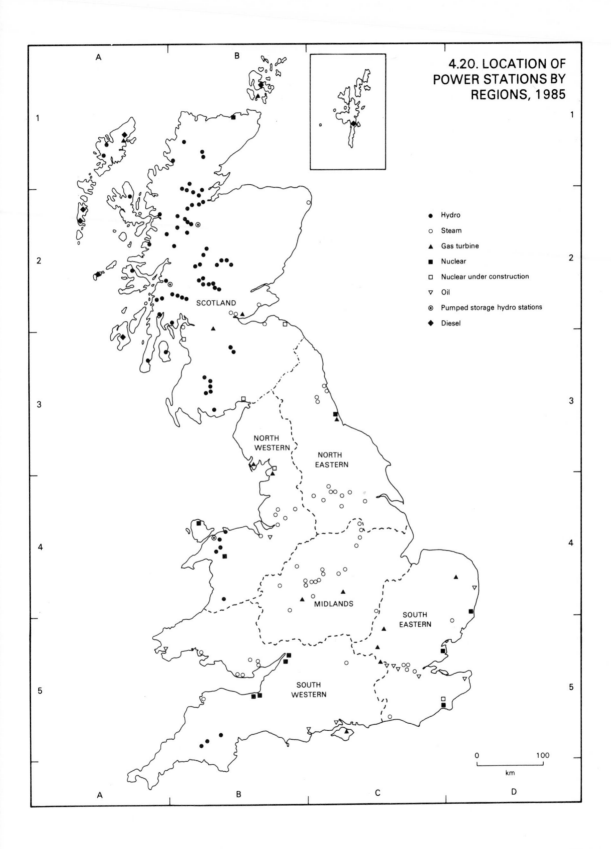

4.20. LOCATION OF POWER STATIONS BY REGIONS, 1985

Hydro
Steam
Gas turbine
Nuclear
Nuclear under construction
Oil
Pumped storage hydro stations
Diesel

SCOTLAND

NORTH WESTERN

NORTH EASTERN

MIDLANDS

SOUTH EASTERN

SOUTH WESTERN

0   100
km

United Kingdom Atomic Energy Authority was created in 1954 and nineteen nuclear power stations were commissioned at a cost per kW three and a half times greater than conventional stations. However, by the time Bradwell in Essex was linked to the Grid in 1962 events had already moved on. The incident at Windscale in 1957, and increased construction costs reflecting concerns about safety and environmental features, served to ensure that the intial investment in nuclear power was far greater than had been anticipated. By 1960 the government had been persuaded to retreat and the stations at Trawsfynydd and Dungeness were postponed.

Stress was laid on expanding oil and coal-fired stations, with large 2,000 MW power stations built on the East Midlands and West Yorkshire coalfields. In the early 1970s, however, industrial disputes in the pits, coupled with the dramatic increase in the price of oil, began to convince both the industry and the government that they had been hasty in curtailing the expansion in nuclear power envisaged in the 1950s. With fuel prices and inflation forcing increased prices of electricity

to the consumer, the industry also found itself being overtaken as a source of power by the reorganized gas industry, with its cheap and plentiful supply of natural gas and its high-power transmission system. By 1985 electricity supplied only 18 per cent of the domestic, 16 per cent of the industrial, and 28 per cent of the commercial demand for power, with less than 5 per cent of the country's energy needs being met by nuclear power. The siting of power stations today (see Map 4.20) reflects the developments outlined above: coal-fired steam-driven power stations can be found grouped in the major coal-producing regions of Yorkshire and the Midlands, oil-powered stations located on the Thames bear witness to the low price of that fuel in the 1950s and 1960s, while in Scotland the industry is dominated by hydro-electric plant. Although the accident at the Chernobyl nuclear station in the USSR in 1986 increased public concern about the safety of this form of generation, a new AGR station has been commissioned for Sizewell, reflecting increased governmental concern about the dependence of the British electricity industry on coal and oil supplies.

Notes

1 By contrast, in Germany a mere twenty undertakings contributed 90 per cent of the nation's coal output by the 1920s.

2 This figure represents statutory undertakings only. *The Gas Industry: Report of the Committee of Inquiry* (Ministry of Fuel and Power), Cmd. 6699 (1945), suggests that the figure in 1882 may have been as high as 800 undertakings.

3 Figures from *The Gas Industry: Report*, Cmd. 6699.

4 The British Electricity Authority took over from the Central Electricity Board in 1948. Six years later, with the creation of the South of Scotland Electricity Board, the BEA became known as the Central Electricity Authority, which was renamed the Central Electricity

Generating Board (CEGB) in 1956. In England and Wales the CEGB sell power to the Area Boards who distribute it to customers.

Map 4.1 is based on statistics from M. Flinn, *The History of the British Coal Industry*, vol. 2, *1700–1830: The Industrial Revolution* (Oxford, 1984). Map 4.2 utilizes material from P. Cromar, 'The coal industry on Tyneside 1771–1800: oligopoly and spatial change', *Economic Geography*, 53 (1977), and R. L. Galloway, *Annals of Coal Mining and the Coal Trade*, vol. 1 (London, 1898). Map 4.3 uses material from R. Church, *The History of the British Coal Industry*, vol. 3, *1830–1913: Victorian Pre-eminence* (London, 1986). Map 4.4 is based on data from C. Jones, 'Industrial relations in the Northumberland and Durham coal industry, 1825–1845', unpublished PhD thesis, CNAA, 1985. Maps 4.5 and 4.6 are based on material contained in *The 'Colliery Guardian' Guide to the Coalfields, 1948* (London 1948). Map 4.7 is based on figures from B. R. Mitchell and P. Deane, *Abstract of British Historical Statistics* (Cambridge, 1962) and B. R. Mitchell and H. G. Jones, *A Second Abstract of British Historical Statistics* (Cambridge, 1971). Maps 4.8 and 4.9 are taken from the *Guide to the Coalfields* (London, 1987). Maps 4.10 and 4.11 are based on data from *Reports Relating to Authorised Gas Undertakings in England and Wales belonging to Local Authorities*, BPP 1882, LXIV, and *Reports Relating to Authorised Gas Undertakings in England and Wales other than Local Authorities*, BPP 1882, LXIV. The material for Maps 4.12 and 4.13 is contained in *The Gas Industry: Report of the Committee of Inquiry*, Cmd. 6699 (London, 1945). Map 4.14 is taken from British Gas, *Energy is Our Business* (London, 1986). Map 4.15 is based on evidence from *Garcke's Manual of Electrical Undertakings and Directory of Officials* (London, 1897). Map 4.16 uses material from the Appendix to J. D. Poulter, *An Early History of Electricity Supply* (Hitchin, 1986). Maps 4.17, 4.18, and 4.19 are reproduced, with the permission of the Central Electricity Generating Board, from R. Cochrane, *Power to the People: The Story of the National Grid* (London, 1985). Map 4.20 is based on material supplied by the Central Electricity Generating Board, the South of Scotland Electricity Board, and the North of Scotland Hydro-Electric Board.

5 TRANSPORT AND TRADE
John Armstrong

Transport

Inland waterways: the 1750s

Great Britain was blessed by nature with an extensive coastline and a framework of navigable rivers, so that the towns developed on these waterways and employed barge or boat as the chief means of transport. This natural endowment was considerably enhanced from the sixteenth century by river improvements – sluices, locks, embankments, cuts to eliminate meanders, dredging, and the construction of wharves and quays. The river system complemented by coastal navigation provided cheap bulk transport for much of the country, for, as Map 5.1 shows, a surprisingly high proportion of the country was within 10 miles of navigable water. Its main drawback was lack of speed – depending on wind or horsepower – and reliability, but these were characteristics common to most pre-industrial forms of transport.

Inland waterways: the 1830s

Canal construction was a logical progression from earlier river improvements but with the civil engineering on a vaster scale. Transport provision on the canal network was similar in kind to riverine: slow, dependent on sail or horse but capable of large loads compared to wagon or cart. The main burst of canal building coincided with the industrial revolution so that by 1830 Britain had an extensive system of internal waterways connecting most industrial

towns. The network was particularly important when heavy cargoes were carried: Cheshire salt, china clay to the Staffordshire potteries, iron, steel, and coal for the metalworking areas of the Black Country and the textile districts of Lancashire. These regions of the Midlands and North-west were well interconnected (see Map 5.2). Construction was both a function of rising economic growth and a contributor to it. However, lack of any central guidance left the system with a variety of widths and lock dimensions and it suffered in parts from summer droughts and winter freezing, reducing reliability. It was, as one recent authority has suggested, 'more suited to an industrialising rather than an industrialised society'.[1]

Coach transport

Although in the period 1760–1830 coaches offered an increasing variety of types of passenger transport, trading celerity against cost, their use was restricted to affluent passengers – businessmen, gentry, and the professions – and small, high-value goods, as prices per mile were high and space restricted. At the top of the range, mail coaches concentrated on reducing their journey times, as shown in Maps 5.3 and 5.4, but this meant higher cost, as horses had to be changed more often and rested longer. Some improvements in road construction, such as graded surfaces leading to greater wear-resistance and faster

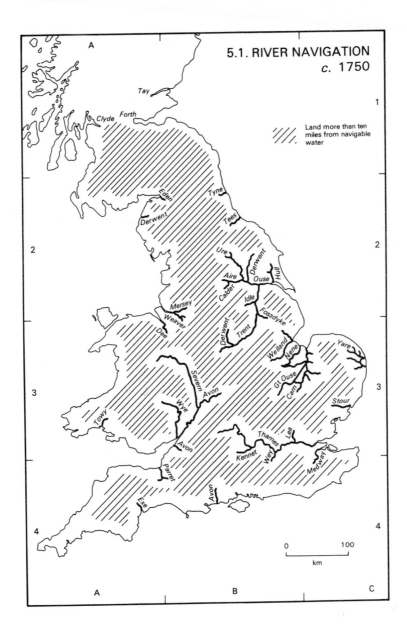

5.1. RIVER NAVIGATION
c. 1750

Land more than ten
miles from navigable
water

drainage as advocated by *inter alia* Macadam and Telford, the turnpike trusts, and better coach design made for more rapid and safer transit. However, the lack of any economies of scale made coaches unsuitable for large-scale goods transport and most important in the carriage of samples and packages, the diffusion of ideas, fashions, and news, and in servicing an upper-crust leisure industry as the wealthy travelled to spas and fashionable resorts such as Bath or Brighton. Coach travel was more important in moving ideas and information than cargo.

Turnpike roads

The first, short-lived section of road on which tolls were collected was part of the Great North

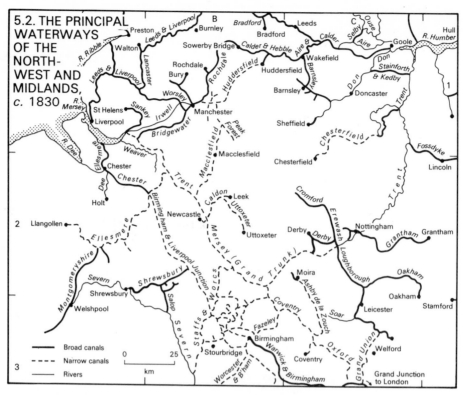

5.2. THE PRINCIPAL WATERWAYS OF THE NORTH-WEST AND MIDLANDS, c. 1830

Broad canals
Narrow canals
Rivers

0   25
km

5.3. COACH JOURNEY TIMES FROM LONDON c. 1750

Edinburgh 12 days winter 10 days summer
Newcastle 5 days
Carlisle 4½ days
York 4 days
Liverpool 3½ days
Manchester 3½ days
Norwich 1½ days
Birmingham 3 days winter 2 days summer
Ipswich 1 day
Oxford 1½ days
LONDON
Bristol 2½ days
Dover 1½ days
Exeter 3 days
Southampton 1½ days
Brighton 1 day

0   100
km

5.4. COACH JOURNEY TIMES FROM LONDON IN THE 1830s

Glasgow 42 hours
Edinburgh 46 hours
Newcastle 36 hours
Carlisle 32 hours
York 20 hours
Liverpool 22 hours
Manchester 18 hours
Norwich 12 hours
Birmingham 15 hours
Ipswich 9 hours
Oxford 6 hours
Bristol 11 hours
LONDON
Salisbury 12 hours
Brighton 4 hours
Dover 8 hours
Exeter 18 hours

0   100
km

Road between Stilton, Huntingdonshire, and Wadesmill, Hertfordshire, open in the period 1663–74. The purpose of turnpikes was to improve the quality of the roads by supplementing statute labour with hired workers, paid for by tolls collected from the road user, so relieving the parish of the financial burden caused by increasing traffic. They were formed mainly as a result of local initiative.

Although there was no national plan, and contrary to the strictures of the Webbs, there was some logic in their development as the roads turnpiked were generally those with the heaviest traffic, especially those into London before 1750, so that before the turnpike 'mania' of 1750–72 routes such as London to Portsmouth, London to Canterbury, and London to Bath were almost completely turnpiked (Map 5.5). By the 1770s nearly 15,000 miles of roads had been gated and tolled,

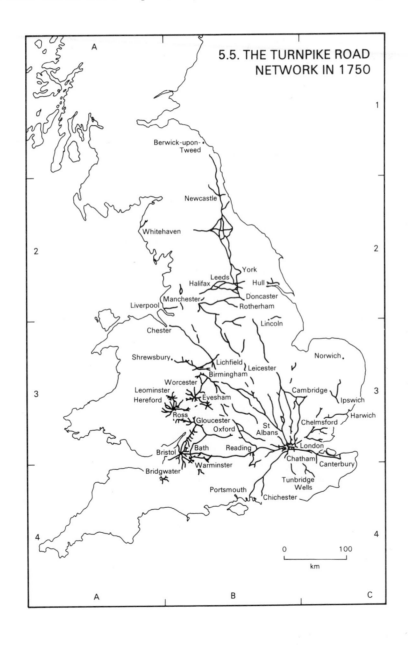

5.5. THE TURNPIKE ROAD NETWORK IN 1750

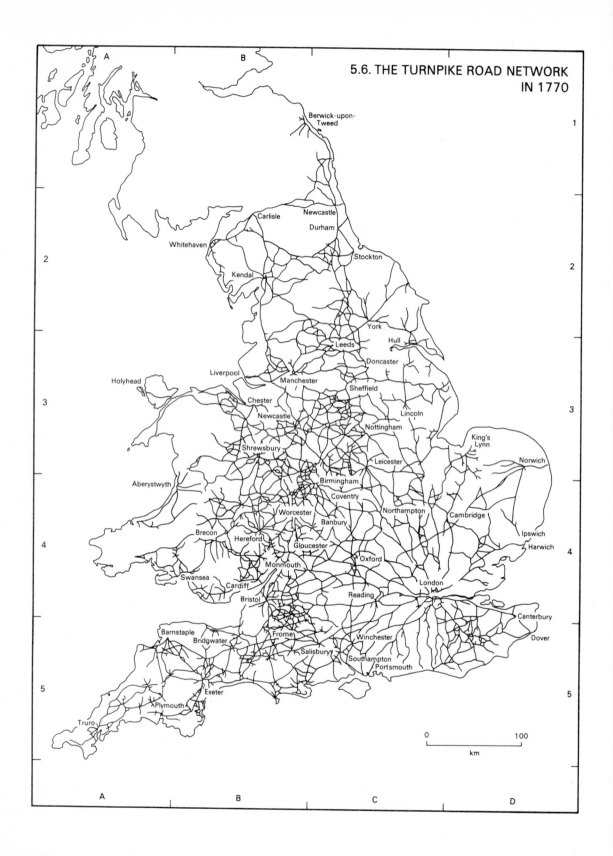

5.6. THE TURNPIKE ROAD NETWORK
IN 1770

Berwick-upon-Tweed

Carlisle
Newcastle
Durham

Whitehaven
Stockton

Kendal

York
Hull
Leeds
Doncaster

Liverpool
Holyhead
Manchester
Sheffield
Chester
Newcastle
Lincoln
Nottingham
King's
Lynn
Shrewsbury
Leicester
Norwich

Aberystwyth
Birmingham
Coventry
Worcester
Northampton
Cambridge
Brecon
Banbury
Ipswich
Hereford
Gloucester
Harwich
Monmouth
Oxford
Swansea
London
Cardiff
Reading
Bristol
Canterbury
Barnstaple
Frome
Dover
Bridgwater
Winchester
Salisbury
Southampton
Portsmouth
Exeter
Plymouth
Truro

0   100
km

100

covering most of the country (Map 5.6). By 1830, this mileage had risen to about 20,000. Finance for the turnpikes came initially from local landed interests who saw indirect benefits via raising the value of land; by the late eighteenth century, *rentiers*, merchants, and manufacturers played a larger though still subordinate role. Despite some maladministration there was an improvement in the road network, through surfacing, drainage, widening, and reduction of gradients, which led to faster, more reliable road transport and possibly some reduction in cost.

Coastal shipping

Coastal shipping (i.e. those ships trading only between UK ports) was ubiquitous from before Tudor times to the First World War, carrying a variety of products in a range of routes. The coaster complemented river traffic, often travelling itself up stream, for the average coastal ship was little bigger than a large barge. The coaster did not require docks or wharves, transshipping direct into river craft or pulling up on a sloping beach and discharging into carts. Not tied to formal ports it was a vital link to villages on creeks and estuaries. When the canals were built the coasters continued to co-operate, providing a method of moving goods cheaply to inland towns. The coaster's carrying capacity was much greater than a cart or wagon and its operating costs were low, using wind power rather than expensive horse power. Thus it carried large cargoes cheaply and, as much of the cost was in loading and discharging, it was particularly suited for long hauls.

Britain was fortunate in having a much-indented coastline and many navigable rivers because industrialization depended on bulky minerals such as coal, iron ore, limestone, salt, and china clay, where cheap water-borne traffic was crucial. Maps 5.7, 5.8, and 5.9 show the changes in the relative importance of ports in the coastal trade. Whitby, Scarborough, and Poole declined, whereas others, such as Cowes with holiday traffic and Southampton

as a liner port, became more important. Some common features persist: the ports receiving most coastal traffic were the major urban centres – London, Liverpool, Bristol, and Glasgow – where population was rising fast and with it the demand for fuel, food, building and industrial raw materials. The ports despatching coastal cargoes were dominated by the coal-producing areas – the North-east, South Wales, the Clyde and Mersey – for coal was the single most important cargo. Grain, sand, stone, and slate were also significant. Before the railway the coaster carried high-value cargoes as well – beer, textiles, cheese, and raisins – but these were the products which the railways captured most easily and by the later nineteenth century the coaster was largely confined to bulk trades: china clay from Cornwall to Runcorn, grain from East Anglia to London, salt from the Mersey to Leith and Newcastle, pig iron and iron rails from Workington and Harrington to Liverpool, and above all coal from the North-east to the Thames and South-east.

Passenger use of coastal ships was widespread in the days of sail, if rather unreliable, depending on the vagaries of wind strength and direction. It boomed with the arrival of the steamer which was faster and more reliable, although dearer. A proliferation of passenger services ensued – on the Thames, Clyde, and other estuaries and across the Irish Channel – virtually every large port was interconnected. The railways by mid-century had made serious inroads into passenger traffic, for the train was more comfortable in rough weather and quicker where the land route was direct, while the sea journey was circuitous, e.g. Bristol to London. The coaster continued to be vital in the traffic to the islands and across channels, and found a new role in the late century providing holiday travel as real wages rose and leisure time grew.

Coastal coal traffic

Coal was the single most important cargo for coastal shipping between 1760 and 1914.

5.7. TOP SIX PORTS IN THE COASTAL TRADE, 1841

Thousand tons of coastal shipping entering or clearing with cargo

500
1,500
3,000

0   100
km

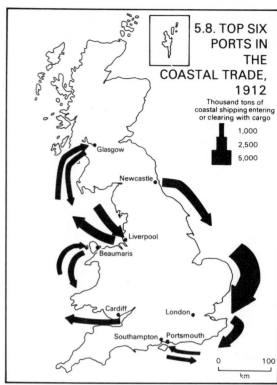

5.8. TOP SIX PORTS IN THE COASTAL TRADE, 1912

Thousand tons of coastal shipping entering or clearing with cargo

1,000
2,500
5,000

0   100
km

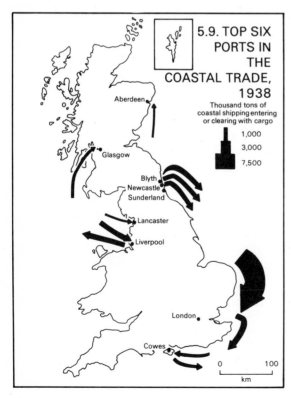

5.9. TOP SIX PORTS IN THE COASTAL TRADE, 1938

Thousand tons of coastal shipping entering or clearing with cargo

1,000
3,000
7,500

0   100
km

Because it was bulky, heavy, and of low intrinsic value, high transport costs priced it out of distant markets. It needed cheap bulk transport by canal barge or coaster. Yet coal was the main fuel of the industrial revolution and demand rose greatly: whereas about 1.6 million tons per annum moved coastwise around Britain in the 1780s, by the 1880s it was over 13 million and by 1913 20 million tons. Coal provided power via the steam-engine, industrial and domestic heat, and lighting through gasworks. As Maps 5.10 and 5.11 show, the main market for coal was the growing urban centres. London dominated this, as most other trades, receiving about half the total coastal coal shipments in the 1780s; this fell to about 36 per cent by the 1820s as industrialization had a greater proportionate effect outside London, but the single largest flow was that from the North-east to the Thames (Map 5.12). Once through rail connections were established the train broke

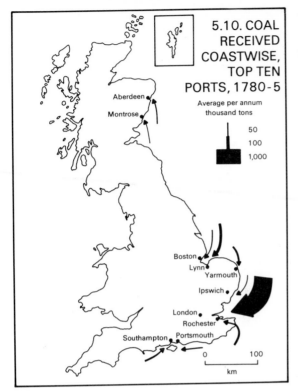

5.10. COAL RECEIVED COASTWISE, TOP TEN PORTS, 1780-5

Average per annum thousand tons

50
100
1,000

Aberdeen
Montrose
Boston
Lynn
Yarmouth
Ipswich
London
Rochester
Southampton Portsmouth

0   100
km

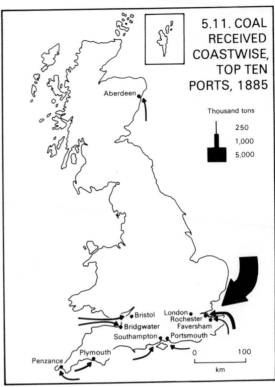

5.11. COAL RECEIVED COASTWISE, TOP TEN PORTS, 1885

Thousand tons

250
1,000
5,000

Aberdeen
Bristol
Bridgwater
London
Rochester
Faversham
Southampton Portsmouth
Penzance Plymouth

0   100
km

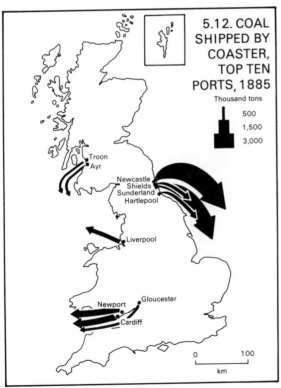

5.12. COAL SHIPPED BY COASTER, TOP TEN PORTS, 1885

Thousand tons

500
1,500
3,000

Troon
Ayr
Newcastle
Shields
Sunderland
Hartlepool
Liverpool
Newport Gloucester
Cardiff

0   100
km

the coaster's monopoly of long-distance bulk traffic, but the introduction of the screw collier, quicker turn-round times through faster loading and discharging using staithes, derricks, and cranes, and all-year-round working, allowed the coaster to regain the lion's share of this trade in the late nineteenth and early twentieth centuries.

Ports

Until the 1880s the number and tonnage of ships entering British ports in the foreign and colonial trades was less than that in the coastal trade. However, overseas trade was more glamorous, bringing higher-value cargoes from exotic ports. The ships were larger and undertook much longer voyages; they paid higher port dues than the coaster, and tariffs were exacted on their cargoes until Britain became 'free trade' in the mid-nineteenth century. There were immense changes in ship technology: ships became larger; the hull, originally built from wood, became composite – iron framed with wood planking – then all iron, and finally steel; the steam-engine captured near trades and, when sufficiently economic in coal consumption thanks to the compound marine engine, dethroned the graceful clipper in the Far Eastern trades; the clumsy paddle wheel gave way to the more manoeuvrable screw propeller; steam hoists, capstans, and derricks speeded loading.

Britain dominated world trade even in the eighteenth century with colonial goods such as sugar, tobacco, and rice being re-exported to Europe. Britain's early industrialization had the twin effects of requiring large imports of industrial raw materials, such as cotton, timber, and ores, and providing a range of cheap, high-quality manufactured exports – cotton yarn and cloth, iron products, later steam-engines, machines, and railway goods.

As the volume of overseas and internal trade grew, so did the tonnage of foreign and coastal shipping entering Britain's ports. This put pressure on the existing port and harbour facilities as early as the eighteenth century and was intensified where individual ports were important in both trades, e.g. London, Liverpool, Newcastle. The pressure was aggravated with the advent of the liner steamship, with its regular sailing dates requiring fast turn-around, and the growth in ship size in the nineteenth century which concentrated overseas trade in those ports which provided the facilities to handle it.

Wharves on a harbour front were no longer adequate and artificial docks had to be constructed enclosing large acreages of water of a guaranteed depth with extensive quay space and adjacent warehouses. Dredging of channels and the construction of piers were also important but insufficient in themselves; the enclosed pool or basin had become essen-

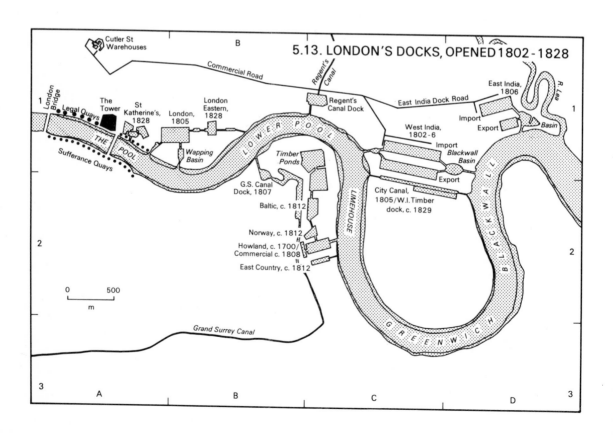

5.13. LONDON'S DOCKS, OPENED 1802-1828

tial by the mid-nineteenth century and rivers such as the Thames and Mersey were lined for miles by these docks (Maps 5.13 and 5.14). These port improvements were often undertaken by local authorities or more commonly by companies seeking to improve trade and earn a return on their investment. These dual aims were incapable of simultaneous maximization and the vested interests so created often hindered further development once their own docks became insufficient to cater for the increased trade. The railways played a large part in port improvements, for example at Southampton and Cardiff, to facilitate their carriage of imports and exports, and became the largest single dock-owner in the UK. To solve the problem of conflicting interests some ports became public trusts with authority over the whole port, e.g. the Merseyside Docks and Harbour Board in 1857, and the Port of London Authority in 1909.

Towards the end of the nineteenth century mechanical methods of loading and discharging assumed importance in order to minimize the time a ship spent on the berth, increasing its earning power and the capacity of the port. Steam and hydraulic cranes, hoists, and conveyors became the key to rapid removal of bulk cargoes.

Railways

British railways, unlike many overseas, were built without government finance, depending entirely on private capital. Like the canals there was no overall plan in their construction and lines were promoted piecemeal as local interests chose, with a mix of gauges which inhibited through traffic. In the promotional manias of the mid-1830s and 1840s the major British towns were linked by rail (Map 5.15). Parliament had an ideal opportunity to exercise control over railway development, as the promoters sought limited liability for their shareholders and power to compel the sale of land through private Acts of Parliament, but the political climate was inimical to government action. Much of the capital came from local merchants and manufacturers keen to improve transport facilities for their raw materials and finished goods and, like canal promotion, over-optimism prevailed in the manias.

The immediate effect of rail transport was to kill long-distance, horse-drawn road transport for both passengers and freight because the train was faster and cheaper. Railways also creamed off some high-value goods, previously carried by the coaster, and much passenger traffic, as by the 1850s the Railway Clearing House had greatly facilitated through traffic over the lines of more than one company. In the third quarter of the nineteenth century much railway construction was devoted to filling out the main skeleton by building branch lines and cross connections. These extended the network mileage, (see Map 5.16) but were often expensive to build and did not generate the anticipated traffic to make them cost-effective. This, with the increased competition offered by the coasters

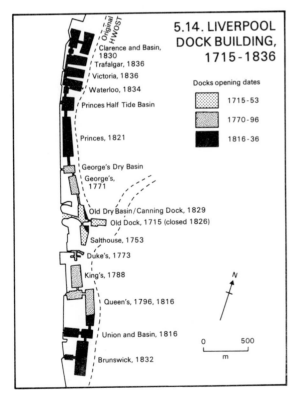

5.14. LIVERPOOL DOCK BUILDING, 1715-1836

Original H'WOST

Clarence and Basin, 1830
Trafalgar, 1836
Victoria, 1836
Waterloo, 1834
Princes Half Tide Basin

Princes, 1821

George's Dry Basin
George's, 1771

Old Dry Basin/Canning Dock, 1829
Old Dock, 1715 (closed 1826)
Salthouse, 1753
Duke's, 1773
King's, 1788
Queen's, 1796, 1816

Union and Basin, 1816

Brunswick, 1832

Docks opening dates

░	1715-53
▒	1770-96
■	1816-36

N

0   500
m

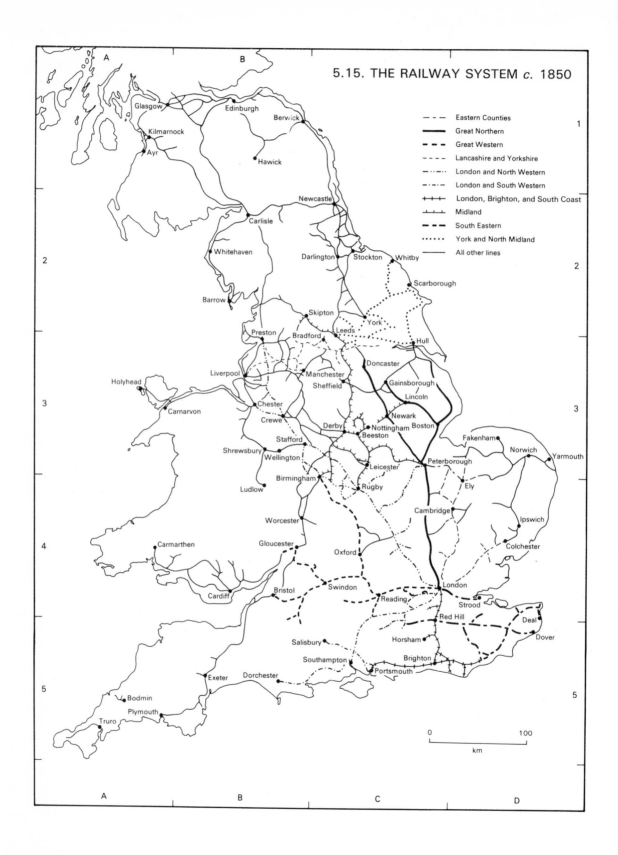

5.15. THE RAILWAY SYSTEM *c.* 1850

– – –	Eastern Counties
——	Great Northern
– – –	Great Western
– – –	Lancashire and Yorkshire
– · – ·	London and North Western
– · · –	London and South Western
+++++	London, Brighton, and South Coast
⊢⊢⊢	Midland
– – –	South Eastern
· · · · ·	York and North Midland
——	All other lines

Glasgow
Edinburgh
Berwick
Kilmarnock
Ayr
Hawick
Newcastle
Carlisle
Whitehaven
Darlington
Stockton
Whitby
Scarborough
Barrow
Skipton
York
Preston
Bradford
Leeds
Hull
Liverpool
Manchester
Doncaster
Holyhead
Sheffield
Gainsborough
Lincoln
Chester
Newark
Carnarvon
Crewe
Derby
Nottingham
Boston
Beeston
Fakenham
Stafford
Norwich
Shrewsbury
Wellington
Leicester
Yarmouth
Birmingham
Rugby
Peterborough
Ely
Ludlow
Worcester
Cambridge
Ipswich
Carmarthen
Gloucester
Oxford
Colchester
Cardiff
Bristol
Swindon
London
Reading
Strood
Deal
Red Hill
Salisbury
Horsham
Dover
Southampton
Brighton
Dorchester
Portsmouth
Exeter
Bodmin
Plymouth
Truro

0   100
km

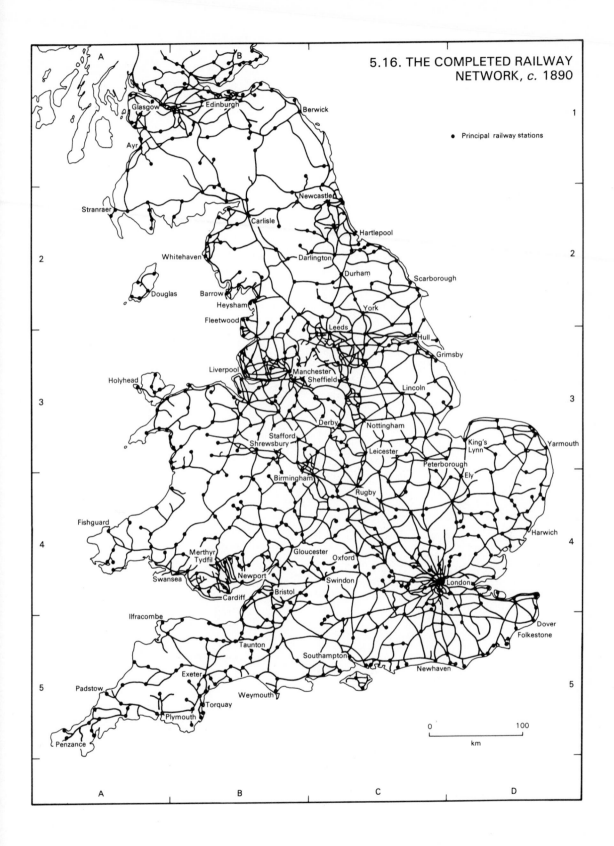

5.16. THE COMPLETED RAILWAY
NETWORK, *c.* 1890

● Principal railway stations

Glasgow
Edinburgh
Berwick
Ayr
Stranraer
Newcastle
Carlisle
Hartlepool
Whitehaven
Darlington
Durham
Scarborough
Douglas
Barrow
York
Heysham
Fleetwood
Leeds
Hull
Liverpool
Grimsby
Holyhead
Manchester
Sheffield
Lincoln
Derby
Nottingham
Stafford
Shrewsbury
Leicester
King's Lynn
Yarmouth
Peterborough
Birmingham
Ely
Rugby
Fishguard
Harwich
Gloucester
Merthyr Tydfil
Oxford
Swansea
Newport
Swindon
London
Cardiff
Bristol
Ilfracombe
Dover
Folkestone
Taunton
Southampton
Newhaven
Padstow
Exeter
Weymouth
Torquay
Plymouth
Penzance

0   100
km

107

which cut their rates on many routes, caused railway profits to stagnate. This in turn boosted the tendency for railway companies to combine or co-operate, apparent earlier, and to acquire control of competing canals.

In the First World War the government ran the railways and this experience led them to believe that excessive competition prevented efficiency. This, and the giant steps toward commercial feasibility made by road transport, encouraged the government to compel a merger of the hundred-plus companies into four regional groupings, as shown in Map 5.17, by the Railways Act of 1921, effective from 1923. However, the railways were not in a strong situation for their staple freights – coal, iron, and textiles – were in decline and road competition began to bite. Technical advances were adopted only slowly: electric traction was used on the London Underground, the North Tyneside suburban lines and some Southern Region routes before

amalgamation. In the inter-war period the Southern Railway carried out a large-scale electrification programme and some lines out of Manchester were converted in the 1930s. Otherwise modernization was slow and diesel locomotives were ignored.

The post Second World War period saw the railways in retreat. Immense growth in motor traffic for both goods and passengers reduced rail ton-mileage and revenue. Some lines, especially those built between 1850 and 1875, had never paid their way and in 1963 a Conservative government, believing road transport cheaper and more flexible, followed the recommendations of the Beeching Report to prune drastically the number of stations, freight wagons, passenger coaches, and route mileage. The result by the 1980s (see Map 5.18) was a much reduced network.

Road construction in the 1930s

Rather like the aeroplane the motor vehicle demonstrated its technical capabilities and military value in the First World War. After the war, cars ceased to be rich men's playthings and became practical transport while short-distance, intra-urban horse and tram traffic was supplemented and ultimately replaced by the motor lorry and bus. Improvements in vehicle design and construction by the 1930s made long-distance journeys economically and technically feasible and as motor vehicle numbers grew – from less than a million in 1920 to over 3 million in 1939 – so did the pressure on the roads. As early as 1909 Lloyd George had established the Road Improvement Fund but until the 1930s most effort was expended on surfacing. In the 1930s some widening of existing roads and the creation of new roads occurred. This was eased by the 1936 Trunk Road Act which transferred 4,500 miles of road from local to national control (see Map 5.19). Despite these measures Britain lagged behind other developed countries in constructing new dual carriageway roads designed for motor vehicles.

5.17.
RAILWAY
GROUPING IN
1921

Great Western

Southern

London and
North Eastern

London, Midland,
and Scottish

0   100
km

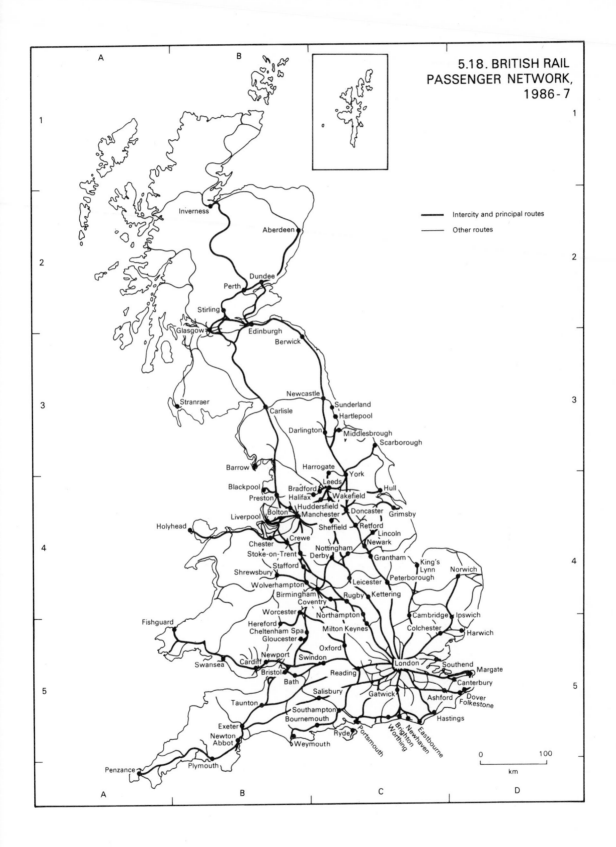

5.18. BRITISH RAIL PASSENGER NETWORK, 1986-7

Intercity and principal routes
Other routes

109

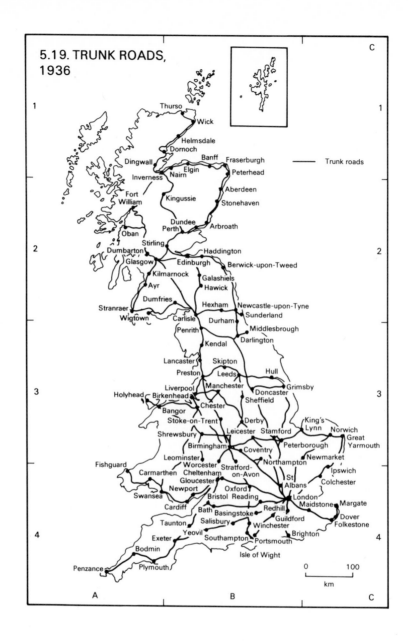

5.19. TRUNK ROADS, 1936

— Trunk roads

Thurso
Wick
Helmsdale
Dornoch
Dingwall
Banff
Fraserburgh
Elgin
Peterhead
Inverness
Nairn
Aberdeen
Fort William
Kingussie
Stonehaven
Oban
Dundee
Arbroath
Perth
Dumbarton
Stirling
Haddington
Glasgow
Edinburgh
Berwick-upon-Tweed
Kilmarnock
Galashiels
Ayr
Hawick
Dumfries
Hexham
Newcastle-upon-Tyne
Stranraer
Sunderland
Wigtown
Carlisle
Durham
Penrith
Middlesbrough
Kendal
Darlington
Lancaster
Skipton
Preston
Leeds
Hull
Liverpool
Manchester
Holyhead
Birkenhead
Doncaster
Grimsby
Bangor
Chester
Sheffield
Stoke-on-Trent
Derby
Shrewsbury
Leicester
Stamford
King's Lynn
Birmingham
Norwich
Coventry
Great Yarmouth
Leominster
Peterborough
Worcester
Northampton
Newmarket
Fishguard
Cheltenham
Stratford-on-Avon
Ipswich
Carmarthen
Gloucester
St Albans
Colchester
Newport
Oxford
Swansea
Bristol
Reading
London
Cardiff
Bath
Basingstoke
Redhill
Maidstone
Margate
Taunton
Salisbury
Guildford
Dover
Winchester
Folkestone
Exeter
Yeovil
Brighton
Bodmin
Southampton
Portsmouth
Penzance
Plymouth
Isle of Wight

0   100
km

Motorway construction 1959–1980s

The earliest British proposals for special roads designed for motor traffic date back to the early years of the twentieth century: Lord Montague proposed them in 1906, the Councillors of Southwark in 1917. However, nothing was done, the schemes being seen as costly, unnecessary given the rail network, and visionary! The example of foreign motor roads – especially the *Autobahnen* in Germany which were visited by a parliamentary delegation in 1937 – caused serious investigation but rearmament and war prevented any action. Pressure from motoring bodies and rising vehicle numbers – there were over 7 ½ million by 1955 – led to government commitment to expenditure on new motorways. In 1958 the

110

8-mile Preston bypass was opened but the first real motorway was the 75-mile London to Birmingham M1 opened in 1959. The system was planned on an initial 'H' shape – M1, M5, and M6 – with restricted access and exit, certain classes of slow traffic banned, and minimal restraints on fast traffic flow. By 1970 over 750 miles had been built and by 1986 nearly 3,000 miles (Map 5.20), when the London orbital motorway, M25, had been completed. Some areas were particularly well served by motorways, for example the North-west, as shown in the inset on Map 5.20. Their effect was to raise average speeds and reduce journey times yet with a lower accident rate than other major roads – though when accidents did occur they could be multiple and horrendous.

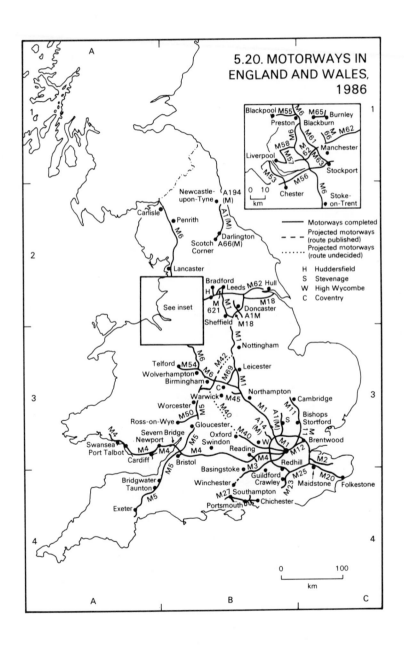

5.20. MOTORWAYS IN ENGLAND AND WALES, 1986

Park Royal: motor transport between the wars

Park Royal developed as an industrial estate between the world wars. The earliest factories were located on the northern edge of the area in the 1900s. They used either the Grand Junction Canal, one firm having its own branch cut right into the factory, or the Euston to Birmingham railway from which sidings were built into the estate. On the southern side of the site the Great Western Railway installed sidings in 1903 for the Royal Agricultural Society to its Paddington to Birmingham line. However, rapid growth of what became the largest industrial estate in southern England really occurred when the road network around it was improved. The A40 Western Avenue was commenced in 1921 at Wood Lane, Shepherds Bush, and by 1943 had reached Denham. The North Circular Road from Chiswick to Southgate was built as a new road in the 1930s. As Map 5.21 shows, these roads

bordered the estate and gave it rapid access to all parts of the large and affluent metropolitan market. Many of the industries established on Park Royal – biscuits, tinned goods, electrical goods, car components, pharmaceuticals, paper, and porter – were aimed at this market. The workforce was catered for by the tube line – North Acton station opened on the Central Line in 1923 – and by the bus network, both motor and trolley. By the end of the 1930s the London Passenger Transport Board was voicing complaints about heavy peak loading at the commencement and completion of work, of buses which were 'definitely uneconomical to run'.

Internal air traffic

The First World War demonstrated the technical feasibility of the aeroplane but commercial success came much later. Many companies were established in the heady post-

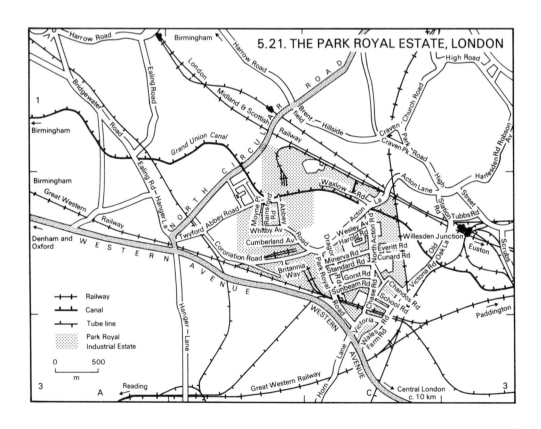

5.21. THE PARK ROYAL ESTATE, LONDON

war days to sink without trace a few years later. Initially the British government left air transport to private initiative but when foreign governments subsidized their airlines Britain followed suit – though parsimoniously. Most of the subsidy between the wars went to overseas routes, via Imperial Airways formed in 1924, which were perceived as important for prestige, strategic, and imperial reasons. A little money went to the internal routes but before the Second World War they were unreliable and expensive, and their speed was little better than a fast train except on journeys over 200 miles or crossing water. They did not capture any significant cargo traffic, no internal mail contracts were awarded until 1934, and their load factors were appallingly low – between 20 and 50 per cent. Virtually no air company made a profit on the domestic routes before 1939, shown in Map 5.22.

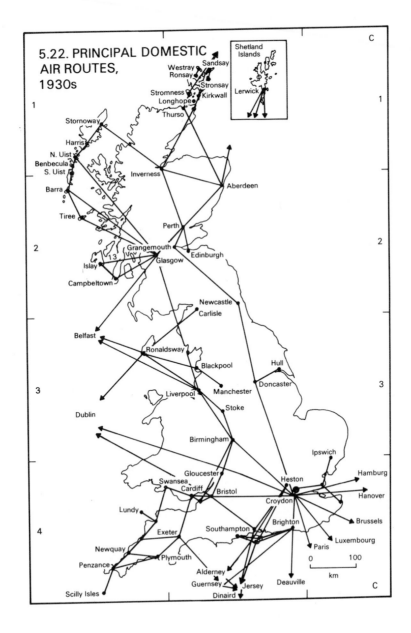

5.22. PRINCIPAL DOMESTIC AIR ROUTES, 1930s

Long-distance air transport became commercially successful after the Second World War when technical changes such as jet engines and radar made for larger-capacity aircraft and greater speed and comfort, and the rising standard of living created a mass leisure industry exploited by tour operators offering package holidays and charter flights. Internal air routes remained the poor relation of this upsurge in air travel. BEA operated over 60 per cent of all domestic air services in the 1960s and although real prices fell and passenger journeys rose from about one million per annum in the late 1950s to over six million in the 1970s, it made no real profit on the routes (Map 5.23). Dissatisfaction with the poor performance led to the 1971 Civil Aviation Act, which established the British Airways Board. The Board recommended a merger of BEA and BOAC with effect from 1973 to increase

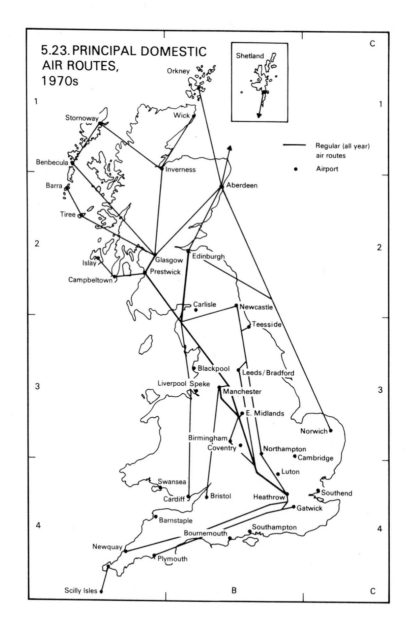

5.23. PRINCIPAL DOMESTIC AIR ROUTES, 1970s

efficiency through operating economies. However, load factors on internal flights remained disappointingly low – about 60 per cent – and air travel faced stiff competition from faster rail journeys, thanks to the 125 diesel train, and from cheap coach fares, after deregulation.

Air traffic: British airports

After the Second World War passenger-carrying aircraft became a commercial proposition as the capacity of successive types of aircraft increased dramatically (from about 40 in a 1950s' DC4 or Comet to over 300 in a 1980s' Boeing 747), their speed rose with the use of the jet engine (from about 250 mph to 600 mph), and radar increased the volume of traffic airports could handle. The growth in real incomes, combined with two or three weeks' holiday becoming the norm, led to a vast

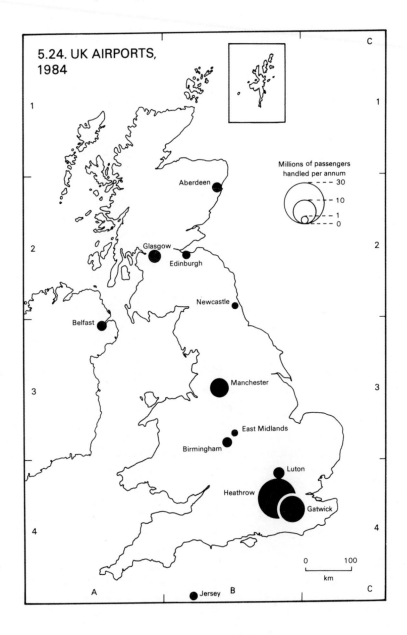

5.24. UK AIRPORTS, 1984

Millions of passengers handled per annum
30
10
1
0

Aberdeen
Glasgow
Edinburgh
Newcastle
Belfast
Manchester
East Midlands
Birmingham
Luton
Heathrow
Gatwick
Jersey

0   100
km

growth in pleasure traffic mobilized by travel firms offering package tours. Consequently, in contrast to inter-war air travel, tourist traffic outweighed business travel and total passengers handled grew dramatically from less than 5 million in the mid-1950s to nearly 65 million in the mid-1980s.

By the 1980s Heathrow Airport had become the 'world's busiest airport' totally dominating UK air traffic, as Map 5.24 shows, with as much traffic as the rest of British airports put together. When the other London airports (Gatwick and Stansted) are added in, they accounted for two-thirds of all UK air traffic, reflecting the attraction of London to foreign tourists and the increasing differential in wealth between the South-east and the rest of the country.

The regional pattern of foreign trade

One significant feature of Britain's trade in the later eighteenth century was the import of tropical products and their re-export to the European mainland. Many of these imports came from Britain's colonial possessions such as India, the British West Indies, and British North America. This trade was encouraged by the Navigation Acts which were intended to promote British shipping and ensure that Britain enjoyed the profits from colonial trade by requiring all goods from the colonies to come to Britain before being re-exported, and all trade to the colonies to be carried in British ships. Hence Britain enjoyed a large entrepôt trade in colonial produce – the 'old' re-exports such as sugar from the West Indies, calicoes from India, and tobacco from America as well as the 'new' re-exports, China tea, Caribbean coffee and American rice. The origins of Britain's imports are shown on Map 5.25. 'South America' imports were largely from the British West Indies; North America provided raw cotton, furs, and some timber; the importance of Asia, still the exclusive preserve of the East India Company, is demonstrated by its 15 per cent contribution to Britain's imports. Britain provided the organization and shipping, taking a profit from each trade as well as earning shipping freights and insurance premiums. By comparison areas later to be of importance as colonial possessions such as Africa and Oceania are of little importance in generating imports to the UK in the eighteenth century, remaining largely unknown and unexplored. Similarly Japan, of crucial significance in twentieth-century trade, was closed to the west before the late nineteenth century by edict of the emperor and a firm belief that the rest of the world was appallingly barbarian. As is true for every period, a large proportion of Britain's imports in the 1770s came from Europe, with the northern countries being much larger-scale providers than the Mediterranean countries, even when (as here) the Levant and Turkish Empire are included in the latter category. This is largely explained by Britain's need of timber and naval stores, such as hemp, flax, tar, and pitch which came from the Baltic, as well as Swedish iron, and, in years when the British harvest was poor, of corn imports.

The geographical pattern of British exports in the eighteenth century shown on Map 5.26 was similar to that of imports, but imports from the tropics exceeded Britain's exports to those areas. Whereas Asia provided 15 per cent of Britain's imports it took only 7 per cent of her exports. Similarly South America, mainly the British West Indies, provided nearly one-third of Britain's imports but it accounted for only one-tenth of her export trade. On the other hand, Europe and North America absorbed a higher proportion of Britain's exports than they contributed to her imports. In the North American case this is largely explained by the high demand for

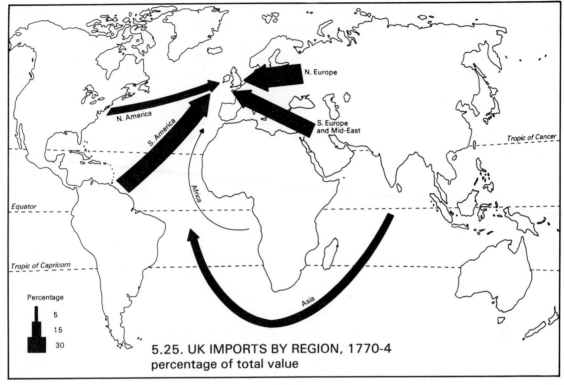

Percentage
5
15
30

5.25. UK IMPORTS BY REGION, 1770-4
percentage of total value

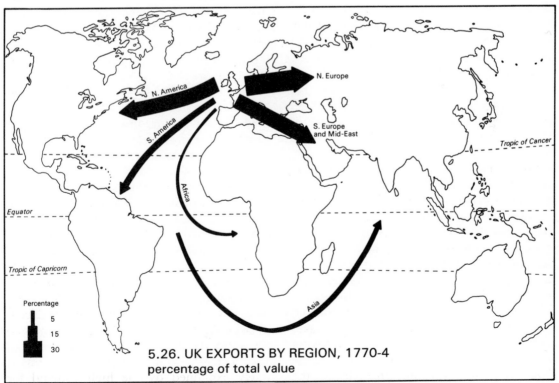

Percentage
5
15
30

5.26. UK EXPORTS BY REGION, 1770-4
percentage of total value

manufactured goods of all kinds to allow the country to be opened up and settlements established – tools, nails, clothing, household goods like pots, pans and bedsteads, axles, stirrups, muskets and ammunition, cloth, axes, and knives. Because Britain endeavoured to suppress manufacture by the colonialists much of these goods had to come from Britain and the primary products which made up their exports did not balance this inflow. The large export trade with Europe was made up partly of the colonial tropical re-exports already mentioned and, of more significance, exports of manufactured goods in which Britain was already excelling – woollen yarn and cloth, manufactures of non-ferrous metals such as brass, copper, and pewter, as well as of iron. The large populations of European countries, their proximity and the relatively high standard of living of some groups, made these obvious markets for Britain's manufactured exports.

By the mid-nineteenth century there were only minor modifications in this geographical pattern of trade, as indicated in Maps 5.27 and 5.28. The relative importance of the imports from the West Indies had declined and with it the South American category. Sugar and tobacco imports did not decline, indeed the former were running at four times their previous value, but rather other imports grew faster. This declining importance of the Caribbean was partly offset by the increased proportion of imports from North America, especially the United States, which had grown significantly in population and area in the intervening century. The imports of raw cotton increased astronomically, nearly fifty-fold – and the great bulk of this was coming from the southern states of the USA. Additionally, that country was now able to export a wide range of other primary products as its vast resources were opened up to commercial exploitation: timber, leather, ores, as well as grains and meat products to feed the rapidly expanding population of the UK which had outgrown the ability of its own farmers to provide even the temperate climate crops. The

other change, though less marked, is the beginning of imports coming from Australia and New Zealand as those countries too were receiving population, capital, and technology from Europe and opening up production of primary products – wool, meat, and minerals.

The changes in the sources of imports were largely mirrored by the changes in the direction of exports. Europe continued to be the single most important area for exports but its domination had diminished, though some of this apparent decline merely reflects the separate recording of statistics for the Middle East. Similarly North America was absorbing a smaller proportion of British exports than it had in the eighteenth century. This is explained by the beginnings of industrialization in these continents which led to home production of some manufactured goods previously bought from Britain, e.g. cotton piece goods and iron products – and in America's case the imposition of tariffs on many manufactured imports from the 1860s, making them too expensive. The other side of this coin was that Britain was sending her manufactured exports to a wider range of countries as they opened up to trade and their demands developed as a result of European colonization and immigration.

By the early twentieth century these trends had been carried further: see Maps 5.29 and 5.30. The UK was importing a yet higher proportion of her requirements from North America and Oceania, while that from Asia fell, and that from South America stagnated. The vast resources of North America and Oceania had still not been fully tapped – the American frontier only closed officially in 1890 – but exploitation was much greater by the early twentieth century. As a result Britain, which increasingly required large quantities of basic foodstuffs and raw materials for her growing population and industries, took a large proportion of America's exports of corn, meat, timber, cotton, and tobacco, and from Oceania, wool, meat, dairy products, and ores. The proportionate decline in Asia's share of British imports was caused by greater

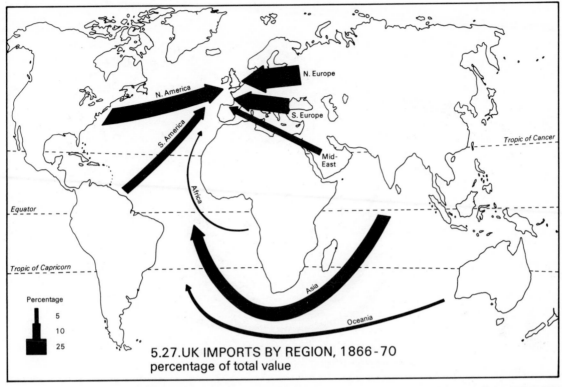

5.27. UK IMPORTS BY REGION, 1866-70
percentage of total value

Percentage
5
10
25

N. Europe
N. America
S. America
S. Europe
Mid-East
Africa
Asia
Oceania

Tropic of Cancer
Equator
Tropic of Capricorn

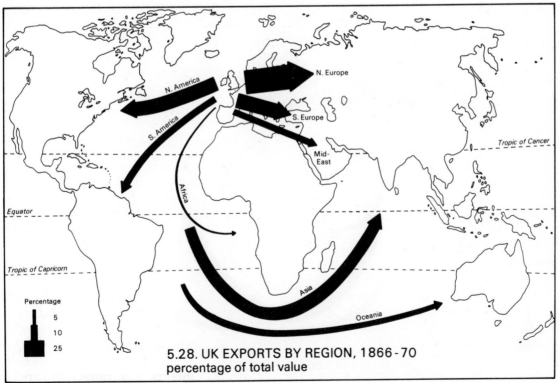

5.28. UK EXPORTS BY REGION, 1866-70
percentage of total value

Percentage
5
10
25

N. Europe
N. America
S. America
S. Europe
Mid-East
Africa
Asia
Oceania

Tropic of Cancer
Equator
Tropic of Capricorn

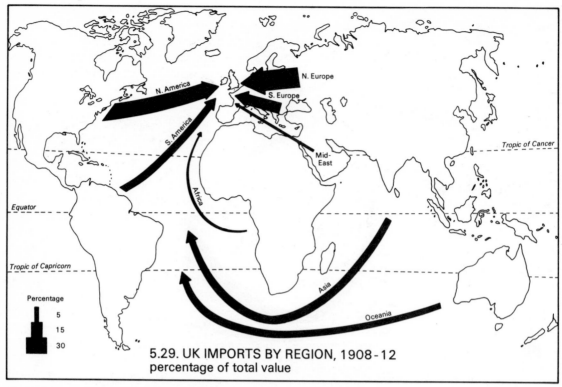

5.29. UK IMPORTS BY REGION, 1908-12
percentage of total value

Percentage
5
15
30

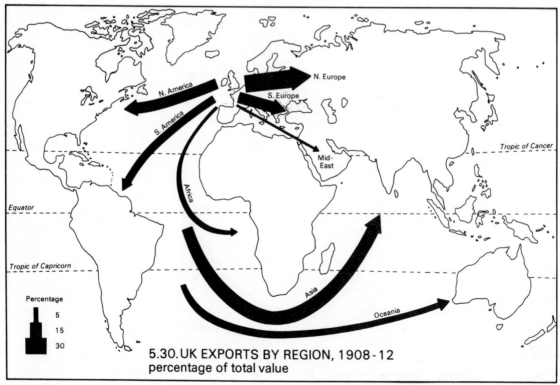

5.30. UK EXPORTS BY REGION, 1908-12
percentage of total value

Percentage
5
15
30

competition in Far Eastern markets as other European powers, North America, and Japan began to take an interest in these potentially vast importers, and by the beginnings of a move, by countries such as India and China, to manufacture the more basic products themselves.

On the export side Europe's share continued to decline as self-sufficiency was developed and home production of manufactures was substituted for imports, and, in some new areas – electrics, synthetic dyes, and motor vehicles – production was initiated earlier or in a more wholehearted manner than in the UK. These trends were aided by increased tariff barriers in Europe from the 1870s, especially on manufactured goods. The countries which increased their share of British exports were those with political links with the UK in Africa, Asia, and Oceania, especially the colonial possessions. As Britain faced stiffer competition in the more developed countries she switched her output of similar products to those areas where development was less advanced or where political ties gave her an advantage.

This shift is even more marked in the 1930s (see Maps 5.31 and 5.32) which saw the high point of Britain's colonial dominance. The high levels of protection in the 1930s are notorious, even the UK eschewing free trade for a general tariff and some countries using quotas, barter, and non-convertibility to limit their imports. In this context the UK directed her trade increasingly to colonial or dominion countries, and this was given political emphasis by the Ottawa conference of 1932. Hence Africa and Oceania's growing share of both imports and exports, the former taking one-eighth of Britain's exports and the latter taking one-tenth and providing over one-eighth of imports. Since protectionism was most rampant in Europe and the United States, the share of Britain's exports to these areas declined further as did her purchases from them.

By the late 1950s Britain's erstwhile European competitors were re-emerging from the destruction and reconstruction of the Second World War. Similarly, in Asia, Japan was coming onto the world scene again as a major economic player. Decolonization, however, had not progressed very far and apart from the Indian sub-continent Britain retained most of her possessions. As a result much of her trade was still orientated towards the Empire (see Maps 5.33 and 5.34), and the rising share of British exports taken by Oceania and Africa is largely explained by this; about 85 per cent of the African imports came from Empire countries, 75 per cent of Asian, about 60 per cent of the Middle Eastern, and virtually all of the Oceanic imports. A similar pattern holds true for exports. The share taken by Europe was at an all-time low, for both exports and imports, because Britain was still so attuned to her Empire; Eastern Europe, the countries making up the Council for Mutual Economic Assistance (CMEA or COMECON), was virtually cut off from trade with the West, and Western Europe was only just emerging from reconstruction. Britain's exports to North America had risen proportionately as a result of the post-war export drive to earn dollars to pay for loans, incurred buying much-needed materials and machinery to restructure British industry from war to peace.

The twenty-five years between the late 1950s and early 1980s saw dramatic changes. The most obvious in Maps 5.35 and 5.36 is the huge increase in the share of trade with the European Economic Community (EEC), rising from about one-seventh to nearly one-half of Britain's trade. Britain entered the community in 1973 when it was enlarged from six to nine members, and barriers to intra-community trade were progressively lowered. Additionally, the post-war world demonstrates that trade grows fastest among developed countries, where real incomes are rising fastest, because the income elasticity of demand for foods is low but is high for manufactured goods, and it is these products which developed economies are best able to produce. The other significant feature is the consistent drop in the shares of the less developed

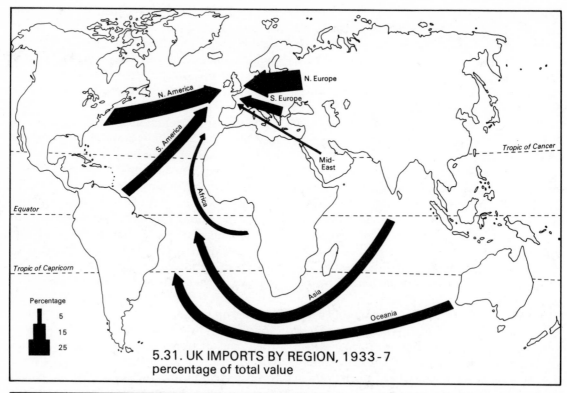

5.31. UK IMPORTS BY REGION, 1933-7
percentage of total value

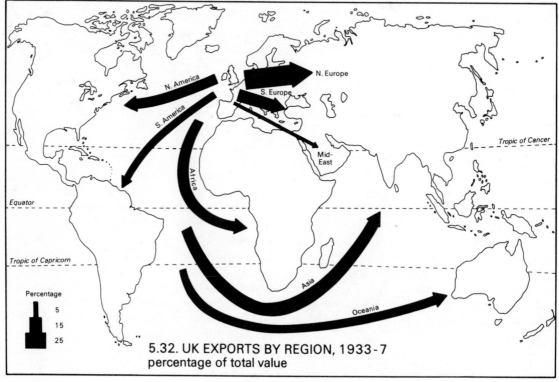

5.32. UK EXPORTS BY REGION, 1933-7
percentage of total value

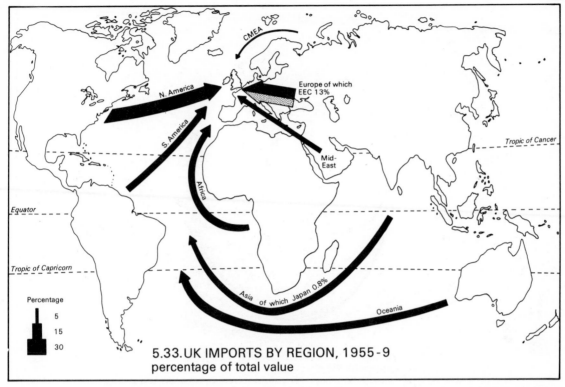

5.33. UK IMPORTS BY REGION, 1955 - 9
percentage of total value

Labels on map: CMEA; N. America; S. America; Africa; Europe of which EEC 13%; Mid-East; Asia of which Japan 0.8%; Oceania

Percentage
5
15
30

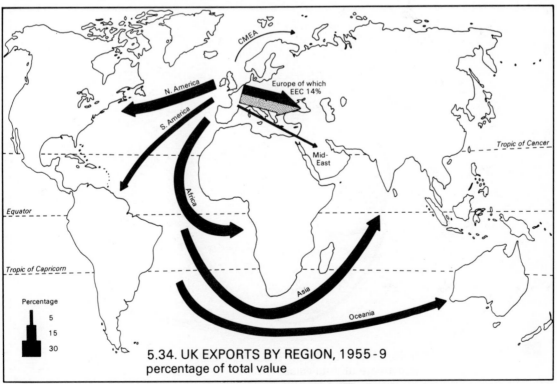

5.34. UK EXPORTS BY REGION, 1955 - 9
percentage of total value

Labels on map: CMEA; N. America; S. America; Africa; Europe of which EEC 14%; Mid-East; Asia; Oceania

Percentage
5
15
30

123

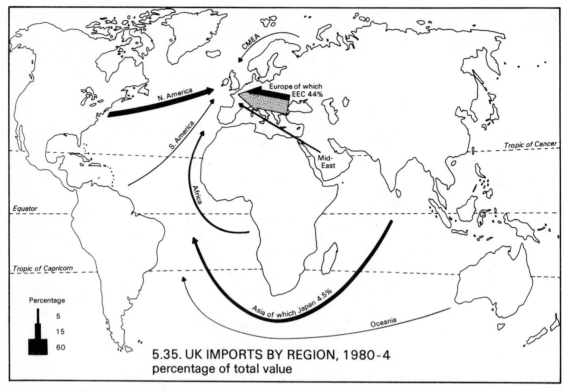

5.35. UK IMPORTS BY REGION, 1980-4
percentage of total value

Percentage
5
15
60

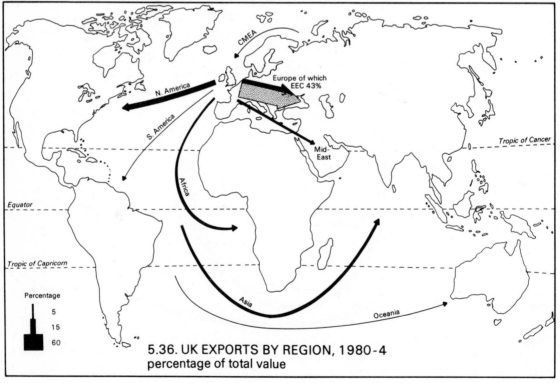

5.36. UK EXPORTS BY REGION, 1980-4
percentage of total value

Percentage
5
15
60

continents, Africa, Asia, South America, and even Oceania. In part of course this is simply a reflection of the dominance of the EEC, but there are specific reasons. By the 1980s Britain's empire was no more and so the formal and informal links which used to translate into physical trade broke down, especially with the efflux of the white minority who enjoyed high standards of living. Additionally these countries made an attempt to be more self-sufficient and to depend less on imports of manufactured goods from traditional sources. The tiny share of South America was affected by the Falklands War of 1983 which stopped trade with Argentina, previously Britain's best market in that continent, but the trend was evident earlier. American firms dominated their 'back yard' and the rising indebtedness of the region made for uncertainty over payment. Within the declining Asian share of British imports in the 1980s the rapid growth of Japanese products is remarkable. A share of less than 1 per cent of British imports in the 1950s had risen to nearly 5 per cent in the 1980s, largely because the Japanese were able to produce the 'high-tech' consumer durables for which demand was rising fastest.

The commodities in British trade

Imports (Figure 5.37)

In the eighteenth and nineteenth centuries the two most important categories of import were raw materials and food, drink, and tobacco. This is obviously the reverse of the situation for exports (see below) and the explanation is similar. As Britain industrialized she required a growing quantity and variety of raw materials to maintain output – ores, timber, raw cotton, hides, and wool. Her own resources were unequal to the task and foreign producers had a comparative advantage in cheaper costs in agricultural production and extractive industries, especially in those parts of the world where European technology, finance, and organization were penetrating, allowing extensive cultivation and extraction at low cost for the first time. Britain's population grew rapidly after 1750 and the demand for foodstuffs rose sharply. For similar reasons as applied to raw materials, from the 1870s an increasing proportion was being imported from newly developing countries in bulk raw state to be processed in the UK. Free trade, resulting in virtually no protection for British agriculture – except during the First World War – meant that the British farmer retreated to niches in which he could compete, leaving many fields fairly free to foreigners.

The Second World War saw a drastic change in government policy towards farming, for strategic reasons. Subsidies were the norm from then on, to encourage a rise in the proportion of home-produced foodstuffs. These subsidies continued into the 1950s and 1960s, and Britain's entry into the EEC with its Common Agricultural Policy increased incentives to produce. This policy combined with a 'green revolution' in agricultural techniques, fertilizers, seed types, and new methods of animal breeding reduced drastically the UK's dependence on imported foods. Additionally the demand for foodstuffs is not income elastic – as incomes rise the proportion spent on food declines – and real incomes rose steadily in Britain between the 1950s and 1980s. The sharp fall in the proportion of raw material imports after the 1950s is largely a function of the decline and shift in Britain's industrial base to lighter industries requiring less bulky material inputs, combined with the desire of the producing countries to part-process their exports in order to get added value. This resulted in a rise in the proportion of semi-manufactures.

Before the twentieth century fuel imports were insignificant because Britain had vast reserves of coal and indeed exported it. The twentieth century saw the advent of

5.37. IMPORTS BY TYPE OF COMMODITY

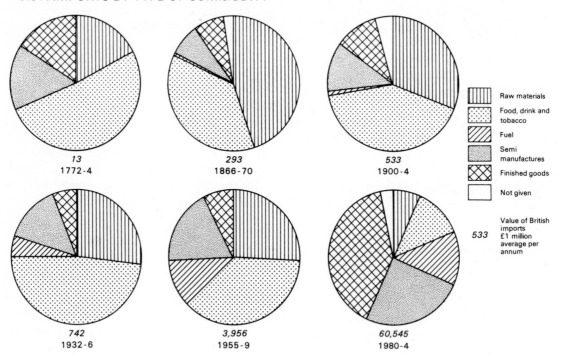

13
1772-4

293
1866-70

533
1900-4

	Raw materials
	Food, drink and tobacco
	Fuel
	Semi manufactures
	Finished goods
	Not given

533 Value of British imports £1 million average per annum

742
1932-6

3,956
1955-9

60,545
1980-4

oil – especially as a fuel for ships and road vehicles and as a chemical feedstock – in which Britain believed herself totally lacking. Hence fuel imports grew as oil became crucial to economic and social life. The discovery of gas and then oil in the North Sea in the 1960s and 1970s changed Britain's position to a net exporter of fuel, although there was still much cross-trading.

Until the very recent past Britain's finished goods imports were a small proportion of total value since Britain produced so much herself and depended on exporting manufactures. However, from the 1870s the UK increasingly imported some manufactured goods especially those embodying new technology, such as dye-stuffs, electrical goods, and motor vehicles before the Great War – as other countries industrialized and took the lead. Between the wars some protection, considered necessary for strategic reasons, saw Britain catch up in these 'new' technologies. The relative desolation of the continental European countries and

Japan compared to Britain gave her an advantage into the 1950s, when they started to catch up and overtake. As UK competitiveness declined in the 1970s the proportion of manufactured goods imports rose sharply and in 1982, for the first time, UK imports of manufactured goods exceeded the value of UK exports of finished goods, and in the following year imports of semi-manufactures exceeded exports so that the UK's balance of payments depended on oil exports and the crucial invisibles to an even greater degree.

Exports (Figure 5.38)

From the late eighteenth century finished goods and semi-manufactures have dominated British exports. The early industrialization of Britain compared to other countries allowed her to produce large quantities of manufactures at low unit cost. Other nations were either unable to produce these products at all or only at much higher cost, and so found it

5.38. EXPORTS BY TYPE OF COMMODITY

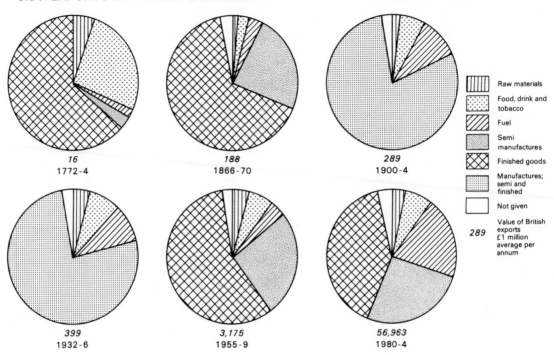

16	188
1772-4	1866-70

289
1900-4

399	3,175
1932-6	1955-9

56,963
1980-4

Legend:

- Raw materials
- Food, drink and tobacco
- Fuel
- Semi manufactures
- Finished goods
- Manufactures; semi and finished
- Not given

289   Value of British exports £1 million average per annum

cheaper to import from Britain. In the late eighteenth century metal and woollen goods were supreme; in the nineteenth, cotton yarn and piece goods took over pole position from wool, and machinery and other manufactures of metal including steam-engines, railway goods, and ships were of crucial significance. Because many of these were capital goods essential to the process of industrialization and modernization, other countries needed to purchase them if they were to catch up with Britain. The UK after the 1830s placed no barriers in the way of exporting this embodied technology, indeed it increasingly espoused free trade, helped to finance the exports by long-term credit, and willingly allowed both permanent and temporary emigration of skilled individuals to help implement the new techniques. The only change in the predominance of manufactured goods has come in the last decade and a half, when their share of

UK export earnings declined as Britain's manufacturing base contracted sharply. This was matched by a rise in the proportion of exports accounted for by fuel. Whereas in the nineteenth century fuel exports were essentially coal (see below, p. 132) with a little culm and patent fuel, in the 1980s this category mainly comprised oil from the North Sea with a little gas. Throughout the whole period Britain was a small-scale exporter of food and drink, mostly manufactured commodities. Until the Second World War, the British Empire played a part, emigrants and expatriates taking with them their taste for Huntley and Palmer biscuits, Guinness stout, or Schweppes soda water. Raw materials were never of great significance as exports, for the UK was a net importer and was comparatively deficient in raw material resources, especially after early intensive exploitation in the industrial revolution.

The main ports in foreign trade

Maps 5.39 to 5.46 give an idea of the growth in value of overseas trade at individual ports. However, because they are in current prices they do not reflect accurately growth in real terms or in volume. Prices fell in the late nineteenth century so the rise in real terms was greater than indicated; conversely price inflation between the 1900s and 1930s, and much more steeply between the 1930s and 1980s, means that the real increase is overstated. In the nineteenth century, because exports were mostly manufactured goods, ports like Liverpool, close to the cotton textile centre of Manchester, Hull and Grimsby near the West Riding woollen and worsted areas, Glasgow, with its shipbuilding, iron and steel, and engineering businesses, and Newcastle and its hinterland of shipbuilders, armaments, engineering, and bulk chemical firms, were crucial export ports. Other towns close to industrial hinterlands and coal pits also feature on Map 5.40: Cardiff and Leith. London had its mass of heterogeneous industries and also acted as a marshalling point for exports. There is little change by the early twentieth century except that Manchester, a totally new creation as a port thanks to the ship canal opened in 1894, appears; although it bit into Liverpool's trade, it did not knock it from top spot. The rapid growth in Southampton's exports was caused by much improved dock facilities attracting the transatlantic liner trade.

Most of the towns which appear on Maps 5.39 and 5.41 as the largest importers also appear on Maps 5.40 and 5.42 among the top ten export locations. For, with their dense populations and heavy industrial base, they were large-scale consumers of raw materials and foodstuffs. Hence London with the largest and most affluent population as well as a wide range of industries heads the imports list in the 1870s, 1900s, and 1930s. Similarly ports like Liverpool, Hull, and Manchester were handling imports for their surrounding populations. Hull, for example, in the 1900s was receiving nearing £10 millions' worth of

grain per annum, much of which it milled into flour for human consumption or feed for animals. It also imported over £3 millions' worth of butter each year. Bristol, too, had a high-value grain trade worth £4 million per annum as well as substantial imports in bacon, butter, cheese, and sugar. Harwich, with its proximity to Holland and Denmark, also had a substantial import trade in bacon and butter. The period from the 1870s had seen a gradual improvement in the diets of the working class, with more money being spent on dairy products, fresh fruit, vegetables, and meat. The increased demand was translated into increased imports, reflected in these maps. Imported industrial inputs are shown in the case of Hull, importing timber and cotton yarn worth respectively £2 million and £3.25 million per annum. Newhaven had a substantial import in silk manufactures, motor cars, and woollen goods, mostly from Europe.

The 1930s saw a reversal of the UK's previous free trade policy. A combination of industrialization abroad, a multitude of tariffs, quotas, and other barriers to foreign trade, and an overvalued pound sterling, at least until 1931, meant that overseas trade stagnated between the wars. This is shown in Map 5.44 where the values of exports at each port show only small increases over those of the 1900s despite the price level more than doubling in the First World War. In real terms there was no rise in most cases; e.g. exports at Liverpool, Glasgow, Hull, and Manchester were all below the rise in retail prices. The nineteenth-century staple industries had made up the bulk of Britain's exports, and the ports serving them were the hardest hit. This is demonstrated by London pushing Liverpool from the top spot. Even if Manchester had not taken some of Liverpool's trade the latter would have been surpassed by London. Southampton was more important as a passenger terminus for the great Atlantic liners run by the White Star, Cunard, and United States lines than for goods

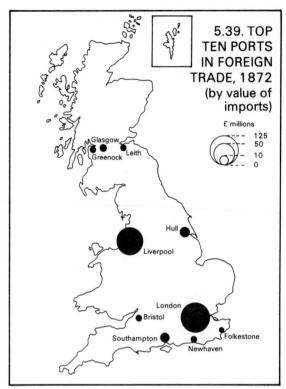

5.39. TOP TEN PORTS IN FOREIGN TRADE, 1872 (by value of imports)

£ millions
— 125
— 50
— 10
— 0

Glasgow
Greenock   Leith
Hull
Liverpool
London
Bristol
Southampton   Folkestone
Newhaven

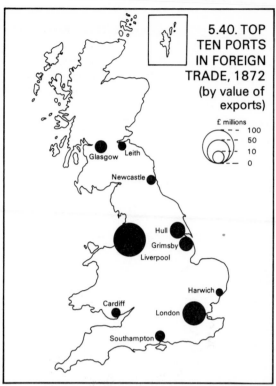

5.40. TOP TEN PORTS IN FOREIGN TRADE, 1872 (by value of exports)

£ millions
— 100
— 50
— 10
— 0

Glasgow   Leith
Newcastle
Hull
Grimsby
Liverpool
Harwich
Cardiff
London
Southampton

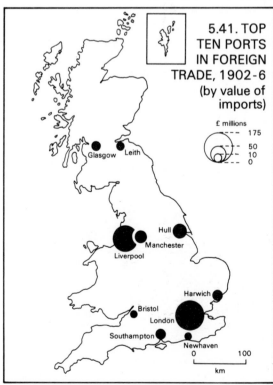

5.41. TOP TEN PORTS IN FOREIGN TRADE, 1902-6 (by value of imports)

£ millions
— 175
— 50
— 10
— 0

Glasgow   Leith
Hull
Manchester
Liverpool
Harwich
Bristol
London
Southampton
Newhaven

0   100

km

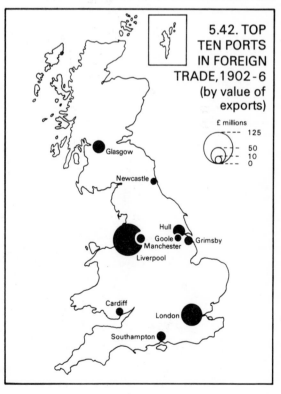

5.42. TOP TEN PORTS IN FOREIGN TRADE, 1902-6 (by value of exports)

£ millions
— 125
— 50
— 10
— 0

Glasgow
Newcastle
Hull
Goole   Grimsby
Manchester
Liverpool
Cardiff
London
Southampton

129

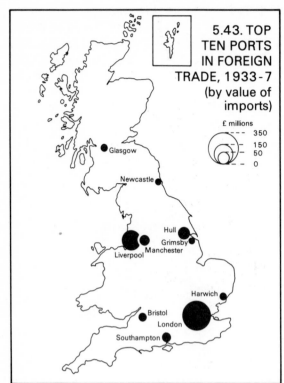

5.43. TOP TEN PORTS IN FOREIGN TRADE, 1933-7 (by value of imports)

£ millions
350
150
50
0

Glasgow
Newcastle
Hull
Grimsby
Manchester
Liverpool
Harwich
Bristol
London
Southampton

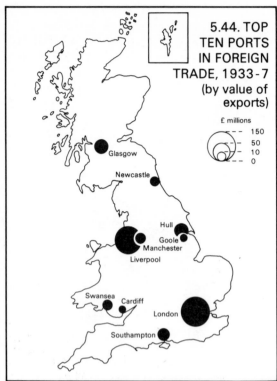

5.44. TOP TEN PORTS IN FOREIGN TRADE, 1933-7 (by value of exports)

£ millions
150
50
10
0

Glasgow
Newcastle
Hull
Goole
Manchester
Liverpool
Swansea
Cardiff
London
Southampton

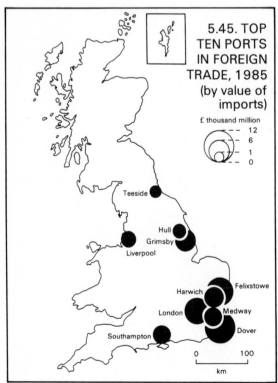

5.45. TOP TEN PORTS IN FOREIGN TRADE, 1985 (by value of imports)

£ thousand million
12
6
1
0

Teeside
Hull
Grimsby
Liverpool
Harwich
Felixstowe
London
Medway
Southampton
Dover

0   100
km

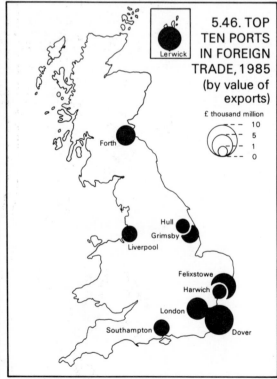

5.46. TOP TEN PORTS IN FOREIGN TRADE, 1985 (by value of exports)

£ thousand million
10
5
1
0

Lerwick
Forth
Hull
Grimsby
Liverpool
Felixstowe
Harwich
London
Dover
Southampton

130

On the import side (Map 5.43), values held up better in the 1930s compared to the 1900s than in the export trade, despite falling primary product prices in the period. The UK was still a large importer of foodstuffs – Harwich was importing bacon and butter; Bristol, as well as grain and tobacco, had a substantial import trade in bananas; Grimsby received more bacon and butter than the more olfactorily obvious fish. There was surprisingly little change between the top import ports of the 1900s and those of the 1930s (Maps 5.41 and 5.43). Of Cardiff's total exports worth over £8 million in 1933-7, more than £7 million was coal and a substantial part of the remainder was manufactured fuel. Swansea's total exports of £14 million included £3.5 million of coal, £7.5 million of iron and steel manufactures, and £1.25 million of nickel. Goole had a wide spread of exports including coal and raw wool, but much higher values of manufactured goods including woollen manufactures, cotton yarn and cloth, and machinery.

The greatest changes in the 'league tables' took place between the 1930s and 1980s for this period saw a revolution in the methods and direction of foreign trade. The increase in the proportion of British trade going to the continent of Europe (see Maps 5.45 and 5.46) meant northern ports were at a disadvantage and southern ports benefited. Hence ports like Dover, Felixstowe, and Harwich appear in the top ten. Their prime position is explained also by the changes in methods of overseas trade. There was a huge increase in the proportion of roll-on-roll-off trade in which cargoes were moved by lorries driving directly onto ferries, thus saving the high costs of loading and unloading. This method was particularly suitable for high-value, low-bulk commodities such as finished goods which were a much higher proportion of UK imports, and for traffic to nearby continental countries with a short sea journey and a long road trip. Dover, Felixstowe, and Harwich dealt with a great deal of 'ro-ro' traffic. The Shetland Isles are represented by Lerwick's presence on Map 5.46 and this is explained by Britain's new role as an oil exporter. Sullom Voe in the Shetlands was the main port for oil tankers to load North Sea oil products. The declining significance of some previously important ports such as London, Liverpool, and Glasgow was caused by their unsuitability for overseas trade in the 1980s. The docks were too far up river to allow access to the much larger ships now in use and their labour-intensive methods of working were superseded by container ports close to deep water with high capital investment in bulk handling equipment for blowing powders and pumping liquids. Some 'old' ports had their own down-river terminals – Tilbury for London, Avonmouth for Bristol, Immingham for the Humber – all of which had commenced operations much earlier but only came into their own as ship sizes increased after the Second World War. Other ports built huge new docks to handle the traffic: Seaforth Dock at Liverpool and Queen Elizabeth II at Hull. Yet other cities had to admit defeat as ports; for example down-river Greenock took over from Glasgow. The net result was a drastic decline in the number of dock workers and the virtual abandonment of the up-river dock areas in cities like Bristol, London, Liverpool, and Glasgow, and plans for their redevelopment for residential and leisure purposes.

Coal exports

Coal exports were of growing importance to the UK in the nineteenth century. By 1870, over 11.5 million tons of coal were sold abroad, accounting for about 5 per cent of total exports by value. By 1910 this had risen to 62 million tons and about 10 per cent of all exports. A further 20 million tons were being shipped out as bunkers for foreign-going steamships, bringing invisible earnings for the UK through freight income. Much coal was going to rapidly industrializing, coal-deficient European countries such as France and Italy, for it was essential to mechanization. Even Russia, which had huge deposits already discovered, found it cheaper to import sea-borne coal from Britain to its western ports than bring it long distances by land or canal.

As can be seen from Maps 5.47 and 5.48, two areas of Britain particularly benefited from this trade: South Wales and the North-east. In 1870 the former accounted for about 30 per cent of all coal exports and the latter for nearly 50 per cent, whereas by 1910 the Welsh ports had risen to 40 per cent and the North-east coast had declined to 30 per cent. Between them they cornered the lion's share – about three-quarters of coal exports. The Welsh share rose because the coal from this region was particularly suitable for steam raising. This export trade helped make the UK the largest producer of coal in the world throughout the nineteenth century, only being surpassed by the USA before the First World War. Because coal-mining was still very labour-intensive huge employment opportunities were created, there being over one million miners in the early twentieth century who were amongst the best-organized groups in the labour force. The export of coal provided outward freights for the large sailing

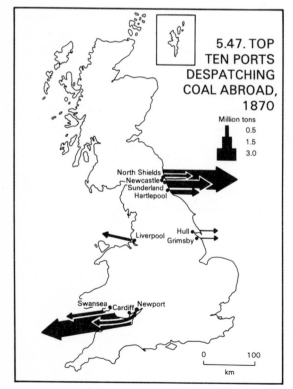

5.47. TOP TEN PORTS DESPATCHING COAL ABROAD, 1870

Million tons
0.5
1.5
3.0

North Shields
Newcastle
Sunderland
Hartlepool

Liverpool
Hull
Grimsby

Swansea Cardiff Newport

0   100
km

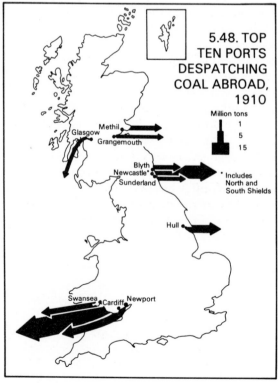

5.48. TOP TEN PORTS DESPATCHING COAL ABROAD, 1910

Million tons
1
5
15

Methil
Glasgow
Grangemouth

Blyth
Newcastle*
Sunderland

* Includes North and South Shields

Hull

Swansea Cardiff Newport

ship, increasingly ousted from higher-value trades by the more rapid and reliable steamship. Coal was bulky and non-perishable so that speed of delivery was less important than cost, and the sailing ship could compete. In this way it provided an outward cargo to balance the sailing ship's continuance in bulk imports such as corn, timber, or nitrate.

Notes

1 B. F. Duckham, 'Canals and river navigations', in D. H. Aldcroft and M. J. Freeman (eds), *Transport in the Industrial Revolution* (Manchester, 1983), p. 125.

Map 5.1 is based on maps in H. J. Dyos and D. H. Aldcroft, *British Transport: An Economic Survey from the Seventeenth Century to the Twentieth* (Leicester, 1969) and D. H. Aldcroft and M. J. Freeman, *Transport in the Industrial Revolution* (Manchester, 1983). Maps 5.2, 5.15, and 5.16 are also derived from material originally presented in *British Transport*. Map 5.22 is reproduced, with permission of the author and the publishers, Leicester University Press, from the same work. Map 5.17 is based on maps in *British Transport* and in P. S. Bagwell, *The Transport Revolution from 1770* (London, 1974). Maps in Bagwell's work also provide the inspiration for Maps 5.3, 5.4 and 5.19. Maps 5.5 and 5.6 are reproduced with kind permission of the author and publishers from E. Pawson, *Transport and Economy: the Turnpike Roads of Eighteenth-century Britain* (London, 1977); Maps 5.13 and 5.14 from Aldcroft and Freeman's *Transport in the Industrial Revolution* with the consent of Manchester University Press. Map 5.9 is based on data from the *Annual Statement of the Navigation and Shipping of the UK* (London, 1940), pp. 20-1. Maps 5.7–5.8 and 5.10–5.12 are based on material in British Parliamentary Papers (BPP) as follows: Map 5.7, BPP 1843, LII, pp. 382-3; Map 5.8, BPP 1913, LXI, pp. 764–85; Map 5.10, BPP 1786, X, pp. 139–40; Maps 5.11 and 5.12, BPP 1886, LX, pp. 203–7. Map 5.18 is based on the British Railways Board's *British Rail Passenger Network, 1986-7*. Map 5.23 is based on, *inter alia*, a map in N.J. Graves and J.T. White's *Geography of the British Isles* (London, 1971); Maps 5.20 and 5.21 on material from road atlases and gazetteers. Map 5.24 is from *The Times*, 26 August 1985. Maps 5.25–5.32 are based on statistics from B. R. Mitchell and P. Deane, *Abstract of British Historical Statistics* (Cambridge, 1962). Maps 5.33 and 5.34 use figures from the *Annual Statement of the Trade of the United Kingdom* (London, 1956–60) and Maps 5.35 and 5.36 use figures from the *Monthly Digest of Statistics*, no. 480 (London, December 1985). Sources for Figures 5.37 and 5.38 are as follows: for 1770-4, R. Davis, 'English foreign trade 1700–1774', in W. E. Minchinton (ed.), *The Growth of English Overseas Trade* (London, 1969); for 1866–70, BPP 1871, LXIII, Pt 2, *Annual Statement of the Trade of the United Kingdom*, Abstract tables 12 and 17; for 1900-4, BPP 1905, LXXIX, *Annual Statement of the Trade of the United Kingdom*, vol. 1, table 6, and *The British Economy, Key Statistics 1900–1970* (London, 1970); for 1932-6, *Annual Statement of the Trade of the United Kingdom, 1936* (London, 1937) and *Key Statistics*; for 1955-9, *Annual Digest of Statistics* (London, 1956–60) and *Key Statistics*; for 1980-4, *Monthly Digest of Statistics*, no. 480. Maps 5.39 and 5.40 use data from BPP 1873, LXIII, pp. 16 and 28; Maps 5.41 and 5.42 data from BPP 1907, LXXXIII, *Annual Statement of the Trade of the United Kingdom for 1906*, vol. 2, table 4; Maps 5.43 and 5.44 are based on figures from the *Annual Statement of the Trade of the United Kingdom, 1937* (London, 1938), vol. 1, table 15; Maps 5.45 and 5.46 use figures from British Ports Association, *Port Statistics 1985* (London, 1986), p. 121. The sources for Maps 5.47 and 5.48 are, respectively, BPP 1871, LXII, p. 10, and BPP 1911, LXXXVI, pp. 407–39.

6 DEMOGRAPHIC CHANGES 1701–1981
Stephen Jackson and Geoff Timmins

It would be difficult to overstate the dramatic impact of population growth in Britain between the early eighteenth and late twentieth centuries. During the early modern period the pattern of change had been varied, with a gradual long-term increase. Less than a million people were added to the population between 1600 and 1700. By the end of the eighteenth century however, there were a further three and a half million and by 1981 the population was more than five times the size it had been in 1801. Also during this period there was a marked transition from the pre-industrial regime of relatively high rates of fertility and mortality, to the modern stable pattern of population growth, characterized by low birth and death rates.

Birth rates and death rates

Figure 6.1 provides some explanation for the causes and timing of this unprecedented growth. A steady and progressive decline in mortality from the mid-eighteenth century to the mid-twentieth century was accompanied by relatively high levels of fertility until the late nineteenth century. From the 1880s onwards there was a sharp downturn in the birth rate, which, over the relatively short space of sixty years, declined to a level close to that of the death rate, resulting in some flattening-out of the population growth curve. In the past, interpretations of this process of demographic transition placed emphasis on the role played by mortality, particularly in the earlier stages of rapid growth. It was suggested that improvements in general health related to higher standards of living, better nutrition, advances in medical knowledge and control over infectious diseases, wore away at the death rate, while fertility remained at pre-modern levels.

More recent research, however, has cast doubt on these views. Seen in the longer term, the changes in mortality in the late eighteenth and early nineteenth centuries were not exceptional, marking a return to more normal levels after the high mortality of the preceding century. What was remarkable was the apparent upturn in fertility between the 1750s and the 1820s. This was the real driving force behind population growth, resulting both from a decline in the average age at marriage and also from an increase of the proportion of people marrying in each generation. Both factors were closely related to economic changes associated with industrialization, particularly the widening opportunity for employment and the abandonment of more traditional constraints on marriage.

The period of rapid expansion in the birth rate was followed by a return to more stable conditions. This arose from the increasing social and economic pressures placed on the

6.1. POPULATION GROWTH : ENGLAND AND WALES, 1701-1981

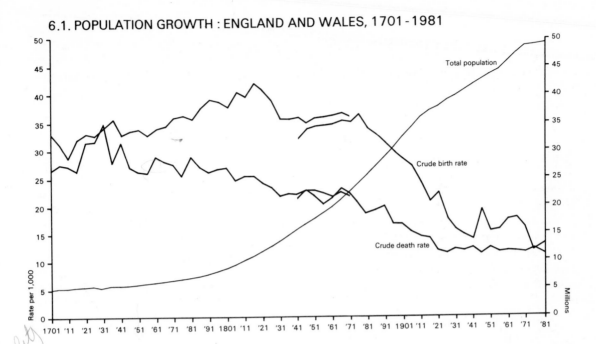

family by the changed circumstances of the Victorian period. Improvements in child survival and changing patterns of work resulted in children becoming an increasing burden on the family budget. These influences, together with a desire for better standards of accommodation and general welfare, led to the association of family size with the quality of life, encouraging many to restrict fertility within marriage to ensure a more secure future for themselves and their children.

During the 1930s birth and death rates came very close together, raising fears at the time that Britain might experience population decline. But in the years after the Second World War there was a marked upturn in fertility. The so-called 'baby boom' of the late 1940s and early 1950s may partly have reflected the delayed marriages and restrictions of the war years, but it was also associated with economic revival and rising real incomes. This situation was repeated in the 1960s with a second peak in fertility. Such cyclical patterns now appear to be the norm for mature societies where relatively minor ups and downs in fertility are governed by the varying sizes of

generational groups and by the influence of economic and social conditions on family formation. Although these fluctuations have only a limited impact on overall population size they do cause considerable problems for governments in forecasting future demands for education, employment, welfare provision, and health care.

Such a generalized picture, however, tends to mask deep-seated diversities within the national population that are associated with social class and differences in the conditions of life. It was the new middle class that led the way, in the late nineteenth century, towards the small family norm, and by the 1920s such families were recording an average of less than two children. On the other hand the decline in both fertility and mortality was retarded for lower-status groups. Unskilled labourers still had an average of more than three children per family in the 1920s and, in the 1930s, the infant mortality rate among children of lower-status groups remained at more than twice the level for children of professional groups.

These patterns have persisted through until the present day. There is still an apparent

135

association between mortality and social class which may in part reflect different life-styles and occupational characteristics. Fertility remains higher for lower social groups with the differences being most marked for younger women. Professional and middle-class groups, as a rule, still marry later and have smaller families, a trend which in recent years has reflected the increasing career opportunities for women and the consequent postponement of family formation until later in marriage.

Population structure

Although the most notable feature of the demographic revolution was the sheer increase in numbers it is also important to remember that it was accompanied by other changes in the structure and distribution of the country's population. For example, average expectation of life from birth improved, as a consequence of declining levels of child and adult mortality (from approximately 37 years in 1701 to 71 years for men and 77 years for women in 1981). Such figures suggest that in the twentieth century, not only were there more people in total, but they were living longer and healthier lives. Changes in the chances of survival

6.2. AGE–SEX STRUCTURE: ENGLAND AND WALES, 1821–1981

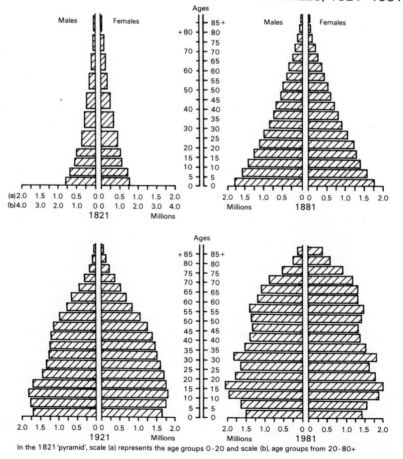

In the 1821 'pyramid', scale (a) represents the age groups 0–20 and scale (b), age groups from 20–80+

are graphically represented by the changing age/sex structure of the population of England and Wales (Figure 6.2). In 1821, the sharply pointed age/sex pyramid indicates the continuing high levels of child and infant mortality in the early stage of transition. By 1881, however, the structure was very similar to that of many of the present developing countries, with a broad base and narrow peak. The late Victorian period was a time when proportionately there were very many more children than today: 36.5 per cent of the population was under the age of 15, compared to only 4.6 per cent over the age of 65 (for 1981 the respective figures are 20.1 per cent and 14.7 per cent). The diagram for 1921 shows some of the effects of the First World War in the relative loss of males in the age-groups 20–40 but also, in general, indicates the slowing down of population growth rates with a broader middle-age spread and a narrower base. Today's population structure is fairly typical for a developed society. It reveals the almost stable condition of population change and the relative shift in emphasis away from the younger age-groups to the middle-aged and elderly categories. Individual groups (10–20 years and 30–35 years) show clearly the effects of the peaks in fertility since the Second World War, but overall it is quite apparent that in the future the post-60-year-old group is going to be of increasing significance within the population as a whole.

Population distribution

There were changes, also, in the geographical distribution of the population with an increasing concentration of numbers in the developing industrial regions (North-west, West Yorkshire, North-east, West Midlands, Central Scotland and South Wales) and the Metropolitan South-east (Maps 6.3–6.6). Much of the increase in numbers and regional variations in distribution can be directly associated with the massive growth of urban areas. In 1801 only approximately 30 per cent of the population were urban dwellers, but by 1981 the figure was in excess of 80 per cent. Certainly, throughout most of the nineteenth century, patterns of internal migration had been dominated by the relentless movement from countryside to town and from the remoter regions of the country to the rapidly expanding urban/industrial core (Maps 6.3 and 6.4).

In the twentieth century this pattern of movement was generally reversed. The depopulation of rural areas had peaked during the later Victorian period and, after the First World War, the suburban expansion of towns and cities created a new form of urban/rural settlement – neither town nor village but an expansive sprawl of residential development on the edges of most major urban centres. This process was continued during the 1950s and 1960s with the establishment of 'new' towns and the decanting of urban populations from inner-city slum clearance areas to newer estates on the periphery of the built-up area. Today the urbanization of the countryside is more or less complete. Apart from a few remote locations, most rural areas are closely tied-in with urban centres and many of those who live in the countryside are living away from the urban focus of their working lives.

In terms of regional patterns the dominant influence in the twentieth century has been the drift towards the southern and Midland counties. Variations in economic prospects between the more traditional manufacturing economies of the older industrial districts and the rapidly expanding commercial economy of the Metropolitan area have strongly influenced the overall pattern of population distribution. A comparison between the maps for 1921 and 1981 (Maps 6.5 and 6.6) shows not only the rapid increase within the

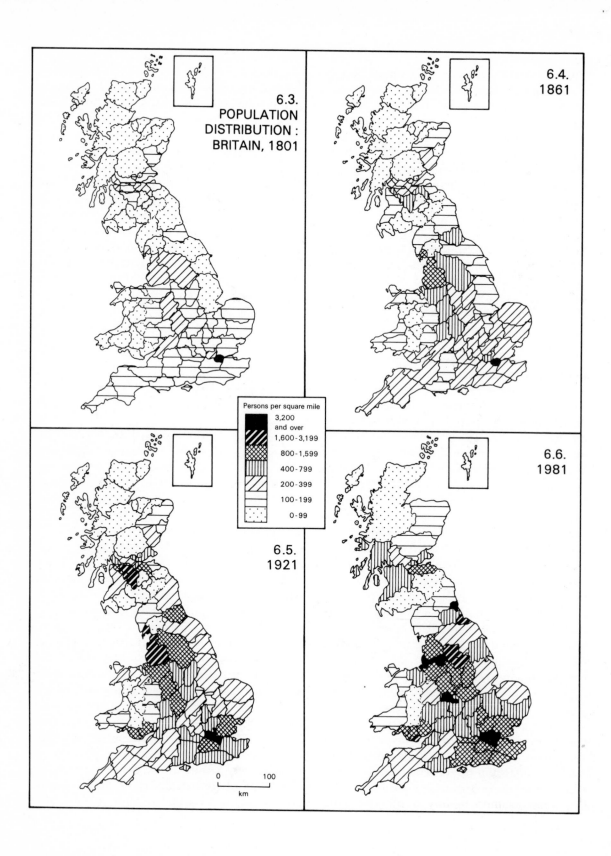

6.3.
POPULATION
DISTRIBUTION :
BRITAIN, 1801

6.4.
1861

Persons per square mile

3,200
and over
1,600 - 3,199
800 - 1,599
400 - 799
200 - 399
100 - 199
0 - 99

6.5.
1921

6.6.
1981

0   100
km

South-east but also its outward expansion so that the Metropolitan economy now influences an area stretching westwards towards Dorset and Wiltshire and eastwards into Suffolk and Cambridgeshire. This process seems likely to continue for the foreseeable future and will exacerbate other differences within Britain relating to the distribution of wealth and chances for employment. In effect, the basic pattern has changed from that of the late nineteenth and early twentieth centuries (see Map 6.5) when the important distinction was between an urban/industrial axis running from North-west to South-east, and a predominantly rural/agricultural western and eastern fringe, to the core–periphery pattern of the late twentieth century with an advanced southern economy and a more slowly developing northern and western periphery (Map 6.6). In these circumstances it is not hard to explain why the pressure for population movement is towards the centre, although other factors such as the housing market, variations in labour/skill requirements and the overall decline in employment prospects have been effective in restricting the flow.

Such shifts in population have been an important factor in determining local variations in demographic patterns. The movement of young adults into the expanding urban centres in the nineteenth century helped to raise levels of natural increase in towns and contributed towards the contrasts between urban and rural areas. In the 1980s geographical variations in fertility and mortality increasingly reflect differences in the conditions of life and the general distribution of different social groups.

Emigration and immigration

Overseas migration also played a part in the general pattern of population change. Throughout the nineteenth century and early twentieth century, England and Wales sustained a continuous net loss of numbers, estimated at 2 million between 1871 and 1931. Figure 6.7 shows a steadily rising trend in inward migration to and outward migration from the United Kingdom between the early years of the nineteenth century and the First World War. Peak years for emigration occurred in the 1850s with the rural exodus from Ireland passing through UK ports; in the 1880s with the opening-up of the Western Frontier in North America and the expansion of territories in Australasia, South America, and Africa; and in the Edwardian period when again the main destinations were North America and the dominion states. A further peak in emigration occurred in the 1950s, at a time when Australia, New Zealand, and Canada were actively recruiting emigrants from the United Kingdom. In recent years this outflow has declined, mainly in response to the reduction in opportunities. All the former recruiting countries now operate strict policies restricting immigration. None the less the pattern is much the same (Figure 6.8); 40 per cent of emigrants in 1981 were destined for the Old Commonwealth and South Africa, although alternative destinations, particularly the Middle East, have become of increasing importance during the last twenty years.

On the other side of the coin, inward movement has shown marked changes over the last two centuries. In the Victorian period immigration was dominated by relatively local origin – notably Ireland, and Central and Northern Europe. In 1851 there were over 700,000 Irish-born in England, Scotland, and Wales; the great majority of these were to be found in Central Scotland, North-west England and in London. Map 6.9 shows the distribution of Irish-born relative to the population of the counties of England, Scotland, and Wales (expressed as a location quotient). The same technique is used in Maps 6.10 and 6.11 to show the distribution of Welsh

6.7. PASSENGERS TO/FROM UNITED KINGDOM PORTS FROM/TO EXTRA-EUROPEAN COUNTRIES, 1815–1935

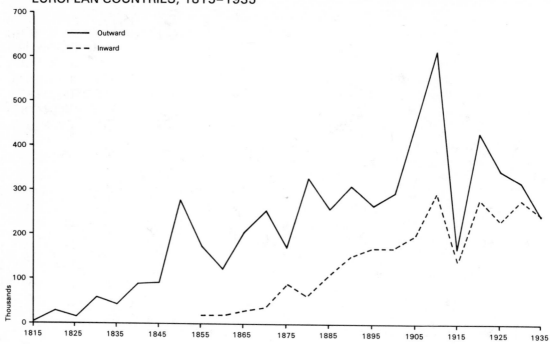

6.8. INTERNATIONAL MIGRATION, 1981

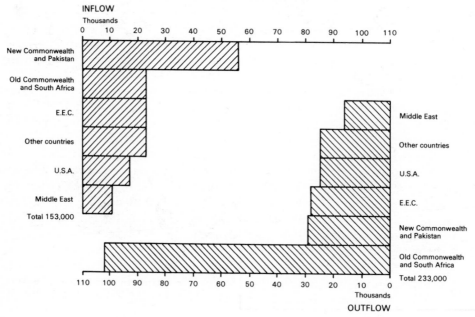

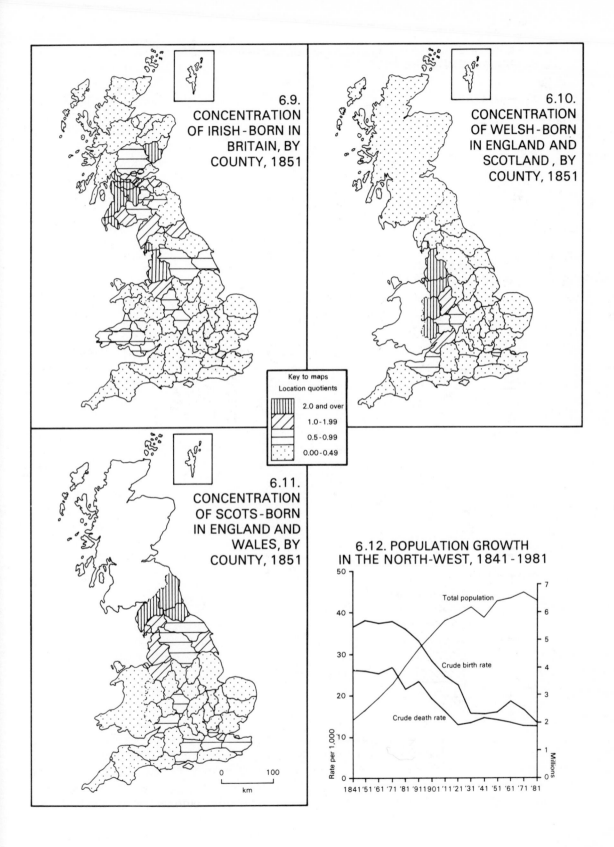

6.9.
CONCENTRATION
OF IRISH-BORN IN
BRITAIN, BY
COUNTY, 1851

6.10.
CONCENTRATION
OF WELSH-BORN
IN ENGLAND AND
SCOTLAND, BY
COUNTY, 1851

Key to maps
Location quotients

2.0 and over
1.0-1.99
0.5-0.99
0.00-0.49

6.11.
CONCENTRATION
OF SCOTS-BORN
IN ENGLAND AND
WALES, BY
COUNTY, 1851

6.12. POPULATION GROWTH
IN THE NORTH-WEST, 1841-1981

Total population

Crude birth rate

Crude death rate

0   100
km

1841 '51 '61 '71 '81 '91 1901 '11 '21 '31 '41 '51 '61 '71 '81

Rate per 1,000

Millions

and Scots migrants who also displayed a marked regional concentration within England.

By the mid-twentieth century the patterns of immigration were more diffuse with an increasing proportion of migrants from the developing world, particularly from those countries that had formerly been part of the British Empire. This directional flow had been encouraged by labour recruitment policies in the 1950s when Britain faced a shortfall in manual and semi-skilled workers. Since the 1960s, however, successive governments have sought to stem this tide by introducing increasingly restrictive immigration regulations. These measures have had the effect of reducing the total numbers of arrivals although the New Commonwealth (and Pakistan) remains the most important area of origin, accounting for 37 per cent of immigrants in 1981 (Figure 6.8).

Population change in the North-west

The extent of growth

Nineteenth- and twentieth-century population statistics are sufficiently detailed to permit intra- as well as inter-regional analysis. To illustrate the type of approaches that may be adopted, one of the country's most populous regions, the North-west, is selected. Until 1973 the region comprised the counties of Lancashire and Cheshire, but since then it has been divided into four sub-regions, the metropolitan boroughs of Merseyside and Greater Manchester being separated from the original counties.

In general, as Figure 6.12 reveals, population growth in the North-west during the last two centuries followed the pattern of the country as a whole. Prior to the Second World War there was a comparatively rapid increase, which slackened markedly thereafter. However, the population of the North-west grew at a faster rate than the national population until the early twentieth century and rather more slowly during subsequent decades. Thus, the national population rose by 38 per cent between 1801 and 1911 and by 37 per cent between 1911 and 1981. The corresponding figures for the North-west were 53 per cent and 20 per cent.

These differences reflect the changing economic fortunes of the North-west region. The prosperous staple industries of the nineteenth century (especially cotton and coal) went into serious long-term decline during the inter-war years and insufficient replacement industry was attracted. Such changes affected rates of population growth in two main ways. Firstly, whereas in the nineteenth century immigration into the region exceeded emigration by an appreciable margin, from the inter-war period the reverse was true. Secondly, it seems probable that migrants to the region in the nineteenth century and from it in the twentieth were mainly young people and that they constituted a fairly numerous group. Accordingly, long-term changes in their pattern of movement would have had a significant influence on general levels of fertility.

Birth rates and death rates

Since the late 1830s, figures of births and deaths in the North-west have been published annually by the Registrar General. For each census year, the figures he provides may be combined with population totals to give crude birth and death rates. These are also shown in Figure 6.12.

Comparison of Figure 6.12 with Figure 6.1 shows that, as with population totals, birth and death rate trends in the North-west were similar to those of the country as a whole. Birth rate consistently exceeded death rate and both showed fairly steady falls from the middle decades of the nineteenth century, before levelling out during the inter-war years. There were times, however, when significant differences occurred between the regional and national figures.

As far as birth rate was concerned, from the 1840s to the 1890s noticeably higher levels were reached in the North-west than in the country as a whole. The gap narrowed with time, but differences of 3 to 4 births per thousand were usually registered. During the twentieth century, very little difference was evident, the national figures actually exceeding the regional, albeit marginally, in 1901 and 1931. Such high birth-rate figures help to explain the comparatively rapid population growth that occurred in the North-west region during the nineteenth century. They also reflect the relatively youthful age structure of the region's population, a high proportion of the inhabitants being of child-bearing age. Thus, whereas 29.5 per cent of the national population were aged 20–39 in 1881, the figure for the North-west was 31.3. per cent.

Throughout the period from 1841 to 1911, crude death rate in the North-west was consistently higher than the national average. As with birth rate, differences of 3 or 4 per thousand were common during the nineteenth century. Moreover, between 1841 and 1871, the death rate in the region as a whole exceeded 23 per thousand, the figure used by the 1848 Public Health Act as a yardstick for establishing local boards of health. That a high proportion of North-west people lived in crowded and often insanitary urban areas, where endemic and epidemic diseases were rife, obviously had a strong influence on prevailing patterns of mortality.

Migration

Parish register evidence suggests that between 1781 and 1800, migrational gains may have increased Lancashire's population by as much as 11 per cent per annum and between 1801 and 1830 by about 6 per cent. During the earlier period, the figure was only marginally below that for natural increase, but was much less significant thereafter. Indeed, census data shows that during the second half of the nineteenth century, migrational increases were moderate (a few per cent per decade) and variable, in both Lancashire and Cheshire. Overall, however, it is clear that growth of the North-west economy during the nineteenth century acted as a powerful attraction to immigrants from less developed regions, especially from Ireland, where, during the mid-nineteenth century, severe economic difficulties arose associated with harvest failure. By 1850, about a quarter of Liverpool's population was Irish-born.

During the twentieth century, the position was reversed. Net migration losses were already being recorded in Lancashire prior to the First World War and they continued to occur during the inter-war years, though less heavily in the 1930s than in the 1920s. After the Second World War further losses arose, which were only partially offset by immigration into the region, chiefly from the New Commonwealth, the Irish Republic, and Europe. By the mid-1960s, net migration from the region was thought to be running at about 17,000 people per annum and during the following decade the average was about 21,000 per annum.

Population density

The rapidity with which the population of North-west England grew during the nineteenth and twentieth centuries varied considerably from district to district (see Maps 6.13–6.16). In comparing the maps, it can be seen that population densities increased in most registration districts throughout the nineteenth century and, in several instances, continued to do so during the first half of the twentieth. The highest concentrations of population, however, developed in south and east Lancashire. The 1801 Census (Map 6.13) showed that Liverpool and Manchester were easily the biggest urban centres in the region,

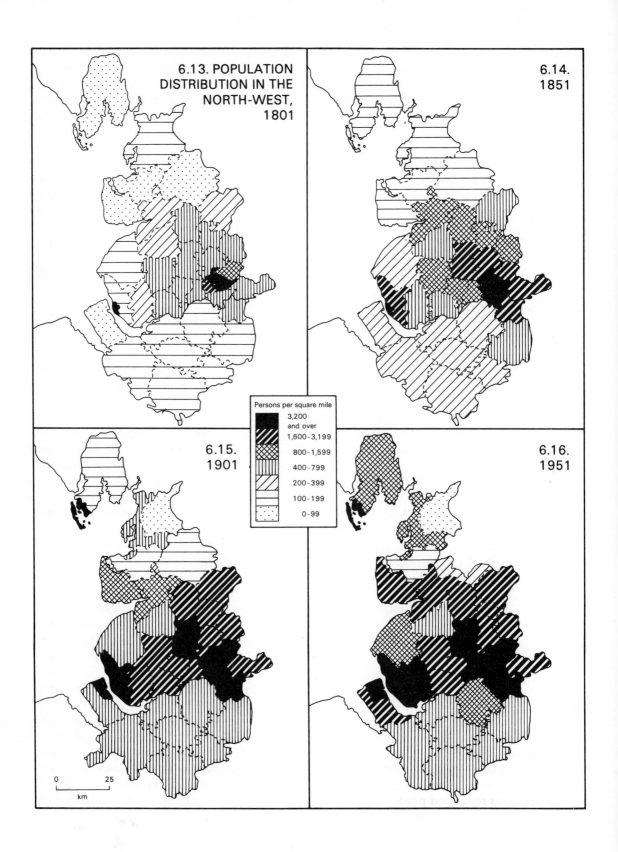

6.13. POPULATION DISTRIBUTION IN THE NORTH-WEST, 1801

6.14. 1851

6.15. 1901

6.16. 1951

Persons per square mile

▨	3,200 and over
▨	1,600 - 3,199
▦	800 - 1,599
▥	400 - 799
▨	200 - 399
▤	100 - 199
⠄	0 - 99

0   25
km

with populations in excess of 75,000. Indeed, they had become the largest provincial towns in England.

Between 1801 and 1851 (Map 6.14) population densities showed marked increases in several neighbouring registration districts, especially those of Salford and Chorlton (to the west and south of Manchester respectively) and of West Derby (to the north of Liverpool). By the mid-nineteenth century, suburban development was becoming important in each of these districts, as commercial and industrial demands placed growing pressure on urban centre land and as the wealthy became increasingly concerned to find more congenial surroundings in which to live. Moreover, appreciable population densities had been achieved in the Bolton, Bury, Oldham, Ashton-under-Lyne, and Stockport districts, a reflection of the continued progress made by the textile industry and its associated trades.

During the second half of the nineteenth century, rising population densities in east and north-west Lancashire and in the mid-Mersey valley were particularly apparent (see Map 6.15). In the former area, this was associated with the continued expansion of the textile trades, mainly weaving, and in the latter with developments in coal mining and chemical production. In the Wirral, too, notable increases in population density occurred, especially in the Birkenhead district, where shipbuilding and general port industries assumed major significance. Elsewhere in the region, though, overall population densities remained appreciably lower than in south Lancashire and north Cheshire, except at Barrow-in-Furness, which emerged as a major steel and shipbuilding centre. It should be noted, however, that in some registration districts population was less thinly spread than the density figures suggest, especially in the west of Lancashire, where Preston and the coastal resorts of Blackpool and Southport became major towns. Meanwhile, large parts of rural Cheshire and of north Lancashire showed only modest increases in population; here agricultural activities remained predominant.

During the first half of the twentieth century, the population of Merseyside and Greater Manchester continued to expand, both areas developing into major conurbations (see Map 6.16). In each case, a powerful influence was large-scale suburban development, promoted by municipal planners and by private enterprise and facilitated by improved transportation. There were also higher densities recorded in the west Lancashire registration districts, where the resorts attracted increasing numbers of commuters and retired people. At the same time, population began to migrate from the coal and cotton districts in the eastern half of Lancashire as the staple industries went into long-term decline.

Population distribution after the Second World War

Much change has occurred in the distribution of the North-west population during the postwar era. The main features have been the reduced numbers living in the Manchester and Merseyside conurbations, population gains in Cheshire and in central and north Lancashire and the continued loss of people from east and north-west Lancashire (Map 6.17).

Between 1961 and 1981 the population of Merseyside fell by 206,271, some 12 per cent of the total. In Greater Manchester, the absolute reduction was 124,160 and the percentage 4.6. Within the cities of Liverpool and Manchester, however, much greater losses occurred. The population of Liverpool fell by 235,769 (31.6 per cent) and Manchester by 213,347 (32.3 per cent). In both cases there have been small natural losses of population, but emigration has been by far the predominant influence. Thus, between 1971 and 1981, the total reduction of Liverpool's population was 16.41 per cent, of which 15.46 per cent could be attributed to migration. Sustained industrial and commercial decline; insufficient jobs arising from replacement industry; and large-scale redevelopment have all contributed to these losses.

In central Lancashire, the population

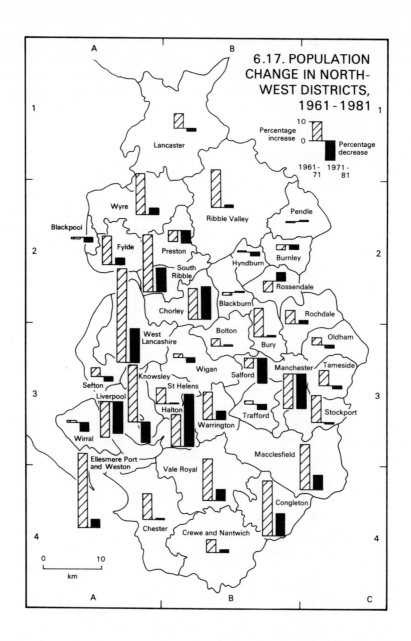

6.17. POPULATION CHANGE IN NORTH-WEST DISTRICTS, 1961-1981

increases have been in the districts of West Lancashire, Chorley and South Ribble. Between 1961 and 1981, the West Lancashire population rose from 61,514 to 107,271 (74.3 per cent), that of Chorley from 67,007 to 91,203 (36 per cent) and that of South Ribble from 66,467 to 97,464 (46.6 per cent). These increases were closely associated with the development of Skelmersdale and Central Lancashire new towns and resulted largely from immigration. In West Lancashire, for example, only 6.45 per cent of the 17.13 per cent increase that took place between 1971 and 1981 resulted from natural causes. This district includes Skelmersdale, to which migration from central Liverpool was heavy. The construction of motorways has helped to diversify the industrial base of central Lancashire, though unemployment has risen to comparatively high levels in recent years. This is reflected in the population losses in the Preston district, again resulting largely from migration.

North of the Ribble, meanwhile, population increases have been recorded in the Lancaster, Wyre, Fylde, and Ribble Valley districts, all of which have become more popular areas for short-distance commuting and for retirement. The rises have been comparatively modest, however. Between 1961 and 1981, they ranged from 5.6 per cent in Lancaster district to 26 per cent in the Wyre district. All have experienced a natural decline in population, which has been associated with smaller proportions of people in the child-bearing age-ranges. During the mid 1980s it was reported that the Fylde and Blackpool districts had the lowest birth rates in Lancashire, as well as the highest death rates.

The growth in the populations of the

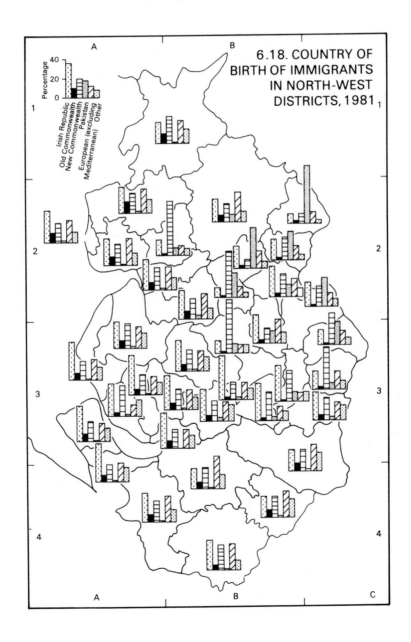

6.18. COUNTRY OF BIRTH OF IMMIGRANTS IN NORTH-WEST DISTRICTS, 1981

147

Cheshire districts have shown marked variations. At the one extreme, the population of Crewe and Nantwich rose by 7.9 per cent between 1961 and 1981; at the other, that of Ellesmere Port and Neston increased by 45.5 per cent. Migration, not least from Liverpool and Manchester, was again more important than natural change in bringing about these increases. At Ellesmere Port, labour was attracted by the growth of a range of industries, but especially oil refining at the vast Stanlow works. However, as the economic difficulties of Merseyside intensified during the 1970s, the Ellesmere Port and Neston district experienced a net loss from migration, the only district in Cheshire where this happened.

The loss of population from north-east Lancashire, already apparent during the interwar years, has continued in recent decades. Yet the reductions have been small. Between 1961 and 1981 the combined population of the Blackburn, Burnley, and Hyndburn districts fell from 322,840 to 315,049, more than 2.4 per cent. Urban clearance programmes, coupled with bleak employment prospects, strongly influenced these losses. In the Pendle and Rossendale districts, however, the reductions of earlier years were marginally reversed during the 1970s. This was far more noticeable in Rossendale, which may have become a more popular area for commuters as communication links with Greater Manchester were significantly improved. Between 1971 and 1981, Rossendale's population rose 5.02 per cent as a result of immigration, though this was partly offset by a natural loss of 1.05 per cent.

Recent immigration

In recent censuses, figures on country of birth have been recorded. They enable assessments to be made of the geographical distribution of immigrants within regions, as well as indicating the relative importance of the various ethnic minorities. The 1981 figures for the North-west are shown in Map 6.18.

Except in the case of Preston, the North-west districts with the greatest proportions of immigrants were in Greater Manchester and East Lancashire, the highest, 11.2 per cent, being in Manchester. Blackburn had 9.2 per cent; Bolton and Trafford 7 per cent; Rochdale 6.5 per cent; Pendle 6 per cent; and Oldham 5.8 per cent. At Preston, the figure was 8.1 per cent. Elsewhere, proportions did not usually exceed more than 2 or 3 per cent.

Immigrants from the Old Commonwealth were relatively unimportant throughout the region, nearly always comprising less than 10 per cent of the total and being virtually absent in east Lancashire. By contrast, those from the Irish Republic commonly formed at least a quarter of the total and as much as 40 per cent in several Merseyside and Greater Manchester districts. Immigrants from Europe and the New Commonwealth were also widely distributed, though the latter formed high proportions in Preston, Blackburn, Tameside, and Bolton. Pakistani immigrants were much more geographically concentrated, however, being found mainly in east and north-west Lancashire. It seems clear that the distribution of Asian immigration was much influenced by the availability of jobs in the textile industry during the 1960s and has not been disrupted by its serious contraction during the past decade.

Notes

Figure 6.1 is based on figures in E. A. Wrigley and R. S. Schofield, *The Population History of England, 1541-1871: A Reconstruction* (London, 1981), B. R. Mitchell and P. Deane, *Abstract of British Historical Statistics* (Cambridge, 1962), *Annual Abstract of Statistics 1938-1981* (London), and *Registrar General's Statistical Review of England and Wales 1941* (London, 1941). Figure 6.2 uses material from Mitchell and Deane, op. cit. and from the Central Statistical Office, *Annual Abstract of Statistics* (London, 1983). Maps 6.3-6.5 are based on figures in Mitchell and Deane, op. cit.; Map 6.6 utilizes *Census 1981: Historical Tables and Surveys* (London, 1982) and *Census 1981: Key Statistics for Local Authorities, Great Britain* (London, 1984). Figure 6.7 uses statistics from Mitchell and Deane, op. cit. Figure 6.8 is based on *Population Trends*, 41 (London, 1985). Maps 6.9-6.11 are based on the Census of 1851. Figure 6.12 is based on *Decennial Census Returns* and on the *Annual Report of the Registrar General of Births, Deaths and Marriages in England*. Maps 6.13-6.16 use data contained in the *Census: County Reports for Lancashire and Cheshire*, 1801, 1851, 1901, 1951, while Maps 6.17-6.18 use data contained in the *Census 1981: County Reports for Lancashire, Merseyside, Greater Manchester and Cheshire* (London, 1982).

7 EMPLOYMENT AND UNEMPLOYMENT
Rex Pope

Employment

In the early eighteenth century, employment was concentrated in agriculture or agriculture-related occupations. In spite of the growth of trade and industry, Porter's distillation of the 1811 Census revealed that agriculture remained the occupation of over 40 per cent of the employed population in 26 of the 42 counties of England.[1] During the nineteenth and early twentieth centuries, however, mining and manufacture became the major employment sectors; by the late twentieth century, this position had passed to the service industries. Emphasis in this analysis is on men's and women's employment as revealed in the Censuses of 1851, 1911 and 1971. The year 1851 is selected since by that time contrasting industrial development was clear; the nine northern and north-western counties of England are used as a case study. For 1911 and 1971, Britain as a whole is depicted: 1911 is selected as representative of the 'Victorian' economy at its most developed, and 1971, rather than 1981, because it offers better opportunities for comparison with the earlier date. County boundaries for the most part remain the same and, while there has been a dramatic shift from manufacturing and mining into service occupations, the collapse of British industrial employment – so marked a feature of the 1970s and 1980s – was yet to occur. Women's employment, where the range of available occupations was at all times more limited, is dealt with separately.

Male employment

Though, during the first half of the nineteenth century, numbers engaged in agricultural work grew to something over 2 million, this represented a declining proportion of the total British labour force, from just over one-third in 1801 to about one-fifth in 1851. The mining, manufacturing, and building industries, by contrast, employed just over two-fifths of the workforce by the latter date. As Maps 7.1–7.4 demonstrate, however, there were wide contrasts even within a limited geographical area. Agriculture remained the largest single sector in six of the nine counties examined, employing as much as 40.6 per cent of occupied males in the North Riding of Yorkshire and 36.7 per cent in Westmorland. Even in Co. Durham (10.5 per cent) and Lancashire (8.5 per cent and over 60,000 in number), it was far from insignificant as a source of work. Within mining and manufacturing, textiles were important in the western counties of Lancashire, the West Riding of Yorkshire and Cheshire. In Lancashire, the work was mainly in cotton, in the West Riding it was mainly in woollens and worsteds while in Cheshire cotton *and* silk were significant employers. Coal-mining was the single most important occupation in Co. Durham but Lancashire, in numerical terms, had more miners (28,834 compared to 28,265). The West Riding, too, contained over 20,000 miners but, as in

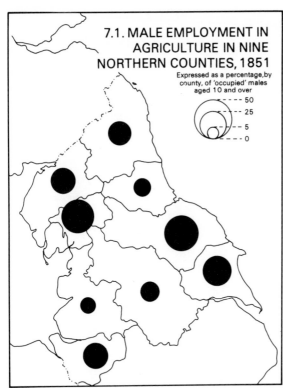

7.1. MALE EMPLOYMENT IN AGRICULTURE IN NINE NORTHERN COUNTIES, 1851

Expressed as a percentage, by county, of 'occupied' males aged 10 and over

- 50
- 25
- 5
- 0

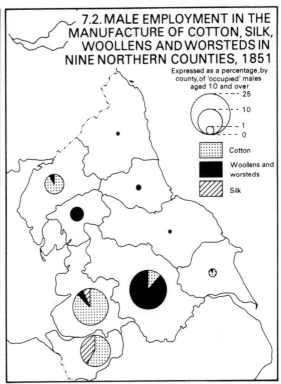

7.2. MALE EMPLOYMENT IN THE MANUFACTURE OF COTTON, SILK, WOOLLENS AND WORSTEDS IN NINE NORTHERN COUNTIES, 1851

Expressed as a percentage, by county, of 'occupied' males aged 10 and over

- 25
- 10
- 1
- 0

Cotton

Woollens and worsteds

Silk

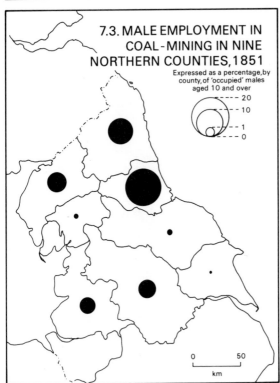

7.3. MALE EMPLOYMENT IN COAL-MINING IN NINE NORTHERN COUNTIES, 1851

Expressed as a percentage, by county, of 'occupied' males aged 10 and over

- 20
- 10
- 1
- 0

0   50
km

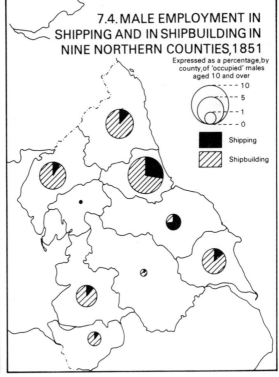

7.4. MALE EMPLOYMENT IN SHIPPING AND IN SHIPBUILDING IN NINE NORTHERN COUNTIES, 1851

Expressed as a percentage, by county, of 'occupied' males aged 10 and over

- 10
- 5
- 1
- 0

Shipping

Shipbuilding

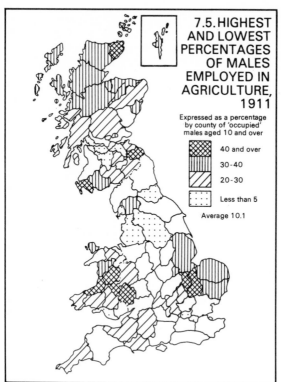

7.5. HIGHEST AND LOWEST PERCENTAGES OF MALES EMPLOYED IN AGRICULTURE, 1911

Expressed as a percentage by county of 'occupied' males aged 10 and over

40 and over

30-40

20-30

Less than 5

Average 10.1

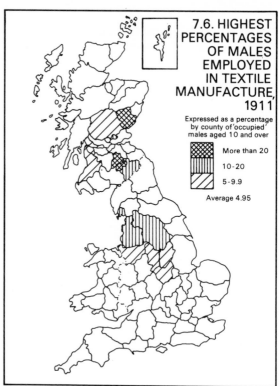

7.6. HIGHEST PERCENTAGES OF MALES EMPLOYED IN TEXTILE MANUFACTURE, 1911

Expressed as a percentage by county of 'occupied' males aged 10 and over

More than 20

10-20

5-9.9

Average 4.95

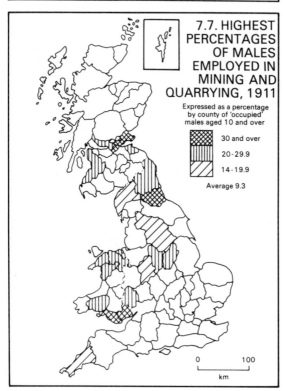

7.7. HIGHEST PERCENTAGES OF MALES EMPLOYED IN MINING AND QUARRYING, 1911

Expressed as a percentage by county of 'occupied' males aged 10 and over

30 and over

20-29.9

14-19.9

Average 9.3

0   100

km

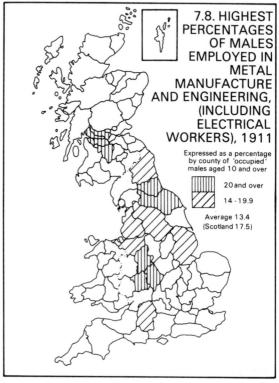

7.8. HIGHEST PERCENTAGES OF MALES EMPLOYED IN METAL MANUFACTURE AND ENGINEERING, (INCLUDING ELECTRICAL WORKERS), 1911

Expressed as a percentage by county of 'occupied' males aged 10 and over

20 and over

14-19.9

Average 13.4
(Scotland 17.5)

Lancashire, this represented under 5 per cent of total male employment. Lancashire, with its huge 'occupied' male population of over three-quarters of a million and the port of Liverpool within its boundaries, also contained nearly 20,000 males employed in seafaring, but Durham's 9,000 were proportionally more significant. Durham, too, including as it did Sunderland, Stockton, the Hartlepools, and South Shields was also the major British shipbuilding county.

By 1911, 10.1 per cent of economically active males were to be found working in agriculture. Contrasts between areas, however, had become more marked (see Map 7.5). In counties containing major industrial and commercial concentrations, agriculture offered employment to under 5 per cent of the working population while in most of Wales, throughout northern Scotland and in much of East and South-west England, the figure remained over 20 per cent. Employment in textiles (4.5 per cent of the British workforce) was heavily concentrated (see Map 7.6) with only Lancashire (cotton), Fife (linen), Angus[2] (jute), and Clackmannan, Roxburgh, Selkirk, Peebles, and the West Riding (all woollens and worsteds) having more than 10 per cent of their male workers so employed. Mining and quarrying (9.7 per cent of the workforce) was rather more widespread. The highest percentages of males working in this sector were found (see Map 7.7) in the coal-mining counties of West Lothian, Fife, Durham, Glamorgan, and Monmouth (all over 30 per cent). Other major centres included the North Wales slate-producing counties of Caernarvon, Denbigh, and Merioneth, and Cornwall (tin and clay). Numerically, the largest concentrations were in Glamorgan and Durham (each over 150,000) and Lancashire (114,000); in each case, these figures largely represented coal-miners.

The employment category loosely defined as the metal manufacturing and engineering trades (including vehicle construction, shipbuilding, and the emerging electrical engineering industry) employed 13.4 per cent of

Britain's working males but 17.5 per cent of those in Scotland. Map 7.8 demonstrates that in Scotland, especially, there was heavy concentration in four central counties of Lanark, Renfrew, Dunbarton, and Stirlingshire. The first three of these had a heavy commitment to shipbuilding while Lanark, like Stirling, was also a centre for iron and steel manufacture. In England, whilst Lancashire with 218,000 employed in this sector had the greatest numbers, the highest percentage concentrations were found in Durham and the North Riding (iron and steel manufacture, shipbuilding and other heavy engineering) and, above all, in the West Midlands counties of Staffordshire, Warwickshire, and Worcestershire, long-established centres of metal manufacture and metalworking. The highest percentages in professional and administrative occupations (Map 7.9) were found in Midlothian (containing Edinburgh) and in London and the adjacent counties of

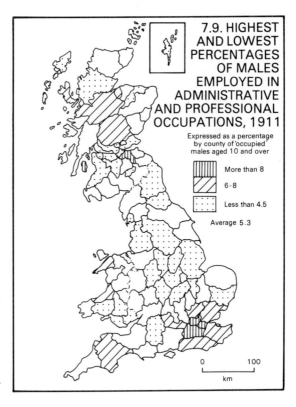

7.9. HIGHEST AND LOWEST PERCENTAGES OF MALES EMPLOYED IN ADMINISTRATIVE AND PROFESSIONAL OCCUPATIONS, 1911

Expressed as a percentage by county of 'occupied' males aged 10 and over

More than 8

6-8

Less than 4.5

Average 5.3

0   100
km

Middlesex and Surrey. Other counties within easy commuting distance of London had the next highest densities. The capital cities, apart from being seats of administration, were important legal, medical, and educational centres. The lowest percentages of males defined as professional and administrative are found in the industrial heartlands of the country (where their numbers are swamped by those of manual workers) and in such predominantly rural counties as Lincolnshire, Huntingdonshire, Suffolk, Banff, or Ross and Cromarty.

By 1971, the proportion of the population employed in agriculture had declined to under 2 per cent. In only seven counties (Kincardine, Kinross, Berwick, and Kirkcudbright in Scotland; Montgomery, Radnor, and Cardigan in Wales) did agriculture provide jobs for more than 20 per cent of the male workforce (see Map 7.10). Mining and quarrying (Map 7.11) was also far less important as a source of employment. The highest percentage of workers so employed (9 per cent) was found in Nottinghamshire; the greatest number (some 57,000) in the West Riding of Yorkshire. The great communities of coalminers had virtually disappeared. Percentages employed in metal manufacture and in engineering (Map 7.12) had, on the other hand, expanded greatly. In all but two small English counties and in most of Wales, over 14 per cent of the working population was to be found in this sector. One reason for the widespread employment picture was the 2–4 per cent of workers, found by now in most counties, employed in the electrical and electronics industries. Traditional and not so traditional industrial areas had over 20 per cent of their workforces concentrated in the metal manufacturing and engineering sectors. Dunbarton, Renfrew, and the West Midland counties remained among those with the highest concentrations so employed, being joined by Bedfordshire with its important motor manufacturing plant.

Service occupations (Map 7.13) had also become much more important and widespread. Even if we exclude those employed in transport and communications, only Montgomery, Radnor, and Carmarthen (in Wales) and a number of rural Scottish counties had under 25 per cent of their economically active males working in this area. The greatest concentrations were close to Edinburgh (Midlothian and Selkirk), Manchester (Cheshire), or London. Buckinghamshire (63.2 per cent) and Surrey (54.8 per cent) had the highest densities not only of service workers in general but also (with 35.4 and 30.4 per cent respectively) of males in professional and administrative occupations.

Female employment

An examination of female employment patterns involves consideration of two interlinked issues that can largely be discounted in relation to men. The first of these is the participation rate which can vary widely according to the nature of the local economy. The other is the extent to which women's work goes unrecorded. Much unpaid domestic service by members of the family or part-time laundry, seamstress, or child-minding employment comes into this category. Census returns, on which all the maps in this section are based, tend therefore to underestimate the percentage of women working.

Maps 7.14–7.17 deal with female employment in the northern and north-western counties of England in 1851. Map 7.14 reveals that the highest percentages of participation were to be found in the textile areas and the lowest, Westmorland apart, in counties with a large commitment to agriculture and mining. The biggest female occupational area across the region (and the country) was domestic service, a form of employment dominated by the young and single. Only in Cumberland, Lancashire, and the West Riding were less than a quarter of employed women found in this sector (see Map 7.15) and, of these counties, Lancashire (86,000) and the West Riding (36,000) contained *numerically* more

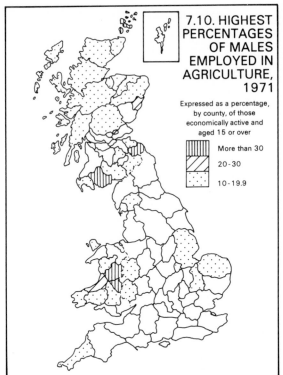

7.10. HIGHEST PERCENTAGES OF MALES EMPLOYED IN AGRICULTURE, 1971

Expressed as a percentage, by county, of those economically active and aged 15 or over

More than 30
20-30
10-19.9

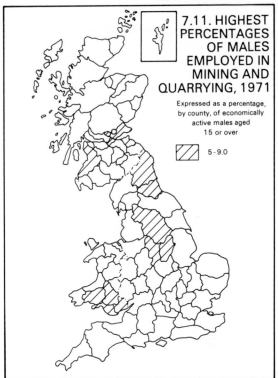

7.11. HIGHEST PERCENTAGES OF MALES EMPLOYED IN MINING AND QUARRYING, 1971

Expressed as a percentage, by county, of economically active males aged 15 or over

5-9.0

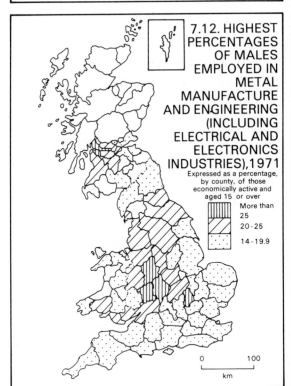

7.12. HIGHEST PERCENTAGES OF MALES EMPLOYED IN METAL MANUFACTURE AND ENGINEERING (INCLUDING ELECTRICAL AND ELECTRONICS INDUSTRIES),1971

Expressed as a percentage, by county, of those economically active and aged 15 or over

More than 25
20-25
14-19.9

0   100
km

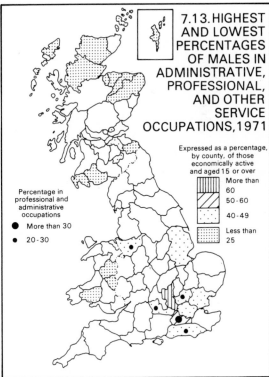

7.13. HIGHEST AND LOWEST PERCENTAGES OF MALES IN ADMINISTRATIVE, PROFESSIONAL, AND OTHER SERVICE OCCUPATIONS,1971

Expressed as a percentage, by county, of those economically active and aged 15 or over

More than 60
50-60
40-49
Less than 25

Percentage in professional and administrative occupations

● More than 30
• 20-30

155

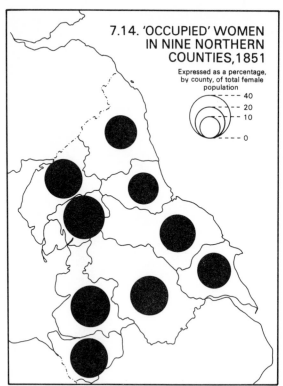

7.14. 'OCCUPIED' WOMEN
IN NINE NORTHERN
COUNTIES, 1851

Expressed as a percentage,
by county, of total female
population

- - - 40
- - 20
- - 10

- - - 0

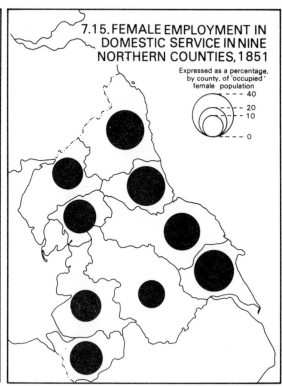

7.15. FEMALE EMPLOYMENT IN
DOMESTIC SERVICE IN NINE
NORTHERN COUNTIES, 1851

Expressed as a percentage,
by county, of 'occupied'
female population

- - - 40
- - 20
- - 10

- - - 0

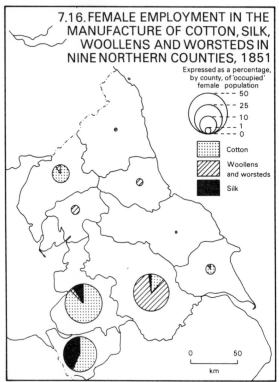

7.16. FEMALE EMPLOYMENT IN THE
MANUFACTURE OF COTTON, SILK,
WOOLLENS AND WORSTEDS IN
NINE NORTHERN COUNTIES, 1851

Expressed as a percentage,
by county, of 'occupied'
female population

- - - 50
- - 25
- - 10
- - 1
- - 0

Cotton

Woollens
and worsteds

Silk

0   50
km

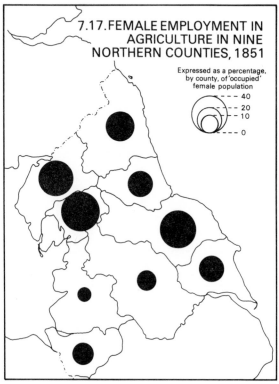

7.17. FEMALE EMPLOYMENT IN
AGRICULTURE IN NINE
NORTHERN COUNTIES, 1851

Expressed as a percentage,
by county, of 'occupied'
female population

- - - 40
- - 20
- - 10

- - - 0

156

domestic servants than any other county in the region.

Textile employment (Map 7.16), like that of males, was geographically concentrated but, expressed as a percentages of the total female workforce of Lancashire, Cheshire, the West Riding, and Cumberland, the figures for women in textiles were markedly higher than those for men. Indeed, in the cotton and silk industries of Lancashire and Cheshire, the absolute numbers of women and girls employed (27,000 in Cheshire, 170,000 in Lancashire) were greater than those of males. Substantial numbers of women were still to be found in agricultural pursuits, mainly working on family farms, and the fact that the counties with the greatest numerical concentrations of women in agriculture (West Riding 24,000, Lancashire 21,000, Cheshire 10,500) were those in which such activity constituted the smallest percentages of female employment (a situation already encountered with regard to domestic service) reinforces the argument that it was the availability of alternative employment to agriculture or service (notably in textiles) that pushed participation rates up.

The impact of the textile industries (particularly cotton and worsted) on the employment of young girls, including half-timers, is revealed in Map 7.18. In 1891, all the ten towns with the highest percentages of girls aged 10–15 employed, from Blackburn with 58.1 per cent to Oldham with 35 per cent, were textile-dominated. The map also shows the ten towns with the lowest percentages of 10–15-year-old girls employed. These fell into two groups. Most were centres of heavy engineering (e.g. the north-eastern towns of Gateshead, South Shields, Sunderland, or Middlesbrough) where job opportunities for women were limited. Tottenham, Leyton, and West Ham, on the other hand, were areas of artisan and clerks' housing where few servants were employed, and girls, once they had left school, would often stay at home and do unpaid housework.

Maps 7.19–7.22 illustrate patterns of female employment in Britain, as a whole, in 1911. As

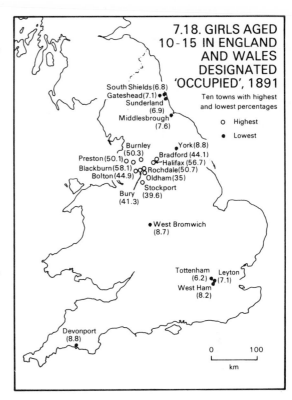

in the 1851 case study of the northern and north-western counties of England, high participation rates were in most cases a consequence of the availability of work in textiles or, in this instance, clothing manufacture. The exceptions were Warwickshire where 30,000 women (19.4 per cent of the county's female workforce) were employed in the metal manufacturing and engineering sectors, and Cardiganshire where an exceptionally high proportion of female workers (25.9 per cent) were employed in small-scale farming. An exception of a different kind was the West Riding where, in spite of having 220,000 women employed in textile and clothing manufacture, the county had an overall female participation level of only 33.7 per cent. Areas with the lowest participation rates were generally those with a heavy commitment to agriculture (e.g. East Anglia and much of Scotland and Wales) or to mining and heavy industry (e.g. Glamorgan and Monmouth, the North-east of England, Central Scotland).

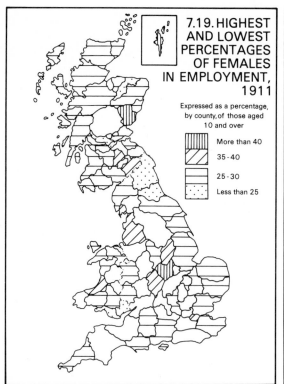

7.19. HIGHEST AND LOWEST PERCENTAGES OF FEMALES IN EMPLOYMENT, 1911

Expressed as a percentage, by county, of those aged 10 and over

More than 40
35 - 40
25 - 30
Less than 25

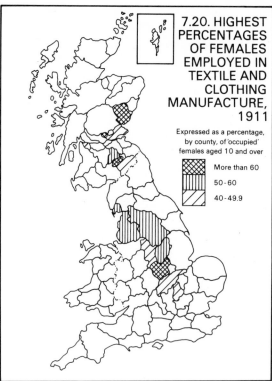

7.20. HIGHEST PERCENTAGES OF FEMALES EMPLOYED IN TEXTILE AND CLOTHING MANUFACTURE, 1911

Expressed as a percentage, by county, of 'occupied' females aged 10 and over

More than 60
50 - 60
40 - 49.9

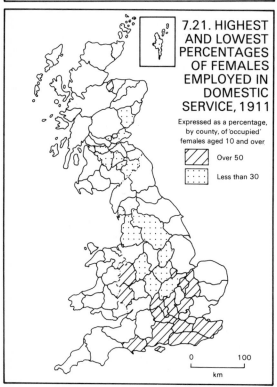

7.21. HIGHEST AND LOWEST PERCENTAGES OF FEMALES EMPLOYED IN DOMESTIC SERVICE, 1911

Expressed as a percentage, by county, of 'occupied' females aged 10 and over

Over 50
Less than 30

0   100
km

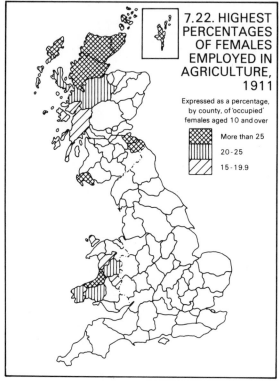

7.22. HIGHEST PERCENTAGES OF FEMALES EMPLOYED IN AGRICULTURE, 1911

Expressed as a percentage, by county, of 'occupied' females aged 10 and over

More than 25
20 - 25
15 - 19.9

Textile and clothing manufacture and domestic service (Maps 7.20 and 7.21) were the two great occupations for women: 31.4 per cent of all occupied women were engaged in the different textile and clothing industries; 35.0 per cent were employed as domestic servants. Within the textile and clothing sectors there was a high degree of regional concentration and specialization. Among major centres not already mentioned were Renfrew (thread manufacture), Nottinghamshire (lace and hosiery), Leicestershire (hosiery, boots and shoes), Northamptonshire (the major centre of the boot and shoe industry), and Bedfordshire (straw hats). The lowest figures for employment of women in domestic service correspond closely with the highest for employment in textiles or (in the case of Warwickshire) engineering. The highest figures occur, for the most part, in counties, mostly around London, with a low overall participation rate and a substantial middle-class population.

Agriculture as a significant source of female employment had, by 1911, been driven to the fringes of the country (see Map 7.22) and was only important in those areas of Wales and Scotland which contained small farms and crofts and little in the way of alternative employment.

By 1971, female occupational distribution had dramatically altered. Due partly to changes in methods of recording or in family size but more to economic changes, agricultural employment, even on the fringes of Wales and Scotland, was minimal. Only seven counties (all in Scotland) had more than 5 per cent of their female workforce employed in agriculture; in only three counties – Orkney (17.9 per cent), Argyll (15.7 per cent), and Kinross (11.9 per cent) – did the figure exceed 10 per cent. Employment in textiles and clothing had also shrunk (see Map 7.24). Roxburgh (28.8 per cent) now had the highest concentration of such workers – thanks largely to the expansion of knitting. Even Lancashire had less than 10 per cent of its women workers in this sector. Private indoor

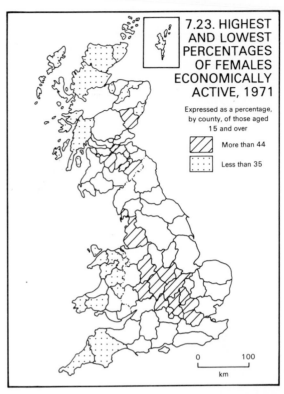

7.23. HIGHEST AND LOWEST PERCENTAGES OF FEMALES ECONOMICALLY ACTIVE, 1971

Expressed as a percentage, by county, of those aged 15 and over

More than 44

Less than 35

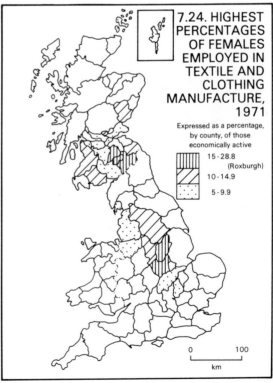

7.24. HIGHEST PERCENTAGES OF FEMALES EMPLOYED IN TEXTILE AND CLOTHING MANUFACTURE, 1971

Expressed as a percentage, by county, of those economically active

15 - 28.8 (Roxburgh)

10 - 14.9

5 - 9.9

domestic service, which had been by far the largest part of the pre-1914 domestic service category, was of even less consequence. Overall, though, in spite of retirement pensions and extended education, the female participation rate had grown to 37.5 per cent, with over 44 per cent defined as economically active in a number of counties, including not only many of the traditional centres of female work but also a great swathe of counties stretching from London to the West Midlands (Map 7.23). Lowest levels of participation were to be found in the extreme west and north – Devon and Cornwall, much of North and West Wales, the Highlands and Islands of Scotland. Women's employment was now overwhelmingly concentrated in service occupations. Excluding those working in transport and communications, no county had less than Carmarthen's 59.4 per cent of its female workers in this sector. Over most of the country, the figure exceeded 65 per cent, and in counties including or close to major administrative and commercial centres, or with a heavy commitment to the holiday trade or, conversely, with little opportunity for industrial employment (e.g. West Wales or the Scottish Highlands), the figure was in excess of 75 or even 80 per cent (Map 7.25).

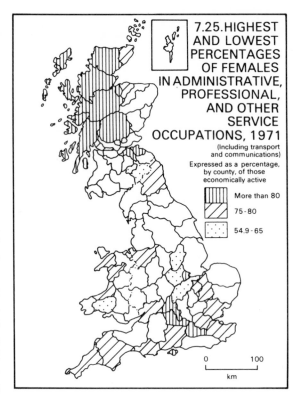

7.25. HIGHEST AND LOWEST PERCENTAGES OF FEMALES IN ADMINISTRATIVE, PROFESSIONAL, AND OTHER SERVICE OCCUPATIONS, 1971

(Including transport and communications)

Expressed as a percentage, by county, of those economically active

More than 80

75 - 80

54.9 - 65

0   100
km

Unemployment

Under-employment is endemic in non-industrial societies; unemployment, varying in cause, incidence, and duration, is a feature of industrialized and advanced economies. Serious analysis of the problem of unemployment only occurred at the turn of the twentieth century and accurate and comprehensive statistics were not available until even later. In consequence, judgements for the period before the First World War are imprecise.

Cyclical unemployment, as a phenomenon, was first observable in the cotton towns of the early nineteenth century. The sheer scale of unemployment in towns like Blackburn at the beginning of the 1840s forced modification in

the application of the New Poor Law. Subsequently, for example in 1885–6 and 1904–5, unemployment associated with trade slumps was to lead to political disturbance and government action in the form of the Chamberlain Circular (1886) and the 1905 Unemployed Workmen Act. Significantly, though, the objectives of policy were essentially to maintain order and avoid demoralization, not to create work.

Seasonal unemployment was evident in outdoor trades like building or agriculture and, in times of exceptionally harsh weather, dockwork. Such winter unemployment aggravated the cyclical problem, e.g. in 1885–6. Other seasonal unemployment, for example in the gas and clothing industries, stemmed from patterns of demand.

More serious for the individual was structural unemployment, the permanent displacement of a worker due to changes in technology (e.g. the replacement of the handloom by the powerloom), changes in work practices (e.g. on the docks after 1889), or in long-term decline in the demand for the product of an industry (e.g. Lancashire cotton after 1920).

Statistical returns made by trade unions to the Board of Trade, published figures of cases dealt with by Distress Committees and evidence from Boards of Guardians, give some indication of levels of unemployment and incidence of hardship. Unfortunately, during the period before 1914, the statistics available give no accurate indication of regional patterns of unemployment. For this we have to wait until the inter-war years when unemployment insurance statistics become available.

These inter-war statistics tend to overstate the percentage unemployed but underestimate the total number. This is because many public sector and transport workers, along with domestic servants and, until after 1934, agricultural workers, were excluded from the scheme. Unemployment returns also omitted many, especially among married women who failed to sign on because they had no right to benefit and little chance of finding work. In spite of this, the figures do give a clear indication of trend and regional variation.

Maps 7.26 and 7.27 show unemployment by county in June 1932 and June 1937: 1932 was the worst year of the slump; 1937 was the best year of economic recovery. June is a month of low seasonal unemployment. In Map 7.26, no county has an unemployment level among insured workers of below 5 per cent. Only counties without any real industrial base (e.g. Sussex, Cambridgeshire) had levels of under 10 per cent. Even Middlesex and Essex came in the 15–19.9 per cent range. Worst hit were the areas where the old staple industries (cotton, coal-mining, shipbuilding, iron and steel) were concentrated. Here, the effects of the slump aggravated difficulties caused by long-term decline in demand for their products. Thus Glamorgan and neighbouring Monmouthshire had unemployment levels in excess of 42 per cent, Dunbartonshire's unemployment stood at 48.2 per cent, Northumberland, Cumberland, Renfrewshire, and Lanarkshire all fell in the range 32–36 per cent. In Lancashire, the worst period for the export-dominated cotton industry came rather earlier (Map 7.28). None the less, in June 1932 cotton towns like Oldham, Padiham, Rawtenstall, Blackburn, and Great Harwood still had over 30 per cent of their insured workforces unemployed, while areas where coal-mining was important were even worse affected, e.g. Hindley (55.4 per cent), Westhoughton (40.6 per cent), Wigan (37.3 per cent). By contrast, the worst figure in the West Midlands county of Warwickshire, with its mixed base of industry catering largely for home demand, was Sutton Coldfield (24 per cent) (Map 7.29).

By June 1937, a recovery based on domestic demand for housing and consumer durables was at its peak. Unemployment among insured workers over much of the South and Midlands stood at under 5 per cent (Map 7.27). In Warwickshire, the highest level was 9.2 per cent at Bedworth, a colliery town. By contrast, unemployment in the electrical engineering centre, Rugby, was 1.2 per cent (Map 7.29). Most of the traditional industrial areas of Scotland, Wales, and the North of England were still experiencing unemployment levels in excess of 13 per cent. In counties like Glamorgan and Monmouthshire, with a heavy commitment to coal-mining, the figure was in excess of 20 per cent. Lancashire's 13.2 per cent overall included 8.8 per cent in Manchester, with its diversified economy, 5.7 per cent in Barrow with its warship yard, and 2.1 per cent in the truck-building town of Leyland. At the other extreme were Westhoughton (27.4 per cent) and Hindley (38.5 per cent), both coal-mining centres, Wigan (cotton and coal) (21.5 per cent) and the cotton towns of Great Harwood (20.9 per cent) and Blackburn (19.6 per cent). Liverpool, too, with the

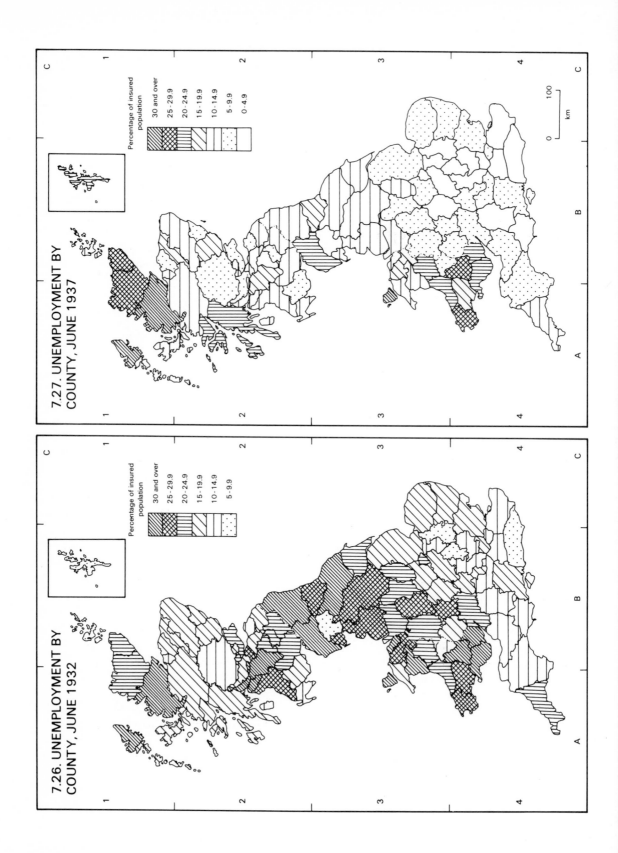

7.27. UNEMPLOYMENT BY
COUNTY, JUNE 1937

Percentage of insured
population

30 and over
25 - 29.9
20 - 24.9
15 - 19.9
10 - 14.9
5 - 9.9
0 - 4.9

0   100
km

7.26. UNEMPLOYMENT BY
COUNTY, JUNE 1932

Percentage of insured
population

30 and over
25 - 29.9
20 - 24.9
15 - 19.9
10 - 14.9
5 - 9.9

162

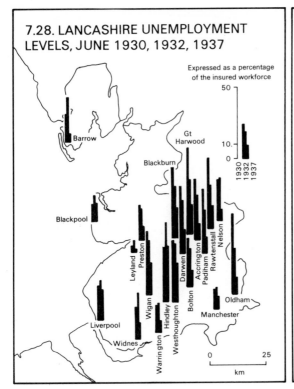

7.28. LANCASHIRE UNEMPLOYMENT LEVELS, JUNE 1930, 1932, 1937

Expressed as a percentage of the insured workforce

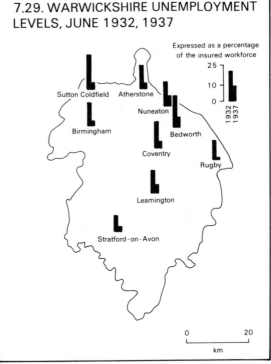

7.29. WARWICKSHIRE UNEMPLOYMENT LEVELS, JUNE 1932, 1937

Expressed as a percentage of the insured workforce

decline in trade, had an unemployment level of 20.9 per cent (Map 7.28).

The late 1930s saw some decline in economic activity but the coming of war, in particular mobilization under the coalition government from 1940, brought with it something close to full employment. By and large, low levels of unemployment were sustained in the twenty-five years that followed the war. This, though, was due more to world economic conditions than to either Keynesian policies of economic management or the regional policies (see below) of different governments. Though overall unemployment levels were at an historically low level, regional variation persisted on much the same pattern as before, with Scotland, Wales, and the North of England having levels in excess of twice those of the South-east of England (Map 7.30).

The 1970s and 1980s have seen a dramatic change in economic fortunes. Overseas competition in areas including textiles, motor vehicles, electrical and electronic goods and shipbuilding, along with a world glut in steel-making capacity, created acute structural unemployment. New technology and the deep slump of 1979–82 added to the number out of work. Map 7.31 shows that in October 1984 no county had a recorded unemployment level of below 5 per cent. Among those with under 10 per cent were Grampian (benefiting from North Sea Oil) and a band of counties in the south of England running from Suffolk to Hampshire and West Sussex. These gained from their good links to home and European centres of demand, their attractiveness to 'hi-tech' and service industries (in part a consequence of their prosperity), and their general lack of any previous commitment to those industries now in decline. Most other counties had unemployment levels in the range 10–19.9 per cent, the industrial West Midlands (with its declining motor vehicle and general metal-work and engineering industries) faring much worse than in the 1930s. Merseyside, with the further decline of the port and associated

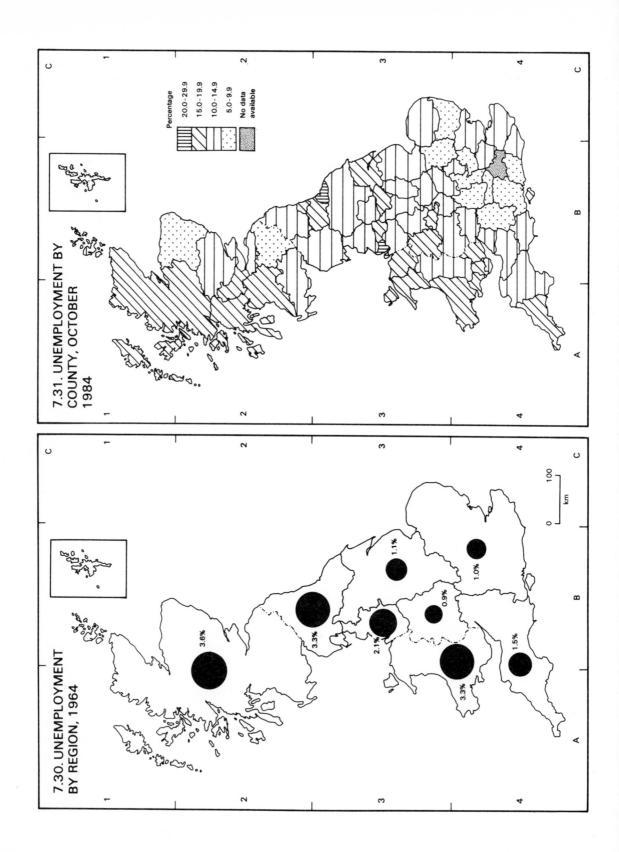

7.30. UNEMPLOYMENT
BY REGION, 1964

7.31. UNEMPLOYMENT BY
COUNTY, OCTOBER
1984

Percentage

20.0 - 29.9
15.0 - 19.9
10.0 - 14.9
5.0 - 9.9
No data
available

industry, and Cleveland, where the workforce of the iron and steel and chemical industries had sharply contracted, were the two worst affected mainland counties. While within counties and particularly in the inner cities there were pockets of more acute unemployment, overall the problem was more evenly spread across the country than it had been during the inter-war years.

Regional policy

Regional policies to combat unemployment have their origins in somewhat reluctant and ineffective action in the 1930s. In 1931 the government sponsored surveys by local universities in five areas associated with the traditional staple industries: the North-east coast, South-west Scotland, South Wales, Lancashire, and Merseyside. Collectively, since 1925 these areas had experienced unemployment levels that were consistently double those of the rest of the country. The surveys estimated that, even in a 'normal' year, the areas could expect 15 per cent of their insured workforce to remain unemployed. If anything, this was an underestimate.

Initially, the government did nothing. Then, in 1934, three of these areas (the North-east coast, South-west Scotland, and South Wales) were the subjects of further government investigation. So was West Cumberland which had been revealed as severely depressed in Jewkes' and Winterbottom's survey of 1933.[3] Lancashire and Merseyside were excluded from further investigation on the grounds that unemployment in those regions was less of a problem. The Special Areas (Development and Improvement) Act, covering parts of the areas investigated and appointing Commissioners for England and Wales, and for Scotland, followed.

The areas designated (see Map 7.32) were determined in an arbitrary and inconsistent way. The South Wales Special Area excluded the coastal strip including Newport, Barry, and Cardiff, coal-exporting ports and centres for the coal-mining villages of the valleys. Similarly Glasgow, which 'formed the centre of a single depressed area and shared its burdens to a very material extent',[4] was excluded from the South-west Scotland Special Area. By contrast, Newcastle-upon-Tyne was included in the North-east Coast Special Area though most of Northumberland, which had higher unemployment, was not.

Special Areas were intended as an experiment. There were restrictions on the Commissioners' activity and firm resistance by the government to any extension of the geographical area covered. At the outset, funds could not be allowed where other government grants were available or to profit-making ventures. In consequence, much of the £2 million initial fund went on public health measures, notably sewerage schemes. Experience, however, led to an extension of activities. In April 1936, the Special Areas Reconstruction Association was set up whereby Treasury loans of up to £10,000 were made available for small business enterprises in the Special Areas. Further assistance became available in December of the same year through a £2 million trust established by Lord Nuffield. The 1937 Special Areas Amendment Act allowed rent and tax allowances, and larger loans, and encouraged the establishment of trading estates. It also allowed, under strict conditions, loans to firms or site companies setting up in hard-hit districts outside the Special Areas, e.g. in the weaving district of north-east Lancashire.

Trading estates are, perhaps, the best-known outcome of the early Special Areas. The most advanced of these, Team Valley at Gateshead in the North-east, had 110 factories employing 3,700 people by July 1939. That sort of figure, along with the 5,000 or so settled on the land by September 1938, indicates the limited potential of this sort of activity in the face of a quarter of a million men unemployed in the Special Areas in 1935.

Another response was to encourage industrial transference, the movement of workers and, if necessary, their families, begun in mining districts in the late 1920s. Grants, loans, and training schemes were offered as incentives to move. For some areas, e.g. Cleator Moor in Cumberland or South-west Durham, this was seen as the only solution. As a method of reducing unemployment, however, it was of limited value. Transference, from all areas (not just or even mainly Special Areas), reached a peak in 1936. In that year, 28,000 adults, 15,400 juveniles, and 10,000 families were transferred. Thereafter, numbers fell off sharply. Not everyone was free or willing to move. Those that were included the young, the enterprising, or the skilled; their loss added to the hopelessness of the district they left. Indeed, transference was quite incompatible with a policy of seeking to attract industry.

Overall, in spite of the extension in activity, Special Areas policy could hardly be designated an unqualified success by 1939. Between 1935 and 1936, unemployment in the South Wales and Cumberland areas had actually risen whilst elsewhere in the country it was declining. Against that, it did rise less in the Special Areas than elsewhere during 1938. As the work of the commissioners began to bear fruit, 1936–8 saw an increasing gap between the number of factories opened in the areas and the number closed. Even so, the Special Areas' 17.1 per cent share of new factories opened in Great Britain in 1938 compared poorly with the 40.6 per cent claimed by Greater London. All the incentives, or pressure put on foreign investors to locate in the Special Areas, failed to offset the disadvantages of distance from markets, poor transport links or non-availability of semi-finished products essential to the fast-growing assembly industries. Further measures, as the 1940 *Report of the Royal Commission on the Distribution of the Industrial Population* recognized, would be required.

War temporarily removed the problem of the Special Areas. In 1945, however, a new Distribution of Industry Act reviewed the policy of regional planning and provided the basis of activity until 1960. The 'Development Areas', as they were now called, were expanded to include major towns previously excluded and an additional area around Dundee was recognized. The population of such areas increased from *c*.4 million to 6½ million. The Wrexham and Wigan–St Helens districts were added in 1946, Merseyside, a nucleus Highland zone incorporating Dingwall and Inverness, and North-east Lancashire in 1948 (see Map 7.33). Responsibility for the policy passed to the Board of Trade. Incentives offered were much as before, though with an initial emphasis on advance factory building and not tax, rent, or rate concessions. The continued existence of wartime building licences and the introduction of Industrial Development Certificates in the Town and Country Planning Act (1947), for new industrial premises of over 5,000 square feet, were further potential policy instruments.

Initially, regional policy was vigorously pursued: 51.1 per cent of all industrial building between 1945 and 1947 was in Development Areas. However, from 1947, when advance factory building was, for the time being, stopped, pressure on businessmen was reduced. By 1954, only 18.1 per cent of new factories were in such areas. The year 1954 also saw the end of building licences and, though Industrial Development Certificates continued, it was not difficult to establish premises in the Midlands or South-east. Regional policy had effectively lapsed because of a boom in the traditional coal-mining, steel, and shipbuilding industries and because unemployment levels in the Development Areas, while higher than elsewhere, were nevertheless low by historical standards. By the end of the 1950s, however, a slowing-up in overall economic growth rates and the uncompetitiveness of Britain's staple industries in increasingly tight markets brought renewed attention to regional issues.

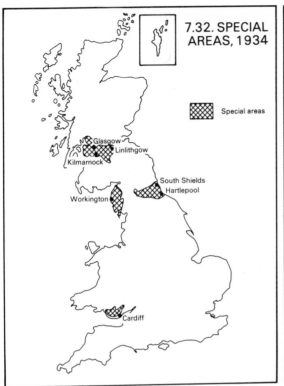

7.32. SPECIAL AREAS, 1934

Special areas

Glasgow
Linlithgow
Kilmarnock

Workington

South Shields
Hartlepool

Cardiff

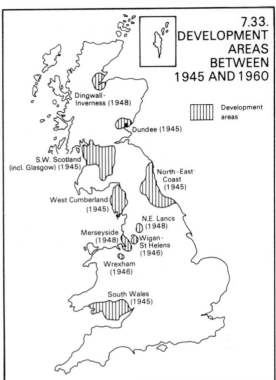

7.33. DEVELOPMENT AREAS BETWEEN 1945 AND 1960

Development areas

Dingwall - Inverness (1948)

Dundee (1945)

S.W. Scotland (incl. Glasgow) (1945)

North - East Coast (1945)

West Cumberland (1945)

N.E. Lancs (1948)

Merseyside (1948)

Wigan - St Helens (1946)

Wrexham (1946)

South Wales (1945)

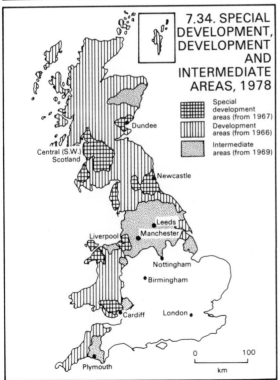

7.34. SPECIAL DEVELOPMENT, DEVELOPMENT AND INTERMEDIATE AREAS, 1978

Special development areas (from 1967)

Development areas (from 1966)

Intermediate areas (from 1969)

Dundee

Central (S.W.) Scotland

Newcastle

Leeds
Manchester

Liverpool

Nottingham

Birmingham

Cardiff

London

Plymouth

0   100
km

7.35. DEVELOPMENT AND INTERMEDIATE AREAS, 1984

Intermediate areas

Development areas

Glasgow

Newcastle

Bradford

Liverpool

Birmingham

Corby

Cardiff

London

After a hasty attempt to add to the Development Areas (1958), the Local Employment Act (1960) instituted a new phase in regional policy. Development Areas were abolished and a system of Development Districts adopted. In general, these were Employment Exchange Districts where 4½ per cent of the workforce was unemployed. Building grants were now made available as was a facility for 'accelerated depreciation' – effectively allowing a firm to defer tax payments. Advance factories had been re-started in 1959. Many rural areas were included, particularly in Britain's Celtic fringe. The use of the 4½ per cent threshold had, however, two distinct disadvantages. Industrialists could not plan investment on the assumption that Development District status, and the attendant incentives, would be maintained. More important, such status was only achieved by unemployment blackspots, the least-favoured areas economically. The concepts of 'travel-to-work areas' or focal points for expansion were ignored. More economically sound were the arrangements for Central Scotland and the North-east of England (1963), two areas beginning to show signs of the inter-war structural problem, where growth points were designated and continuity of status assured.

A potentially sounder policy was instituted by the Labour government in 1966. Large Development Areas including all of Scotland (except Edinburgh), the North, most of Wales and much of the South-west were instituted. Development Area status was not tied to a given level of unemployment, hence there was scope for industrial planning. However, the rationale of the system was undermined by the further creation, in 1967, of Special Development Areas. These were based on declining coal-mining districts and there were additional incentives to lure companies to them. In 1969, Intermediate Areas were created. Thus, in the 1970s, areas occupied by 42–43 per cent of Britain's population were receiving some form of assistance (see Map 7.34). Spending on regional policy rose, meantime, from £34 million (at 1975 prices) in 1960/61 to £661 million in 1975/6.

Industrial Development Certificates were used as instruments of regional policy by both Conservative and Labour governments in the 1960s and early 1970s. So, too, were controls on office development. Regional Employment Premiums were introduced from 1967. To these must be added aid to particular ailing industries (as under the Industry Act, 1972) and attention to infrastructure. The cumulative effect of the different measures was a sizeable shift of investment and jobs (perhaps 350,000 between 1965 and 1980) to the assisted areas. This, though, was at high cost and only marginally affected regional economic imbalance. Moreover the policies were associated with preserving an ossified employment structure in the assisted regions (e.g. in shipbuilding), with paying too little attention to the geographical relocation of labour rather than industry, and with contributing to low productivity and general diseconomies resulting from split operations (e.g. in motor vehicle manufacture).

Deteriorating general economic conditions in the late 1970s demonstrated the frailty of many of the firms or plant established in the assisted areas. Attention also shifted away from regional policy. The Conservative government, from 1979, instituted a sharp reduction in regional support – reducing expenditure immediately to just over £300 million and cutting down on the areas eligible for assistance (see Map 7.35).

Notes

1. See G. R. Porter, *Progress of the Nation*, vol. 1 (1836).
2. The modern names for Scottish counties (e.g. Angus rather than Forfarshire) are used throughout.
3. J. Jewkes and A. Winterbottom, *An Industrial Survey of West Cumberland* (Manchester, 1933).
4. *Reports of Investigations into Industrial Conditions of Certain Depressed Areas: IV – Scotland*, Cmd. 4728 (1934), p. 232.

Maps 7.1–7.4 and 7.14–7.17 are based on the *Census* of 1851; 7.5–7.9 and 7.19–7.22 on the *Census* of 1911, and 7.10–7.13 and 7.23–7.25 on the *Census* of 1971. The data for Map 7.18 is to be found in Board of Trade Labour Dept., *Report by Miss Collet on the Statistics of Employment of Women and Girls*, C. 7564, BPP 1894, LXXXI, Pt 2. The material for Maps 7.26–7.29 can be found in the Ministry of Labour's *Local Unemployment Index* for June 1930, 1932, and 1937. Map 7.30 is based on figures contained in the Department of Employment's *British Labour Statistics, Historical Abstract 1886–1968* (London, 1971), p. 329, and Map. 7.31 is reproduced by permission of the Controller of Her Majesty's Stationery Office from *Regional Trends*, no. 20 (London, 1985). Maps on 'Special' or Development Areas (7.32–7.35) are based on material in S. R. Dennison, *The Location of Industry and the Depressed Areas* (London, 1939), G. McCrone, *Regional Policy in Britain* (London, 1969), D. Maclennan and J. B. Parr (eds), *Regional Policy: Past Experience and New Directions* (London, 1979), and *Regional Trends*, no. 22, (London, 1987).

Particular thanks are due to Matthew and Branca Pope for their work in converting census figures into percentages.

8 URBANIZATION AND LIVING CONDITIONS
Callum Brown

The industrial revolution produced exceptionally rapid changes in the location and living conditions of the British people. Population became increasingly concentrated in towns and cities, and acute social and health problems emerged. Whilst the urbanization of the British people ended early in the twentieth century, changes in the urban map of the country have continued. This has helped to ease many urban problems, but, as this section shows, conditions in the countryside have often been slower to improve.

Urban growth

Before the nineteenth century, Britain's city society was by international comparison rather underdeveloped. With the exception of London, which had a population of over a million in 1801, the rest of urban Britain was composed of a series of small market towns and ports, the largest of which before 1750 was Norwich. There was nothing to compare with the large provincial centres of the continent like Lyons and Marseilles in France, nor with the relatively urbanized societies of Northern Italy and the Low Countries. Britain was one of the least urban-centred societies, having no cities in the middle range of size (between small commercial centre and giant metropolis). Consequently, there was little experience in Britain of urban living, problems, and government as there was in Europe where cities had already started – however ineffectively – tackling issues like urban renewal and the control of street layout. In this way, Britain was in many respects the least prepared for rapid urbanization.

In 1801 (Map 8.1) there were only seven cities in Britain in which the number of people exceeded 50,000, and Greater London with 1.1 million inhabitants was more than twice the size of the other six put together. Of the six, Edinburgh was a former capital, playing host until 1707 to the Scots parliament, and remaining thereafter a major legal and ecclesiastical centre. The other cities were based on more recent and commercial foundations. Birmingham was developing a distinctive economy of workshop metal trades; Manchester and Glasgow were the principal centres of the cotton industry; whilst Glasgow along with Liverpool and Bristol had developed during the eighteenth century as Atlantic trading ports. From being modest towns of around 10,000 people in 1700, Glasgow, Manchester, and Liverpool had grown within a hundred years to upwards of 70,000, and were to remain the frontrunners during the early stages of British industrial urbanization.

By 1851, (Map 8.2), not only were those three cities much expanded (with populations of 316,000 to 376,000), but clusters of industrial towns and villages had sprung up around them. In southern Lancashire significant industrial communities like Bolton, Oldham,

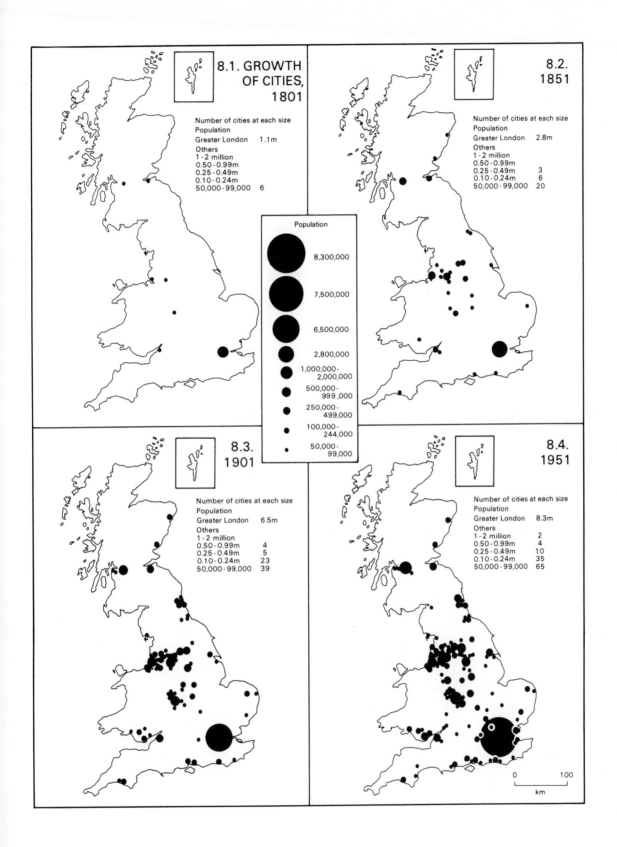

8.1. GROWTH OF CITIES, 1801

Number of cities at each size
Population
Greater London   1.1m
Others
1 - 2 million
0.50 - 0.99m
0.25 - 0.49m
0.10 - 0.24m
50,000 - 99,000   6

8.2. 1851

Number of cities at each size
Population
Greater London   2.8m
Others
1 - 2 million
0.50 - 0.99m
0.25 - 0.49m   3
0.10 - 0.24m   6
50,000 - 99,000   20

Population
8,300,000
7,500,000
6,500,000
2,800,000
1,000,000 - 2,000,000
500,000 - 999,000
250,000 - 499,000
100,000 - 244,000
50,000 - 99,000

8.3. 1901

Number of cities at each size
Population
Greater London   6.5m
Others
1 - 2 million
0.50 - 0.99m   4
0.25 - 0.49m   5
0.10 - 0.24m   23
50,000 - 99,000   39

8.4. 1951

Number of cities at each size
Population
Greater London   8.3m
Others
1 - 2 million   2
0.50 - 0.99m   4
0.25 - 0.49m   10
0.10 - 0.24m   35
50,000 - 99,000   65

0   100
km

171

Preston, and Salford emerged to emphasize the county's pre-eminence in the economic life of the nation. It was generally the textile industries which promoted the provincial urban growth of the first half of the nineteenth century. Outside the main textile counties of Lancashire, Cheshire, West Yorkshire, and Lanarkshire, urbanization was geographically more sporadic: the east-coast port of Hull, the spa town of Bath, the naval ports of Plymouth and Portsmouth, and the east-coast Scottish cities of Dundee and Aberdeen. Regions like Tyneside and Wearside, and South Wales, were little developed in 1851, but they urbanized rapidly in the second half of the nineteenth century with the rise of heavy industries like shipbuilding, coal, and iron. Whilst sporadic urban centres still appeared (such as the shipbuilding community of Barrow in the northwest corner of Lancashire), the trend to clustering (or 'conurbations') was sustained with nearly twenty cities of over 50,000 people in the Liverpool–Manchester region, with Birmingham forming the focus for a much smaller though rising cluster of some nine cities, and with smaller zones of urban development such as that of Leeds and Bradford (see Map 8.3).

At the beginning of the twentieth century the great process of urbanizing the British people was ending. In 1911 four-fifths of the population lived in cities, and that proportion has remained roughly constant since then. The urban experience of twentieth-century Britain has not, however, been without profound change. For example, there have been significant movements in the *location* of urban population. Between 1901 and 1951 the large industrial cities of Glasgow, Liverpool, and Manchester barely grew at all, but their satellite towns mushroomed. In the 100 miles between Birkenhead and Leeds, there were by the middle of the present century three cities with over half-a-million inhabitants each, one of 292,000, ten of between 100,000 and 250,000, and thirteen of 50,000–100,000 (Map 8.4). Within the traditional industrial

regions, population was being redistributed from large cities to small ones.

This trend could be seen in almost every region. The Birmingham urban area was growing steadily, but significantly there was a movement towards sporadic urban growth in the southern half of England. With the advent of a national grid in the 1930s, electricity freed modern (and especially consumer) industries from dependence upon the coal-mining regions, permitting a significant shift towards smaller towns and greenfield sites in the South where workers could enjoy higher standards of environmental amenity and firms could gain easy access to the London market. Thus, old and often medieval towns which had changed remarkably little for centuries became the centres for new factories, housing estates, and in-migration of workers from the northern industrial regions. The university towns of Cambridge and Oxford doubled in size between 1901 and 1951, whilst the newer community at Luton tripled. One of the most spectacular growth rates was achieved by Coventry in the West Midlands where the population rose from 70,000 to 258,000. London continued its seemingly inexorable expansion, attracting migrants, as it always had done, from all parts of the country, swelling its population to nearly 8.5 million. Seaside resorts grew dramatically as their infrastructures became increasingly geared to residential holiday-makers rather than day-trippers. Blackpool, with a mere 3,000 inhabitants in 1851, reached 147,000 a century later, whilst Southend-on-Sea rose from virtually nothing in the mid-nineteenth century to 152,000 in 1951, doubling in size every decade in the first half of the present century. Overall, the economic power of the country was drifting southwards, relocating urban growth away from the traditional industrial areas.

This trend accelerated after 1950 when the population of most major cities started to decline. The Second World War gave rise to a massive state-sponsored programme to ease inner-city congestion. Schemes of comprehensive urban planning were drawn up for the first

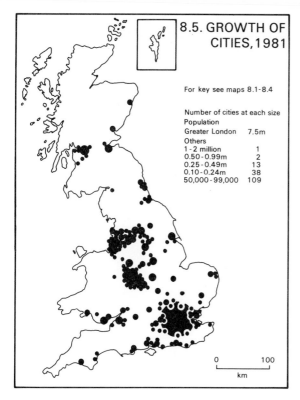

8.5. GROWTH OF CITIES, 1981

For key see maps 8.1-8.4

Number of cities at each size
Population

Greater London	7.5m
Others	
1 - 2 million	1
0.50 - 0.99m	2
0.25 - 0.49m	13
0.10 - 0.24m	38
50,000 - 99,000	109

0   100
km

time, including the demarcation of 'green belts' around large cities in which the erection of buildings was to be practically banned, and the 'overspilling' of urban population to new and expanded satellite towns. Between 1951 and 1981 (Map 8.5), the number of towns in the population range 50,000–100,000 increased from 65 to 109. Although overspill was very important to the industrial cities of the North like Glasgow, Manchester, and Liverpool, the most dramatic impact was felt in the Midlands, the London region and the south coast.

At the same time as small cities expanded (including those between 25,000 and 50,000 people), the number of cities with over 500,000 population halved during the period 1951–81 from six to three. The population of Liverpool dropped from 789,000 to 539,000; that of Manchester from 703,000 to 438,000, and that of Glasgow from 1,090,000 to 755,000. Of the provincial giants, only Birmingham stayed relatively buoyant, falling from 1,113,000 to

1,014,000. But government decentralization of urban population was not confined to cities with ailing economies; London's population fell by almost a million in thirty years. By the early 1970s, the policies of planners were appearing too successful, leaving depopulated and run-down inner-city areas in which conditions of life for remaining residents (often Blacks and Asians) were deteriorating at the same rate as the Victorian housing stock. As a result, the policy of overspill was put in reverse with the creation of inner-city development schemes which in the late 1980s are starting to bear fruit. Central and dockland districts of large cities are being renovated to encourage the return of working-class families from peripheral housing estates, though in some instances (such as London and Glasgow) precedence may be going to gentrified 'merchant cities' inhabited by the upwardly-mobile young.

A significant by-product of overspill policy was the creation of the British new towns (Map 8.6). Twenty-eight were designated by the government between 1946 and 1970 – with two main objectives. The great majority were designed to receive decanted population from existing large cities like London, Manchester, Liverpool, Glasgow, and Newcastle; thus, many new towns were to assist in solving the housing crisis. But in other cases, new towns were created to act as centres of economic regeneration in regions suffering badly from the decline of the old staple industries. Many involved designating existing communities: as with medieval towns like Peterborough, or with decaying industrial towns like Preston, Leyland, and Chorley which were collectively made Central Lancashire New Town in 1970. In the case of Newtown (Mid Wales), a small community was established in an isolated area in order to stem rural depopulation.

The new towns have had mixed fortunes. Some have flourished, like Milton Keynes where the pressure of expansion has not relented. But some have merely decanted chronic housing and unemployment problems from old large cities to new small ones;

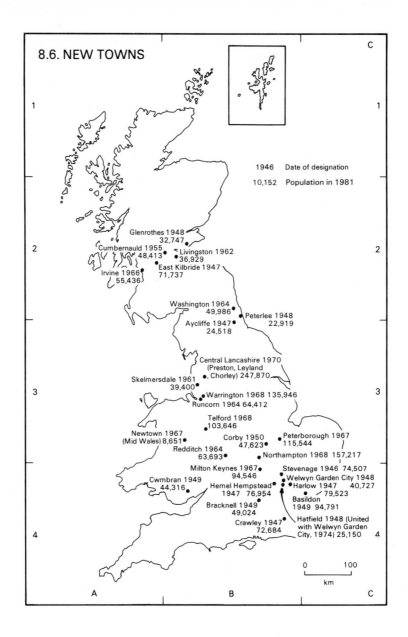

8.6. NEW TOWNS

1946   Date of designation

10,152   Population in 1981

Glenrothes 1948
32,747

Cumbernauld 1955   Livingston 1962
48,413   36,929

Irvine 1966   East Kilbride 1947
55,436   71,737

Washington 1964
49,986   Peterlee 1948
Aycliffe 1947   22,919
24,518

Central Lancashire 1970
(Preston, Leyland
, Chorley) 247,870
Skelmersdale 1961
39,400   Warrington 1968 135,946
Runcorn 1964 64,412

Telford 1968
103,646

Newtown 1967   Corby 1950   Peterborough 1967
(Mid Wales) 8,651   47,623   115,544
Redditch 1964   Northampton 1968 157,217
63,693

Milton Keynes 1967   Stevenage 1946 74,507
94,546   Welwyn Garden City 1948
Cwmbran 1949   Harlow 1947   40,727
44,316   Hemel Hempstead   79,523
1947 76,954   Basildon
Bracknell 1949   1949 94,791
49,024
Crawley 1947   Hatfield 1948 (United
72,684   with Welwyn Garden
City, 1974) 25,150

0   100

km

Skelmersdale in Lancashire, for example, has replicated some of the worst features of Liverpool. As overspill policy has been reversed in the 1970s, so new-town growth has been slowed down. By 1980, less than 4 per cent of the total British population lived in areas designated as new towns.

The problems of the older cities stemmed very much from the rapidity of their early growth and the characteristic way in which increasing population was housed within small areas. Map 8.7 shows the physical growth of the built-up area of Glasgow after 1700. Glasgow was not untypical in its experience, growing from around 12,000 inhabitants in 1700 to 77,000 in 1800, reaching 762,000 in 1900 and just over a million in 1911–51. As in Liverpool and Manchester, the height of population growth was reached in Glasgow between 1780 and 1910, yet spatial growth was

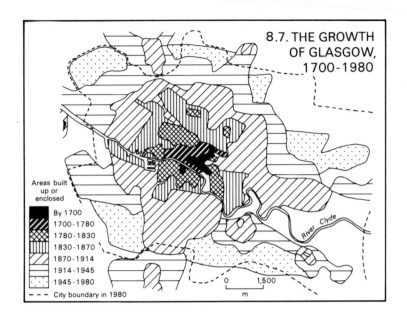

constricted. This resulted in part from the general absence before the 1880s of the technology to provide cheap transportation. Urban areas had to be 'walking cities' to enable the bulk of the population – the working classes – to reach their place of work fairly easily. The main spatial expansion took place within a later time-span – between 1870 and 1945. The advent of tramways facilitated large-scale middle-class suburbanization to commence in 1870–1914 – a process that was quickened in most cities (especially in the south of England) in the late 1920s and 1930s.

But of importance to urban expansion after 1920 was subsidized council housing. Between 1919 and 1965, 41 per cent of dwellings built in England and Wales, and 87 per cent of those in Scotland, were owned and rented out by local authorities. By 1981, 30 per cent of the total housing stock in Britain (including houses built before 1919) was rented out by public agencies, but in Glasgow, where the housing crisis was most intractable, the figure rose to 70 per cent. In this way, the state's social policy objectives came to have a major impact upon the spatial configuration of the modern city. In Glasgow's case, four massive council estates (of up to 50,000 inhabitants each) consumed much of the territory built up between 1945 and 1980. Though these estates were larger than many new towns, the failure to provide comprehensive amenities (none of Glasgow's housing estates had public houses before 1970), and to integrate local sources of employment, helped to create dismal and isolated lives for those deprived by slum clearance of the warmth and friendship of older, inner-city working-class communities.

Housing conditions

The slow spatial growth of industrial cities before the last quarter of the nineteenth century was a major cause of social problems. Instead of the housing expanding at the same rate as population grew, landlords made ready profits by cramming extra families into existing houses, or by subdividing houses. The latter practice reached its height in Scotland where the prevalent tenemental style of housing allowed the 'making-down' of three-

175

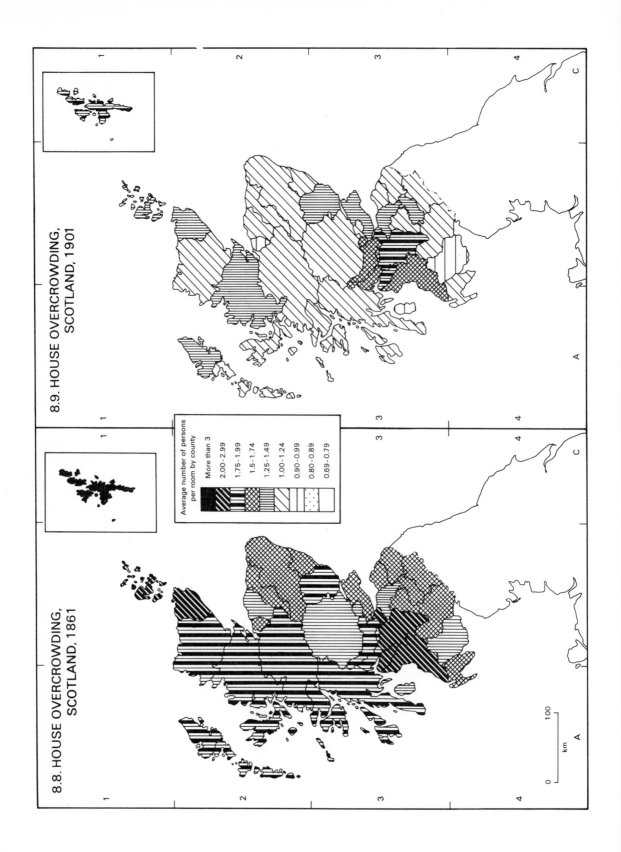

8.9. HOUSE OVERCROWDING, SCOTLAND, 1901

8.8. HOUSE OVERCROWDING, SCOTLAND, 1861

Average number of persons
per room by county

More than 3
2.00 - 2.99
1.75 - 1.99
1.5 - 1.74
1.25 - 1.49
1.00 - 1.24
0.90 - 0.99
0.80 - 0.89
0.69 - 0.79

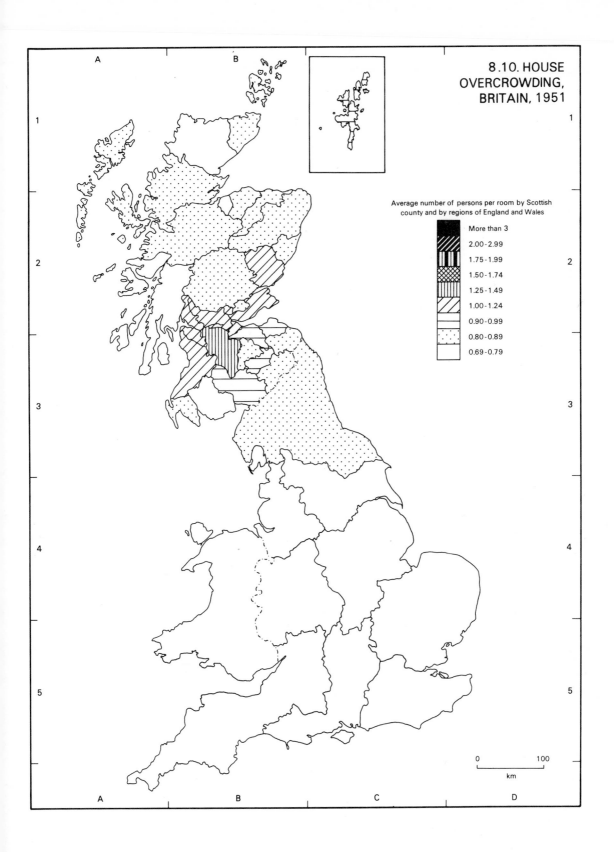

8.10. HOUSE
OVERCROWDING,
BRITAIN, 1951

Average number of persons per room by Scottish
county and by regions of England and Wales

More than 3
2.00 - 2.99
1.75 - 1.99
1.50 - 1.74
1.25 - 1.49
1.00 - 1.24
0.90 - 0.99
0.80 - 0.89
0.69 - 0.79

0   100
km

and four-roomed flats into one- and two-roomed ones. By 1901, 26 per cent of Glasgow families lived in one-roomed houses and a further 44 per cent lived in two-roomed houses. Maps 8.8–8.10 show the extent of overcrowding in Scotland in 1861–1901, and its sustained severity in 1951 compared to the rest of Britain. Glasgow contained the most overcrowded houses of any major city. In 1891, 59 per cent of families lived more than two persons to a room compared to 35 per cent in Newcastle, 10 per cent in Liverpool and 8 per cent in Manchester. But the position was worse in the smaller Scottish towns and some rural areas. The average number of persons per room (p.p.r.) stood at 2.04 in Glasgow in 1861 when it was 2.68 in Coatbridge and 2.76 in Rutherglen (both nearby towns), and 2.11 in the northern county of Caithness and 3.18 in the Shetland Islands.

Forty years later, as Map 8.9 shows, overcrowding was easing somewhat overall, though it worsened or remained static until the 1920s in industrial towns like Falkirk, Greenock, and Port Glasgow. While the level of overcrowding halved in most Scottish towns between 1861 and 1951, the heritage of 'made-down' tenement flats still left the Scottish home smaller and more overpopulated than anywhere in Britain. As Map 8.10 shows, the p.p.r. of 0.84 for the northern region of England was comparatively high, but neither it nor the figure of 0.74 for England and Wales as a whole compared to Scotland's average of 1.05.

The nature of the problems afflicting the domestic environment differed in other parts of Britain. Maps 8.11–8.14 show the shortage of basic conveniences in 1951. By two of these measures (piped water and WCs), houses in England and Wales were deficient in comparison to Scotland (Maps 8.11–8.13). Homes in rural areas of England and Wales were particularly badly equipped, more than a fifth lacking piped water supply, and more than a third lacking WCs. East Anglia and to a lesser extent Wales were the most deficient regions south of the Tweed, whilst homes in the South-east and the industrial counties of Lancashire and Yorkshire were comparatively well equipped with these necessities. But even houses in the conurbations of England and Wales were not as well provided as those in the larger Scottish cities. Indeed, provision of these facilities was exceptionally good in Scotland, especially in industrial counties like Lanarkshire and Renfrewshire, though it worsened appreciably in the rural areas, reaching a peak in the northern crofting counties and in Orkney and Shetland.

Cooking facilities (Map 8.12) were generally more common than other appliances, though deficiency was relatively high in Wales and rural areas of Scotland. The most stark shortage was of fixed baths (Map 8.14). In England, cities were generally better provided than rural areas, but in Scotland the position was poor. Fifty per cent of homes in Glasgow lacked this amenity, but by far the worst shortage existed in the Northern Isles with figures of 70 and 72 per cent in Orkney and Shetland respectively. However, it is instructive to remember that even as late as 1951, 30 per cent of homes in the relatively affluent London and the South-east lacked baths.

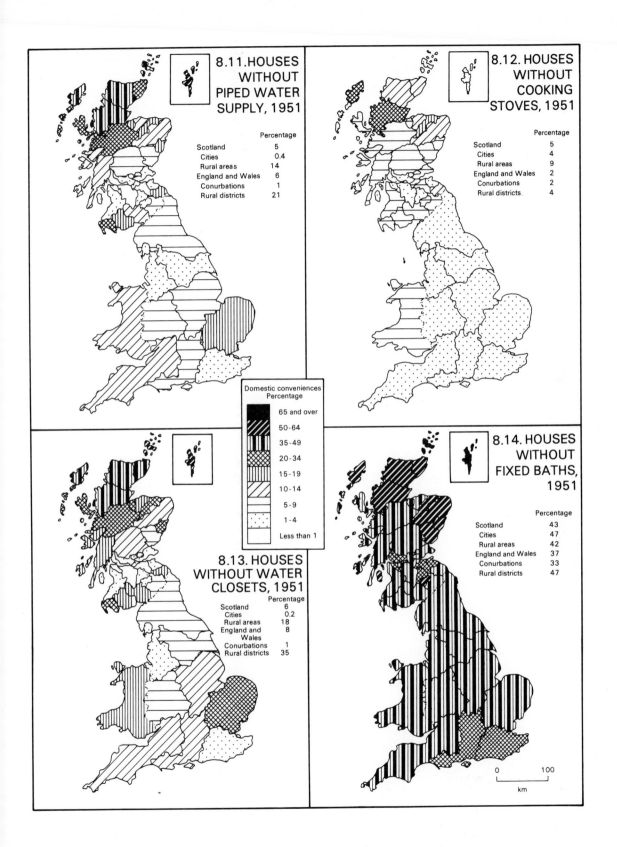

8.11. HOUSES WITHOUT PIPED WATER SUPPLY, 1951

	Percentage
Scotland	5
Cities	0.4
Rural areas	14
England and Wales	6
Conurbations	1
Rural districts	21

8.12. HOUSES WITHOUT COOKING STOVES, 1951

	Percentage
Scotland	5
Cities	4
Rural areas	9
England and Wales	2
Conurbations	2
Rural districts	4

Domestic conveniences Percentage

65 and over
50-64
35-49
20-34
15-19
10-14
5-9
1-4
Less than 1

8.13. HOUSES WITHOUT WATER CLOSETS, 1951

	Percentage
Scotland	6
Cities	0.2
Rural areas	18
England and Wales	8
Conurbations	1
Rural districts	35

8.14. HOUSES WITHOUT FIXED BATHS, 1951

	Percentage
Scotland	43
Cities	47
Rural areas	42
England and Wales	37
Conurbations	33
Rural districts	47

0   100
km

Health

Whilst conditions of housing and domestic equipment were undoubtedly slower to improve in rural areas after 1900, life was usually more unhealthy in cities than in the countryside. There is no single measure of health, but Maps 8.15–8.19 display one of the most revealing. Infant mortality rate (i.m.r.) records the number of children that die during the first year of life. Until the 1920s, when medical clinics for mothers and young children started to appear, infancy accounted for a significant proportion of all deaths. In such circumstances, i.m.r. provides a good gauge of the combined effects of living conditions, diet, and general health upon child-rearing women and their offspring. Even after the 1920s, strong regional patterns of i.m.r. were not completely eroded by differential regional and social access to, and take-up of, the new neonatal and post-natal medical services.

Taken together, the maps from 1841 to 1951 indicate a northward drift in the location of the areas of high infant mortality. In 1841 (Map 8.15), high levels of i.m.r. were spread over a wide area, focused on the centre of England but reaching south to London, north to Northumberland, east to Norfolk and west to Monmouth. Counties with in excess of 170 infant deaths per 1,000 live births were geographically and economically diverse: Cambridgeshire (175.0), Lancashire (177.8) and the East Riding of Yorkshire (184.4). But they enclosed practically all of central England where the rate for most counties was over 140.

By 1872 (Map 8.16), by which time data on Scotland had become available, the areas of high infant mortality were radiating out from the Home Counties. London (158.2) remained bad, but rates were diminishing fairly rapidly in counties like Gloucestershire and Hertfordshire, and Cambridgeshire's i.m.r. had dropped markedly to 140. By the same token, the position in the industrial periphery was deteriorating as industrial and urban congestion deepened and spread. Whilst Monmouth improved, the position was

worsening in 1841–72 in North Wales (the rate rising from 113 to 121) and South Wales (115–129), in the tin-mining county of Cornwall (101–148), and in the industrial parts of the Midlands and North, where Durham (156–179) and Leicestershire (151–186) emerged as the least healthy counties in which to give birth. In Scotland, infant death rates were (and remained for many decades) markedly better; whilst the English average was 150 in 1872, it was only 124 in Scotland, with the majority of rural counties recording rates of under 100 (Orkney's was 42).

The process was continuing in 1901 (Map 8.17); rural counties throughout Britain were generally improving whilst many of the main industrial counties were experiencing a very deep crisis. The rate rose to over 170 in South Wales, remained unchanged at 179 in Durham, and rose from 158 to 182 to propel Northumberland to the status of the worst British county. But while the English average i.m.r. climbed in the late nineteenth century to reach its all-time peak of 163 in 1899, Scotland's rate was falling (to 131 in that year) with most industrial areas improving (except notably the expanding mining counties of Fife and West Lothian).

There have been major changes in infant mortality during this century. On the one hand there has been an enormous improvement throughout Britain which year-by-year statistics indicate occurred particularly during the 1940s (when rates in many counties halved); by 1951, i.m.r. had fallen to 30 in England and Wales, overtaking Scotland at 37. Thirty years later, in 1980, rates had fallen to around 12 for practically all of Britain. Clearly, the provision of medical facilities has had an enormous bearing. Improvement occurred especially during the Second World War and immediately after it in the late 1940s with the formation of the National Health Service and the integrated welfare state.

Infant mortality becomes less useful as a

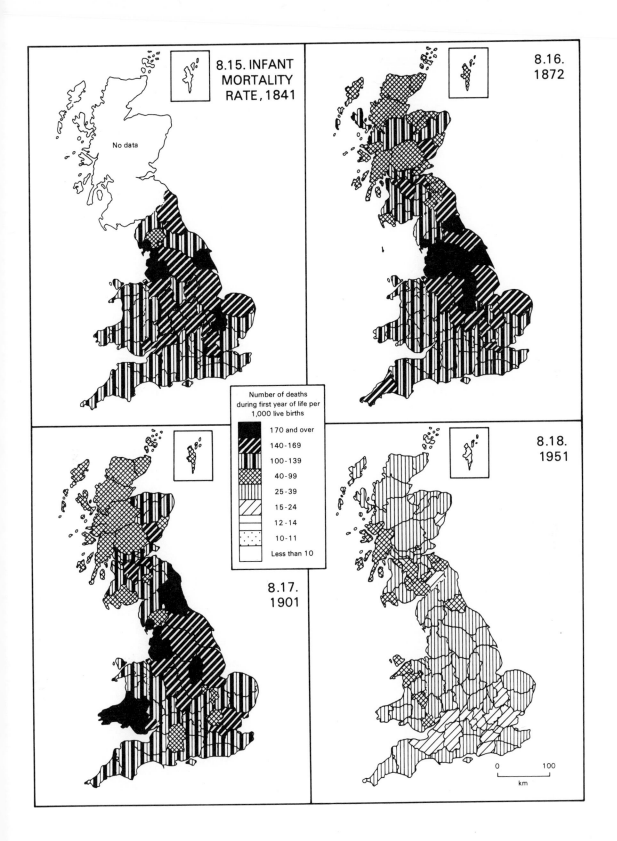

8.15. INFANT MORTALITY RATE, 1841

No data

8.16. 1872

8.17. 1901

8.18. 1951

Number of deaths during first year of life per 1,000 live births

170 and over
140 - 169
100 - 139
40 - 99
25 - 39
15 - 24
12 - 14
10 - 11
Less than 10

0   100
km

181

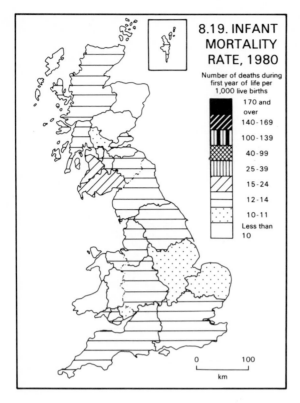

8.19. INFANT MORTALITY RATE, 1980

Number of deaths during first year of life per 1,000 live births

170 and over
140 - 169
100 - 139
40 - 99
25 - 39
15 - 24
12 - 14
10 - 11
Less than 10

0   100
km

guide to general health as we move through the century, yet the regional patterns established last century were still perceptible in 1951 (Map 8.18). The lowest rates of infant death were to be found in the agricultural counties stretching from the Severn estuary to East Anglia. London with a rate of 24 had advanced further than most other urban or industrial areas like Lancashire (34), Northumberland (34), Yorkshire's East Riding (39), Co. Durham (41), and Lanarkshire (45). Still higher rates were to be found in some rural counties – Radnor 48, Anglesey 55, Wigtownshire 51, and Berwickshire 55 – suggesting that improvements in medical provision were slow to penetrate outlying areas. By the 1970s and 1980s, regional variation has become very small (Map 8.19), and where it occurs local health authorities tend to react swiftly with increased medical provision.

Notes

Maps 8.1–8.5 are based on material from B. R. Mitchell and P. Deane, *Abstract of British Historical Statistics* (Cambridge, 1962), pp. 24–7; *Census of Great Britain, 1851: Population Tables*, vol. 1.1, pp. cciv–ccvii; *Census of England and Wales 1901: Preliminary Report*, pp. 21–41; *Census of Scotland 1901: Preliminary Report*, vol. 1, pp. 40–4; *Census of England and Wales 1951: Preliminary Report*, pp. 45–7; *Census of Scotland 1951: Preliminary Report*, pp. 43–4; *Census 1981: Key Statistics for Urban Areas: Great Britain*, pp. 8–11 (definitions), 22–38. Map 8.6 uses material from M. Aldridge, *The British New Towns: A Programme without a Policy* (London, 1979); *Census 1981:*

New Towns Report, England and Wales, Pt 1, pp. 3–4; *Census 1981, Scotland: New Towns*, vol. 1, p. 2. Maps 8.8–8.14 use data from the *Census 1951 England and Wales: Housing Report*, pp. 12–22 and 58–63, and the *Census 1951 Scotland*, vol. 2, pp. 72–4 and 108–11. Maps 8.15–8.19 are based on data in, or calculated from, the *Registrar-General's Annual Reports (England and Wales)*, 1841, 1872, 1901; *Registrar-General (Scotland) Annual Reports*, 1872, 1901, 1951, 1981; *Registrar-General's Statistical Review of England and Wales 1951*, text volume, pp. 62–111; *Local Authority Vital Statistics*, ser. US no. 7, pp. 30–5.

9 LABOUR MOVEMENTS
Keith Laybourn

Luddism 1811–17 and Luddism in Yorkshire 1812–13

Machine-wrecking was by no means uncommon throughout the eighteenth century, but came to a head in Yorkshire, Nottinghamshire, Derbyshire, and Lancashire between 1812 and 1813 (see Map 9.1). The starting-point was a set of disturbances in Nottingham, in March 1811. A demonstration of stockingers was dispersed by the military; as a result sixty stocking-frames were broken at the large village of Arnold. This was followed by several weeks of disturbances, mainly at night, throughout the hosiery villages of north-west Nottinghamshire. Although the stockingers or hosiers did obtain some improvements in pay, Luddism declined in 1812; the movement was revived on several occasions, and did not entirely disappear until early 1817.

The events in Nottinghamshire, which had spread over into Derbyshire, stimulated similar activity in Lancashire and Yorkshire. Lancashire cotton weavers began to form secret committees in early 1812 to help secure improved wages after several years of agitating and petitioning for a minimum wage. For a few weeks they resorted to machine-wrecking activities. They attacked the Stockport warehouse of William Ratcliffe, one of the first

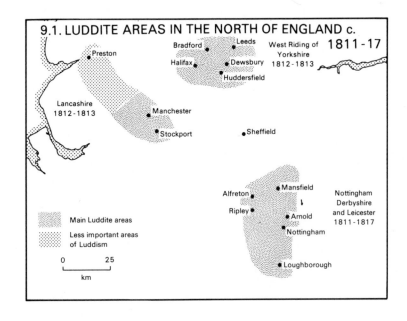

9.1. LUDDITE AREAS IN THE NORTH OF ENGLAND c. 1811-17

West Riding of Yorkshire 1812-1813

Lancashire 1812-1813

Nottingham Derbyshire and Leicester 1811-1817

Main Luddite areas

Less important areas of Luddism

0   25
km

manufacturers to use the powerloom, on 20 March. But these Luddites were the new expanding working-class of the industrial revolution, not the declining and threatened traditional workforce, and machine-wrecking soon died out in Lancashire giving way to politically inspired demonstrations – as occurred at the Manchester Exchange on 8 April. Indeed, Lancashire machine-wrecking reached its climax on 20 April with the attack upon Daniel Burton's powerloom mill at Middleton – which saw the death of at least seven Luddites. Thereafter, the Lancashire Luddites appear to have been divided between groups prepared to petition Parliament and others who may have been preparing for insurrection.

In Yorkshire, the main reason for the rise of Luddism was economic: shearing men, or croppers, were being put out of work by the introduction of the shearing-gig machinery. The traditional skills of cropping, a process in the finishing of wool pieces whereby the nap of the cloth was raised by teazels and then cropped with large cropping shears, were being challenged. Initially the croppers, and the cottage weavers who were worried by allied trends, petitioned Parliament to prevent the introduction of the new machinery which was strictly illegal under ancient legislation. Indeed, a Select Committee of the House of Commons was set up to examine the conditions of the wool trade and took evidence between 1803 and 1806. However, it concluded that the new machinery and factory production presented no threat to existing skills and that the new innovations should be allowed. As a result new machinery was introduced and the 3,000 to 5,000 Yorkshire croppers took to machine-smashing and murderous activities as a last resort.

The Yorkshire map (9.2) indicates the major Luddite attacks which occurred in the Yorkshire textile district. As you will note,

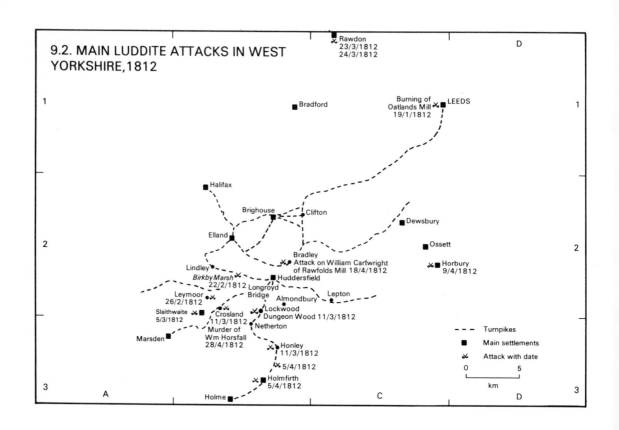

9.2. MAIN LUDDITE ATTACKS IN WEST YORKSHIRE, 1812

Rawdon
23/3/1812
24/3/1812

D

Bradford

Burning of
Oatlands Mill LEEDS
19/1/1812

Halifax

Brighouse   Clifton

Dewsbury

Elland

Ossett

Bradley
Attack on William Cartwright
of Rawfolds Mill 18/4/1812

Horbury
9/4/1812

Lindley
Birkby Marsh
22/2/1812   Longroyd
Bridge
Leymoor
26/2/1812
Slaithwaite
5/3/1812

Huddersfield

Lepton
Almondbury
Lockwood
Crosland
11/3/1812   Dungeon Wood 11/3/1812
Murder of   Netherton
Wm Horsfall
28/4/1812

Marsden

Honley
11/3/1812
5/4/1812

Holmfirth
5/4/1812

Holme

Turnpikes

Main settlements

Attack with date

0   5

km

Huddersfield was the centre of activities. Indeed, it was John Wood's finishing shop at Longroyd Bridge, Huddersfield, which was the headquarters of Luddite activity, for it employed George Mellor, William Thorpe, Thomas Smith, and Benjamin Walker – the leading activists.

The Yorkshire Luddite movement went through a number of phases. In January 1812 there was a spontaneous attack upon Oatlands' Mill, Leeds. This was followed by a spate of more organized attacks upon isolated workshops, mainly in the Huddersfield area, during February, March, and early April 1812. Later, the machine-breaking reached its climax with attacks upon two Liversedge Mills. With the failure of the second attack, during which two Luddites were killed, Luddism practically came to an end in Yorkshire. At this stage, threats were made to the mill owners who employed the new machinery. William Cartwright, the owner of Rawfolds Mill, was attacked in Bradley Woods, and William Horsfall, the Marsden Mill owner, was murdered on Crosland Moor, outside Huddersfield.

Yet, by the end of April 1812, Yorkshire Luddism had lost its momentum. The authorities had moved thousands of troops into the area to protect the mills and the chief Yorkshire Luddite leaders had been arrested, being brought to trial in January 1813. The eventual execution of seventeen Luddites at York, including George Mellor, the nearest thing Yorkshire had to a Luddite general, brought an end to the episode. The croppers accepted their fate and by 1816 there were only about 1,000 croppers in the West Riding of Yorkshire – many of them young and relatively unskilled men who were supervising the new machinery.

These militant 'Luddite' events have, of course, given rise to a vast amount of interpretative literature. Some modern historians have seen Luddism as evidence of a clash between the rival moralities of capitalism and the working class. In other words, it was an early example of class conflict in Britain. The difficulty of this approach is that the Luddites varied from region to region. In Yorkshire and Nottinghamshire they were drawn largely from the declining trades threatened by capitalism. In Lancashire, on the other hand, they were the new industrial workforce attempting to control their conditions of employment. Not surprisingly, then, other modern historians have seen Luddism as a set of disturbances responding to specific local industrial problems. It is not seen as an attempt at insurrection and, it has been noted, the subject of revolution concerned the authorities more than it did the Luddites.

Chartism in Britain
c. **1836** to *c.* **1848**

Chartism (Map 9.3) had its origins in the constitutional movement begun by the London Working Men's Association (LWMA) in 1836 and was taken up by the revived Birmingham Political Union (BPU) in 1837. The Charter was drawn up by the LWMA, with the help of a number of Radical MPs, and accepted by the BPU. Officially put forward on 8 May 1838, it contained six demands: the vote for all men over 21, voting by secret ballot, the abolition of the property qualification for MPs, payment for MPs, equal electoral districts, and annual Parliaments.

At one time, historians wrote of Chartism as a unified movement led by a few notables such as Feargus O'Connor, MP and editor of the *Northern Star*. However, in the last twenty-five years it has become clear that Chartism varied regionally and locally in its strategy, support, and impact. Historians now place less emphasis upon the question 'why did Chartism fail?' and have sought to understand the immense variety of Chartist responses.

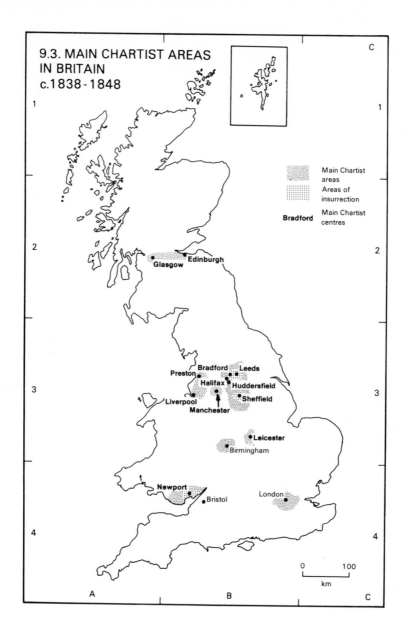

9.3. MAIN CHARTIST AREAS IN BRITAIN c.1838-1848

Main Chartist areas

Areas of insurrection

Bradford Main Chartist centres

Edinburgh

Glasgow

Bradford   Leeds

Preston

Halifax   Huddersfield

Liverpool

Manchester   Sheffield

Leicester

Birmingham

Newport

Bristol

London

0   100

km

Despite the changing balance of opinion, which now takes the view that Chartism was a fractured, divided, and limited movement rather than a unified revolutionary working-class movement, it is clear that certain events provide the shape of the whole Chartist period.

In early 1839 a National Convention of the Industrious Classes was held in London to help present a petition to Parliament in May calling for the Charter. When that petition was rejected the 'physical force' Chartists, such as George Julian Harney, John Frost, and Bronterre O'Brien, felt justified in calling for revolution. On 3 November 1839 John Frost led some 3,000 colliers to rescue Henry Vincent, the leading orator of the LWMA, from Newport gaol and to seize the town. But the plot became known to the authorities who easily crushed the colliers' revolt and arrested Frost. The risings in the West Riding and

Sheffield in January 1840 were also abortive.

It was at this juncture that O'Connor began to make his mark. He helped form the National Charter Association at Manchester which presented the second Chartist petition to Parliament in April 1842. The rejection of this petition led to a brief industrial reaction which was chiefly marked by an abortive attempt to call a general strike, or Grand Holiday, and the 'plug plots' – in which plugs were drawn from the boilers of steam-engines, thus bringing mills to a halt. From 1842 to 1847 those who remained active in the Chartist movement directed their attention towards land schemes and industrial co-operation.

The depressed economic conditions of 1847 and 1848 led to the revival of Chartist activities and the presentation of the third petition on 10 April 1848. When that was also rejected by Parliament a National Assembly was formed, though quickly adjourned and never to meet again, in order to act as an alternative government, and violence erupted in the provinces. Since much unrest occurred in industrial areas where there was a significant Irish presence, it was sometimes assumed by the authorities that Chartism was in part an extension of the movement for Irish independence. However, in this 'year of revolutions' in Europe the Chartist disturbances were easily contained. By the summer of 1848 Chartism was effectively dormant – although it continued to exist, in a variety of forms, until the late 1850s.

Bradford Chartism 1848

Chartism reached its zenith on 10 April 1848 with the presentation of its third petition to the House of Commons. As on the previous occasions in 1838 and 1842, it was rejected. Yet the Charter and its demands were particularly potent in some northern industrial towns faced with serious cyclical and structural unemployment.

Bradford was one of these towns. Something like 40 per cent of the workforce was unemployed at the peak of depression, many facing structural unemployment as wool-combing machinery replaced hand wool-combers. One observer noted that:

> Bradford would be a disaffected town for a good many years in consequence of a large body of workmen in the town and immediate vicinity being thrown out of employment by the introduction of combing machines. One firm, Messrs Walker & Co used to employ 1,700 combers, now they do not employ 400. They attribute their unfortunate position to what they call class legislation and (sic) that the Charter would find them plenty of good work and good wages if it became the law of the land.[1]

The poor economic situation and the rejection of the Charter thus provoked the Chartists into much threatening activity. It was claimed that they were holding regular meetings, making pikes and

> marching in military style with the captains in red and green caps and divided into sections and companies, keeping step with true military precision carrying tricolor flags and others bearing horrible inscriptions such as 'more pigs and less parsons' [a reference to a by-law of the vestry banning the keeping of pigs in pokes], 'down with the aristocracy'. . . (ibid.)

Indeed, on 15 May the unemployed Chartists sent a deputation to the Court House and subsequently held meetings in the area.

The Bradford authorities initially raised a local militia from the middle classes, the specials/embodied pensioners, but on 24 May called in 800 troops to supplement the 70 police and 1,500 specials/embodied pensioners. Bradford was, therefore, practically in a state of military occupation. The government felt that there was going to be a northern rebellion and that Bradford was likely to be its flashpoint.

The main aim of the authorities was to advance into the Irish centre of disaffection along Manchester Road (see Map 9.4) to arrest 'Wat Tyler', Isaac Jefferson, a blacksmith who was making pikes at his home in Adelaide Street. It was decided to foray up

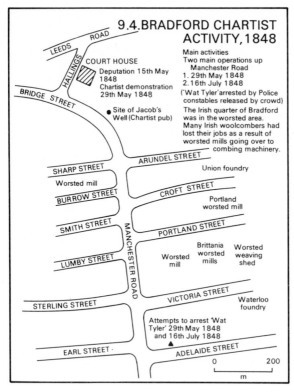

9.4. BRADFORD CHARTIST ACTIVITY, 1848

LEEDS ROAD

HALLINGS

BRIDGE STREET

COURT HOUSE
◪ Deputation 15th May 1848
Chartist demonstration 29th May 1848

● Site of Jacob's Well (Chartist pub)

Main activities
Two main operations up Manchester Road
1. 29th May 1848
2. 16th July 1848
('Wat Tyler' arrested by Police constables released by crowd)

The Irish quarter of Bradford was in the worsted area. Many Irish woolcombers had lost their jobs as a result of worsted mills going over to combing machinery.

ARUNDEL STREET

SHARP STREET

Worsted mill

BURROW STREET

SMITH STREET

LUMBY STREET

STERLING STREET

EARL STREET

MANCHESTER ROAD

CROFT STREET

PORTLAND STREET

VICTORIA STREET

ADELAIDE STREET

Union foundry

Portland worsted mill

Worsted mill
Brittania worsted mills
Worsted weaving shed

Waterloo foundry

Attempts to arrest 'Wat Tyler' 29th May 1848 and 16th July 1848 ▲

0   200
m

Manchester Road on Monday, 29 May at 9.00 a.m. The foray was made, but while 'Wat Tyler's' premises were being searched a crowd developed and 'stones and bric-a-brac' fell about like hail on the constables. The force was driven down Manchester Road and back to the Court House. Later the same day, about 4.00 p.m., the Bradford Magistrates sent 50 police with cutlasses, 500 special constables and 200 dragoons and infantry back up Manchester Road to Adelaide Street. About a dozen stone-throwers were arrested and later committed for trial at York Castle.

Thereafter, violence in and around Bradford was sporadic. The occasional Chartist march was thwarted, there were a number of attempts to arrest 'Wat Tyler' and eventually he was arrested at the hamlet of Swilling, near Halifax, on 13 September 1848.

Bradford 'physical force' Chartism disappeared quickly in the face of military authority and some gradual improvement in trade conditions. In its wake, Bradford manufacturers such as Titus Salt, who built the industrial community of Saltaire, began to attempt to improve the lot of the working classes in the region.

Trade unionism in the nineteenth century

There are no accurate figures for trade union membership in the United Kingdom until the late 1880s and early 1890s when the Labour Department of the Board of Trade and Beatrice and Sidney Webb conducted detailed surveys of membership. There are many reasons for this, the main one being that trade unions, organizations of workers willing to take strike action to defend and improve their wages and conditions, were illegal before the repeal of the Combination Acts in 1824, and of doubtful legality thereafter. Some were able to develop under the guise of being friendly societies, but the Combination Acts of 1799 and 1800 reiterated the illegality of organizations which were in restraint of trade – that is, willing to take strike action.

For a decade, between 1824 and 1834, trade unions were legal under certain constraints and many small unions emerged, usually of skilled workers. The most famous national body was Robert Owen's Grand National Consolidated Trade Union which developed in the early 1830s. But in 1834 this greater freedom for trade unionism came to an end when some Dorchester labourers, the 'Tolpuddle Martyrs' were imprisoned and eventually sent to Tasmania, for meeting in

9.5. TRADE UNION STRENGTH, 1867

Leeds ● Main trade union centres

Main coalfields

Edinburgh
Glasgow
Bradford Leeds
Liverpool Hull
Manchester Sheffield
Birmingham
Bristol London

0   100
km

secret to improve their agricultural wages and conditions. Thereafter, trade unions were on the defensive and secretive.

It was not until the 1850s and 1860s, the period of so-called mid-Victorian prosperity, that trade unions began to grow again (see Map 9.5 for main areas of strength). The relatively good economic conditions were propitious for the development of small groups of skilled workers – such as engineers, builders, and carpenters – into unions. Indeed, the earliest attempts at national organization occurred amongst these groups and gave birth to bodies such as the Amalgamated Society of Engineers (1851). Nevertheless, there were attempts to organize unskilled and semi-skilled groups, such as the miners. Indeed, by the 1860s there were two major national miners' unions – the Amalgamated Association and the National Union which between them could claim upwards of 100,000 members. Indeed, the formation of the Trades Union Congress in

1868 reflected the growth of trade unionism amongst a substantial number of relatively unskilled workers. In the early years the leaders of the craft unions, nicknamed the 'Junta' by the Webbs, would not join the TUC.

One of the main reasons for this split within trade unionism was the fact that the main skilled unions were attempting to give the impression that they were peaceable organizations dedicated to providing friendly-society benefits for their members. The intimidation and outrages conducted by the skilled cutlery and light-metal workers of Sheffield in the 1860s, the 'Sheffield outrages', had called into question the continuance of trade unionism. As a result of their persuasive powers they encouraged a Royal Commission on Trade Unions to suggest the official registration of unions. Indeed in 1871 a Trade Union Act was passed to this effect. Those unions which registered, and not all did, would have their funds protected in the sense that they could prosecute anyone absconding with the funds.

In the mid-1870s, however, the legal position of trade unions was less important than the economic depression and deflation which reduced the movement to a 'craft' rump of its previous organization. Most unions were still relatively small and had a great propensity to collapse during bouts of bad trade and from employer pressure. It was only the trade revival in the late 1880s, and the work of socialists within the ranks of the unskilled, which led to the substantial trade union revival known as 'new unionism'. The 1891 Webb survey (see Map 9.6) thus picked up trade unionism at a moment of expansion in its membership:

Date	Members	Date	Members
1851	100,000 (est.)	1884	379,000 (est.)
1867	800,000 (est.)	1888	568,000 (est.)
1876	1,600,000 (est.)	1891	1,507,000

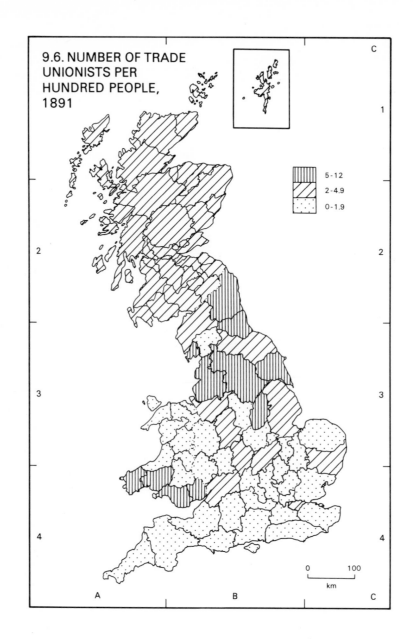

9.6. NUMBER OF TRADE UNIONISTS PER HUNDRED PEOPLE, 1891

5-12
2-4.9
0-1.9

0   100
      km

The Labour movement
c. 1890–1914: the West Riding of Yorkshire

It was not until the late 1880s, in the wake of local and parliamentary legislation which widened the franchise and removed many of the restrictions on candidature, that the independent political Labour movement was able to emerge. In some areas, such as Lancashire and London, the spark came from socialist groups such as the Social Democratic Federation, a quasi-Marxist organization. In other areas, most prominently the West

Riding of Yorkshire, the stimulus came from a broad group of frustrated Liberal Radicals and trade unionists who began to believe that the Liberal and Conservative parties were not the political vehicles for achieving working-class aspirations.

In Bradford, the birthplace of the national Independent Labour Party in January 1893, a major industrial dispute at Manningham Mills led to the formation of a Labour Union (later ILP) in 1891. This collective organization captured the support of the Trades Council in 1892 and sponsored the unsuccessful parliamentary campaigns of Ben Tillett in the 1892 and 1895 general elections, and of Keir Hardie in the Bradford East by-election of November 1896. It was eventually successful in returning Fred Jowett for Bradford West in the 1906 general election.

In Halifax, the financial support of John Lister, a Fabian and owner of the Shibden Hall estates, plus some considerable support from

the Trades Council, led to the formation of the Halifax Labour Union. In contrast the Leeds Trades Council was slow to respond to the demands of the local branches of the ILP and it was not until 1900, when the Labour Representation Committee, the forerunner of the Labour Party, was formed, that the local trade unions decided to ally with the embryonic Labour Party.

Map 9.7 indicates a number of features about the Labour movement in the West Riding of Yorkshire. First of all, it stresses the fact that the dominant political organization was the ILP. In Bradford there were in fact about twenty-nine branches of the ILP in the early 1890s, with up to 2,000 members. In Halifax there were eight branches with about 500 members. Together they provided more than half the fee-paying membership of the ILP in this region – a region which was the most important ILP centre in the nation. Secondly, it is clear that the SDF never carried

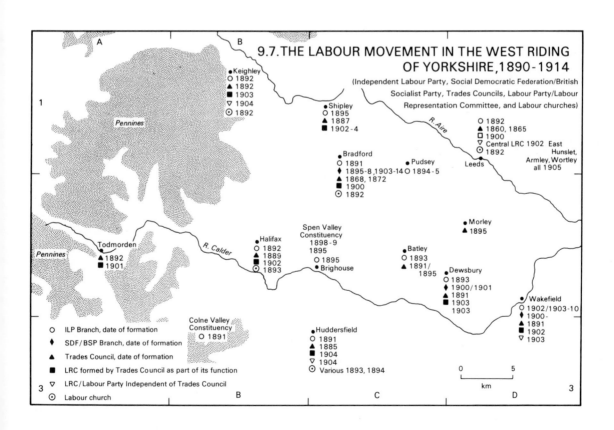

9.7. THE LABOUR MOVEMENT IN THE WEST RIDING OF YORKSHIRE, 1890-1914

(Independent Labour Party, Social Democratic Federation/British Socialist Party, Trades Councils, Labour Party/Labour Representation Committee, and Labour churches)

much support in the district. In 1894 there were nineteen SDF branches in Lancashire with a membership of 1,021. In the West Riding there was none. The first to be formed opened in Bradford in 1895, had a mere twenty-seven members, and collapsed in 1898. It was in fact revived in 1903 but never carried a substantial membership. About 1900 another branch was formed at Dewsbury, out of the local ILP branches, but never had more than fifty members. A third branch of the SDF (which soon became the British Socialist Party) emerged in Leeds before the First World War. The flurry of activity to form the British Socialist Party in 1910 and 1911 produced some increased support for the BSP/SDF but it quickly faded away.

Despite the growing political support for the early Labour movement, there were political setbacks. The disastrous 1895 General Election set the ILP back on its heels and was dubbed the 'most expensive funeral since that of Napoleon'. During the next few years the movement was very largely sustained by the development of a small but hard core of support around the cultural activities of the movement. ILP clubs provided the focus for book clubs, theatre groups, and football and cricket competitions. The Clarion movement encouraged the formation of vocal unions and glee unions. In this respect, a third point to note about the map is the existence of Labour churches. Although they lacked any coherent theology, other than a faith in brotherhood, they did help to 'make socialists' through offering a forum for the leading Labour speakers of the day to address local audiences.

This cultural development kept the heart of the movement beating and, once the LRC/Labour Party won more trade union support, paved the way for the political successes in 1906, when Fred Jowett was returned to Parliament for Bradford West, James Parker for Halifax, and James O'Grady for Leeds East. On the heels of these successes followed Victor Grayson's success at Colne Valley in the 1907 by-election.

The West Riding of Yorkshire was a Labour heartland in the quarter of a century before the First World War and, as the map indicates, this was facilitated by a strong link between the ILP and trade unionism. It is also interesting to note that the LRC/Labour Party did not challenge the supremacy of the ILP in the Labour politics of this area until the end of the First World War.

Syndicalism and militant industrial action c. 1910–14

From about 1910 until 1924 the level of industrial militancy rose throughout the United Kingdom. This was particularly marked before the First World War. In 1910 the number of working days lost in disputes rose to more than 4 million for only the second time (the previous occasion had been 1908), and from 1911 to 1914 it averaged 18 million, with 40 million days being lost in 1913. In seeking explanations for this burst of militancy most historians now agree that relatively good trade conditions allowed trade unions to organize more effectively and to pursue strike action to improve the wages and conditions of their members. This is seen as the general explana-tion of the bewildering array of transport strikes and miners' strikes, including the Miners' National Strike which took place in the early months of 1912. Nevertheless, a few historians have been prepared to suggest that syndicalism was an important stimulant to such militancy before the First World War.

British syndicalism appears to have drawn its philosophy and approach from two main sources; American De Leonism and French syndicalism. Daniel De Leon, the American syndicalist leader, believed in the need to create revolutionary unions outside the existing trade union movement. The French syndicalists, on the other hand, maintained the need to 'bore from within', to capture and change existing trade unions and to make them revolutionary. Although syndicalist views varied enormously, they could at least agree upon the need to create one industrial union for each industry and that a parliament of such unions could call a general strike to overthrow capitalist society. Coherence was given to the syndicalist movement by Tom Mann, who had helped to organize the London Dock strike in 1889, when he returned to Britain from Australia and went to France to learn about syndicalist ideas. In 1910 he formed the Industrial Syndicalist Education League which expressed the need for revolutionary trade unionists to work through the existing unions.

Nevertheless, of the fourteen major industrial disputes which took place between September 1910 and 1914 (see Map 9.8), only three appear to have had any significant syndicalist presence. The first was the strike of the coal-miners at the Eli Colliery of the Cambrian Combine in the Rhondda. This started as a dispute over rates of pay for opening up and working difficult seams but built up into a major dispute which eventually involved 30,000 miners. It began in September 1910 and finished, with defeat, in August 1911, and was entirely organized by miners who were not syndicalist. Nevertheless, the dispute attracted the attention of Tom Mann who wrote of his experiences on the picket line in his journal *The Industrial Syndicalist*. Notoriety surrounded this dispute because of the clashes at Tonypandy which led to the death of one striker on 17 November 1910. And, indeed, from these events sprang a small but influential South Wales group of syndicalists, of up to 150 or 200 in strength, who produced *The Miners' Next Step* in early 1912. This pamphlet outlined the way in which the revolutionary rank and file could capture the miners' union and pave the way for society based upon syndicalism.

Mann was also involved in the Liverpool Dock Strike, which at various times involved seamen, dockers, carters, and railwaymen between June and August 1911, effectively as leader. There was considerable violence, and indeed two strikers were killed in the dispute on 15 August 1911 attempting to prevent some strikers being removed to prison. It was also one of the few occasions when most of the strikers won their demands. Yet even this 'syndicalist' success was incidental to normal demands of trade unionists, and Liverpool, allegedly the second most important syndicalist centre in Britain, could only muster about fifty syndicalists. Elsewhere, there were a few syndicalists in London, Huddersfield, and Birmingham, where there was a branch of about twenty members led by Leonard Hall. But syndicalist influence was always marginal and even the engineering dispute in the Black Country in 1913 displayed little evidence of syndicalist support. The only other major evidence of syndicalist presence occurred in the unsuccessful Dublin Transport Strike, led by Jim Larkin, a man with both syndicalist and Irish nationalist sympathies.

The inescapable conclusion is that syndicalism was incidental to the industrial militancy of the pre-war years and latched upon the move towards trade union amalgamations and strike activity that was occurring. Its support was always limited and in 1912 the Industrial Syndicalist Education League split and moved towards De Leonist ideas. Mann, who was briefly imprisoned for his part in publishing the famous 'Don't Shoot' leaflet had gone off lecturing in the United States in 1912 but subsequently returned to form an Industrial Democracy League, based upon the policy of changing unions by 'boring from within'. In the end, however, a fragmented syndicalist movement, just as much as a unified syndicalist organization, failed to exert much influence upon the industrial events of the pre-war years.

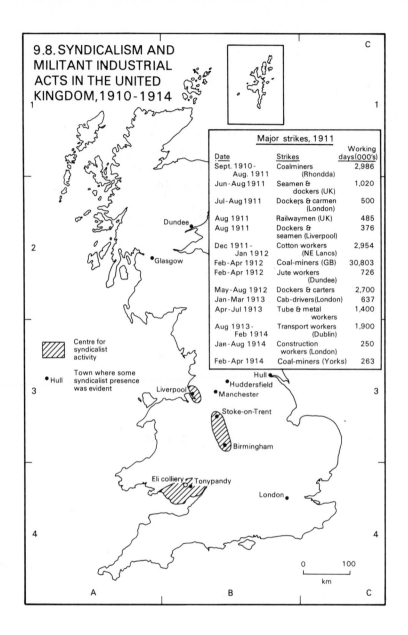

9.8. SYNDICALISM AND MILITANT INDUSTRIAL ACTS IN THE UNITED KINGDOM, 1910-1914

Major strikes, 1911		
Date	Strikes	Working days(000's)
Sept. 1910- Aug. 1911	Coalminers (Rhondda)	2,986
Jun-Aug 1911	Seamen & dockers (UK)	1,020
Jul-Aug 1911	Dockers & carmen (London)	500
Aug 1911	Railwaymen (UK)	485
Aug 1911	Dockers & seamen (Liverpool)	376
Dec 1911- Jan 1912	Cotton workers (NE Lancs)	2,954
Feb-Apr 1912	Coal-miners (GB)	30,803
Feb-Apr 1912	Jute workers (Dundee)	726
May-Aug 1912	Dockers & carters	2,700
Jan-Mar 1913	Cab-drivers(London)	637
Apr-Jul 1913	Tube & metal workers	1,400
Aug 1913- Feb 1914	Transport workers (Dublin)	1,900
Jan-Aug 1914	Construction workers (London)	250
Feb-Apr 1914	Coal-miners (Yorks)	263

Centre for syndicalist activity

Town where some syndicalist presence was evident

The General Strike of 1926 and Yorkshire

The General Strike, which took place between 3 and 12 May 1926, is a unique event in British history. It is the only occasion on which the Trades Union Congress has ever called out some sections of the British trade union movement on indefinite sympathetic strike action.

The reasons for this event are complex and interconnected. The most obvious point is that poor industrial relations between coal-owners and coal-miners paved the way for a major coal dispute. Nevertheless, industrial conflict in the coal industry was partly induced by the decision of Baldwin's Conservative government to return to the gold standard in April 1925, along with an immediate increase of the parity of the pound sterling against other currencies by about 10 per cent. Such an action demanded that employers needed to cut their costs by 10 per cent in order to compete with foreign producers on the same terms as they had done before. This resulted in a number of attempts to reduce wages, the most celebrated being the coal-owners' demand for wage reductions and changes in the condition of services amongst miners. It appeared that a coal lock-out was on, as from 31 July 1925. But the government intervened at the last moment – on that day which subsequently became known as 'Red Friday' – and offered a nine-month subsidy to allow the coal industry to be examined by the Samuel Commission. It is clear that the decision of the TUC to

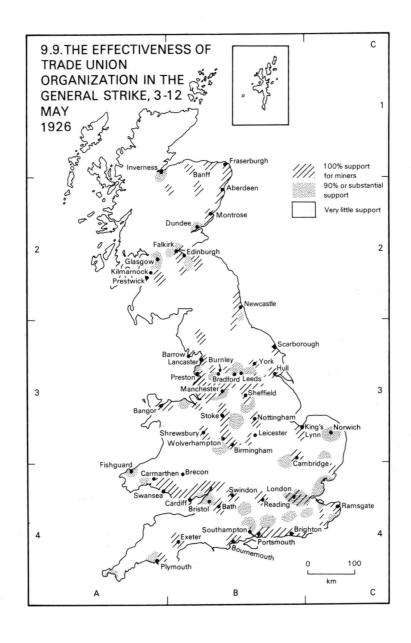

9.9. THE EFFECTIVENESS OF TRADE UNION ORGANIZATION IN THE GENERAL STRIKE, 3-12 MAY 1926

100% support for miners
90% or substantial support
Very little support

support the miners had forced the government to intervene. And the TUC felt itself obligated to do so since part of the function of the General Council had been to ensure that the events of 'Black Friday', 15 April 1921 – when the railway workers and the transport workers failed to come out in support of a miners' strike – did not occur again.

It is clear that the government bought time. The Samuel Commission solved nothing and the subsidy ran out on 30 April 1926. From 1 May 1926 the coal-miners were locked out and soon afterwards the TUC called out the transport unions and began a 'national strike in support of the miners' which is usually known as the General Strike.

Support for the miners is not easy to assess for the strike was very confused and activities varied from area to area. Though only the miners and the transport workers should have been involved in strike action, some workers – such as the textile workers in Yorkshire – came out despite the fact that they were never called out. The two 'General Strike' maps (9.9 and 9.10) should therefore be considered as notional. They are in fact based upon a survey produced by the Plebs League, though there are one or two modifications to allow for the evidence produced by Emile Burns's *Councils in Action* (1927). What they demonstrate is that the General Strike was most complete in the mining areas, where the local trade unions firmly supported the miners. Elsewhere, support was fragmented and normally dependent upon significant activity in some major industrial town. There was also very little support in rural areas – where the workforce had always been badly organized. This is particularly evident in the case of the eastern and northern rural areas of Yorkshire.

In Yorkshire, the most significant support appears to have occurred in the textile and coal areas which extended between Bradford and Leeds to the north and Sheffield to the south (Map 9.10). Nevertheless, even in this area there was great fluctuation of support. For instance, despite the Plebs League survey,

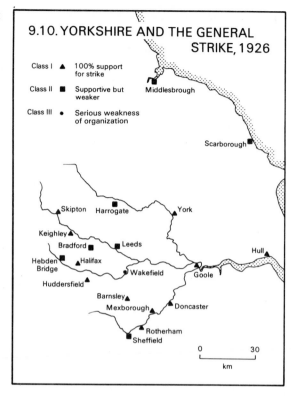

9.10. YORKSHIRE AND THE GENERAL STRIKE, 1926

Class I ▲ 100% support for strike
Class II ■ Supportive but weaker
Class III • Serious weakness of organization

there were those who regarded Leeds 'as the worst organized' town in England. The problem appears to have been that not only was there a Council of Action based upon the Trades Council but a rival committee formed by the 'transport unions'. Both were attempting to run the strike in the locality and both claimed the exclusive right to issue permits for the movement of food supplies. In fact, the transport committee was right, for the General Council of the TUC had only called for the formation of committees of the 'local transport unions' to organize strike activity.

The TUC's decision to call off the strike after nine days provoked great disillusionment amongst trade unionists and fuelled charges of 'betrayal'. It is clear that it came as a great shock throughout Yorkshire. In Hull it was argued that there was 'Alarm – fear – despair – a victorious army disarmed and handed over to its enemies.' At Wakefield, it was claimed that 'The spirit was magnificent, and dismay prevailed when the news came that the strike was called off'.

In the end, the miners were left to fight against wage reductions alone. It is true that they did receive some financial support from the British trade union movement but despite this they were forced back to work, normally at reduced wage rates, in November 1926.

The General Strike was clearly a defeat for the British trade union movement. Nevertheless, it did serve to warn both employers and government that a continued assault on the monetary wages of British workers was not to be considered lightly.

Notes

1. Binns to Home Office, 25 May 1848, PRO. HO 45/2410.

Maps 9.1 and 9.2 are based on material from M. I. Thomis (ed.), *Luddism in Nottinghamshire* (London, 1972) and E. P. Thompson, *The Making of the English Working Class* (Harmondsworth, 1986 edn). Map 9.3 uses material from A. Briggs (ed.), *Chartist Studies* (London, 1959); D. Jones, *Chartism and the Chartists* (London, 1975); and D. Thompson, *The Chartists* (London, 1954). Sources for Map 9.4 are Disturbance Records (PRO Home Office Papers); O. S. map for Bradford, 1852 (1848 Survey); and D. G. Wright, *The Chartist Risings in Bradford* (Bradford, 1987). Map 9.5 is based on evidence from The Royal Commission on Trade Unions (1867–9) and Webb MSS (British Library of Political and Economic Science). Map 9.6 uses evidence from the inquiries of the Royal Commission of Labour (1891–4) and S. and B. Webb, *The History of Trade Unionism, 1666–1920* (London, 1920 edn), Appendix V. Material for Map 9.7 is drawn from the Francis Johnson (ILP) collection; the Labour Representation Committee, Correspondence and Labour Party Archives; *Labour Leader; Bradford Labour Echo; Bradford Pioneer, Forward* and the *Yorkshire Factory Times*. The sources for Map 9.8 are the strikes and lockout *Reports* (Labour Department of the Board of Trade) and H. A. Clegg, *A History of British Trade Unions since 1889*, vol. II, *1911–1933* (Oxford, 1985). Maps 9.9 and 9.10 are from the TUC Survey of the Strike, published in M. Morris, *The General Strike* (London, 1976).

Particular acknowledgement must be made to Julia M. Laybourn for her work in drafting the maps contained in this section.

10 EDUCATION: LATE NINETEENTH-CENTURY DISPARITIES IN PROVISION

Bill Marsden

The Education Census of 1851 identified, more authoritatively than had been the case before, the demographic imperative which had and was still to plague public educational planning and provision in England and Wales. Its architect, Mann, formulated a base-line for such provision. He suggested that schools were needed for approximately one-sixth of the nation's population. In the event, it was found that for the rapidly growing towns and cities this was an underestimate, and even a one-fifth calculation hardly enough. Among other achievements the Education Census confirmed also the findings of earlier and less accurate surveys, that blatant regional disparities in educational provision were present,[1] and that the large industrial and commercial towns and cities posed particular difficulties.

The next important survey of the nation's education emerged from the Newcastle Commission of 1858. Generally regarded as of malign influence because its recommendations led to the 'Payment by Results' system, it also had its positive outcomes. Its terms of reference were to examine the state of popular education. While its regional sampling unfortunately excluded too many significant provincial cities, its case-study approach through detailed investigations of agricultural, manufacturing, mining, maritime, and metropolitan areas was revealing of important regional differences in attitudes and access to education. More significant, though prone to deploy the term 'the education of the poor', the Commission exposed the anachronistic nature of the concept through its findings that large

portions of the working-class population were respectable, aspiring, living above the poverty line, and were far from hostile to education, so long as it was tuned to their perceived needs.

The chief providers of elementary education remained the voluntary bodies; the National Society (Anglican), the British Society (Nonconformist) and the Catholic Poor Schools Society. The religious tensions which dogged nineteenth-century educational advance resulted among other things in a lack of co-ordination of provision, including duplication in some areas and overall neglect in others. Maps 10.1, 10.2, and 10.3 reveal the impact of religious differentiation of the educational system in England and Wales. They are based on figures collected by the Newcastle Commissioners. Overwhelmingly apparent is the dominance of the established church, mostly though not entirely through the auspices of the National Society. Thus even in counties in which they were relatively least influential, they provided over half the elementary day schools. Map 10.1 shows how Church of England schools dominated from the Wash to the Severn estuary (excluding London), the south-eastern heartlands of Anglican influence, and also the rural shires of Shropshire,[2] Worcestershire, and Herefordshire, and in Cumbria. The position was less strong in heavily urbanized counties and in Wales.

For all its relative wealth, and the attention it devoted to early provision in manufacturing counties such as Lancashire,[3] the Church of England was never comfortable in providing for the urban proletariat. Like the Wesleyans, it preferred to cater for more respectable children and to establish schools with higher fees to keep them relatively select.[4] The established church also tried hard to assist the colonialist official thinking which sought to extinguish Welsh-language teaching in the elementary day schools of Wales by providing Anglican English-language schools.[5] The strategy was in its turn subverted by the more potent impact on the local population of indigenous, chapel-provided Sunday schools in which Welsh was the medium of instruction.

The British Society, though first in the field in the early years of the century in the dissemination of the monitorial or 'New Plan' system, was always less well resourced and organized than the National Society,[6] and at most provided not more than 20 per cent of the elementary day schools in any English county, excluding the marginal case of Monmouthshire. Map 10.2 shows its main contribution, predictably, as being in Wales, leaving aside the more Anglicized counties of Pembrokeshire, Flintshire, and Radnorshire. The map does not, however, do justice to the early efforts of this society in the major towns and cities, where large and important day schools were established, such as the Royal Lancastrian School in Manchester. The Lancastrian system of the British Society was also taught in many more than British Schools as such. These, by mid-century, were adjusting their sights upwards in the sense of seeking to attract more respectable children by increasing fees. More supportive of the School Boards than the Anglicans or Catholics, the British Society built few schools after the Education Act of 1870, and indeed transferred some of their own to the Boards.

The position of the Catholic Poor Schools Society was different. The Catholic Church inevitably had to accept the responsibility for providing for the many Catholic children among the labouring classes in the towns and cities in which the influx of the poor Irish from the 1840s was concentrated, if these children were to have an appropriate religious education, following the failure of the Liverpool Corporation School experiment to create a cross-denominational schooling system.[7] Map 10.3 illustrates the concentration of Catholic provision in particular urban areas, and especially in Lancashire, where over 15 per cent of the day-school population was in Catholic schools, a figure rising much higher in places in which Catholic population was concentrated, such as Liverpool, Bootle, Preston, and St Helens.

In addition to this religious differentiation, variations in local attitudes to provision created gross regional disparities. All the surveys of accommodation up to 1870 revealed great deficiencies in the densely populated counties, notably Lancashire and Middlesex, and also in Wales and some adjoining counties. In contrast, provision was more adequate in less highly populated areas, and distinctly good in the extreme northern counties. Northumberland, Cumberland, and Westmorland were picked out for the extent and quality of their schooling, seen as reflecting the benign influence of Scotland with its envied parochial system, and the favourable attitudes towards education stemming from the social stability of the native population.[8]

It should not be inferred that counties such as Lancashire were universally deficient in provision, however. While some smaller counties were relatively homogeneous in terms of accommodation and attendance levels, others were more differentiated. Attendance at school was strongly influenced by the amount of accommodation available, and Map 10.4 shows the position in Lancashire on census day, 1851. The leading areas for attendance were the Furness district, hinged on to Cumbria, matched by the Fylde. These were followed by south-west Lancashire, in which Liverpool stood out as deficient. Lagging behind were the coal-mining and cotton-manufacturing areas of south-east Lancashire. It must be stressed that the Anglican and then the Catholic Church had made great efforts to keep up with the demand. While the former was unsuccessful, at least enough had been done to pre-empt the need for School Boards in

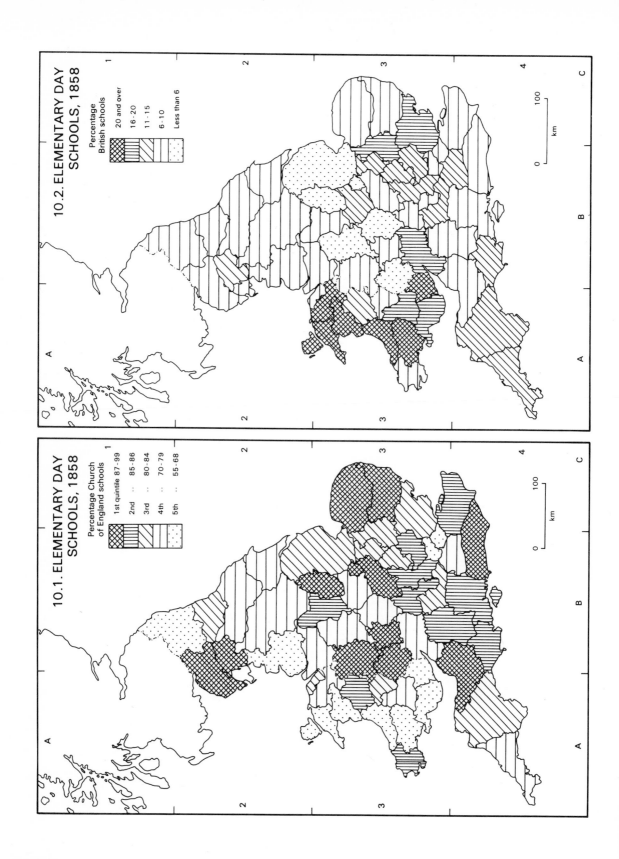

10.1. ELEMENTARY DAY SCHOOLS, 1858

Percentage Church of England schools

1st quintile 87-99
2nd   85-86
3rd   80-84
4th   70-79
5th   55-68

10.2. ELEMENTARY DAY SCHOOLS, 1858

Percentage British schools

20 and over
16-20
11-15
6-10
Less than 6

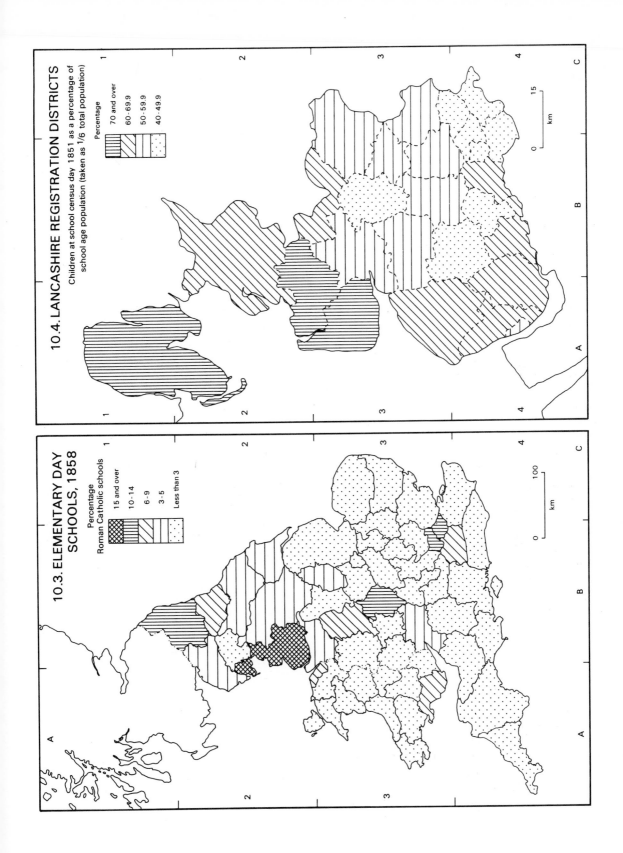

10.3. ELEMENTARY DAY SCHOOLS, 1858

Percentage
Roman Catholic schools

15 and over
10 - 14
6 - 9
3 - 5
Less than 3

0   100
km

10.4. LANCASHIRE REGISTRATION DISTRICTS

Children at school census day 1851 as a percentage of
school age population (taken as 1/6 total population)

Percentage

70 and over
60 - 69.9
50 - 59.9
40 - 49.9

0   15
km

a significant number of Lancashire towns, including Preston, Warrington, St Helens, Southport, and Bury. But the overwhelming weight of numbers defeated the churches in the largest towns and cities such as Liverpool, Manchester, Salford, and Bolton.

Low attendances were not only a result of deficient accommodation, however. Lancashire in particular suffered from the confusion caused by the incompatibilities between the Education Acts and the Factory and Workshops legislation. In Lancashire children were very important in the coal-mines and cotton mills, and on some School Boards, notably Salford's and Burnley's, the influence of members was directed to protecting manufacturing rather than educational priorities.[9]

Similarly the pattern on Map 10.1 conceals as much as it reveals about the schools of Cumberland, Westmorland, Herefordshire, and Monmouthshire. Apart from Monmouthshire, these are shown as counties in which the established church was dominant. But it does not demonstrate the wide variations in actual uptake. Accepted nationally as a leading region, Cumbria (Map 10.5) had only one registration district on census day with less than 50 per cent attendance. All other districts had over 60 per cent attendance and most of Westmorland over 70 per cent. At the other extreme, no district of Monmouthshire or Herefordshire surpassed 60 per cent, while in Monmouthshire itself only one achieved 50 per cent (Map 10.6). The deficiencies in these areas were variously ascribed to rural apathy in the case of Herefordshire and rapid industrialization in Monmouthshire.[10]

At a different level of resolution, however, certain urban areas were in advance both in accommodation and attendance. As Map 10.7 indicates, a considerable number of smaller towns had more day scholars at school on census day in 1851 than the suggested norm of one-sixth of the population. These were mostly old-established market towns, located particularly in the counties south-east of a line from the Wash to the Severn. Clearly such towns had advantages over the rapidly growing industrial towns and commercial cities. In the first place they often benefited from long-standing endowments and a populace acclimatized to the notion of subscribing to schooling. They were also places which typically had experienced gradual rather than dramatic population growth, at a rate with which the voluntary agencies could cope. Further, there was sufficient distancing from the often reactionary sway of the rural squire, parson, and farming lobby to allow the advance of educational provision.

On the other hand, the demographic pressures in industrializing and urbanizing Britain gradually overtook the ability of the voluntary agencies to meet the demand, particularly in a context in which it was also escalating because more favourable attitudes to schooling were being engendered, while legislation was being tightened in the direction of compulsory attendance, implemented through official enforcement agencies including attendance committees and offices. The support of local rates administered through School Boards became urgent, and was enshrined in the Education Act of 1870. The voluntary bodies were given breathing space to plug the gaps, but over vast areas of rural England and Wales, and in most towns with a large proletariat, they did not succeed in doing so. In these circumstances, School Boards had to be established. But many places took the initiative without pressure from Whitehall. Map 10.8 shows the first boards to be established, at the end of 1870, and of course many more were soon to follow. The contrast with Map 10.7 could hardly be more striking. Of the towns shown on the former, only Stockton appears on Map 10.8. Additionally, apart from the special case of London, only Bridgewater is south of the line from the Wash to the Severn estuary. Most of the early boards were in industrial areas of the Midlands, Lancashire, the West Riding, and the North-east, ill-provided for by earlier endowments.

The School Boards were graded in size according to the local population, and ranged from five members in small communities to

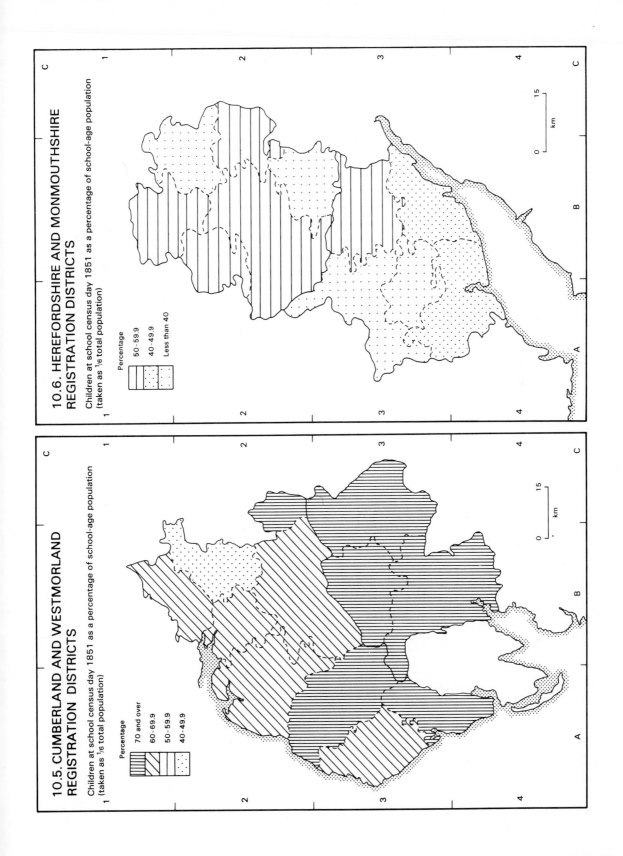

10.5. CUMBERLAND AND WESTMORLAND REGISTRATION DISTRICTS

Children at school census day 1851 as a percentage of school-age population
1 (taken as ⅙ total population)

Percentage

70 and over
60 - 69.9
50 - 59.9
40 - 49.9

0   15
|————————|
km

10.6. HEREFORDSHIRE AND MONMOUTHSHIRE REGISTRATION DISTRICTS

Children at school census day 1851 as a percentage of school-age population
1 (taken as ⅙ total population)

Percentage

50 - 59.9
40 - 49.9
Less than 40

0   15
|————————|
km

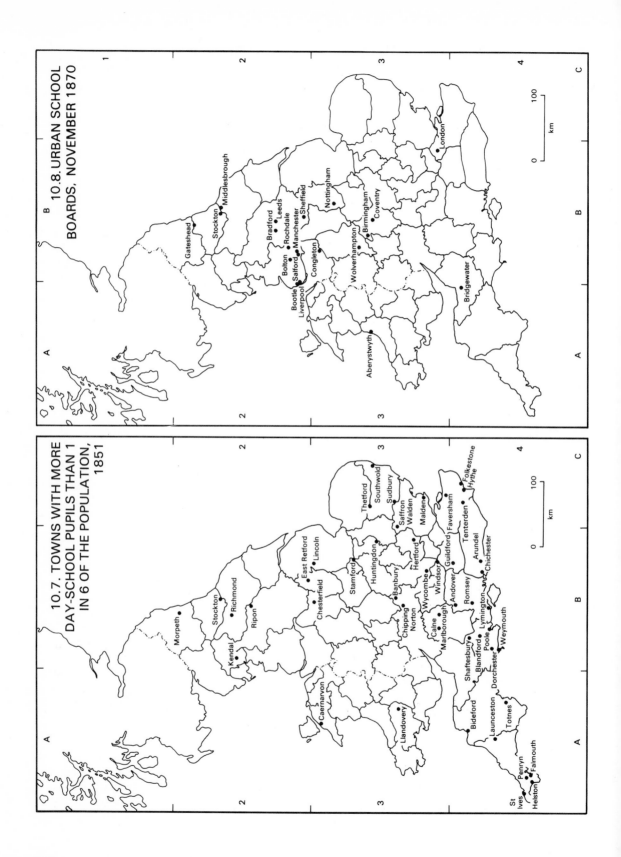

10.7. TOWNS WITH MORE DAY-SCHOOL PUPILS THAN 1 IN 6 OF THE POPULATION, 1851

B 10.8. URBAN SCHOOL BOARDS, NOVEMBER 1870

fifteen in the large cities, of which Liverpool, Manchester, and Salford were examples in Lancashire. London was, uniquely, much larger than this. The motivation of School Boards, in places which were apparently similar in nature and in need, differed according to which lobbies gained power. Some saw as their priority the obvious one of building schools, an expensive responsibility, however. Such boards included London, Birmingham, Sheffield, Bradford and, in Lancashire, Bolton and Liverpool. Others of which Salford and Manchester were prime examples, blatantly saw themselves as protectors of voluntary interests. Both these boards were chaired by H. Birley, a prominent textile manufacturer.[11] Bootle was a classic example of a board perfectly timed to meet the demands presented by a rapidly growing, youthful, and proletarian population which followed the expansion into the borough of the Mersey docks. But for fifteen years it successfully resisted building schools, attempting to justify its existence by a rigorous though not always effective school-attendance policy.[12]

Bootle in fact exemplifies the many demographic, economic, and social pressures which so exercised the providers of urban schools.[13] Before 1850 the town was split into the original agricultural village, sited at the junction of coastal marshes and a sandstone rise behind, and a growing commuter suburb of Liverpool, located along the Mersey shore. Hit by Mersey dock expansion during the 1850s, its population grew rapidly from 4,000 in 1851 to 16,000 in 1871, and to nearly 50,000 in 1891.[14] Before 1860 it had only one National School, designed for a much more respectable intake than the incoming casual labouring population. As problematic as the population growth was the socio-economic slippage, the percentage of the child population drawn from the gentleman/professional categories (socio-economic groupings I and II) declining from 32 per cent in 1851 to 15 per cent in 1871, and that in the semi- and unskilled labouring categories increasing from 37 per cent in 1851 (many at this date being from agricultural labouring families) to 48 per cent in 1871. Maps 10.9 and 10.10 show the territorial variation which existed at the time of the 1871 Census. The greatest concentration of child population and particularly that in socio-economic groupings IV and V (semi- and unskilled labouring) was in the south-western dockland corner of the borough, which had almost overnight evolved into a notorious slum, particularly enumeration districts 7 and to a lesser extent 5 and 6.[15] The Leeds and Liverpool Canal and Liverpool–Southport railway served as a convenient physical barrier between this ghetto and middle-class enclave which developed on the slopes of Breeze Hill in enumeration district 3, on the edge of the old Bootle village. Note here the predominance of population in socio-economic groupings I and II. Enumeration district 4 formed a buffer zone of relatively respectable working-class population (SEG III) between the canal and the railway. By the 1890s, the whole of the Mersey shore was built up (Map 10.11) and the dockland slums had spread to the north-west corner of the borough.

As in other major towns and cities, a minutely detailed correspondence developed between social and school grading. As Map 10.11 suggests, the middle-class enclave was not visited by the attendance officers as most of the children were sent to schools such as Merchant Taylor's at Crosby or Liverpool Collegiate, if not to boarding-schools further afield or indeed to the local proprietary school, Bootle College, located on Breeze Hill (Map 10.11). Away from this area were the zones of population requiring public provision.

Bootle's first National School, St Mary's, long predated dockland development and, as Bootle's sole Anglican elementary establishment by the early 1860s, was discomfited by the violent social change in its immediate catchment area. So the position was ripe for Christ Church, established in the mid-1860s in a middle-class fringe area, to take over as Bootle's most prestigious elementary school. Meanwhile St John's Parish, if it was to provide schooling at all, had to cater from the

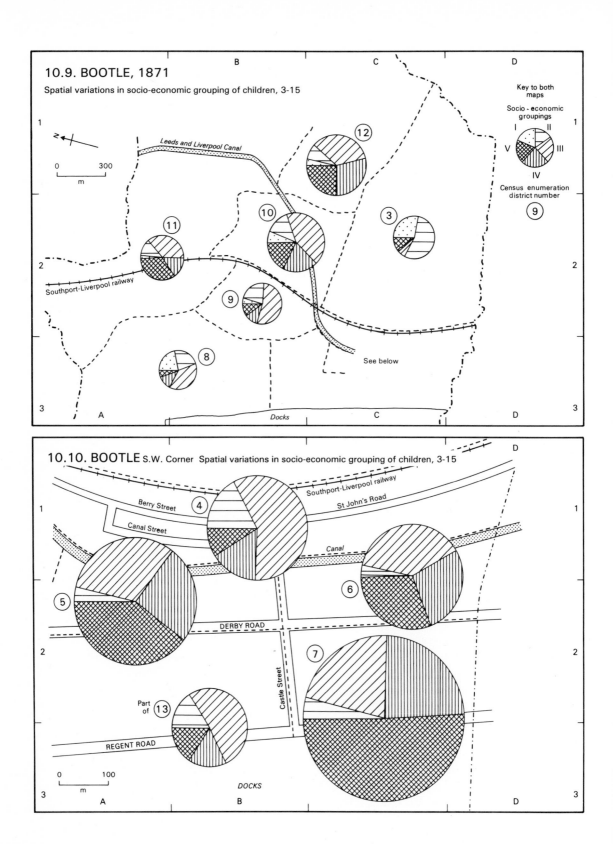

10.9. BOOTLE, 1871

Spatial variations in socio-economic grouping of children, 3-15

Leeds and Liverpool Canal

Southport-Liverpool railway

Key to both maps

Socio - economic groupings

Census enumeration district number

See below

Docks

10.10. BOOTLE S.W. Corner Spatial variations in socio-economic grouping of children, 3-15

Southport-Liverpool railway

Berry Street

Canal Street

St John's Road

Canal

DERBY ROAD

Castle Street

Part of 13

REGENT ROAD

DOCKS

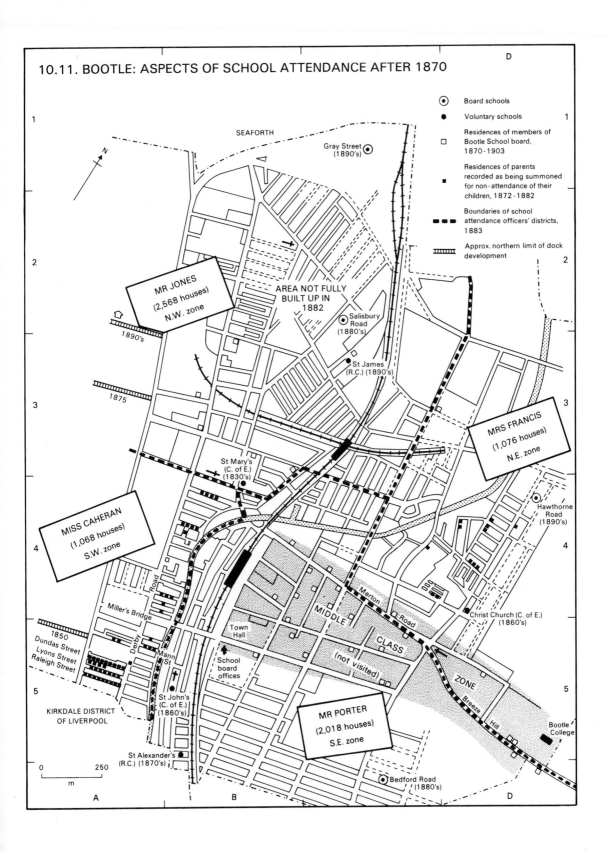

10.11. BOOTLE: ASPECTS OF SCHOOL ATTENDANCE AFTER 1870

Board schools

Voluntary schools

Residences of members of
Bootle School board,
1870-1903

Residences of parents
recorded as being summoned
for non-attendance of their
children, 1872-1882

Boundaries of school
attendance officers' districts,
1883

Approx. northern limit of dock
development

SEAFORTH

Gray Street
(1890's)

MR JONES
(2,568 houses)
N.W. zone

AREA NOT FULLY
BUILT UP IN
1882

1890's

Salisbury
Road
(1880's)

1875

St James
(R.C.) (1890's)

MRS FRANCIS
(1,076 houses)
N.E. zone

St Mary's
(C. of E.)
(1830's)

Hawthorne
Road
(1890's)

MISS CAHERAN
(1,068 houses)
S.W. zone

Road

Miller's Bridge

MIDDLE

Merton
Road

Christ Church (C. of E.)
(1860's)

1850

Town
Hall

CLASS

Derby

Dundas Street
Lyons Street
Raleigh Street

Mann
St

School
board
offices

(not visited)

ZONE

Breeze

Hill

KIRKDALE DISTRICT
OF LIVERPOOL

St John's
(C. of E.)
(1860's)

MR PORTER
(2,018 houses)
S.E. zone

Bootle
College

0   250

m

St Alexander's
(R.C.) (1870's)

Bedford Road
(1880's)

A   B   D

207

start for the non-Catholic dockland children. The vicar of the parish (in the mid-1860s) urgently appealed to the National Society to provide funds, as the middle classes were moving out and the local population was poor. In the Catholic sector St James's School was established in 1848 but moved to a new location in 1872. It took the precaution also of providing a 'Select' school in separate premises, with higher fees, because the shop-keeping classes were reluctant to allow their children to mix with those of casual dock labour. St Alexander's began in the 1860s but moved (at the beginning of the School Board period) into a tall purpose-built school just over the Liverpool boundary. It was designed to take two-thirds of its children from Bootle and the rest from Liverpool, but mostly from the dockland environment, and it was the school with the most pressing social problems.

With so much activity in the 1860s and early 1870s, members of the Bootle School Board clearly felt enough school building had been accomplished by the voluntary bodies, and their main duty would be to enforce attendance. Officers were cumulatively appointed and Map 10.11 shows the boundaries of the districts of the four officers in 1883, and the number of houses they covered. It also depicts the location of residences of parents recorded as being summoned for non-attendance in the 1872–82 period. Many more than this were involved but exact addresses not recorded. But this, and evidence about the residences of parents claiming remission of fees from the Board,[16] a procedure allowed up to 1876, makes it clear that the south-western corner of Bootle was the area in deepest distress. The social divide in the town was symbolized by the territorial polarity between the residences of the members of the Bootle School Board over its period of office, and those of the parents they summoned for non-attendance of the children. The School Board offices (Map 10.11) were located, with an apposite social verisimilitude, on the margin of the segregated residential zones.

From early in its period of office, the School Board came under pressure from the Education Department to meet an increasing deficiency in accommodation. The Board thereupon fought a long rearguard action to avoid the cost on the rates of building new schools. In order to demonstrate adequate provision, the Board meticulously recorded accommodation provided in private venture schools, of which there were scores in the borough and many in the working-class areas, as well as that in inspected voluntary schools. Most of the private schools were in unsuitable premises and some were no more than child-minding institutions. Yet all but a handful were given some kind of seal of approval from the Board. In 1878, for example, the Board counted nearly 700 children on the registers of such schools as being in accommodation it had certified. Many of these were in the middle-class quarter, taking children for which the Education Department did not expect the Board to provide. By 1881, the approximate number requiring elementary accommodation was over 5,000. There was actual accommodation for 4,000. The Board had to bow to the inevitable and built two board schools at the ends of the borough, Bedford Road serving a newly developed and reasonably respectable working-class quarter in the south, and Salisbury Road new dockland development in the north. These two were by themselves inadequate to meet the continuing population growth, and further schools were provided in the 1890s at Hawthorne Road and Gray Street (Map 10.11). Almost predictably, Hawthorne Road became the most prestigious of the board schools, followed by Bedford Road. Salisbury Road, on the other hand, found itself in an area of rapid social decline, and taking disadvantaged children, in some cases offloaded by the voluntary schools.[17]

By the end of the School Board period in 1903, therefore, this town of approximately 60,000 people had epitomized many of the social forces impinging on mass educational provision, tensions between central government legislation and local responses, and the complexities which added to the educational planners' concerns, not only caused by the presence of the dual system, but also by duplication of effort within the voluntary sector. Symptomatic of this was the chagrin of the Bootle School Board in having to build Gray Street because of overcrowding at Salisbury Road, when there were many empty places in the Catholic schools, to which of course Nonconformist parents, in the vanguard of those clamouring for rate-aided board school accommodation, would not send their children. The religious problem therefore continued to harass the providers in a situation in which they no doubt considered the demographic and social difficulties more than sufficient to contend with.

Notes

1 See W. B. Stephens, *Education, Literacy and Society 1830–1870: The Geography of Diversity in Provincial England* (Manchester, 1987); and W. E. Marsden, *Unequal Educational Provision in England and Wales: The Nineteenth-century Roots* (London, 1986).

2 See E. J. Green, *Elementary Education in Shropshire during the First Fifteen Years of the School Board Period* (unpublished PhD thesis, University of Liverpool, 1985) for detailed information on variations within Shropshire.

3 See W. E. Marsden, 'Diffusion and regional variation in elementary education in England and Wales 1800–1870', *History of Education*, 11 (1982), pp. 183–7.

4 See W. E. Marsden, 'Social stratification and nineteenth-century English urban education', in R. K. Goodenow and W. E. Marsden (eds), *Urban Educational History in Four Nations: the United States, the United Kingdom, Australia, and Canada* (New York, forthcoming).

5 See Marsden, op. cit. (1982), p. 194.

6 ibid., pp. 177–82.

7 See J. Murphy, *The Religious Problem in English Education: The Crucial Experiment* (Liverpool, 1959).

8 See Marsden, op. cit. (1982), pp. 187–91.

9 See W. E. Marsden, 'Variations in educational provision in Lancashire during the School Board period', *Journal of Educational Administration and History*, 10 (1978), pp. 18–19.

10 See Marsden, op. cit. (1982), pp. 191–2.

11 See Marsden, op. cit. (1978), p. 18.

12 See W. E. Marsden, 'Social environment, school attendance and educational achievement in a Merseyside town 1870–1900', in P. McCann (ed.), *Popular Education and Socialization in the Nineteenth Century* (London, 1977), pp. 208–14.

13 See W. E. Marsden, 'Education and urbanisation in nineteenth-century Britain', *Paedagogica Historica*, 23 (1983), pp. 85–124.

14 See W. E. Marsden, 'Census enumerators' returns, schooling and social areas in the late Victorian town: a case study of Bootle', in R. Lowe (ed.), *New Approaches to the Study of Popular Education, 1851–1902*, History of Education Society Occasional Publication no. 4 (1979), p. 21. Maps 10.9 and 10.10 are taken from that publication and I am grateful to the History of Education Society for permission to reproduce.

15 See W. E. Marsden, 'Ecology and nineteenth-century urban education', *History of Education Quarterly*, 23 (1983), pp. 40–53, for an account of schooling and community in this area; also Chapter 9 in Marsden, op. cit. (1986).

16 See Marsden, op. cit. (1977), pp. 209–10.

17 See W. E. Marsden, 'Education and the social geography of nineteenth-century towns and cities', in D. A. Reeder (ed.), *Urban Education in the Nineteenth Century* (London, 1977), pp. 63–4.

Maps 10.1, 10.2, and 10.3 are based on Tables of Weekday Schools by Denominations, 1858, in vol. 1 of the Reports of the *Newcastle Commission* (1861). Maps 10.4–10.7 are based on materials in the *Census of Great Britain: Reports and Tables on Education in England and Wales* (Education Census, 1851).

Map 10.8 is based on material in the *Reports of the Committee of Council on Education* (1871/2). Maps 10.9 and 10.10 are based on the *Census Enumerators' Returns* for Bootle for 1871, while Map 10.11 is based on information in the *Annual Reports of the Bootle School Board.*

11 RELIGION

Callum Brown

Before the mid-nineteenth century, there was little collection of statistics on the religious habits of the British people. This neglect reflected the pre-industrial primacy of the established churches of England, Scotland, and Wales, and a general satisfaction at the level of religious observance. Things had changed by 1851 when the first and only state census of religion was taken. Dissenting churches had grown enormously in membership, and industrialization and urbanization had created large centres of population in which the habit of going to church for Sunday worship appeared to contemporaries to have fallen into abeyance – especially amongst the working classes. By the twentieth century, religion played a much smaller part in British social life, and this resulted in statistical information about religion being even scarcer as government became unconcerned about the issue. The social investigator is thus left to rely upon voluntary and less reliable surveys, such as a series conducted by the Bible Society in 1979–84. Despite severe problems of inaccuracy, these two censuses, taken some 130 years apart, provide a valuable insight into changing habits of religious worship, and into regional variations in church-going and denominational alignment.

Levels of church-going, 1851 and 1979–84

When the results of the government's religious census became known in the 1850s, considerable alarm was aroused at the apparently 'low level' of church attendance. The census compiler, Horace Mann, set the tone when he wrote in his report that 'a sadly formidable portion of the English people are habitual neglecters of the public ordinances of religion'. However, what strikes the modern eye in the census results (Map 11.1) is not the low but the high level of church-going in 1851. The number of attendances on census Sunday throughout Great Britain was 11,807,292, representing 56.7 per cent of the total population. However, a significant proportion of these attendances were by 'twicers' and 'thricers' – that is, worshippers who attended two or three of the services during the day. Unfortunately, it is impossible to make an accurate allowance for multiple church attendances, but we can say that the minimum number of individual worshippers were those recorded at the highest-attended diet, the morning service, who were enumerated at 5,169,182, or 24.8 per cent of the population. A further difficulty is that both of these figures make no allowance for non-returns which were particularly high in Scotland (20 per cent), because of the lack at that time of local Registrars to supervise the enumeration; non-returns in England and Wales, where there were Registrars, were significantly lower

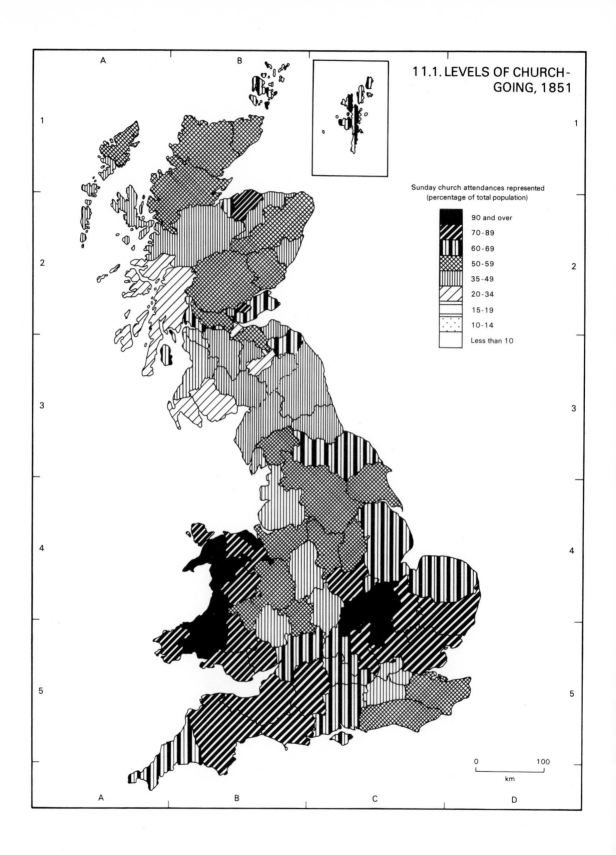

11.1. LEVELS OF CHURCH-GOING, 1851

Sunday church attendances represented
(percentage of total population)

- 90 and over
- 70 - 89
- 60 - 69
- 50 - 59
- 35 - 49
- 20 - 34
- 15 - 19
- 10 - 14
- Less than 10

0   100
km

(4 per cent). If non-returning congregations are assumed to have been the same size as returning ones, the proportion of population attending church rises to 26.9 per cent for morning services and 60.8 per cent for all three services. In reality, the true figure lay somewhere in between, possibly around 40 to 45 per cent. Contrast this with the figure for average Sunday attendances in 1979–84 of 11.3 per cent. Clearly, church-going played an enormous part in the lives of the British people in the mid-nineteenth century, but much less so today.

Because the relative popularity of morning, afternoon, and evening church services varied in different parts of Britain in 1851, it is most accurate when looking at regional and local variation to present the number of attendances at all three diets as a percentage of population. (This means that the indices of attendance for some districts are over 100 per cent of population because of 'twicers' and 'thricers'.) Map 11.1 shows how varied was the pattern of attendances. There was an enormous difference between the county with the highest return, Bedfordshire, with attendances accounting for 105 per cent of population, and the county with the lowest return, Argyllshire in the West Highlands of Scotland, with 26 per cent. Great variation existed in Scotland where there was a highly localized pattern of attendance. Pockets of high attendance were to be found in Morayshire (74 per cent) and Nairn (68 per cent) in the north, and at Kinross (89 per cent), Berwickshire (62 per cent), and Dumbartonshire (65 per cent) in respectively the east, south-east and west of the Lowlands. Counties with very low figures were equally scattered. Argyllshire (26 per cent) in the West Highlands, West Lothian (27 per cent) in the Central Lowlands, and Selkirkshire (29 per cent) in the Borders of the south-east. In so far as we can generalize at all, church-going was higher on the east coast than in the west. Significantly, no appreciable difference emerged between industrial and agricultural counties.

By contrast, church-going patterns in England and Wales were highly regionalized with very little variation within each area. We can easily identify two main regions of high attendance. The first lies in a band of mostly agricultural and rural counties stretching from Cornwall in the south-west to the Wash in the north-east, within which there were two zones of very high attendance: the first centred on the three counties of Northamptonshire (90 per cent), Huntingdonshire (94 per cent), and Bedfordshire (105 per cent) and the second centred on Wiltshire (86 per cent) and Dorset (78 per cent). The other region of high attendance lay in Wales with its central zone stretching along most of the western seaboard from Carmarthen (92 per cent) and Cardigan (102 per cent) in the south, to Merioneth (93 per cent) and Caernarvon (100 per cent) in the north. Practically all the other Welsh counties had strong attendance rates above 76 per cent – the only exception being Radnor (50 per cent) in the centre of the principality. Apart from the North Riding of Yorkshire (63 per cent), the rest of England fell into two regions of low attendance: one in the South-east incorporating London (37 per cent), Surrey (42 per cent), Sussex (57 per cent), and Kent (57 per cent), and the other stretching from the Severn estuary northwards through the Midlands to take in nearly all the northern counties on both sides of the Pennines. Interestingly, attendances were particularly low in the most industrialized areas: in Lancashire (44 per cent), Staffordshire (49 per cent), and County Durham (43 per cent). Industrialization and urbanization thus seems to have had different effects on Scotland and England: compare Glasgow (43 per cent), Edinburgh (55 per cent), and Dundee (58 per cent) with Manchester (34 per cent), Birmingham (36 per cent), London (37 per cent), and Liverpool (45 per cent). However, low church-going also afflicted English agricultural counties like Cumberland (37 per cent), Northumberland (42 per cent), Warwickshire (49 per cent), and Herefordshire (49 per cent).

Although the statistics of church attendance shown by Map 11.2 are not directly

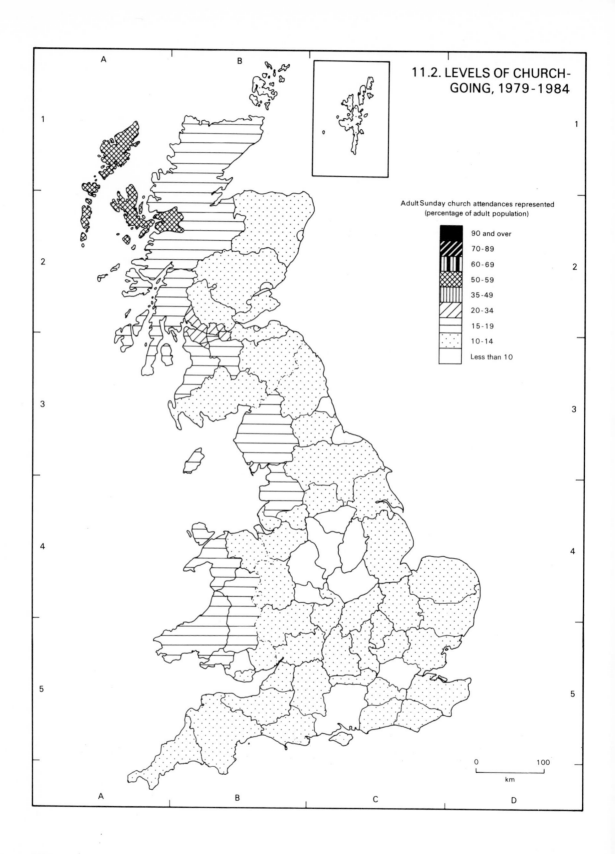

11.2. LEVELS OF CHURCH-GOING, 1979-1984

Adult Sunday church attendances represented
(percentage of adult population)

- 90 and over
- 70-89
- 60-69
- 50-59
- 35-49
- 20-34
- 15-19
- 10-14
- Less than 10

comparable with Map 11.1 (because of the different manner of enumeration), it is quite justifiable to conclude that there has been a massive fall in the church-going habit. The secularization of leisure (through the motor car, radio, and television) and a wider abandonment of religious ideology and habits have taken a heavy toll on the churches. Moreover, there has been a reversal of nineteenth-century trends: Lancashire ranked seventh from bottom of the English counties in 1851, but first in 1979; Cumberland ranked second bottom (after London) in 1851, but its modern near-equivalent, Cumbria, ranks second top. The counties with low rates are now spread across different parts of England, but many of them are large urban conurbations: Cleveland, the West Midlands, Greater London, West Yorkshire and Tyne and Wear with 8 to 9 per cent. Counties of higher attendance are far more numerous in Scotland and Wales. Only two of the eight Welsh counties (Mid Glamorgan and Gwent), and only one out of twenty enumeration areas in Scotland (Aberdeen city) fall below the British average. Still, 'secular' culture has invaded the Celtic fringes, producing wide areas with mid-range attendance rates of between 10 and 14 per cent. These areas are, notably, in the eastern half of Wales bordering England, and in southern and eastern parts of Scotland.

Overall, the social significance of the churches has been falling fast. Church membership has plummeted in England (to 18 per cent of population), and whilst it has remained higher in Wales and Scotland (24 and 47 per cent respectively), this has been offset by a dramatic fall in the frequency of members' church attendance: in Wales in 1982, less than one member in two attended church each Sunday, and in Scotland in 1984 just over one in three. Only in two types of area has the decline been slower: first, in the highland and western maritime regions of Scotland and Wales where puritanical dissenting presbyterian churches have sustained great loyalty amongst isolated communities; and second, in areas like Lancashire and west central Scotland around Glasgow where there are large concentrations of Catholics. Indeed, the presence of Catholics sustains church-going levels in all areas – notably in large conurbations like Merseyside and Greater Manchester which have average attendance rates rather than low ones. In some areas of low attendance, Catholics make up around half the church-goers and keep rates above a negligible level. But for the high turnout of Catholics in Cleveland, Greater London, and Tyne and Wear, church-going rates on Sundays would fall to around 5 per cent of the adult population. However, it is worth observing that in areas like Merseyside, Lancashire, and Glasgow, sectarian awareness and animosity sustains high levels of church-going amongst both Catholics and Protestants. In this way, the areas of religious diversity and geographical isolation which often recorded low rates of church-going in the nineteenth century are now in the later twentieth century the places where religious observance is strongest.

Denominational alignment in England and Wales

Maps 11.3 to 11.10 show the relative popularity of the different religious denominations in England and Wales in 1851 and 1979–82. In the nineteenth century, by far the largest was the Church of England – the established or state church. Its power base lay in the southern half of the country, in the predominantly agricultural counties and also in London. Anglican density tended to be greatest in the counties of high church-going, though Sussex and Herefordshire were notable exceptions, having lower than average attendance but the highest densities of Anglicans in the country (68 and 66 per cent respectively).

The Church of England felt at its most secure in the southern provinces where the parishes tended to be the best endowed, had higher social standing, and were thus favoured by Anglican clergy. The high density of rural population in these fertile areas reinforced the community role of the parish church, and parishioners were generally more assured of a space on a pew at Sunday service than in other regions. Anglican parishes were large in the North, often covering hill country where the population density was lower and the distance to church greater. The industrial revolution reinforced this tendency by loosening the traditional ties between land, labour, and church, and by propelling a rapidly rising population towards urban centres and waged labour. The Church of England was slow to develop an empathy for the inhabitants of industrial society, and the legal and self-imposed restraints on the creation of new parishes in the growing cities of the North resulted in a significant loss of its adherents.

The impact of the industrial revolution upon the Anglican periphery in the North is apparent from Map 11.4 which shows the strength of the various branches of Methodism in 1851. The growth of Methodism from the 1740s was contemporaneous with first the surge of population growth and then with industrialization after 1770. The strongest levels of Methodist adherence were in counties with significant degrees of manufacturing, metallurgy, or mining: in the tin-mining county of Cornwall, for instance, where 65 per cent of church-goers were Methodist, and in the North in the three Ridings of Yorkshire, in Durham and Derbyshire (40–47 per cent). Further south, the density dropped to between 25 and 37 per cent and then to less than 25 per cent in the South-east with the lowest figures coming in London, Essex, and Surrey (7–9 per cent).

But dissent from the established church dated from before the time of John Wesley. Map 11.5 shows the concentration of other Nonconformist churches – most of them, like the Congregationalists, Baptists, Presby-terians, and Quakers, dating from before the mid-seventeenth century. Despite their fairly even distribution, Nonconformist density was highest in a zone around and to the north of London, and in the West Country. The most regionalized of the denominations was the Catholic Church which had maintained a following of recusants in the North of England during the seventeenth and eighteenth centuries, to be reinforced and overtaken in the nineteenth century by Irish immigration. Map 11.6 demonstrates how the immigrants came in through ports like Liverpool, settled near where they disembarked, and then fanned out into adjacent industrial counties or headed, like many other immigrant groups, for London and the South-east.

The position in Wales differed greatly. The Church of England (later called the Church in Wales) was very insecure as the state church, and was in fact disestablished in 1914. Its strength was greatest inland in Radnor (44 per cent), falling to between 21 and 25 per cent in the majority of counties, but reaching only 9 to 13 per cent in the industrial south and the north-west. Methodism too was weak, especially in the south and north-west (4 per cent in Carmarthen), though it ranged between 17 and 26 per cent in some of the northern and inland counties. The main feature of religion in Wales was the dominance of Nonconformity, and especially the Baptists, Congregationalists, and Calvinistic Methodists (who later became known as the Welsh Presbyterians). In only one county (Radnor) did this group fail to equal or outnumber all other church-goers, and in six counties it accounted for between 75 and 80 per cent of the total. In all types of Welsh society – agricultural, urban, and pit villages – the Nonconformist chapels formed powerful foci for working-class and lower-middle class communities for whom religious ties of deference with an Anglican landowning class had been savaged by economic change and, over the longer term, by cultural and linguistic differences.

Maps 11.7–11.10 show that by 1979–82 there had been some significant changes in

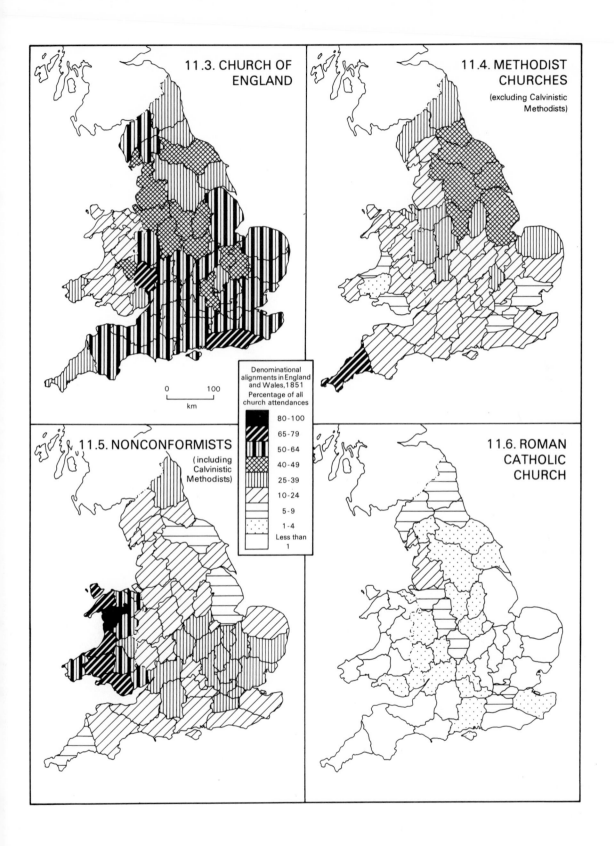

11.3. CHURCH OF ENGLAND

11.4. METHODIST CHURCHES

(excluding Calvinistic Methodists)

11.5. NONCONFORMISTS

(including Calvinistic Methodists)

11.6. ROMAN CATHOLIC CHURCH

Denominational alignments in England and Wales, 1851
Percentage of all church attendances

80-100
65-79
50-64
40-49
25-39
10-24
5-9
1-4
Less than 1

0   100
km

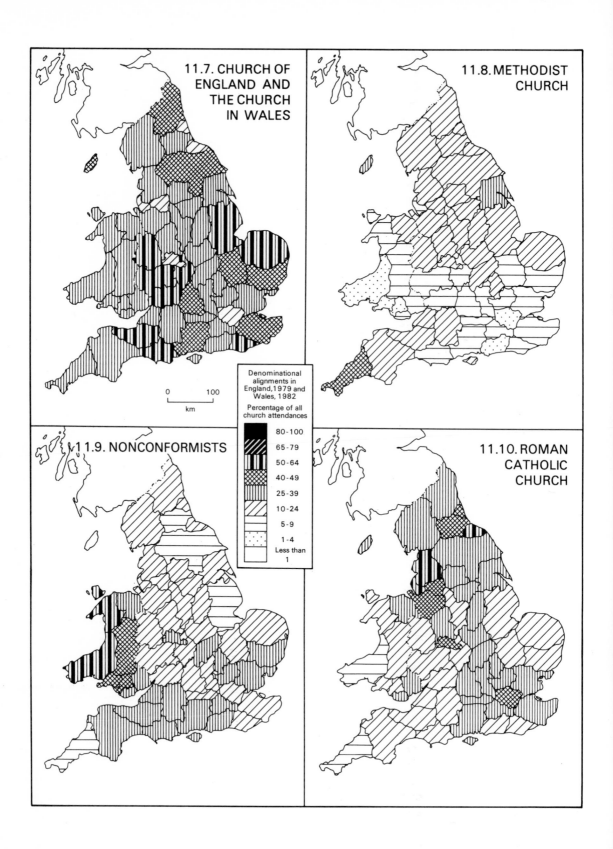

11.7. CHURCH OF ENGLAND AND THE CHURCH IN WALES

11.8. METHODIST CHURCH

11.9. NONCONFORMISTS

11.10. ROMAN CATHOLIC CHURCH

Denominational alignments in England, 1979 and Wales, 1982

Percentage of all church attendances

80-100
65-79
50-64
40-49
25-39
10-24
5-9
1-4
Less than 1

0   100
km

denominational alignment in England and Wales. All the Protestant churches have diminished in relative strength whilst the Catholic Church has expanded. The national percentage share of church-goers fell for practically every major Protestant denomination between 1851 and 1979–82: from 49 to 31 per cent for the Church of England, 22 to 11 per cent for the Methodist Church, and from 25 to 23 per cent for all other Protestant churches. The Catholic share, on the other hand, rose from 4 to 34 per cent. Though the British constitution is still overtly sectarian (forbidding a monarch to be Catholic), few realize that the Catholic Church is now the largest denomination in terms of church-goers in the country (in England, Scotland, and Britain as a whole).

The Protestant churches have suffered a double blow: sharply declining rates of church attendance, and a falling share of active worshippers. During this decline, the Protestant churches have retained some though not all of their regional characteristics. Methodism, for instance, remains strongest in the industrial or formerly industrial periphery (in Cornwall with 48 per cent of church-goers, the North-east and the Midland counties), whilst it remains weakest in the Home Counties and the South-east (with a density in London of 8 per cent in 1851 and 5 per cent in 1979). The Nonconformists remain strong on the west coast of Wales (62 per cent in Dyfed), whilst in England they are weak in the North. However, the former Nonconformist centre of support in the counties to the north of London has been eroded, to be replaced by a new centre of strength in the South-west (in Somerset, Dorset, and most notably Devon where their density has risen from 24 to 32 per cent during 1851–1979). Some change has also occurred in the Church of England's regional pattern, with a marked erosion pushing out from its southern centre. Anglican density in London has fallen from 61 to 24 per cent. One cause has been the phenomenal rise of the Catholic share of the capital's worshippers (from 6 to 46 per cent), but also of importance has been the spectacular collapse of religious habits amongst London's elites and professional middle classes.

Denominational alignment in Scotland

The religious structure of Scotland has been very different from that of England, and to a lesser extent from that of Wales. Scotland was the only part of the British Isles where the established church became presbyterian after the Reformation, reflecting the growth of puritanism in theology, the law, and social mores in a rather backward early-modern economy. But in the eighteenth century, economic progress became exceptionally rapid in Scotland, with industrialization and agricultural improvement causing a profound modernization of the social structure. An industrial society emerged in which the fractures of social class often took religious forms.

By 1851, there were two strong and influential dissenting presbyterian denominations: the United Presbyterian (UP) Church; and the Free Church, formed in May 1843 by the secession of more than a third of the clergy, elders, and adherents of the Church of Scotland. The religious census showed that by 1851 the Church of Scotland and the Free Church each accounted for 32 per cent of worshippers whilst the UP Church's share was 19 per cent. But these national statistics conceal Scotland's marked regional variations in denominational alignment. Maps 11.11–11.14 show that the greatest loss of the Church of Scotland's support occurred in the Highlands and Hebrides as a result of the formation of the Free Church. The Church of Scotland was left with exceptionally few worshippers in this region: 4 per cent in Caithness and

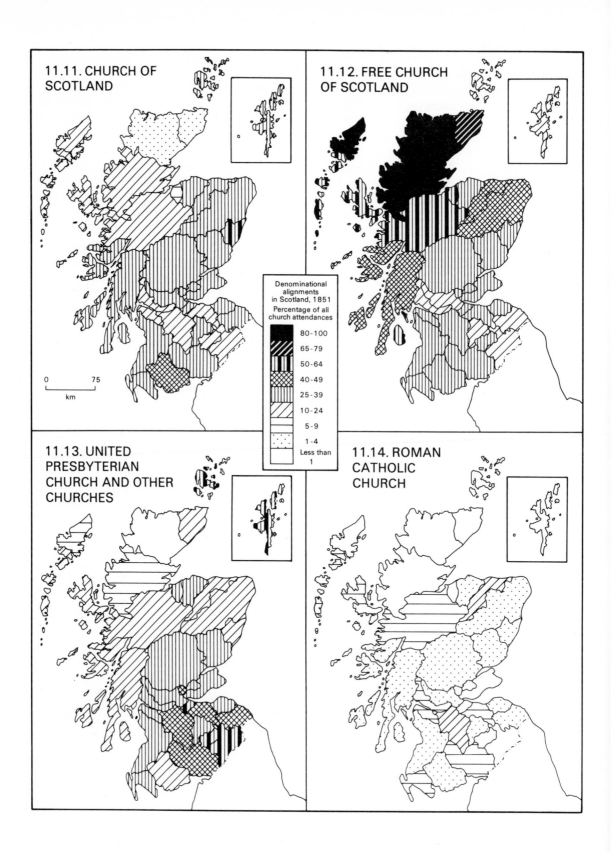

11.11. CHURCH OF SCOTLAND

11.12. FREE CHURCH OF SCOTLAND

11.13. UNITED PRESBYTERIAN CHURCH AND OTHER CHURCHES

11.14. ROMAN CATHOLIC CHURCH

Denominational alignments in Scotland, 1851
Percentage of all church attendances

80-100
65-79
50-64
40-49
25-39
10-24
5-9
1-4
Less than 1

0 75
km

Sutherland, rising to 10 per cent in Ross and Cromarty, and to 20 per cent in Inverness-shire. Conversely, the Free Church was exceptionally strong, accounting for 61 per cent of worshippers in Inverness-shire, 74 per cent in Caithness, 85 per cent in Ross and Cromarty, and for a staggering 96 per cent in Sutherland. In the Lowlands, the Church of Scotland was stronger but still locally weak – especially in the South-east and the cities like Edinburgh where it attracted only 16 per cent of attendances. The figures for the Free Church in the Lowlands ranged from around 40 per cent in the North-east to around 25–35 per cent in the majority of other counties. But in the cities, the northern isles of Orkney and Shetland, and in the south-eastern counties, the UP Church was very strong, attracting along with minor Protestant churches some 63 per cent of attenders in Selkirkshire, 59 per cent in Roxburghshire, and over 35 per cent in most counties of central Scotland. Only in the Highlands and Hebrides were the UP and other minor Protestant churches insignificant – having for instance no recorded attenders in Sutherland.

Finally, Map 11.4 shows the distribution of the Catholic population in Scotland in 1851. Practically all the Catholics were Irish immigrants or their offspring, arriving during the century (and especially after the 1846 potato famine) through west-coast ports such as Glasgow and Greenock, from where they spread out into Lowland counties in search of industrial employment. However, there were some native Scots Catholics in the northern counties, collected into small and isolated communities stretching in a narrow band from the Outer Hebridean islands of Barra and South Uist eastwards as far as Aberdeenshire on the north-east coast.

Two dramatic changes in denominational alignment have taken place since 1851. As Maps 11.15–11.18 show, the major change has been the collapse of presbyterian dissent, which in all but the Hebrides and parts of the West Highlands has virtually disappeared. The cause has been ecumenical reunions; the first in 1900 which brought most of the Free and UP Churches together to form the United Free Church, and the second in 1929 when that denomination was absorbed by a newly disestablished Church of Scotland. Accompanying this reunification of Scottish presbyterianism was the disappearance in the Lowlands of distinctively Calvinist theology and presbyterian puritanism. In revolt against this trend, most of the crofter-fishermen of the north-west refused to participate in the erasure of tradition and strict religious rules (over the keeping of the Sabbath, for instance) and continued in separate denominations: the Free Church and the Free Presbyterian Church. Other Protestant dissenting churches (like the Baptists, Congregationalists, and the Episcopalians) have sustained a small presence throughout the country, though they are exceptionally strong in the Shetland Isles (64 per cent) where Methodism – otherwise insignificant in Scotland – has been a major attraction since the early nineteenth century.

The other important change has been the advance of Catholic adherence. Some 46 per cent of Scottish church-goers are Catholic, and in the industrial communities in and around Glasgow they account for between 54 per cent (Lanark, East Kilbride, and Hamilton) and 68 per cent (Motherwell and Monklands). But as in England and Wales, the Catholic community has spread out into most parts of the Scottish Lowlands, making up for instance 46 per cent of worshippers in Lothian and 45 per cent in Dundee, and their numbers in rural areas have risen slowly (even reaching 15 per cent of church-goers in the Borders of the south-east). But it is important to remember that church-going and church membership are still strong in Scotland compared to the rest of Great Britain, and that this applies to Protestants as well as Catholics. In part, secularization has not proceeded quite so far in Scotland; but in part also, Catholic–Protestant antagonisms are generally stronger here than anywhere in the British Isles – with the notable exception of Northern Ireland, with which there are in Scotland strong religious and family ties on both sides of the sectarian divide.

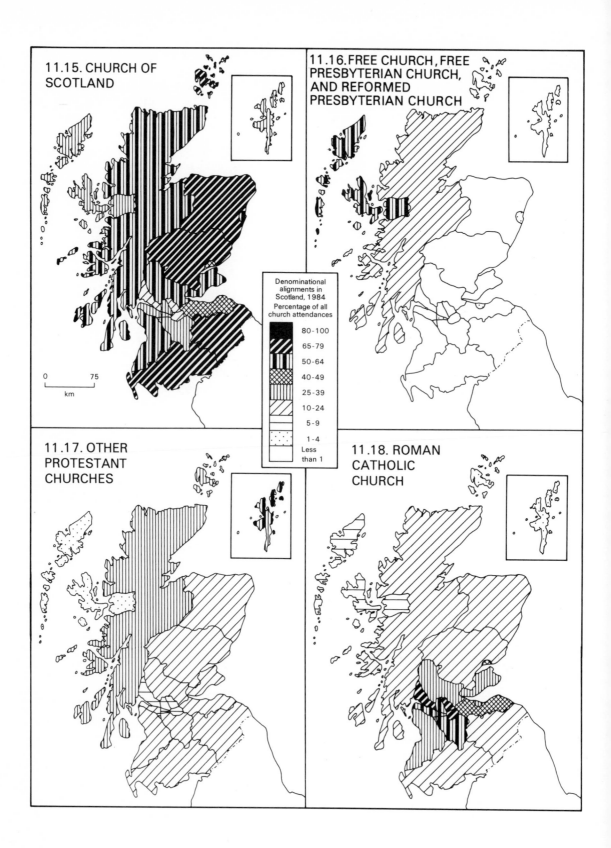

11.15. CHURCH OF SCOTLAND

11.16. FREE CHURCH, FREE PRESBYTERIAN CHURCH, AND REFORMED PRESBYTERIAN CHURCH

Denominational alignments in Scotland, 1984
Percentage of all church attendances

80-100
65-79
50-64
40-49
25-39
10-24
5-9
1-4
Less than 1

0   75
km

11.17. OTHER PROTESTANT CHURCHES

11.18. ROMAN CATHOLIC CHURCH

Notes

Map 11.1 shows total attendances at morning, afternoon, and evening worship on Sunday, 30 March 1851 in each county, expressed as a percentage of total population and calculated from data in the *Census of Great Britain, 1851: Religious Worship, England and Wales*, BPP 1852-3, LXXXIX, and *Religious Worship and Education (Scotland): Report and Tables*, BPP 1854, LIX, p. 301. Map 11.2 shows estimates of the attendances (all services) on an average Sunday in England in November 1979, in Wales in May 1982 and in Scotland in March 1984, in each county and metropolitan authority for England and Wales, and in each region or sub-region for Scotland, expressed as a percentage of adult population. The figures on which the map is based are taken from P. Brierley (ed.), *Prospects for the Eighties: From a Census of the Churches in 1979* (London, 1980); P. Brierley and B. Evans (eds), *Prospects for Wales: Report of the 1982 Census of the Churches* (London, 1983), and P. Brierley and F. Macdonald (eds), *Prospects for Scotland: Report of the 1984 Census of the Churches* (London, 1985). Maps 11.3–11.6 are based on data in the *Census of Great Britain, 1851: Religious Worship, England and Wales*. Maps 11.7–11.10 use figures calculated from data in Brierley, op. cit. and Brierley and Evans, op. cit. Maps 11.11–11.14 use data from the *Census of Great Britain, 1851: Religious Worship and Education (Scotland): Report and Tables*. Maps 11.15–11.18 use figures calculated from data in Brierley and Macdonald, op. cit.

12 LEISURE
Stephen G. Jones

In recent years leisure has emerged as a respectable historical discipline, and scholarly studies have appeared on a wide range of themes from sport to seaside holidays and cinema. It is important to stress at the outset that these studies have been informed by the need to situate leisure within the determining economic, social, and political context. Leisure is after all a 'determined' form of conduct for it is inextricably linked to the economic and social totality, and the various categories which make up that totality – population, work, the ownership of property, the structure of power, and the ideological formation. In other words, it is necessary to consider leisure in relation to the various other sections which appear in this Atlas.

During the course of industrialization in the eighteenth and nineteenth centuries the leisure of the British people was radically transformed. In traditional, pre-industrial society, there was little division between work and leisure, and popular recreations were largely determined by the rhythm of the agricultural cycle. Indeed, as Robert Malcolmson has shown, public festivities such as the annual parish feast, market, or fair, with their excessive eating and drinking, blood sports, and general sociability, were related to wider rural and agricultural influences. Needless to say, many of these rural sports and pastimes were unregulated and very boisterous. With the rise of industrial capitalism and a new urban society, however, there gradually emerged a new and clear separation between the quite distinct spheres of work and leisure. To be sure, capitalist modes of industrial organization in factories meant that labour was constrained by the exigencies of work and time discipline, the face of the clock and the whistle of the hooter. As working time became standardized, leisure was increasingly perceived as that free time left over after work had been completed. Moreover, leisure time itself slowly became subservient to the needs of production. For instance, it was in the interests of employers to stamp out irregular holidays and promote longer, standardized ones which were more efficient than many short, disruptive breaks from work.

In order to meet market orders and delivery dates, employers also required a disciplined, temperate, and reliable workforce. Leisure activities which went against this objective were therefore to be countered. Drinking, gambling, blood sports, and other rowdy pursuits which led to absenteeism and a fall in labour productivity were discouraged. In their place, masters, supported by religious interests, temperance advocates, the new police, and even professional Labour leaders, sponsored rational recreation in the form of regulated amusement, organized sport, and public provision – libraries, parks, and museums. Thus many authorities took the opportunity to establish public libraries under an Act of 1850. The total stock of books in public libraries in British towns increased up to the First World War, in aggregate terms from 1,062,000 in 1875–7 to 1,405,000 in 1913–14. By this later date the distribution of books

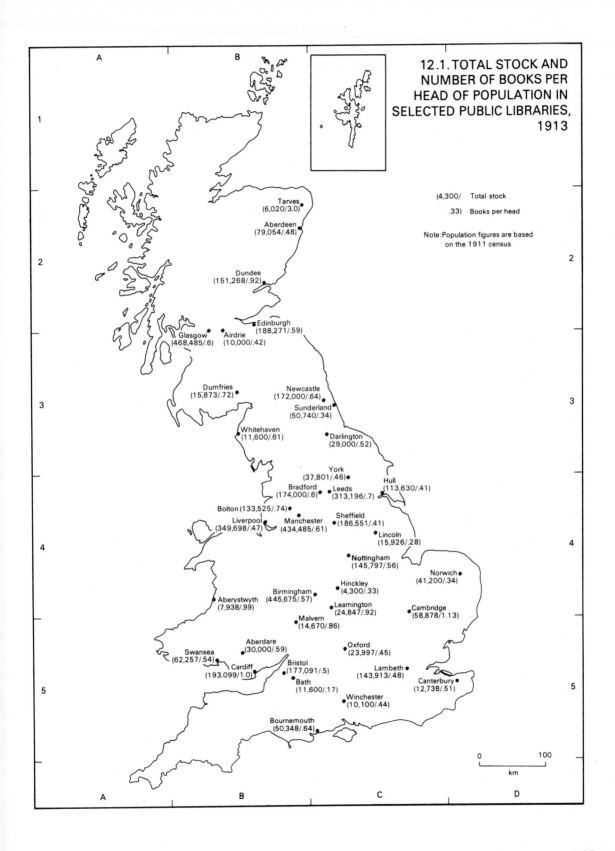

12.1. TOTAL STOCK AND NUMBER OF BOOKS PER HEAD OF POPULATION IN SELECTED PUBLIC LIBRARIES, 1913

(4,300/ — Total stock

.33) — Books per head

Note: Population figures are based on the 1911 census

Tarves (6,020/3.0)
Aberdeen (79,054/.48)
Dundee (151,268/.92)
Edinburgh (188,271/.59)
Glasgow (468,485/.6)
Airdrie (10,000/.42)
Dumfries (15,873/.72)
Newcastle (172,000/.64)
Sunderland (50,740/.34)
Whitehaven (11,600/.61)
Darlington (29,000/.52)
York (37,801/.46)
Hull (113,630/.41)
Bradford (174,000/.6)
Leeds (313,196/.7)
Bolton (133,525/.74)
Liverpool (349,698/.47)
Manchester (434,485/.61)
Sheffield (186,551/.41)
Lincoln (15,926/.28)
Nottingham (145,797/.56)
Norwich (41,200/.34)
Hinckley (4,300/.33)
Birmingham (445,675/.57)
Leamington (24,847/.92)
Cambridge (58,878/1.13)
Aberystwyth (7,938/.99)
Malvern (14,670/.86)
Aberdare (30,000/.59)
Oxford (23,997/.45)
Swansea (62,257/.54)
Cardiff (193.099/1.0)
Bristol (177,091/.5)
Lambeth (143,913/.48)
Canterbury (12,738/.51)
Bath (11,600/.17)
Winchester (10,100/.44)
Bournemouth (50,348/.64)

0   100
km

per head of the population varied significantly across the country (Map 12.1). Readers in the textile towns of Leeds, Bradford, Bolton, and Manchester thus had a greater choice of books than did readers in the less industrialized towns of Oxford, Bath, Winchester, and Canterbury. Though the selection of books could not be controlled, reading was a rational recreation *par excellence*.

However, employers and like-minded groups were not always successful in fashioning working-class behaviour. Robert Storch and others have shown that traditional cultural practices were remarkably durable, and many 'irrational' leisure activities survived until the late nineteenth century and beyond. As is now well established, in a number of regions workers continued to keep the first day of the working week as a traditional holiday, known as St Monday, after 1850. It is true, as Hugh Cunningham has claimed, that people defended and even 'clung to customs whose original meaning had been lost'. Also interesting is the fact that the working class was often resentful of patronage, and in turn was able to re-shape middle-class provision to accord with their own needs and tastes. Workers were therefore able to take over the Working Men's Club and Institute Union (founded 1862) from the temperance advocate, the Reverend Henry Solly, and thereby introduce alcohol. In fact, by the end of the century drinking was still a primary hobby, and public houses and other outlets for drink still central social institutions. For instance, York spawned 338 drink licences for a population of 77,793. As Map 12.2 shows, most of the licensed houses were found in the old streets of the city centre, inhabited by the poorest classes. Not surprisingly, the difficulty of being precise about the character and function of popular recreation has given rise to debate between historians as to whether leisure was a means of bourgeois social control or working-class expression.

Either way, most historians agree that a new world of leisure had emerged by the 1880s and 1890s. What did this new leisure world consist of? First, basic weekly hours of work had been gradually established, and specific periods for holidays were in the process of being established. At the same time, successes had been recorded in the development of new codes of regulated and organized recreation. Here the state provided the essential means of control; appropriate legislation, amenity provision, and of course regulatory agencies in the guise of the police and the courts. Even more important was the penetration of commercial forces into the leisure sphere and the emergence of an embryonic leisure industry, essentially within an urban context. Thus, in the view of Charles Critcher,

> Leisure looked very much as it would be defined and recognized today: something which went on outside working hours; at regular times; in specially provided places (where frequently one person's pleasure was another's profit) unequally distributed between classes and sexes.

It must be added, however, that this was not the end of the leisure story: the twentieth century was again to recast the culture and recreation of the people.

More specifically, the last quarter of the nineteenth century witnessed a growth of leisure forms. There were perhaps four factors in this. The first factor was the increase in purchasing power. Notwithstanding the fact that poverty continued to be a major social problem, it is generally agreed that wages began to rise from the 1850s. Estimates show that real wages rose by about one-third between 1875 and 1900, falling off slightly until the First World War. Unfortunately, there is a lack of evidence as to expenditure patterns and family budgets, but it is possible that increased income was spent on leisure goods and services. Also, presumably the fall in beer consumption when it came towards the end of the century freed income into other leisure products. Certainly, impressionistic evidence suggests that more money was being spent at football matches, seaside resorts, music halls, and cycling shops.

Second, the 54-hour-week norm had been

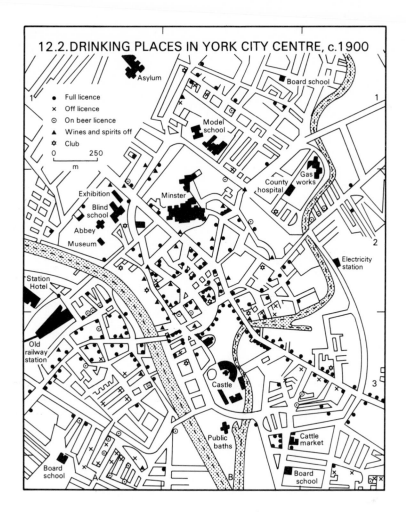

12.2. DRINKING PLACES IN YORK CITY CENTRE, c.1900

Legend:
- • Full licence
- × Off licence
- ⊙ On beer licence
- ▲ Wines and spirits off
- ✿ Club

0 — 250 m

Labels on map: Asylum, Board school, Model school, Gas works, County hospital, Exhibition, Minster, Blind school, Abbey, Museum, Electricity station, Station Hotel, Old railway station, Castle, Public baths, Cattle market, Board school, Board school

established in the 1870s, bringing with it more free time, though there were many groups of workers such as shop assistants and agricultural labourers who worked far longer hours. In addition, a longer weekend evolved with the widespread introduction of the Saturday half-holiday. This provided the opportunity for Saturday afternoon football, and was undoubtedly a factor in the rise of the organized professional game. The participants in the opening season of the Football League in 1888–9 are shown in Map 12.3. As can be seen, the league catered for clubs in the industrial heartland of the North-west and the Midlands, the South remaining the preserve of the amateur game.

Closely associated with the increase in available leisure time was an extension of holiday entitlements. The holiday legislation of 1871 and 1875 led to the August Bank Holiday, particularly important in southern counties where the day trip became common. Londoners would visit Southend or Leigh-on-sea, or perhaps venture further south to Brighton. In the Lancashire and Yorkshire textile industry standardized summer holidays of one week were gained, though it must be added that other regions were not so fortunate. Since paid leave was the privilege of white-collar workers, savings clubs provided the necessary finance, but again almost exclusively in the textile districts. In any case, seaside resorts began to grow (see Map 12.4). By the end of

227

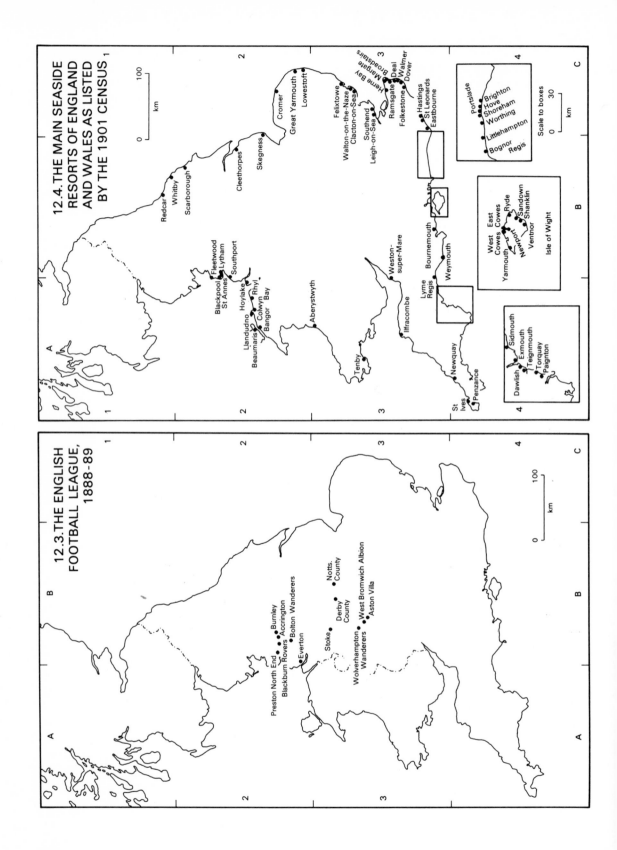

12.4. THE MAIN SEASIDE RESORTS OF ENGLAND AND WALES AS LISTED BY THE 1901 CENSUS

Redcar
Whitby
Scarborough
Cleethorpes
Skegness
Cromer
Great Yarmouth
Lowestoft
Felixtowe
Walton-on-the-Naze
Clacton-on-Sea
Southend
Leigh-on-Sea
Herne Bay
Margate
Broadstairs
Ramsgate
Deal
Walmer
Folkestone
Dover
Hastings
St Leonards
Eastbourne

Fleetwood
Blackpool
St Annes
Lytham
Southport
Llandudno
Beaumaris
Hoylake
Colwyn Bay
Bangor
Rhyl
Aberystwyth
Tenby
Weston-super-Mare
Ilfracombe
Lyme Regis
Bournemouth
Weymouth
Newquay
St Ives
Penzance

Portslade
Brighton
Hove
Shoreham
Worthing
Littlehampton
Bognor Regis

Scale to boxes
0   30
km

West Cowes
East Cowes
Cowes
Yarmouth
Newport
Ryde
Sandown
Shanklin
Ventnor
Isle of Wight

Dawlish
Sidmouth
Exmouth
Teignmouth
Torquay
Paignton

0   100
km

12.3. THE ENGLISH FOOTBALL LEAGUE, 1888-89

Preston North End
Burnley
Blackburn Rovers
Accrington
Bolton Wanderers
Everton
Stoke
Derby County
Notts. County
Wolverhampton Wanderers
West Bromwich Albion
Aston Villa

0   100
km

the nineteenth century the popular seaside resorts of today had been created.

The third factor was the commercialization of leisure, together with the application of technology to entertainment. Again there is a paucity of data, but clearly heavily capitalized entertainment increasingly featured as more investment and labour were used in the leisure industries. Leisure had been commercialized since the eighteenth century, but it was only in the last decades of the Victorian era that large-scale capital investment was channelled into music-halls, pleasure piers, hotels, and sports stadia, no doubt encouraged by limited liability and more efficient financial structures. Asa Briggs has portrayed 1896 as something of a hinge year in the leisure transition, with the arrival of Marconi in England, the presentation of the first moving picture show in London, the first motor race between London and Brighton, and the founding of the *Daily Mail*. All of these of course involved the application of technical innovations to leisure, in the form of electronically induced entertainment, the adoption of the internal combustion engine or the use of new rotary presses and Linotype typesetting in the production of newspapers.

The fourth and final factor in the expansion of leisure was the influence of transport. The railway had stimulated travel and leisure for many decades, but it was only from about the 1870s that the working-class outing became popular and firmly established. Excursion trains were laid on to race meetings, football matches, and seaside resorts. But pehaps more important was the improvement of urban public transport systems and the increasing use made of trams and omnibuses in and around town centres, widening market choice.

By the Edwardian period modern forms of leisure were being established, albeit falteringly and with many gaps. This should not lead us to believe, however, that the new leisure revolution was received in the same way through all levels of society. As in other areas of life, there was inequality in leisure and significant differences in experience according to class, age, and gender. Despite the development of an all-pervasive mass entertainment which exerted an influence over everyone, certain leisure activities remained essentially for the middle classes: sports such as tennis, golf, hockey, and badminton. There was a kind of social zoning between classes in their leisure, as was the case at seaside resorts. Class differentiation in leisure was not simply determined by different levels of income, but was the inevitable outcome of different value systems, mores, and cultures. Yet income was clearly a crucial factor. For the poor, many leisure products were beyond their reach. And even for the not-so-poor, non-commercial alternatives were often preferred. Workers banded together in an array of autonomous clubs and institutions, from working men's clubs to horticultural societies. The accessibility to leisure also depended upon age and sex. The scope of and opportunity for leisure were clearly different for children and youths than for adults. As for women, it appears that the public house, football ground, racecourse, and other places of entertainment were male preserves. For the working-class woman, particularly if she was the mother of a family, leisure was essentially a domestic and private affair spent in the home. As one Preston woman remarked, 'It was all bed and work.'

With the coming of the twentieth century there was again to be much change in leisure. Leisure was constrained during the First World War, not simply because hours of work rose, but also due to the state's restriction, supervision, and regulation of various pastimes, most notably drinking. The years between the two world wars did witness, however, a considerable expansion of leisure. By the end of the 1930s there was more money being spent on leisure, more voluntary organizations working in leisure, and more public amenities for leisure than there had ever been. Most crucial was the increasing commercialization of leisure time. Leisure industries of all descriptions, fed by rising real wages and shorter hours of work, expanded at an unprecedented rate. For instance, the

12.5. THE ENGLISH AND SCOTTISH FOOTBALL LEAGUES, 1935-36

(1898/   Year of formation
/1)   Division in 1935-36 season
1)   First
2)   Second
3N)   Third north
3S)   Third south

1   Cowdenbeath (1905/2)
2   Dunfermline (1907/1)
3   Stenhousemuir (1884/2)
4   Falkirk (1876/2) & E. Stirling (1894/2)
5   Airdrie (1878/1)
6   Albion R. (1881/1)
7   Motherwell (1885/1)
8   Preston N.E. (1880/1)
9   Blackburn R. (1871/1)
10   Accrington (1886/3N)
11   Bradford C. (1903/2) & Bradford P.A. (1907/2)
12   Halifax T. (1911/3N)
13   Huddersfield T. (1908/1)
14   Barnsley (1887/2)
15   Oldham A. (1899/3N)
16   Rochdale (1900/3N)
17   Bury (1885/2)
18   Manchester C. (1887/1) & Manchester U. (1880/2)
19   Stockport C. (1883/3N)
20   Everton (1878/1) & Liverpool (1892/1)
21   Crewe (1877/3N)
22   Port Vale (1874/2)

a GLASGOW
Celtic (1888/1)
Clyde (1877/1)
Partick T. (1876/1)
Queen's Park (1867/1)
Rangers (1873/1)
Third Lanark (1868/1)

b EDINBURGH
Hearts (1873/1)
Hibernian (1875/1)
Edinburgh C. (1928/2)
St Bernards (1878/2)

c LONDON
Arsenal (1886/1)
Brentford (1880/1)
Charlton A. (1906/2)
Chelsea (1904/1)
Clapton Orient (1881/3S)
Crystal Palace (1905/3S)
Fulham (1880/2)
Millwall (1885/3S)
Queens Park Rangers (1885/3S)
Tottenham Hotspur (1882/2)
West Ham U. (1900/2)

Aberdeen (1903/1)
Brechin C. (1906/2)
Montrose (1879/2)
Forfar A. (1885/2)
St Johnstone (1884/1)
Arbroath (1878/1)
Dundee (1893/1) & Dundee U. (1910/2)
King's Park (1875/2)
East Fife (1903/2)
Alloa (1878/2)
Raith R. (1883/2)
Dumbarton (1872//2)
Morton (?/2)
St Mirren (1876/2)
Leith A. (1887/2)
Kilmarnock (1869/1)
Hamilton A. (1870/1)
Ayr U. (1910/1)
Queen of the South (1919/1)
Newcastle U. (1882/2)
Gateshead (1899/3N)
Sunderland (1879/1)
Carlisle (1903/3N)
Hartlepool U. (1908/3N)
Darlington (1882/3N)
Middlesbrough (1876/1)
Barrow (1901/3N)
York C. (1903/3N)
Burnley (1883/2)
Leeds U. (1904/1)
Hull C. (1904/2)
Blackpool (1887/2)
Southport (1881/3N)
Bolton W. (1874/1)
Doncaster R. (1879/2)
Grimsby T. (1878/2)
New Brighton (1921/3N)
Rotherham U. (1884/3N)
Tranmere R. (1883/3N)
Sheffield W. (1867/1) & Sheffield U. (1889/2)
Chester (1884/3N)
Chesterfield (1866/3N)
Lincoln C. (1883/3N)
Wrexham (1873/3N)
Mansfield T. (1905/3N)
Stoke C. (1863/1)
Derby C. (1884/1)
Notts F. (1865/2) & Notts C. (1862/3N)
Wolves (1877/1)
West Brom (1879/1)
Leicester C. (1884/2)
Norwich C. (1905/2)
Walsall (1892/3N)
Aston Villa (1874/1) & Birmingham C. (1875/1)
Coventry C. (1883/3S)
Northampton T. (1897/3S)
Luton T. (1885/3S)
Swansea T. (1900/2)
Newport C. (1911/3S)
Swindon T. (1881/3S)
Watford (1891/3S)
Southend U. (1906/3S)
Cardiff (1899/3S)
Bristol R. (1883/3S) & Bristol C. (1894/3S)
Reading (1871/3S)
Gillingham (1893/3S)
Aldershot (1927/3S)
Exeter C. (1908/3S)
Southampton (1885/2)
Brighton (1898/3S)
Bournemouth (1890/3S)
Portsmouth (1898/1)
Plymouth A. (1910/2)
Torquay U. (1921/3S)

0   100
km

sports industry and all its various ancillary activities, from the manufacture and retailing of sports products to the printing and publication of specialist papers, matured into a fully-fledged commercial operation. Association football had thus made enormous strides since its late-nineteenth-century origins, with large attendances, large stadia, and clubs belonging to the Scottish and Football Leagues found in all the important industrial areas, especially Clydeside, the Midlands, the textile communities and the major ports, as can be seen from Map 12.5. The same pattern can be discerned across the leisure spectrum. The inter-war years, in brief, witnessed the introduction of all kinds of novel entertainments which were cheap and plentiful, catering almost exclusively for the lower end of the market – charabanc trips to the seaside, the football pools, the tote, popular broadcasting, the talkies, Penguin paperbacks, children's comics, Wembley Cup Finals, cheap gramophone records, the Saturday-night dance, and much more besides. Urban leisure had arrived. As shown in Map 12.6, the centre of Manchester had a wide array of public places of amusement well served by the city's transport network.

It is perhaps the cinema which best captures the changing leisure landscape. By the beginning of the 1920s there were already over 4,000 cinemas in Great Britain. What is important about the inter-war years was the massive rebuilding programme, whereby many of the rather primitive pre-war picture theatres were demolished and replaced by larger, more comfortable and sophisticated cinemas, designed in ornate Moorish, Egyptian, or Gothic architectural styles. Most well known were the huge dream palaces or super cinemas with their plush surroundings and Wurlitzer organs emerging magically from below ground. By the 1930s most cinemas had been converted to sound, and along with television, the talking picture was to become the most pervasive cultural influence of the twentieth century, ushering in new modes of mass, standardized entertainment. In overall terms, the number of cinemas in Britain approached the

5,000 mark by 1938. In some urban sprawls cinemas were ubiquitous. Map 12.7 sets out the increases which took place in the textile districts of the North-west, a region, interestingly enough, which had a greater concentration of cinemas than the relatively more prosperous southern counties.

Throughout the length and breadth of Britain, cinema audiences consisted of members of all social groups from the very poor to the well-off. Even the unemployed and the working-class housewife, usually starved of leisure, were frequent patrons, particularly at cheap matinées. However, this should not disguise the fact that the underprivileged classes simply could not afford the expense of many of the new forms of marketed leisure. It is also as well to remember that leisure was linked to trends in the business cycle. Rugby Union in the Welsh valleys thus suffered due to industrial stagnation and rising unemployment, while the cyclical fluctuations of the economy were reflected in attendance receipts at racecourses. There was of course a spatial aspect to this, for the industrial North, and South Wales, savaged by the decline of the old staples of mining, shipbuilding, iron and steel, and textiles, had less resources for leisure than the relatively prosperous Midlands and South with their new industries of electrical engineering, motor vehicles, and the rest.

Commercialization did not undercut voluntary forms of leisure. The working class may have spent more of their income at the football match, the seaside resort or the racecourse, yet they still continued to sponsor and support their own class-based organizations. There was, for example, a wide range of cultural agencies attached to the Labour movement catering for sport, film, drama, travel, education, and even temperance activity. It was the working man's club which was one of the most important of proletarian social institutions. The Working Men's Club and Institute Union was more than a supplier of drink; an array of facilities was provided, satisfying members' tastes for all kinds of indoor and outdoor recreation. By the end of the 1920s there were

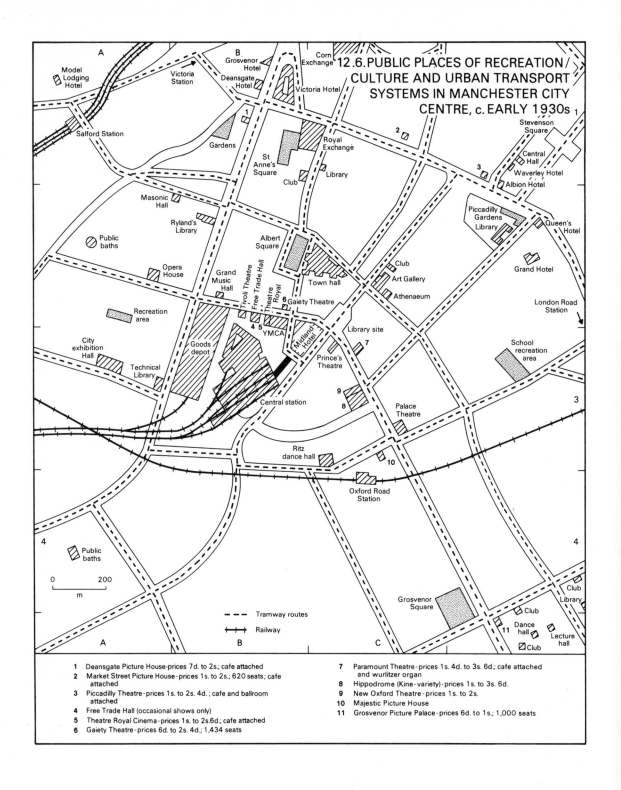

12.6. PUBLIC PLACES OF RECREATION/ CULTURE AND URBAN TRANSPORT SYSTEMS IN MANCHESTER CITY CENTRE, c. EARLY 1930s

Model Lodging Hotel

Victoria Station

Salford Station

Grosvenor Hotel

Deansgate Hotel

Corn Exchange

Victoria Hotel

Gardens

St Anne's Square

Royal Exchange

Club

Library

Stevenson Square

Central Hall

Waverley Hotel

Albion Hotel

Masonic Hall

Ryland's Library

Public baths

Opera House

Grand Music Hall

Albert Square

Town hall

Piccadilly Gardens Library

Queen's Hotel

Grand Hotel

Recreation area

Tivoli Theatre

Free Trade Hall

Theatre Royal

Gaiety Theatre

Club

Art Gallery

Athenaeum

City exhibition Hall

Technical Library

Goods depot

YMCA

Midland Hotel

Library site

London Road Station

School recreation area

Central station

Prince's Theatre

Palace Theatre

Ritz dance hall

Oxford Road Station

Grosvenor Square

Club Library

Dance hall

Lecture hall

Club

Public baths

0   200
m

- - - Tramway routes
—|—|—|— Railway

1   Deansgate Picture House-prices 7d. to 2s.; cafe attached
2   Market Street Picture House-prices 1s. to 2s.; 620 seats; cafe attached
3   Piccadilly Theatre-prices 1s. to 2s. 4d.; cafe and ballroom attached
4   Free Trade Hall (occasional shows only)
5   Theatre Royal Cinema-prices 1s. to 2s.6d.; cafe attached
6   Gaiety Theatre-prices 6d. to 2s. 4d.; 1,434 seats
7   Paramount Theatre-prices 1s. 4d. to 3s. 6d.; cafe attached and wurlitzer organ
8   Hippodrome (Kine-variety)-prices 1s. to 3s. 6d.
9   New Oxford Theatre-prices 1s. to 2s.
10 Majestic Picture House
11 Grosvenor Picture Palace-prices 6d. to 1s.; 1,000 seats

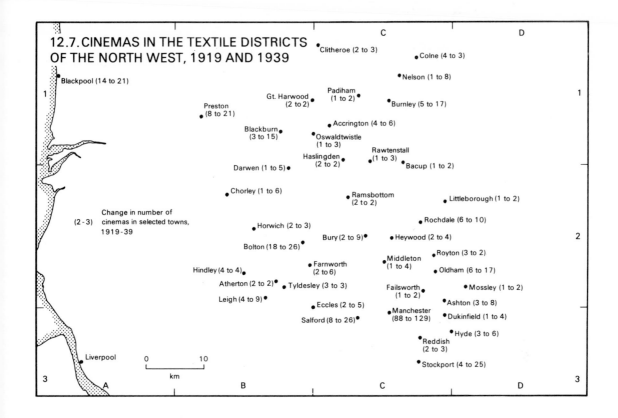

12.7. CINEMAS IN THE TEXTILE DISTRICTS OF THE NORTH WEST, 1919 AND 1939

Clitheroe (2 to 3)
Colne (4 to 3)
Nelson (1 to 8)
Blackpool (14 to 21)
Gt. Harwood (2 to 2)
Padiham (1 to 2)
Burnley (5 to 17)
Preston (8 to 21)
Accrington (4 to 6)
Blackburn (3 to 15)
Oswaldtwistle (1 to 3)
Rawtenstall (1 to 3)
Haslingden (2 to 2)
Bacup (1 to 2)
Darwen (1 to 5)
Chorley (1 to 6)
Ramsbottom (2 to 2)
Littleborough (1 to 2)
Rochdale (6 to 10)
Horwich (2 to 3)
Bury (2 to 9)
Heywood (2 to 4)
Bolton (18 to 26)
Royton (3 to 2)
Farnworth (2 to 6)
Middleton (1 to 4)
Oldham (6 to 17)
Hindley (4 to 4)
Atherton (2 to 2)
Tyldesley (3 to 3)
Failsworth (1 to 2)
Mossley (1 to 2)
Leigh (4 to 9)
Ashton (3 to 8)
Eccles (2 to 5)
Manchester (88 to 129)
Dukinfield (1 to 4)
Salford (8 to 26)
Hyde (3 to 6)
Reddish (2 to 3)
Liverpool
Stockport (4 to 25)

(2-3) Change in number of cinemas in selected towns, 1919-39

0   10
km

2,626 clubs affiliated to the Union, with particular strength in the industrial North: there were 654 clubs in Yorkshire, compared to 227 in the Home Counties. Group-created leisure as dispensed by the Club and Institute Union provided male workers with a degree of control and autonomy in their spare time, in much the same way as Miners' Welfare Institutes, brass bands, choirs, Sunday football teams, and homing societies did.

In conclusion, it should be noted that leisure has again been transformed in the period since the Second World War. Again, consumers of leisure have benefited from a growth in real income and a fall in working hours, together with paid holiday concessions. Again, the leisure industry has expanded and is now one of the most important sectors of the British economy. Again, voluntary organizations have survived and been able to compete against commercial alternatives. Indeed, since the industrial revolution, there has been a great deal of inventiveness and independence in people's leisure time, and class-based recreational and cultural institutions have been able to adapt to economic change and new demands. But possibly the most far-reaching innovation since 1945 has been the growing importance of the state. Central and local government and quasi-official bodies such as the Sports Council and the Arts Council play a crucial role in providing resources for and regulating the organization of leisure. In all British towns there is a range of public recreational facilities, from libraries to leisure centres. Our final Map 12.8 thus provides a geographical breakdown of one important aspect of public provision in the 1980s, namely National Parks and designated Areas of Natural Beauty.

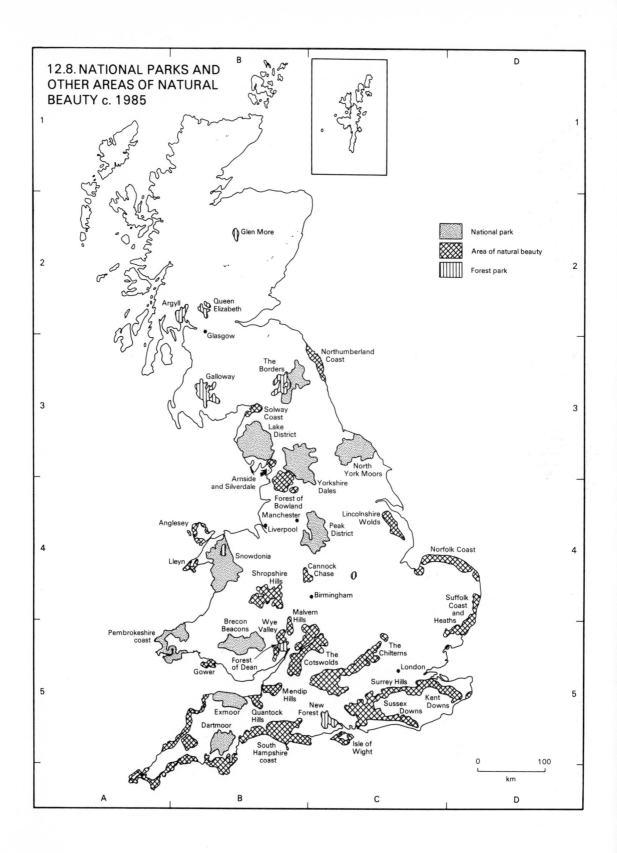

12.8. NATIONAL PARKS AND OTHER AREAS OF NATURAL BEAUTY c. 1985

National park

Area of natural beauty

Forest park

Glen More

Argyll
Queen Elizabeth
Glasgow

Northumberland Coast

The Borders
Galloway
Solway Coast
Lake District

North York Moors

Arnside and Silverdale
Yorkshire Dales
Forest of Bowland
Manchester
Liverpool

Lincolnshire Wolds

Peak District

Norfolk Coast

Anglesey

Lleyn
Snowdonia
Shropshire Hills

Cannock Chase

Birmingham

Suffolk Coast and Heaths

Malvern Hills
Brecon Beacons
Wye Valley

Pembrokeshire coast

The Cotswolds
The Chilterns

Forest of Dean
London

Gower

Surrey Hills

Mendip Hills
Kent Downs

Exmoor
Quantock Hills
New Forest
Sussex Downs

Dartmoor
South Hampshire coast
Isle of Wight

0   100
km

Notes

Map 12.1 is based on information from T. Kelly, *A History of Public Libraries in Great Britain, 1845–1975* (London, 1973). Map 12.2 is taken with permission from B. Seebohm Rowntree, *Poverty: A Study of Town Life* (London, 1901). Maps 12.3 and 12.5 are drawn from miscellaneous sources including football year-books, directories, etc. Map 12.4 is based on material from the Census of 1901.

Map 12.6 uses information from the *Kinematograph Year Book*, various Manchester newspapers and *Bartholomew's Pocket Atlas and Guide to Manchester*. Map 12.7 is based on information from the *Kinematograph Year Book*. Map 12.8 is based on information in the *Ordnance Survey Road Atlas of Great Britain* (London, 1985).

FURTHER READING

What follows is a brief guide to further reading. Contributors have indicated up to twenty or so sources (mostly in book-form) which they consider particularly useful. The *General* section includes edited collections (Aldcroft (1968), Baber and Williams (1986), British Association (1934, 1936) Buxton and Aldcroft (1979), Church (1980), Elbaum and Lazonick (1986), and Langton and Morris (1986)) which incorporate valuable chapters on individual industries.

General

Aldcroft, D. H. (ed.) (1968) *The Development of British Industry and Foreign Competition, 1875–1914*, London: Allen & Unwin.

—— (1986) *The British Economy*, vol. 1, *Years of Turmoil 1929–1951*, Brighton: Harvester Press.

Ashton, T. S. (1972) *The Eighteenth Century*, London: Methuen.

Baber, C. and Williams, L. J. (eds) (1986) *Modern South Wales: Essays in Economic History*, Cardiff: University of Wales Press.

Barker, T. H. and Drake, M. (eds) (1982) *Population and Society in Britain, 1850–1980*, London: Batsford.

Berg, M. (1985) *The Age of Manufactures 1700–1820*, London: Fontana.

Best, G. (1979) *Mid-Victorian Britain 1851–75*, London: Fontana.

British Association (1935) *Britain in Depression*, London: Pitman.

British Association (1938) *Britain in Recovery*, London: Pitman.

Buxton, N. K. and Aldcroft, D. H. (eds) (1979) *British Industry Between the Wars*, London: Scolar Press.

Church, R. (ed.) (1980) *The Dynamics of Victorian Business*, London: Allen & Unwin.

Crafts, N. (1985) *British Economic Growth During the Industrial Revolution*, London: Oxford University Press.

Crouzet, F. (1982) *The Victorian Economy*, London: Methuen.

Dean, P. and Cole, W. A. (1967) *British Economic Growth, 1688–1959*, Cambridge: Cambridge University Press.

Department of Employment (1971) *British Labour Statistics, Historical Abstract, 1886–1966*, London: HMSO.

Elbaum, B. and Lazonick, W. (eds) (1986) *The Decline of the British Economy*, Oxford: Clarendon Press.

Floud, R. and McCloskey, D. (eds) (1981) *The Economic History of Britain since 1700*, 2 vols, Cambridge: Cambridge University Press.

Fothergill, S. and Vincent, J. (1985) *The State of the Nation*, London: Pan.

Glynn, S. and Oxborrow, J. (1976) *Inter-war Britain: a Social and Economic History*, London: Allen & Unwin.

Halsey, A. H. (1972) *Trends in British Society since 1900*, London: Macmillan.

Harrison, J. F. C. (1971) *The Early Victorians, 1832–51*, London: Weidenfeld & Nicolson.

Langton, J. and Morris, R. (eds) (1986) *Atlas of Industrialising Britain 1780–1914*, London: Methuen.

Law, C. M. (1980) *British Regional Development since World War I*, Newton Abbot: David & Charles.

Lee, C. H. (1971) *Regional Economic Growth in the United Kingdom since the 1880s*, Maidenhead: McGraw-Hill.

Mathias, P. (1979) *The Transformation of England*, London: Methuen.

—— (1983) *The First Industrial Nation*, 2nd edn, London: Methuen.

Musson, A.E. (1978) *The Growth of British Industry*, London: Batsford.

Pawson, E. (1979) *The Early Industrial Revolution*, London: Academic Press.

Pollard, S. (1983) *The Development of the British Economy, 1914–1980*, London: Edward Arnold.

Stevenson, J. and Cook, C. (1977) *The Slump: Society and Politics during the Depression*, London: Quartet Books.

Sturgess, R. W. (ed.) (1981) *The Great Age of Industry in the North-East, 1700–1920*, Durham: Durham Local History Society.

Agriculture

Agrarian History of England and Wales (1978) vol. 8, ed. E. H. Whetham; (1985) vol. 5 (2 parts), ed. J. Thirsk, Cambridge: Cambridge University Press.

Chambers, J. D. and Mingay, G. E. (1966) *The Agricultural Revolution, 1750–1880*, London: Batsford.

Gonner, E. C. K. (1912) *Common Land and Inclosure*, London: Macmillan.

Hasbach, W. (1908, 1966) *The History of the English Agricultural Labourer*, London: Frank Cass.

Holderness, B. A. (1985) *British Agriculture since 1945*, Manchester: Manchester University Press.

Hoskins, W. G. (1955) *The Making of the English Landscape*, London: Hodder & Stoughton.

Minchinton, W. E. (1968) *Essays in Agrarian History*, 2 vols, Newton Abbot: David & Charles.

Mingay, G. E. (1963) *English Landed Society in the Eighteenth Century*, London: Routledge & Kegan Paul.

Ministry of Agriculture, Fisheries, and Food (1968) *A Century of Agricultural Statistics: Great Britain 1866–1966*, London: HMSO.

Orwin, C. S. and Whetham, E. H. (1964) *History of British Agriculture 1846–1914*, London: Longman.

Perry, P. J. (1974) *British Farming in the Great Depression 1870–1914; An Historical Geography*, Newton Abbot: David & Charles.

Slater, G. (1907) *The English Peasantry and the Enclosure of Common Fields*, London: London School of Economics.

Thompson, F. M. L. (1963) *English Landed Society in the Nineteenth Century*, London: Routledge & Kegan Paul.

Turner, M. E. (1980) *English Parliamentary Enclosure: Its Historical Geography and Economic History*, Folkestone: Dawson.

Yelling, J. A. (1977) *Common Field and Enclosure in England*, London: Macmillan.

Textiles

Baines, E. (1835, 1966) *History of the Cotton Manufacture of Great Britain*, London: Frank Cass.

Board of Trade Working Party on Cotton (1946) *Report*, London: HMSO.

Board of Trade Working Party on Wool (1946) *Report*, London: HMSO.

Chapman, S. D. (1967) *The Early Factory Masters*, Newton Abbot: David & Charles.

—— (1972) *The Cotton Industry in the Industrial Revolution*. London: Macmillan.

—— (1981) 'The Arkwright mills – Colquhoun's census of 1788 and archaeological evidence', *Industrial Archaeology Review*, VI, pp. 5–26.

Farnie, D. A. (1979) *The English Cotton Industry and the World Market: 1815–1896*, Oxford: Clarendon Press.

Gregory, D. (1982) *Regional Transformation and the Industrial Revolution: A Geography of the Yorkshire Woollen Industry*, London: Macmillan.

Harte, N. B. and Ponting, K. (eds) (1972) *Textile History and Economic History: Essays in Honour of Miss Julia de Lacy Mann*, Manchester: Manchester University Press.

Heaton, H. (1965) *The Yorkshire Woollen and Worsted Industries*, Oxford: Clarendon Press.

Jenkins, D. T. and Ponting, K. G. (1982) *The British Wool Textile Industry 1770–1914*, London: Heinemann.

Ramsay, G. D. (1982) *The English Woollen Cloth Industry, 1500–1750*, London: Macmillan.

Robson, R. (1957) *The Cotton Industry in Britain*, London: Macmillan.

Rodgers, H. B. (1962) 'The changing geography of the Lancashire cotton industry', *Economic Geography*, XXXVIII, pp. 299–314.

Sandberg, L. (1974) *Lancashire in Decline*, Columbus: Ohio State University Press.

Timmins, J. G. (1977) *Handloom Weavers' Cottages in Central Lancashire*, Lancaster: University of Lancaster, Centre for North West Regional Studies.

Wadsworth, A. P. and Mann, J. de L. (1931) *The Cotton Industry and Industrial Lancashire, 1600–1780*, Manchester: Manchester University Press.

Chemicals

Clow, A. and Clow, N. L. (1952) *The Chemical Revolution*, London: Batchworth.

Haber, L. F. (1971) *The Chemical Industry, 1900–1930,* London: Oxford University Press.

Hardie, D. W. F. and Pratt, J. D. (1966) *A History of the Modern British Chemical Industry*, Oxford: Pergamon Press.

I. P. C. Publications (1983) *Chem-facts 1983*, Sutton: I. P. C. Business Press.

Musson, A. E. (1965) *Enterprise in Soap and Chemicals: Joseph Crosfield and Sons Ltd, 1815–1965*, Manchester: Manchester University Press.

Reader, W. J. (1970–5) *Imperial Chemical Industries: A History*, 3 vols, London: Oxford University Press.

Warren, K. (1980) *Chemical Foundations: The Alkali Industry in Britain to 1926*, London: Oxford University Press.

Wilson, C. H. (1954) *The History of Unilever*, 2 vols, London: Cassell.

Iron and steel industries

Birch, A. (1879, 1967) *The Economic History of the British Iron and Steel Industry, 1784–1879*, London: Frank Cass.

Burn, D. (1939) *The Economic History of Steelmaking*, Cambridge: Cambridge University Press.

Burnham, T. and Hoskins, G. O. (1943) *Iron and Steel in Britain, 1870–1939*, London: Allen & Unwin.

Heal, D.W. (1974) *The Steel Industry in Post-war Britain*, Newton Abbot: David & Charles.

Hyde, C. *Technological Change and the British Iron Industry, 1700–1870*, Princeton, NJ: Princeton University Press.

McCloskey, D. N. (1973) *Economic Maturity and Entrepreneurial Decline: British Iron and Steel, 1870–1913*, Cambridge, Mass.: Harvard University Press.

Riden, P. (1977) 'The output of the British iron industry before 1870', *Economic History Review*, 2nd ser., XXX, 3, pp. 442–59.

Roepke, H. G. (1956) *Movements of the British Iron and Steel Industry – 1720 to 1851*, Urbana, Ill.: University of Illinois Press.

Warren, K. (1970) *The British Iron and Steel Industry since 1840*, London: Bell.

Shipbuilding

Clarke, J. F. (1977) *Power on Land and Sea: A History of Hawthorn–Leslie*, Wallsend: Clark Hawthorn.

Dougan, D. (1968) *A History of North-East Shipbuilding*, London: Allen & Unwin.

Pollard, S. (1951) 'The decline of shipbuilding on the Thames', *Economic History Review*, 2nd ser., III, 1, pp. 72–89.

Pollard, S. and Robertson, P. (1979) *The British Shipbuilding Industry, 1870–1914*, Cambridge, Mass.: Harvard University Press.

Shields, J. (1947) *Clyde Built: A History of Shipbuilding on the Clyde*, Glasgow: William MacLellan.

Motor vehicles

Church, R. (1979) *Herbert Austin: the British Motor Car Industry to 1941*, London: Europa.

Durnett, P. (1980) *The Decline of the British Motor Industry*, London: Croom Helm.

Overy, R. J. (1976) *William Morris, Viscount Nuffield*, London: Europa.

Richardson, K. (1977) *The British Motor Industry, 1896–1939*, London: Macmillan.

Saul, S. B. (1962–3) 'The motor industry in Great Britain to 1914', *Business History*, V, pp. 22–44.

Thoms, D. and Donnelly, T. (1985) *The Motor Car Industry in Coventry since the 1890s*, London: Croom Helm.

Williams, K., Williams, J., and Haslam, C. (1987) *The Breakdown of Austin Rover*, Leamington Spa: Berg.

Aerospace

Fearon, P. (1969) 'The formative years of the British aircraft industry, 1913–1924', *Business History*, XLIII.

—— (1974) 'The British airframe industry and the state, 1918–1935', *Economic History Review,* 2nd ser., XXXVII.

Gardner, C. (1981) *British Aircraft Corporation,* London: Batsford.

Reed, A. (1973) *Britain's Aircraft Industry,* London: Dent.

Scott, J. D. (1963) *Vickers – a History,* London: Weidenfeld & Nicolson.

Other engineering

Aldcroft, D. H. (1966) 'The performance of the machine tool industry in the inter-war years', *Business History Review*, XL, pp. 281–96.

Hume, J. and Moss, M. S. (1979) *Beardmore's: the History of a Scottish Industrial Giant,* London: Heinemann.

Saul, S. B. (1967) 'The market and the development of the mechanical engineering industries in Britain, 1860–1914', *Economic History Review,* 2nd ser., XX.

—— (1968) 'The machine tool industry in Britain to 1914', *Business History*, X.

Coal-mining

Ashworth, W. (1986) *The History of the British Coal Industry*, vol. 5, *1946–1982: The Nationalised Industry*, London: Oxford University Press.

Buxton, N. K. (1978) *The Economic Development of the British Coal Industry*, London: Batsford.

Church, R. (1986) *The History of the British Coal Industry*, vol. 3, *1830–1913: Victorian Pre-eminence*, London: Oxford University Press.

Flinn, M. (1984) *The History of the British Coal Industry*, vol. 2, *1700–1830: The Industrial Revolution*, London: Oxford University Press.

Gas

Barty-King, H. (1984) *The New Flame: The Illustrated History of Piped Gas*, Tavistock: Graphmitre.

Peebles, M. W. H. (1980) *The Evolution of the Gas Industry*, London: Macmillan.

Williams, T. I. (1981) *A History of the British Gas Industry*, London: Oxford University Press.

Electricity supply

Cochrane, R. (1985) *Power to the People: the Story of the National Grid*, Twickenham: Newnes.

Hannah, L. (1979) *Electricity before Nationalisation*, London: Macmillan.

—— (1982) *Engineers, Managers and Politicians*, London: Macmillan.

Simpson, E. S. (1966) *Coal and Power Industries in Post-war Britain*, London: Longman.

Transport: general

Aldcroft, D. H. (1975) *British Transport since 1914: An Economic History*, Newton Abbot: David & Charles.

Aldcroft, D. H. and Freeman, M. J. (eds) (1983) *Transport in the Industrial Revolution*, Manchester: Manchester University Press.

Bagwell, P. S. (1974) *The Transport Revolution from 1770*, London: Batsford.

Barker, T. C. and Savage, C. I. (1974) *An Economic History of Transport in Britain*, London: Hutchinson.

Dyos, H. J. and Aldcroft, D. H. (1969) *British Transport: An Economic Survey from the Seventeenth Century to the Twentieth*, Leicester: Leicester University Press. Reprinted Harmondsworth: Penguin Books, 1974.

Turnbull, G. L. (1979) *Traffic and Transport: An Economic History of Pickfords*, London: Allen & Unwin.

Road transport

Albert, W. (1972) *The Turnpike Road System in England, 1663–1840*, Cambridge: Cambridge University Press.

Barker, T. C. (ed.) (1986) *The Economic and Social Effects of the Spread of Motor Vehicles*, London: Macmillan.

Pawson, E. (1977) *Transport and Economy: the Turnpike Roads of Eighteenth-century Britain*, London: Academic Press.

Canals

Hadfield, C. (1969) *British Canals: An Illustrated History*, Newton Abbot: David & Charles.

Rolt, L. T. C. (1950) *The Inland Waterways of England*, London: Allen & Unwin.

Ward, J. R. (1974) *The Finance of Canal Building in Eighteenth-Century England*, London: Oxford University Press.

Railways

Gourvish, T. R. (1980) *Railways and the British Economy, 1830–1914*, London: Macmillan.

Perkin, H. (1970) *The Age of the Railway*, London: Granada.

Simmons, J. (1978) *The Railway in England and Wales, 1830–1914*, Leicester: Leicester University Press.

Overseas trade

Davis, R. (1979) *The Industrial Revolution and British Overseas Trade*, Leicester: Leicester University Press.

Imlah, A. H. (1958) *Economic Elements in the Pax Britannica: Studies in British Foreign Trade in the Nineteenth Century*, London: Oxford University Press.

Minchinton, W. E. (ed.) (1969) *The Growth of English Overseas Trade*, London: Methuen.

Saul, S. B. (1960) *Studies in British Overseas Trade, 1870–1914*, Liverpool: Liverpool University Press.

Schlote, W. (trans. 1952) *British Overseas Trade From 1700 to the 1930s*, Oxford: Blackwell.

Employment and unemployment

Aldcroft, D. H. (1984) *Full Employment: the Elusive Goal*, Brighton: Harvester Press.

Dennison, S. R. (1939) *The Location of Industry and the Depressed Areas*, London: Oxford University Press.

Glynn, S. and Booth, A. (1987) *The Road to Full Employment*, London: Allen & Unwin.

Hannington, W. (1937) *The Problem of the Distressed Areas*, London: Gollancz.

John, A. V. (ed.) (1986) *Unequal Opportunities: Women's Employment in England, 1800–1918*, Oxford: Blackwell.

Lee, D. (1980 edn) *Regional Planning and the Location of Industry*, London: Heinemann.

McCrone, G. (1969) *Regional Policy in Britain*, London: Allen & Unwin.

Maclennan, D. and Parr, J. B. (eds) (1986) *Regional Policy: Past Experience and New Directions*, Oxford: Martin Robertson.

Pilgrim Trust (1938) *Men Without Work*, Cambridge: Cambridge University Press.

Demographic change

Darby, H. C. (1976) *A New Historical Geography of England after 1600*, Cambridge: Cambridge University Press.

Flinn, M. W. (1970) *British Population Growth 1700–1850*, London: Macmillan.

Freeman, T. W., Rogers, H. B., and Kinrig R. H. (1966) *Lancashire, Cheshire and The Isle of Man*, London: Nelson.

Lancashire County Planning Department (1982) *People in Lancashire*, Preston: LCPD.

—— (1984) *Census Atlas of Lancashire*, Preston: LCPD.

Mitchell, B. R. and Deane, P. (1962) *Abstract of British Historical Statistics*, Cambridge: Cambridge University Press.

Mitchison, R. (1977) *British Population Change since 1860*, London: Macmillan.

NorthWest Joint Planning Team (1973) *Strategic Plan for the North West*, London: HMSO.

Tranter, N. L. (1985) *Population and Society, 1750–1940: Contrasts in Population Growth*, London: Longman.

Wrigley, E. A. and Schofield, R. S. (1981) *The Population History of England, 1541–1871: A Reconstruction*, London: Edward Arnold.

Labour movements

Brown, K. D. (ed.) (1985) *The First Labour Party*, London: Croom Helm.

Clegg, H. A. (1985) *A History of British Trade Unions since 1889*, vol. II, *1911–1933*, Oxford: Clarendon Press.

Clegg, H. A., Fox, Alan, and Thompson A. F. (1964) *A History of British Trade Unions since 1889*, vol. I, *1889–1910*, Oxford: Clarendon Press.

Fraser, W. (1974) *Trade Unions and Society: The Struggle for Acceptance, 1850–1880*, London: Allen & Unwin.

Howell, D. (1983) *British Workers and the Independent Labour Party, 1888–1906*, Manchester: Manchester University Press.

Laybourn, K. and Reynolds, J. (1986) *Liberalism and the Rise of Labour 1890–1918*, London: Croom Helm.

Marquand, D. (1977) *Ramsay MacDonald*, London: Jonathan Cape.

Morris, M. (1976) *The General Strike*, Harmondsworth: Penguin Books.

Pelling, H. (1954) *The Origins of the Labour Party, 1880–1900*, London: Oxford University Press.

Phelps Brown, H. (1986) *The Origins of Trade Union Power*, London: Oxford University Press.

Phillips, G.A. (1976) *The General Strike*, London: Weidenfeld & Nicolson.

Price, R. (1986) *Labour in British Society*, London: Croom Helm.

Thompson, D. (1984) *The Chartists*, Hounslow: Temple Smith.

Thompson, E. P. (1963) *The Making of the English Working Class*, London: Gollancz.

Urbanization and living conditions

Briggs, A. (1968) *Victorian Cities*, Harmondsworth: Penguin Books.

Burnett, J. (1978) *A Social History of Housing 1815–1970*, London: Methuen.

Cartwright, F. F. (1977) *The Social History of Medicine*, London: Longman.

Checkland, S. G. (1964) 'The British industrial city as history: the Glasgow case', *Urban Studies*, 1.

Corlfield, P. J. (1982) *The Impact of English Towns, 1700–1800*, London: Oxford University Press.

Daunton, M. (1983) *House and Home in the Victorian City: Working-Class Housing 1850–1914*, London: Edward Arnold.

Dennis, R. (1984) *English Industrial Cities of the Nineteenth Century: A Social Geography*, Cambridge: Cambridge University Press.

Dyos, H. and Wolf, M. (eds) (1973) *The Victorian City: Images and Realities*, 2 vols, London: Routledge & Kegan Paul.

Gauldie, E. (1974) *Cruel Habitations: A History of Working-Class Housing 1780–1918*, London: Allen & Unwin.

Gibb, A. (1983) *Glasgow: The Making of a City*, London: Croom Helm.

Gordon, G. (ed.) (1986) *Regional Cities in the U.K. 1890–1980*, London: Harper & Row.

Smith, F. B. (1979) *The People's Health*, London: Croom Helm.

Waller, P. (1983) *Town, City and Nation: England 1850–1914*, London: Oxford University Press.

Walvin, J. (1984) *English Urban Life 1776–1851*, London: Hutchinson.

Education

Aldrich, R. (1972) *An Introduction to the History of Education*, London: Hodder & Stoughton.

Ball, N. (1983) *Educating the People: a Documentary History of Elementary Schooling in England 1840–1870*, London: Temple Smith.

Cruickshank, M. (1981) *Children and Industry: Child Health and Welfare in North-west Textile Towns during the Nineteenth Century*, Manchester: Manchester University Press.

Digby, A. and Searby, P. (1981) *Children, School and Society in Nineteenth-Century England*, London: Macmillan.

Evans, K. (1985) *The Development and Structure of the English School System*, London: Hodder & Stoughton.

Gardner, P. (1984) *The Lost Elementary Schools of Victorian England*, London: Croom Helm.

Gordon, P. (1980) *Selection for Secondary Education*, London: Woburn Press.

Grace, G. (ed.) (1984) *Education and the City: Theory, History and Contemporary Practice*, London: Routledge & Kegan Paul.

Hurt, J. S. (1971) *Education in Evolution: Church, State, Society and Popular Education 1800–1870*, London: Hart-Davis.

—— (1979) *Elementary Schooling and the Working Classes 1860–1918*, London: Routledge & Kegan Paul.

McCann, P. (ed.) (1977) *Popular Education and Socialization in the Nineteenth Century*, London: Methuen.

Murphy, J. (1972) *The Education Act 1870: Text and Commentary*, Newton Abbot: David & Charles.

Parsons, C. (1978) *Schools in an Urban Community: A Study of Carbrook 1870–1965*, London: Routledge & Kegan Paul.

Reeder, D. (ed.) (1977) *Urban Education in the Nineteenth Century*, London: Taylor & Francis.

Seaborne, M. and Lowe, R. (1971 and 1977) *The English School: Its Architecture and Organisation*, vol. I, *1370–1870* (1971), vol. II, *1870–1970* (1977), London: Routledge & Kegan Paul.

Silver, H. (1980) *Education and the Social Condition*, London: Methuen.

—— (1983) *Education as History: Interpreting Nineteenth- and Twentieth-Century Education*, London: Methuen.

Silver, P. and Silver, H. (1974) *The Education of the Poor: The History of a National School*, London: Routledge & Kegan Paul.

Simon, B. (1974) *The Two Nations and the Educational Structure 1780–1870*, London: Lawrence & Wishart.

—— (1974) *Education and the Labour Movement 1870–1920*, London: Lawrence & Wishart.

Sutherland, G. (1973) *Policy-Making in Elementary Education 1870–1895*, London: Oxford University Press.

West, E. G. (1975) *Education and the Industrial Revolution*, London: Batsford.

Religion

Brown, C. G. (1987) *The Social History of Religion in Scotland since 1730*, London: Methuen.

—— (1988) 'Did urbanisation secularise Britain?' *Urban History Yearbook*.

Coleman, B. I. (1980) *The Church of England in the Mid-Nineteenth Century: A Social Geography*, London: Historical Association.

Cox, J. (1982) *The English Churches in a Secular Society: Lambeth 1870–1930*, London: Oxford University Press.

Davies, E. T. (1965) *Religion in the Industrial Revolution in South Wales*, Cardiff: University of Wales Press.

Gilbert, A. D. (1976) *Religion and Society in Industrial England: Church, Chapel and Social Change, 1740–1914*, London: Longman.

McLeod, H. (1973) 'Class, community and region: the religious geography of nineteenth-century England', in M. Hill (ed.) *The Sociological Yearbook of Religion in Britain*, 6.

—— (1984) *Religion and the Working Class in Nineteenth-Century Britain*, London: Macmillan.

Sellers, I. (1977) *Nineteenth-Century Nonconformity*, London: Edward Arnold.

Wilson, B. (1966) *Religion in Secular Society*, Harmondsworth: Penguin Books.

Leisure

Bailey, P. (1978) *Leisure and Class in Victorian England: Rational Recreation and the Contest for Control*, London: Routledge & Kegan Paul.

Briggs, A. (1960) *Mass Entertainment: The Origins of a Modern Industry*, Adelaide: Griffen Press.

Critcher, C. (1982) 'The politics of leisure – social control and social development', in *Work and Leisure: The Implications of Technological Change*, Edinburgh: Edinburgh University Tourism and Recreation Unit.

Cunningham, H. (1985) 'Leisure', in J. Benson (ed.) *The Working Class in England 1875–1914*, London: Croom Helm.

Jones, S. G. (1986) *Workers at Play: A Social and Economic History of Leisure, 1918–39*, London: Routledge & Kegan Paul.

Kelly, T. (1973) *A History of Public Libraries in Great Britain 1845–1975*, London: Library Association.

Malcolmson, R. (1973) *Popular Recreations in English Society 1700–1850*, Cambridge: Cambridge University Press.

Mason, T. (1980) *Association Football and English Society 1863–1915*, Brighton: Harvester Press.

Richards, J. (1984) *The Age of the Dream Palace: Cinema and Society in Britain 1930–1939*, London: Routledge & Kegan Paul.

Rowntree, B. Seebohm (1901) *Poverty. A Study of Town Life*, London: Macmillan.

Walton, J. K. (1983) *The English Seaside Resort: A Social History 1750–1914*, Leicester: Leicester University Press.

INDEX

aerospace industries 58-60, 66; aero-engine manufacturers 58-60; airframe manufacturers 58-60; amalgamations in 1920s-30s 58; British Aerospace 59-60; changes in labour force 59; civil aircraft, comparison with USA 59-60; effect of war 58-9; Government support 58-9; growth of output 58, 62; international co-operation 60; locations 59-61; military aircraft post-1945 60; missile systems 60; satellite equipment 60

agricultural depression 6-12

agricultural machinery manufacturers 61, 63; locations in Eastern England 61, 63

agriculture 1-22; barley 16-17; cereals area 8-9; commons and wastes 3-4; enclosure 1-5; farm size 18-19; foreign competition 6, 8, 13; in war 3-5, 13-15; livestock 6; mechanization 11, 13, 18, 22; milk production 6-8, 10, 17-18; open fields 1-3; poultry 19-21; rents 6; subsidies 18; tax assessments 7; tillage area 13-17; use of fertilizers 13, 18, 22; wages 11-12; wheat 6, 8, 17, 21-2; *see also* employment

air traffic 112-16; airports 115-16; Civil Aviation Act, 1971 114-15; growth 1950s-80s 116; Imperial Airways 112-16; inland traffic 112-16, British European Airways 114, poor performance 113-15, principal routes 1930s 113, principal routes 1970s 114; size and speed of aircraft 115; tourist 115-16

boilermakers 61, 63, 65

carpets 24-5

Chartism 185-8; in Bradford 1848 187-8, authorities' reaction 187-8; Feargus O'Connor 185, 187; 'Grand Holiday' 1842 187; Irish presence 187; land schemes and industrial co-operation 187; main

areas of activity 186; National Charter Association 187; National Convention of the Industrious Classes 1839 186; Newport Rising 186; 'plug plots' 187; variations in 185

chemical industries 36-44; Alkali Acts 36; alkali manufacture: Le Blanc Process 36, 39-40, Solvay Process 36, 39; ammonia 43; ammonium nitrate manufacture by nitrogen fixation 39; ammonium sulphate 39-41; bakelite 41; Beechams 41; benzene 41-2; bleaching powder 39-40; British Petroleum 42-3; Brunner Mond 36, 39 41; butadiene 41-2; changing location 38-9, 42-4; celluloid 41; cellulose acetate 39; chlorine 39-40; chlorohydrocarbons 41; detergents 43; dyestuffs 38-9, 41; Dyestuffs (Import Regulations) Act, 1920 39; Esso Chemicals 42-4; ethylene 41-2; exports 36-8, 41; in First World War 39; gross output (in £) 42; hydrochloric acid 36, 38-9; Imperial Chemical Industries 41-2; imports 41; nitric acid 38-40, 43; Nobel Industries 41; petro chemicals 41-4; petroleum by hydrogenation of coal 41; pharmaceuticals 38, 41, 44; polyethylene 41; polymethylmethacrylate 41; propylene 41-2; rayon production 41; Shell Chemicals 42-3; sodium carbonate 43; synthetic drugs *see* pharmaceuticals; synthetic fertilizer (chemical manure) 36, 39-41; toluene 39; United Alkali Company 36-7, 39, 41

churches, falling social significance of 215

churchgoing 211-23; Bible Society Surveys 1979-84 211; decline 1851-1979/84 211; effects of industrialization and urbanization 211; highest in Scotland 1979-84

214-15; high levels in Wales 1851 212-13; localized patterns in Scotland 1851 213; low levels in industrial areas 1851 213; overall levels 1851 211, 213; overall levels 1979-84 214; Religious Census 1851 211; variations 1851 212-13; variations 1979-84 214-15

cinemas 231-2; audiences 231; growth in North-west textile district 1919-39 231; inter-war rebuilding 231; Manchester centre, early 1930s 232; talkies 231

coal-mining industry 68-81; adoption of Newcomen engine 68; changing means of transporting coal 68, 70; Coal Industry Act, 1967 79; Coal Mines Act, 1930 73; depth of pits 68, 70; effect of war 73; expansion and prosperity in 1950s 73; exports 70, 73, 132-3; inter-war experience 73; loss of markets 73, 79-81; mining costs 70; Mining Industry Act, 1926 73; National Coal Board 73, 80; nationalization 73; new production techniques 73; North-east collieries: early dominance 68-9, mid-nineteenth century 72, 1940s 76-7, Tyne pits 1780s-1800 70; North-east deep mines 1987 79; output 68-71, by region 68-71, 78-80; pit closures 79-81; *Plan for Coal* 1974 80; profits 70; rationalization and the 1984-5 strike 81; Sankey Commission 1919 73; use of Davy Lamp 68; Yorkshire coalfield 70, 74-5; *see also* employment

coastal navigation 96, 101-3; cargoes 101; coal traffic 101-3; main ports 101-2; passenger traffic 101; size and capacity of coasters 101

computer ware, expansion in Cambridgeshire 66

cotton 24-33; Arkwright-type mills in Nottinghamshire and Derbyshire 1788 25; Blackburn cotton mills 1894 27-9; Cotton Industry

Reorganization Act, 1959 27; decline 26–9; early mills 25–6; exports 26–7; finishing trades 27; imports 27; separation of spinning and weaving 26; *see also* employment

Courtaulds 27, 41, 43

demographic changes 134–49; age at marriage 134, 136; 'baby boom' 1940s, 1950s 135; birth rates 134–7, 142–3; changing age and sex structure 136–7; death rates 134–5, 142–3, by social class 136; emigration 139–40, destinations 139, peak years 139; expectation of life from birth 136; family size 135; fear of population decline 1930s 135; fertility *see* birth rates; geographical distribution 137–9, 143–5, movement to South-east and Midlands 137–9, twentieth-century suburbanization 137–8; immigration 139–43, 147–8, areas of origin 139–43, 147–8; migration 139, 141, 143, from Scotland 141, from Wales 139, 141; mortality *see* death rates; North-west England 142–8, age structure 143, birth rates 142–3, death rates 142–3, effect of new towns 146, falling population of old centres 145–8, geographical distribution 143–5, growth of commuting and retirement areas 145, 147, immigration to 143, 147–8, migration from 143, migration into 143, migration to Cheshire 148, population growth 141–2; population growth (England and Wales) 1701–1981 134–5; *see also* rural depopulation; urban growth

education 198–210; in Bootle, attitude of School Board 208–9, Board schools 208–9, claims for remission of fees 208, effect of religious differences 209, growing population and changing needs 205–6, National schools 205, 207–8, non-provision for middle classes 205, private venture schools 208, Roman Catholic schools 207–9, summoned for non-attendance 207–8, voluntary sector activity in 1860s–70s 205, 208, zones of School Attendance Officers 205, 207–8; British schools, attendance 1851 200; British Society 198–9, contribution in Wales 199, efforts in major towns 199, monitorial system 199, supportive of school boards 199; Church of England schools 198–200, 202, 205, 207–9,

charging higher fees 199, dominant position 198, National Society 198–9, 202, preference for respectable children 198–9, school attendance 1858 200; Education Act, 1870 202; Education Census 1851 198, estimated school needs 198, regional disparities in school provision 198; increasingly favourable attitudes to schooling 202; late-nineteenth century disparities in provision 198–210; Liverpool Corporation School experiment 199; Newcastle Commission 1858 198, regional contrasts in attitudes and access to education 198; Roman Catholic schools 198–9, 201, 207–9, attendance 1858 201; Catholic Poor Schools Society 198–9, 201, concentration in Lancashire 199; school accommodation 199, 202, attempts by voluntary agencies to meet demand 199, 202, deficiencies in densely-populated areas 199, inability of voluntary agencies to meet demand 202, quality in northern English counties 199; school attendance 199, 201–4, child labour in cotton and coal-mining industries 203, effect of accommodation available 199, move towards compulsion 202, towns with above norm attendance 1851 202, 204, variations within Cumberland and Westmorland 1851 202–3, variations within Hereford and Monmouthshire 1851 202–3, variations within Lancashire 1851 199, 201; School Boards 202, 204–5, contrasting objectives 205, earliest established 202, 204, Lancashire towns lacking them 202; Scottish parochial system 199; Wales: Anglican English-language schools 199, chapel-provided Sunday schools 199

electrical engineering 61, 64–6; geographical concentration 61, 65; gross output (£'000) 65; growth rate post-1945 66; location pre-1914 61, 64; manufacturers of cables location 1910 64; manufacturers of dynamos and/or electric motors location 1910 64; manufacturers of transformers location 1910 64; *see also* employment

electrical goods: increasing use of 90–1; Swan and Edison's electric light bulb 87

electricity supply industry 75, 79, 81, 87–94; British Electricity Authority 91; Central Electricity Board 90; comparisons with USA and

Germany 90; decline in private generation 91; diversification of sources of power 91, 93–4; effect of war 91; growth in numbers of homes connected 90–1; growth of generating capacity 89–90; lack of co-ordination 89–90; location of power stations by regions 93; loss of customers to gas 94; National Grid 90–2, 94, power flow pattern 1982–3 91; supply undertakings: 1888 87, 89, 1896 88, London 1896 88, London 1907 89, municipal 87–9, private 87–9

employment 150–60; collapse of industrial employment 150; female 154, 156–60, administrative, professional, and other services 1971 160, agricultural 156–9, in clothing industries 157–9, domestic service 154, 156–60, of girls aged 10–15 1891 157, limited range of occupations 150, in nine northern counties 1851 154, 156–7, in textiles 156–9, unrecorded 154, 157, varying participation rates 154–8, 160; male 150–5, agricultural 150–5, in metal manufacturing and engineering 152–5, in mining and quarrying 150–5, in nine northern counties 1851 150–1, 153, professional, administrative, and other services 153–5, in shipbuilding 151, 153, in shipping 151, 153, in textiles 150–3; *see also* unemployment, regional policy

engineering 66; capital expenditure by region 1983 66; overseas competition 66; *see also* agricultural machinery manufacturers; boilermakers; computer ware; electrical engineering; employment; locomotive manufacturers; machine tool industry; marine engineering; mechanical engineering; railway carriage and wagon works; railway company workshops, location of; steam engine manufacture; textile machinery manufacture

exports *see* foreign trade

food 5, 13; prices 5; self-sufficiency 13
football 226–9, 231, 233; the Football League 1888–9 227–8, based on North and Midlands 227, 1935–6 230–1; the Scottish League 1935–6 230–1; Sunday football teams 233
foreign trade 103–4, 116–33; coal exports, main ports 1870 and 1910 132, role of sailing ships 132–3; commodities 116, 118, 121, 125–7, exports by type 126–7, imports by type 125–6; Council for Mutual

Economic Assistance (CMEA) 121; importance of empire 116, 118, 121, Ottawa conference 1932 121; importance of Europe 116–17, 119–24, European Economic Community (EEC) 121–5; importance of North America 118–19, 123; Japan 116, 121, 125; main ports 128–31, decline of up-river ports 131, growth of those close to Europe 130–1, importance of hinterlands 128, roll-on-roll-off traffic 131; Navigation Acts 116; re-exports 104, 116, 118; regional patterns 116–25, 1770–4 116–18, 1866–70 118–19, 1908–12 118, 120–1, 1933–7 121–2, 1955–9 121, 123, 1980–4 121, 124–5; protection 118, 121, 128

gas industry 79, 81–7; British Gas Corporation 86; competition from electricity 84; effect on coal-mining industry 83; Gas Council 84, 86; Gas Industry Act 84; gas undertakings: 1830 81, 1892 82–3, 1912 83, 1945 85, amalgamations 81, 84, Gas Light and Coke Company 81, 83–4, 86, in London 1882 83, 1945 86, Sheffield Gas Company 84; Heyworth Committee 1944 84; high-pressure transmission system 84, 86–7; loss of customers 84; nationalization 84; natural gas 84, 86–7, liquidified 84, North Sea gas 84, 86–7; number of consumers: 1912 83, 1938 84, 1984/5 86; prices to consumers 81, 83–4; privatization 86; *see also* chemical industries
General Strike 1926 73, 194–7; assessment of 197; 'Black Friday' 1921 196; effectiveness of trade union organization 195–7; industrial relations in coal-mining industry 194–6; 'Red Friday' 1925 195; return to gold standard 195; role of General Council of the Trades Union Congress 195–7; Samuel Commission 1925–6 195–6; in Yorkshire 196–7

hosiery industry 23, 159; employment of women in 159
housing conditions 175–9; availability in 1951: of cooking stoves 178–9, fixed baths 178–9, piped water 178–9, water closets 178–9; overcrowding 175–8, in Britain 1951 177–8, in Scotland 1861 and 1901 175–6, 178

imports *see* foreign trade
infant mortality 135, 180–2; infant

mortality rates: 1841 180–1, 1872 180–1, 1901 180–1, 1951 180–2, 1980 180–2, urban/rural contrasts 180–2; by social class 135
inland waterways 96–8; canals 96, 98, in Midlands and North-west 96, 98, uses and drawbacks 96; river improvements 96–7
iron and steel industry *see* iron industry; steel industry
iron industry 45–7; bar iron 45; 'black band' ores 46; Cort's processes 45; Darby's process 45; forges 45; furnaces 45; locations: in eighteenth century 45, in nineteenth century 46–7; Neilson's 'hot blast' 46; pig iron output 45–7; regenerative 'hot blast' 46; sources of ores 46

labour movement 190–2; Social Democratic Federation 190–2; in West Riding of Yorkshire 1890–1914 190–2, Clarion Clubs 192, Independent Labour Party 191–2, labour churches 191–2, Labour Representation Committee 191–2, political success 192, Social Democratic Federation 191–2, trades councils 191; *see also* Chartism; General Strike; luddism; strikes; trade unionism
leisure 224–35; August Bank Holiday 227; autonomous working-class institutions 229; brass bands and choirs 233; class differences 226, 229; durability of traditional practices 226; effect of war 229; holidays 227, savings clubs 227, Yorkshire and Lancashire textile industries 227; inter-war period 229, 231–2, amusement places in Manchester centre 231–2, charabanc trips 231, children's comics 231, cultural agencies of the labour movement 231, effect of economic fluctuations 231, football pools 231, gramophone records 231, growth of leisure activity 229, Saturday Night dance 231, the sports industry 231; lack of opportunity for women 226, 229; late nineteenth century 226–9, commercialization 226, 229, cycling shops 226, fall in beer consumption 226, 54-hour week 226, growth of purchasing power 226, influence of transport developments 229, role of the state 226, and technology 229; Miners' Welfare Institute 233; post-war 233–4, Areas of Natural Beauty 233–4, Arts Council 233, effect of incomes, hours of work and paid

holidays 233, growth of importance of state 233, leisure centres 233, National Parks 233–4, Sports Council 233; pre-industrial society 224, agricultural influences 224, little division between work and leisure 224; race meetings 231; rational recreation 224; removal of irregular holidays 224; Rugby Union and depression in Welsh valleys 231; rural sports and pastimes, irregular and boisterous 224; 'St Monday' 226; Saturday half-holiday 227; separation of work from leisure 224; and standard working time 224; working-class resentment of patronage 226; *see also* cinemas; football; music halls; public houses; public libraries; seaside resorts; Working Men's Club and Institute Union
locomotive manufacturers 61–2; North British Locomotive Company 61–2
luddism 183–5; authorities' reaction to 185; in Lancashire and Stockport 183–5; in Nottinghamshire 183, 185; in Yorkshire 183–5; varied objectives 183–5

machine tool industry 66
marine enginering 49–54 *passim*, 62
mechanical engineering 65–6; gross output (£'000) 65; growth rate post-1945 66
motor vehicle manufacture 55–8; amalgamations 57–8; British Leyland 57–8; closure of plant and loss of jobs 1960s–80s 57–8; comparison with American and French production 55, commercial vehicle manufacture in Lancashire and North Cheshire 57; development in South-east 57; development in West Midlands 55–7, pre-1914 55–6, 1920s–30s 57; effect of war 57; expansion 55, 57, 62, 1900–14 55, 1920s–30s 55, 57, 62; Ford and production line techniques 55; *The Future of the British Car Industry* 58; major car manufacturing plant 1960s–80s 57; tariff protection at home 55
motor vehicle manufacturers 1913 56
motor vehicles 55, 57; exports 55, 57; imports 57; *see also* road transport
music halls 226, 229, 232; in Manchester centre 232

overseas trade *see* foreign trade

Park Royal 112
population *see* demographic changes
port improvements 103–5; in Liverpool 105; in London 104

public houses 226-7, 229; in York 226-7
public libraries 224-6, 233; books per head 225-6; bookstock 224

railway carriage and wagon works 61-2; Metropolitan Amalgamated Carriage and Wagon Company 61-2
railway company workshops, location of 61
railways 101, 105-8; British Rail passenger network 1986 109; combination or co-operation 105, 108; competition from roads 108; completed network *c*. 1890 107; electrification 108; extension of network 105-7; grouping 1921 108; high value cargoes 101; lack of planning 105; passenger traffic 101; and port improvement 105; reduction of network 108-9; system *c*. 1850 106
re-exports *see* foreign trade
religion 211-23; puritanical dissenting presbyterian churches, loyalty of isolated communities 215; sectarian awareness and animosity 215, 221; strength of Roman Catholicism 1979/84 215, 218-19, 221; *see also* churches; churchgoing; religious denominations; religious habits
religious denominations 215-22; alignments 1851: England and Wales 217, Scotland 220; alignments 1979-82: England and Wales 218; alignments 1984: Scotland 222; Church of England 215-17, 219, large northern parishes 216, loss of adherents in northern cities 216, loss of southern support 1979-82 219, southern power-base 1851 215-17; Church of Scotland 219-21, loss of Highland and Hebridean support 219-21; collapse of presbyterian dissent 221-2; decline in protestant strength by 1979/84 219; Free Church 219-21; Free Presbyterian Church 221; Methodism 216-17, 219, 221, strength in mining and manufacturing areas 1851 216-17, strength in Shetlands 221, strongest in industrial periphery 1979-82 219; non-conformist churches, even distribution in England 216-17; regional concentration of Roman Catholicism 1851 216-17, 220-1; United Presbyterian Church 219-21; Wales 1851: strength and role of non-conformists 216-17, weakness of Church of England 216-17; Wales 1979-82: non-conformists remain strong 219; *see*

also churches; churchgoing; religion; religious habits
religious habits, deficiencies of statistics on 211
Report of the Royal Commission on the Distribution of the Industrial Population 1940 166
road improvements 96-7, 99-101, 108, 110-11; in the seventeenth, eighteenth and nineteenth centuries 96, 99-101; trunk roads 1936 108, 110; turnpikes 97, 99-101; twentieth-century motorways 110-11
road transport 96-8, 105, 108, 112; coaches 96-8, 105, journey times 96, 98, mail coaches 96; in eighteenth century, uses and drawbacks 97; in nineteenth century, effect of railways 105; in twentieth century 108, 112, effect on Park Royal 112, motor vehicle numbers 108
rural depopulation 173

Safeguarding of Industries Act, 1920 39
seaside resorts 226-9; pleasure piers 229; *see also* urban growth
shipbuilding 49-54; average tonnage launched 1985-6 53; capacity in early nineteenth century 49; closure of yards on Tyne and Wear 51, 53-4; collapse of British industry 53; comparison with Japan 53; developing shipbuilding technology 49; effect of war 51, 53; growth in North-east England and on Clyde 51; labour force 53; loss of exports 53; National Shipbuilding Securities Ltd 51; output 51, 53, 1913 51, 1931-4 51, 1948-61 53, 1985-6 53; principal centres (tonnage launched) 50, 52, 1825 50, 1870 50, 1913, 1938, 1953, 1963 52; size of yards 49, 51; world over-capacity 51, 53, in 1930s 51, in 1970s 53; *see also* employment
steam engine manufacture 61
steel industry 46, 48-9; basic oxygen process 49; basic process 46; Bessemer converter 46; British Iron and Steel Federation 49; British Steel Corporation 49, plant closures 49; electric arc and induction processes 49; Government intervention 46, 49; location 46, 48-9; output 46, 48-9; Seimens' open hearth 36; war and production 49
strikes 192-4; militant industrial action 1910-14 192-4, Liverpool dock strike 1911 193, Rhondda

miners' strike 1910-11 193, Tonypandy clashes 193; working days lost 1910-14 192; *see also* Chartism; General Strike; syndicalism
syndicalism 192-4; Dublin transport strike 193; marginal influence 193; *The Miners' Next Step* 1912 193; origins 192-3; Tom Mann 193, Industrial Democracy League 193, *The Industrial Syndicalist* 193, Industrial Syndicalist Education League 193

textile machinery manufacture 61-3; major textile engineering firms 1914 63; output 61
textiles 23-36; handloom weaving 29-32; local textile specialization *c*. 1900 25; power looms 30-3; use of steam power 26, 33-6; use of water power 33-6; *see also* carpets; cotton; hosiery industry; wool textiles
trade unionism 188-90, 192-7; Combination Acts, 1799 and 1800 188; effect of 1870s depression 189; emergence of skilled unions in 1850s-60s 189; formation of Trades Union Congress 1868 189; Grand National Consolidated Trade Union 188; lack of membership statistics 188; membership 1851-91 189; miners' unions in 1860s 189; Sheffield outrages' 189; strength 1867 189; 'Tolpuddle martyrs' 188-9; Trade Union Act, 1871 189; trade unionists per hundred people 1891 190; *see also* General Strike
transport 96-116; *see also* air traffic; coastal navigation; inland waterways; port improvements; railways; road improvements; road transport

unemployment 160-9; Chamberlain Circular 1886 160; by county 161-4, June 1932 161-2, June 1937 161-3, October 1984 163-4; cyclical 160, 163; Lancashire unemployment levels June 1930, June 1932, June 1937 161, 163; low unemployment 1945-70 163; more evenly spread in 1980s 165; persistent regional variations 163-5; regional policy 165-8, Conservative reduction in support 168, Development Areas 1945-60 166-8, Development Areas 1966-84 167-8, Development Districts 168, effectiveness by 1939 166, effectiveness 1970s 168, Industrial Development Certificates 168, Intermediate Areas 167-8, inter-war surveys 165, Regional

Employment Premiums 168,
Special Areas 165–7, Special
Development Areas 167–8, trading
estates 165, transference 166;
seasonal 160; statistical deficiencies
161; structural 161, 163;
Unemployed Workmen Act, 1905
160; Warwickshire unemployment
levels June 1932, June 1937 161
163
United Kingdom Atomic Energy
Authority 94
urban growth 137–8, 143–5, 170–5;
absence, before 1800, of large
provincial centres 170; around
heavy industry from 1851 172;

around textile industries before
1851 172; clustering of towns
170–2; effect of tramways 175;
effects and deficiencies of council
estates 175; growth of cities 170–3,
1801 170–1, 1851 170–2, 1901
171–2, 1951 171–2, 1981 172–3;
limited spatial expansion 174–5,
Glasgow 174–5; London 171–3,
attracting migrants 172, population
1801–1951 171, 1981 173; North-
west England 143–5; seaside resorts
145, 172; twentieth-century in
southern England 171–3
urban planning 172–5; 'green belts'
173; new towns 173–4, mixed

fortunes 173–4; overspill 173–4;
regeneration of inner cities 173

Von Tunzelmann, G.N., and use of
steam power 33

wool textiles 23–5, 27–30; exports
27–9; imports 27; locations 1946
29; numbers employed 1835 and
1867 24; output 23; traditional
centres 23; Yorkshire area
specializations *c.* 1800 24; *see also*
employment; textiles
worsted *see* wool textiles
Working Men's Club and Institute
Union 226, 231, 233